D1456784

REVISED EDITION
# COMPETING
## FOR
# CLIENTS
## IN THE

# 90s

A DYNAMIC
GUIDE TO
MARKETING,
PROMOTING
& BUILDING A
PROFESSIONAL
SERVICES
PRACTICE

# BRUCE W. MARCUS

**PROBUS PUBLISHING COMPANY**
Chicago, Illinois
Cambridge, England

ISBN 1-55738-230-1

Printed in the United States of America

BC

1   2   3   4   5   6   7   8   9   0

To
Mana and Lucy
with thanks for your love

and

Peter Horowitz and Ken Wright
with thanks for your friendship

# Contents

# Acknowledgements

If the effort to produce this book is dedicated to those who energized and sustained me during its writing—my wife, Mana, and my daughter, Lucy—then the intellectual thrust must be dedicated to the two friends and colleagues who most constructively challenged and supported the book's rationale—Kenneth Wright and Peter Horowitz. This book could not have moved one inch from its predecessor without them. While a large number of professional marketers of very high caliber contributed substantially, Peter and Ken inspired and challenged and brought perspective and incandescence to the subject. That they are the undisputed leaders in the field of marketing professional services is beyond question, although the small number of their peers is increasing. But no one has matched these two in moving the boundaries of professional services marketing farther and farther out. If this book in any way goes beyond the mundane, it's because Ken and Peter have spent so many hours with me, testing ideas, feeding me new ones, knocking down my straw men, and showing me where the bricks are to build new and useful edifices in the rocky fields of the practice.

My esteem for them, and my awe at their capabilities, in no way diminishes my regard for other practitioners of this new and arcane art, who have also contributed substantially.

The truth is that professional service marketing has gotten too big for any one person to know all the answers.

That's why a great many people have had to be brought into this venture. In fact, the vast amount of new information in this book comes from picking the best brains in professional services marketing. Not the theoreticians or academics, but the people who really make this stuff work—who shape practices and bring in clients through their marketing activities.

We would still be in the dark ages of professional services marketing were it not for a growing body of exceptional marketing professionals, including those who eagerly proffered help, advice, guidance, and just plain "this is what we do and this is how it works." Never mind the encouragement, of which, thank goodness (literally) there was plenty. I'm talking about the movable feast of information they used in their own practices, and that now, thanks to their good offices, you can use.

Patrick McKenna and Gerry Riskin, of The Edge Group, are probably the leading consultants in the world in marketing for lawyers. Not hyperbole. Though based in Canada, they are so many light years ahead of almost everybody else that their clientele is indeed world wide. They are truly multinational. They are also, I'm proud to say, dear and valued friends.

The privilege of having the input of such leading practitioners of this arcane art as August Aquila—an old and cherished friend—and Les Garnas—a new and no less cherished friend—has been invaluable. They are pioneers who daily bring new insights into the practice.

The advisory committee of *The Marcus Letter on Professional Services Marketing* has been a constant source of intelligence about this rapidly changing field. Diane Cramer, Yona Rogosin, Judith Fisher, and Robert Segal are a credit to professional services marketing, as is Sally Schmidt, who elevates the standards of marketing consulting with every consulting engagement. She has taught us all new tricks.

Contributors to *The Marcus Report*, predecessor to *The Marcus Letter*, have produced some of the most lucid thinking in the field. Noteworthy are Tim Powell, who is probably the practitioner in the use of computers in marketing, and Mattie Mola, who, with her sister Mary, have always produced fresh views from their corners of the marketing world. Elaine Goldman has graciously contributed her extraordinary wisdom on the difficult subject of hiring and managing marketing people. She brings grace and talent to the executive search field.

I was fortunate to be able to call upon the experience and expertise of such people as Diane DeMailly, who knows how to put a newsletter together that really works; Ruth Sheridan, who has probably done more than anyone to elevate the art of proposal writing to a new level of success; Steve Lebetkin, who, as both a CPA and a telemarketer, has made telemarketing both successful and respectable in our field; Sam Kingsley, who knows both the truth and consequences of marketing research; Alex Stanton, of Dorf & Stanton, who contributed from the depth of his experience in crisis management; Dan Cohen, of Price Waterhouse, who lent his knowledge of the advertising industry; Byron Sabol, who, as marketing director for a leading national law firm, practices successfully what others merely preach; and Neil Rackham, who knows more about selling and sales training than all of the others in that business put together. This profession owes more to Neil than they know.

James Emerson, Morrie Helitzer, Lee Berton, Donis Ford, George Burns, and Bob LaVine, journalists and artists all, have moved professional services beyond the ordinary, and made many a lawyer, accountant, and consultant aware of the significant values in professional services marketing. Lotus' Alexandra Trevelyan, who is responsible for a great deal of the good will that exists toward that company, was particularly helpful with the computer chapter. I owe them all thanks, and the professions owe them thanks.

Ray Newkirk, publisher of *The Marcus Letter*, deserves thanks as well. Without his support, there would be no *The Marcus Letter*. Without *The Marcus Letter*, this book might not have happened. Ray and his excellent staff are dedicated publishers, and I'm proud to be part of the team.

Much of the material in this edition has appeared before, in various iterations, in a variety of publications, including *The Marcus Letter, The Marcus Report,* Accounting Today, AAME (Association of Accounting Firm Marketing Executives) MarketTrends, New Accountant, and in speeches before a great many (again, thank goodness) accounting, consulting and law firms, and accounting and bar associations in both the United States and Canada. My thanks to the good graces of publishers, editors, and association executives.

Certainly, my thanks to the myriad professional firm clients, both mine and those of others, who allowed the material in this book to be tested under that hottest fire—producing clients and revenue. To both their profit and ours, I trust.

The state of the art would be in decline were it not for such organizations as AAME and NALFMA, the National Law Firm Marketing Association. They nurture the future of this business.

And finally, I owe deep thanks to the good folk at Probus, who are not only my publishers, but my friends as well. Wayne McGuirt runs the best business book publishing operation around, thank goodness. Mike Jeffers puts up with my author's shenanigans beyond any other publisher's endurance, and for this I'm grateful. His idiosyncrasies and my idiosyncrasies are constantly wrestling, but I guess that's what makes useful books. Pam van Giessen, my good editor, has more patience with me than I deserve. These are all good people.

Competing for clients is a continuing saga. Every month, it will be updated in *The Marcus Letter* and elsewhere, as the ardent and intelligent marketing professionals continue to learn from the rigors of their daily experience. You see, the state of the art is a fluid state. If we didn't have the help of all of these people, and many more than I could fit into this space, we would all drown in that fluid state.

Thanks, friends.

Bruce W. Marcus

New York, New York

# Introduction to the First Edition

In 1978, the United States Supreme Court, in an astonishing and far-reaching decision, overturned those aspects of the canons of ethics of professional societies that, until then, had effectively precluded frank marketing.

Until then, and for many years before that, lawyers, doctors, dentists, accountants and others in certificated, client-serving professions could not advertise, could not promote, could not solicit clients uninvited. So long had these restrictions prevailed, in fact, that they had become ingrained in the professional demean of practioners. Self-promotion, or anything that might be construed as self-promotion, was not only prohibited by fiat, but was frowned upon by other professionals, and frequently by clients as well. The prohibition became more than a function of ethical codes; it became a tenet, a way of life. To behave otherwise was clearly (horrors forfend) "unprofessional."

Which doesn't mean that there wasn't some form of "practice development" in common use. Clearly, something was being done that propelled some law firms and accounting firms to international size and stature, even as their fellows remained small. Some doctors thrived well beyond the success of their colleagues, and giant consulting firms emerged from small partnerships and solo practices. Even among non-certificated professionals, such as public relations firms and advertising agencies, some thrived while others stagnated or languished, and not always as a measure of either superior performance our astute management.

What was done, in the way of practice development, could hardly be called marketing, as we commonly think of the word. One simply made one's presence more obvious and ubiquitous. One joined the right clubs—those with prospective clients or patients as members. One gave speeches before learned groups of fellow business people, in which skill and expertise were exposed. An occasional seminar for business people imparted helpful information, perhaps about the new tax law, or the advantages of one kind of corporate structure over another. Brochures and newsletters on crucial subjects for clients were common, and if they found their way into the hands of non-clients, that was not inappropriate, if it was done "ethically" and professionally.

But flagrant promotion was a taboo. Advertising was strictly prohibited by all professional societies and governing bodies. And perhaps the strictest prohibition of all—of the most unthinkable and heinous of crimes—was soliciting another professional's clients. Frank marketing was simply unthought of . . . out of the question . . . unprofessional.

And then came the Supreme Court decision. The prohibitions against frank marketing were struck down.

For generations, concepts of probity had pervaded the professions. Accountants were not to be merely independent, but well beyond the fray of public quarrel or exposure. Lawyers, even in their advocacy, were to be beyond the pale of commerce. The privacy of the medical profession, with its freedom from the demands of the marketplace, was sacrosanct. Even so amorphous a profession as public relations had a code of ethics that prohibited soliciting other firms' clients. And now comes marketing, the crux of which is visibility and commercial interchange.

Realistically, only two things were changed by the Supreme Court ruling. First, professionals were suddenly allowed to advertise. This opened a number of possibilities, all of which, thus far, have for the most part been explored only tentatively or (with notable exceptions) primatively.

The second and infinitely more important change was the new ability to directly solicit clients—even the clients of other professionals.

This was more than a change in law—it was a change in tradition, and it fell upon professionals like a hail storm on a clear July day. It began a chain of events that continues to barrel along at breakneck speed, altering forever the texture of professional practice.

Most significantly, as doctors, dentists, lawyers, accountants, consultants and other professionals began to explore ways to function under the new rules, competitiveness acquired a new demean. Timidly, tentatively at first—you can legislate a change in the rules much more easily than you can legislate a change in decades of ingrained tradition—the professionals explored marketing. And then, suddenly, they began to realize that they no longer competed with one another with skills and reputation alone. They competed in marketing as well. Today, in the professions, the firms that succeed best will be not just those that perform best, but those that market best.

And realizing this, there was a sudden surge in marketing activities. Marketing consultants were brought in and specialists in the several disciplines of marketing were hired. There was a scramble for advertising agencies and public relations firms. Within two years, for example, at least four of the Big Eight accounting firms were competing for the top two national public relations firms. Law firms, slightly more gun shy, took a little longer, but then began having discreet "discussions and explorations" with public relations firms and advertising agencies.

Several Big Eight accounting firms, attempting to be first to market, started advertising almost immediately. Arthur Young was the first in print with several full page ads in Fortune, Business Week and the like, followed by Deloitte, Haskins & Sells.

In law, medicine and dentistry, on the other hand, it was the smaller practitioner who moved quickly to advertising. The legal clinic serving the small client sprang into existence, virtually an invention of advertising. Dental clinics opened in shopping malls, aided by advertising and direct mail. It was the first example, in professional services, of market feedback, in which serving the perceived needs of a market created a new service vehicle. In fact, the new legal, medical, and dental clinics institutionalized their performance of the professions, turning personalized service into something that could be sold like a loaf of bread. Like bank services, this uniform professional service became a commodity that could be sold under the old rules of marketing.

The classic professional, however, discovered something fascinating. The old rules of marketing—the techniques that so readily sold products and such nonprofessional services as banks and airlines—just didn't seem to work. Other professionals, such as architects and engineers, had the same revelation.

No sudden flocking of new clients, nor burst of public name recognition, nor ripples of excitement in the firmament.

It was more than just a matter of advertising that didn't work, or of press releases not appearing in the papers. It was, rather, the sudden realization that there was a lack of rationale for what was being done. And without a rationale, the target was missed by the marketing shots being fired.

An ad for a product is a relatively simple thing. If you advertise lollipops for sale, you know how effective your ad is because you know how many lollipops you sell. If you have a heavy campaign for soap, and your share of market increases, you know how well your campaign worked.

But the professional services consumer, unlike the lollipops consumer, may not be ready to retain those services just at the moment the ad appears. Is the advertising wasted? How do you know if it works? How do you know what, if anything, works?

With introspection and experience, some significant differences began to emerge. For example, can you advertise that you do a better audit, or a better tax return, or that your firm wins more cases in court than any other, or that you do neater appendectomies? Of course not.

All professionals perform essentially the same services. How do you persuade somebody—particularly on a large-scale marketing basis—that you perform those services better, or that you're smarter than your competitor?

You can, of course, advertise that you understand the issues of the day, and that you are the "businessman's" accountant or lawyer; this is what the first Big Eight accounting firm ads tried to do. That comes under the heading of institutional advertising. If you spend many millions of dollars doing it, you may ultimately impress some people sufficiently for them to turn to you when they need a lawyer or an accountant. But considering the kind of budget you'd need for it to work, you'd be bankrupt by the time the first prospect responded to the campaign.

And while the ingredients and process of a product may be quality controlled, how do you do that in a service, in which every individual, and every business, has a different and perhaps unique need?

That's what began to dawn on professionals first—that frank marketing requires a new way for the professional to reach out to prospects. It requires a different kind of advertising and public relations, and even selling.

What, then, *is* marketing? And why didn't traditional marketing techniques work for professional services?

There are as many definitions of marketing, I suppose, as there are marketing people. Ultimately, it's a discipline and a process that moves products or services to market effectively, and therefore profitably. It can be broken down into four very basic elements:

- Define your market
- Define your product (or service)
- Define your marketing tools
- Manage your marketing tools

Every marketing professional knows that—it's basic marketing.

But when the service you offer is a professional service, tailored to the needs of myriad individual clients, and is as multifarious as it is in any professional practice, then you don't fathom your market the way you do for a product. The body of knowledge about why women buy soap is vast. Every airline marketer knows why people choose one airline over another, and every bank marketer knows a great deal about how to get a customer to switch his account from one bank to another, or to buy another bank service. Who knows, though, how to get an audit committee to switch from one accounting firm to another, or what really motivates an individual or a corporate executive to choose one law firm over another?

It's not that this information isn't discernible. It's that nobody ever had to get it before. Beyond knowing the basic needs that people have for professional services, professionals simply never had to find out what the markets for their services really are, and what those markets really want, or even who the decision makers in the marketplace really are, and so they didn't know how to do find out.

In traditional marketing, when you know what your market wants, you adjust your product—or the way you position or present it—to meet the needs of the marketplace. The classic story, of course, is the one about Henry Ford, who said you can have any color car you want so long as you want black. He lost out to General Motors, which realized that people wanted their cars in different colors.

If the professional service you have to offer is so varied, so individualized, then obviously you can't package or position it in the same way you would a cake of soap or even an investment vehicle—products or services cherished for their consistency and uniformity. It becomes infinitely more complex than anything the marketing professionals have ever had to face before. And because it had never been done before, thoughtful marketing professionals were perplexed; others marched blindly forward, enthusiastically repeating expensive mistakes. Nothing from the past seemed to fit just right.

As for the tools—advertising, public relations, direct mail, and even straight selling—these new disciplines bedazzled the professionals. Not only did they scarcely understand them, but the tools themselves had to be used in a new and unfamiliar way. Moreover, these tools work best only in a total marketing context, and not as abstracts. If you don't clearly understand the marketing context, then how do you devise an ad campaign that makes sense, or judge one devised by an ad agency? How do you develop a public relations program that isn't more than wasted energy? When you can't rely on professional salesmen, and must depend upon the professional who performs the service to do the selling, what do we draw from traditional selling skills to close the sale and bring in the client?

In managing the tools, from where is the expertise to come? Internally, from a partner who is a lawyer or an accountant? Externally, from a marketing professional who doesn't understand law or accounting or medical practice?

As if these factors alone didn't add enough confusion, there is the problem of the nature of the firms that perform professional services. They are, for the most part, partnerships. Even in professional corporations, every member is a professional, and therefore the equivalent of a partner.

In a classic corporation, there are the marketing professionals, and there is the chief executive officer or the board of directors. When the powers of a corporation approve a marketing program, then the rest of the people get out of the way and let the professionals work. In a partnership, however, where the marketing expense comes out of every partner's profits, then every partner is a participant in the program, and will have his say.

And even in the broad context of all professions, there are strategies that are unique to each profession.

Accounting firms, perhaps because of the broad range of services they offer and the stronger competition they face, have been more aggressive in marketing than any of the other professions. The larger firms, with offices in many cities throughout the country and the world, have been more aggressive in their national marketing efforts, although they are learning that professional marketing techniques function best on a local level.

Law firms, tend not to be national in the sense that accounting firms are, although that's changing. Still, a major accounting firm may have eighty or a hundred offices; few law firms have more than two or three. And while many large law firms draw their clients nationally, there has been virtually no national advertising. In fact, except for the legal clinics and the smaller practitioners, lawyers have been somewhat more reluctant than other professionals to move into advertising and frank marketing.

Medicine and dentistry face a somewhat different problem. Obviously, their practices are local and usually limited to a single geographic area. And except for the clinics, certain medical and dental disciplines are more promotional than others. Ads for plastic surgeons abound; ads for brain surgeons do not. And then, of course, is the significant difference that these professions seek patients—individuals who come to the practitioner's site—rather than clients, who usually function within the realm of their own business (personal or otherwise).

Architects, consultants, and others are somewhat freer in their marketing efforts in that they can be more imaginative and expansive in projecting their capabilities.

The distinctions among the professions that make one profession more or less aggressive in marketing than the others are rapidly breaking down as the competition for clients becomes more acute. Still, functioning within the prescribed boundaries of professional ethics requires more skill and imagination, and this competition is bringing these qualities to the fore.

With all of the traditions of professionalism that impede marketing breaking down and eroding, and as some firms within each profession succeed more substantively than others, the whole area for marketing professional services becomes more active.

The techniques for competing for clients are clearly present and available. What is yet to be developed is experience, skill, and the imagination to use these techniques in ways that bring successful competition in the professional marketplace.

What is emerging are clear and overriding factors that define the distinction between marketing a professional service and marketing a product or a non-professional service, and that dictates developing new marketing techniques.

There may be a thousand people behind a product—those who finance it and design it and manufacture it and distribute it. But the interface between all of those people and the consumer is the product itself. It's all the consumer ever sees or knows about the company.

The interface between the consumer of the professional service and the professional firm that supplies that service, on the other hand, is the professional who performs the service. An entire firm can rise or fall on the performance of its individuals.

When the consumer buys a box of soap, he or she does so without a second thought that the quality and characteristics of that box might in any way differ from that of the last box he or she bought. The quality and characteristics of the service performed by each professional is a function of the next job he or she performs, and not the last.

Virtually all non-professional services—banking and other financial services, airlines, even dry cleaning—are discrete and limited, and are virtually commodities. They they are uniform and consistent, and may be described in a finite way, even as can be a product. Certainly, this is not so of a professional service, where the performance fits the unique needs of the individual client, and where, therefore, the range of services is practically infinite. You can warehouse soap; there is no way to inventory professional services.

How, in the face of all of this, does one market a distinction from one's competitors? How does one credibly and ethically project quality and expertise?

Even if traditional ethical practices allowed such distinctions to be made in public utterances, how can they be proven—particularly where professional services are offered by individuals, and not by quality-controlled machines? And particularly where all professions offer the same service (although the quality of delivery may differ). There is an answer, of course, to both this and other questions raised thus far—else why this book? But the answer doesn't come from the traditional practices of marketing.

And therein hangs the tale. Marketing professional services is very different from marketing anything else. It is new and pioneering territory, with only a few years of practical experience.

But it is a growing body of knowledge. More and more professionals are doing it, and learning how to do it well. They are learning by trial and error, and they are learning by recognizing the distinctions between the old and the new, and using old skills imaginatively to make new rules. The thinking is different, and comes from a different point of view. And thinking there is, which is beginning to show good results.

The following pages are devoted to exploring the techniques of marketing professional services, in the context of the new experience and the new thinking. It is, to an extent, old wine in new bottles. But it is, as well, a new brew of the old wine.

A word about how this book is organized.

It really consists of two parts—a discussion of how and why marketing professional services differs from other aspects of marketing, as a basis for planning a marketing strategy, and a breakdown of the techniques of the various disciplines of marketing. A handbook and a kind of a "how-to," if you will. This last is necessary, I feel, because many of the basic techniques take on a different cast when applied to professional services. Good copywriting is good copywriting, but in a world in which you can't say "we do better audits," good copywriting is an idea of a different color.

In detailing these techniques, there is no overt attempt to try to turn accountants and doctors and lawyers and consultants into advertising or public relations technicians. Presumably, you'll hire professionals in those fields. But if you understand the processes, you'll be better able to participate in your own marketing planning, and to instruct, guide, and judge the performances of those who must function for you. In other words, the attempt here is to make you a better consumer of marketing services.

For the marketing professional, it is fondly hoped that this book will serve to help you rethink your skills in terms of the unique needs of the professional for whom you must function.

I recognize, also, that while this book is organized in the order of a textbook, and is structured as a handbook, life—and especially professional life—is not a textbook case history. Most of you are now active in your own practices, and as much concerned, perhaps, with keeping the clients you have as with getting new ones. Keeping clients, of course, is as much an objective of marketing as is practice development. And many of you have well-established practice development structures. You may find, then, that this book will serve you best as both an overview and as a source of ideas.

That's fine. It's purpose is to serve—to be useful in any context. It is assumed, in fact, that a mark of a professional is that he or she doesn't abdicate intelligence in the face of expertise from another discipline. Marketing is as much an art form, given the basic skills, as it is a set of rules, and both the professional marketer and the consumer of marketing services must bring a large dollop of imagination to the table.

In fact, a singular purpose of this book is to function not as a final word on the subject, but rather as a beginning—a foundation to a new and important structure that will grow, develop, and change with experience and the infusion of wisdom beyond these pages and this time.

When, in 1978, the United States Supreme Court, in an astonishing and far-reaching decision, overturned those aspects of the canons of ethics of professional societies that, until then, had effectively precluded frank marketing, they created an opportunity that has a great distance to go to reach its outer limits.

# Introduction to the Revised Edition

Things change.

Thank goodness, sometimes.

When the first edition of *Competing for Clients* was published in 1986, marketing for professionals was very—well, relatively—new. Although Bates vs. The State Bar of Arizona, the case that resulted in throwing out the canons of ethics that prohibited frank marketing by professionals, had been ruled on in 1977, by 1986 there were just the first few awakenings of marketing in the professions. Accounting firms were somewhat ahead, with more marketing professionals than the lawyers or consultants or architects had. But the effort was primarily in the larger firms. Only the Big Eight firms (not all of them) and a few others had marketing departments, and a few of the middle-sized firms had "somebody." Law firms and the others, except for the very largest, also had "somebody." That "somebody" was a person (usually a woman, because they work cheaper, right?) who might have been anybody from an elevated secretary to a thoroughly experienced (but, as we shall see, frustrated) public relations professional. There were, indeed, isolated cases of full-blown professionalism in marketing, but they were very rare. Certainly, there were too few professional marketers serving the professions to have their own organizations.

## What Bates Did

That's one part that's changed. In the past five years, there's been a growing recognition of the role of that foreign substance called marketing in a new competitive world. What Bates did, people now realized, was more than just to allow advertising where it hadn't been permitted before. It allowed real competition to enter the professions—a competition that had to be fought on some new and unfamiliar (to the professionals) level.

As this arcane and unfamiliar fact dawned on the accountants and lawyers and architects and consultants, they lurched out to build some kind of marketing capability. Thus began a new era of marketing. The reality of it is encapsulated in the fact that two organizations of marketing professionals serving the professions—NALFMA (National Association of Law Firm Marketing Administrators) and AAME (Association of Accounting Firm Marketing Executives) have each grown to memberships in the hundreds—in less than 5 years.

xxiii

Changed, too, have been the canons of ethics in the several states, for both law and accounting. Prohibitions have fallen, one by one, such as those against direct mail campaigns, slogans, specific appeals to prospective clients based upon knowledge of need, and so forth. It's not quite open season, but there are almost as few prohibitions in marketing for professionals now as in product marketing. *Almost*, but not quite, as we shall see.

It's interesting to note that Canadian professionals, while obviously not subject to the ukases of the U.S. Supreme Court, quickly paralleled U.S. professionals in allowing their own professionals to market. After a brief lag, the United Kingdom followed suit. Obviously, marketing is the idea that's time has come.

But these changes that have taken place in the decade since *Bates* are the smallest manifestation of the vast and profound metamorphosis in not only the professions, but in the economy and society they serve. As with any decade-long metamorphosis, it's been difficult to observe and fathom on a day-to-day basis, but when seen in perspective, it's overwhelming. The exception, of course, has been the big event—the megamerger, for example, that turned the Big Eight into the Big Six. And even there, a great many people failed to see it for what it was—a marketing action to allow the participating firms the opportunity to increase share of market. The idea that's time has come.

Look at the state of the professions at the time of *Bates*. Only a decade ago, professional prestige was a given. In fact, the cash value of the mystique of a professional was at least equal to the cash value of the service he or she performed. Overwhelming ethical concerns pervaded the professions, guaranteeing that there would be no overt competition—which further enhanced professional prestige.

The economics of practice, then, were very different. As partnerships, revenues, profits, and margins were hidden. Professionals could charge anything they pleased. After all, there was a sort of professional monopoly. Only lawyers could handle legal problems; only accountants could handle auditing and accounting problems. That fees were arbitrary is no surprise—it was almost as if the rules of free enterprise didn't apply to the professions. The strength of the spine of traffic and what it will bear—not market forces—dictated pricing.

The local or regional firm, in all professions, was generally free from national contamination. Even local accounting firms saw little competition from the local offices of national firms, and there were very few national law firms.

The practice was collegial, and the professions were for gentlemen. Management—firm governance—wasn't important. The senior partners were chosen because they were the best rainmakers, or the best firm politicians, or the partners responsible for the firm's largest clients. Certainly, there was no competitive need for professionals to be businesspeople. And as self-governing professions, lawyers made the laws and accountants made the accounting rules, and all professions protected themselves with canons of ethics which, as the Supreme Court neatly pointed out, were self-serving and restraint of trade.

And there was no marketing to muddy the water.

*Bates*—with the help of a few other socioeconomic factors—changed all that. Just look at what's happened since then to change the context of the professions.

New laws and regulations, and changes in regulatory controls and philosophy—a legacy of the Reagan Administration and the Reagan Court—have not only proliferated, but have substantially changed the texture of law. This includes not only new tax laws, but new accounting regulations that have put new spotlights on accounting practice.

The accelerating internationalization of business has substantially changed the nature of domestic commerce, and the nature of the corporation. Capital flows across borders have increased substantially. There is a new corporate climate, dictated by the borderless corporation and the technology that makes it possible. New opportunities in the European community and the Eastern bloc countries, and new structures and laws to deal with them, affect even those parts of the profession that don't participate directly in international business.

The new financial markets, and new financial instruments, have opened up vast opportunities for lawyers, accountants, and consultants. There are now approximately 600 financial instruments in which one can invest, or which can be traded.

New technology has bred new industries, such as computers and genetic research, all of which have expanded opportunities for all the professions. The new technology also accelerates process in the professions, with immediate access to legal research and computer auditing.

## The Changing Attitude toward Professionals

At the same time, the decade has produced a substantial change in attitudes towards professionals. The decline in awe for lawyers and other professionals, including doctors, has contributed to the growing competitive picture. This increasing skepticism about the professions has contributed to an increase in litigiousness on the part of the public, which is also fostered by publicity about the high rewards of successful litigation.

The popularization of law and the legal process by television, films, and the press also has altered the view of these and other professionals. This has also led to a substantial increase in the number of lawyers and an increased number of non-professionals, both administrative and paralegal, in law firms and in other professions.

And further altering professional practice is the growth of the professional clinic, both legal and tax, and the development of do-it-yourself professional software, such as legal programs to help you write your will and other simple legal documents, tax programs, and bookkeeping and accounting programs. The clinic and the computer program are, of course, pure manifestations of marketing. Lawyers are no longer needed for all legal problems, nor accountants for all accounting and tax problems.

The power that has enabled all of these factors to impinge on the professions since the *Bates* decision has been the growth of marketing as a management force, which impels firms to compete by functioning as professional companies, and not simply collegial firms. The paradox is that this one crucial factor is scarcely recognized by an overwhelming proportion of professionals.

If the collegial partnership structure that was sufficient to manage the professional firm a decade ago has been eroded, it has moved the professions, for the first time, into the new world of free enterprise.

Where the professional firm was once driven by the practice itself, it's now driven by the market—a force with which most professionals are not familiar by training, experience, or temperament. But this, too is changing.

Firms in all the profession are now becoming acquainted with new concepts and disciplines, none of which are taught in law or accounting school. Terms such as "market share" now float through the air of professional firms. Subjects such as productivity, economics, demographics, pricing in a competitive situation, management of profits, problems of getting and keeping good people, and long-range planning now become the concern of professionals who never worried about such things before. And they are shocked to discover that long-range planning is really *marketing*. What indeed is planning if not a projection of—or a wish for—a size and configuration of a firm and its practice? And how else is that projection—or wish—fulfilled except in relation to a marketplace that's constantly changing? And in fathoming and dealing with that marketplace, what discipline is more central than marketing?

Significantly, there is now more professionalism in the marketing. As more people got into it, and realized that the differences between marketing professional services and marketing products were significant, new bodies of knowledge and techniques and skills had to be developed. The first edition of this book dealt with that, to some degree. This edition attempts to chronicle the overwhelming body of new knowledge and skill that has been developed in these past five years. And is still, fortunately, growing.

### More Marketing Tools

In this context, more marketing tools and devices are being used than ever before—things that were once thought to be highly unlikely. Billboards? Radio and TV? Telemarketing? In the past five years, all of these have been used, some with such success as to now be standard practice. The phrase "not in my lifetime" is heard less and less from lawyers and accountants and other practitioners. "Telemarketing? Billboards? Not in my lifetime." What's fascinating is that as these marketing disciplines are brought into action, they go through the same process as did advertising, public relations, and the others—they are changed and adapted to professional services marketing.

Marketing has changed the practice of law and accounting as well. The ability to advertise has, to a large extent, helped to develop the concept of the legal clinic—the low cost legal center where you can get a simple but perfectly legal and effective will for two or three hundred dollars, and sometimes less. Without advertising, these clinics certainly couldn't thrive as they have. And for good or ill, advertising and marketing for personal injury lawyers has developed into virtually a profession of itself. In accounting, the clinics of tax preparers, the H & R Blocks, are ubiquitous.

On another scale, marketing has changed practices in ways that benefit the consumers of professional services. First, it's served to educate these consumers. The outreach of professional firms means projecting expertise in all aspects of a service. This is done through the press, through seminars, through advertising, and through publications—the whole raft of communications devices. The result is that more people know about their rights under the law, and how to think about taxes, and how to set up and run a business, and when to call a lawyer or an accountant, than ever before. This is all courtesy of recent marketing efforts by professionals.

But even more important is that in learning to compete, professionals have had to learn to listen more carefully to what their markets really need and want, and to adapt accordingly. In the old days, a lawyer was a lawyer and an accountant was an accountant, and that's all there was to it. Today, professionals increasingly cast their services in terms of what the consumer wants—and that's frequently more than just an accountant or a lawyer. New needs breed new skills, so that the lawyer hones his specialties to the needs of his or her market—be it matrimonial or intellectual properties or corporate law—and the accountant, now more than simply an auditor, does financial planning, or computers, or special programs that integrate the business and personal financial need of the entrepreneur.

### The Role of the Partnership Structure

One crucial factor that's emerged in these past several years has been to define an obstacle, not an opportunity. It's an obstacle that's probably been a greater deterrent to successful marketing than any other. That obstacle is the difference between the culture of the practitioner and that of the marketer. It manifests itself most outrageously in the partnership structure.

In a manufacturing corporation, marketing is accepted as a consequential part of the operation. The company will have grown on marketing. The marketers are recognized as professionals in their own right. They report to senior executives who themselves understand marketing, and who perhaps may have themselves been marketers. And while the cost of marketing and marketers may be high, it's expected to be high, and it doesn't come from the pockets of individuals.

In a partnership, there's virtually no experience of marketing—the professions have been allowed to do it for only slightly more than a decade—and the cost of marketing comes from every partner's pocket. Every partner feels every penny spent on marketing. And because marketing activities are most often not brought to fruition in the short term, the older partners—the ones with the voting clout—tend to feel that they won't be around to benefit from the effort, so they vote against it. The younger partners, who want to build for the future, don't have the voting clout. A paradox.

And in a partnership structure, where every partner is presumably equal (some more equal than others, of course), every partner becomes a participant in the marketing operation—regardless of qualification, or more likely, lack of qualification.

It's the peculiar nature of marketing professional services that every practitioner becomes a part of the process. In a manufacturing corporation, only those executives directly concerned with marketing are involved, and they're usually trained or experienced in the subject. In a partnership, particularly in a profession for which marketing is only a decade old, people of no training or experience exercise a great deal of authority over marketers.

The point is that unlike any other areas, marketing professional services is shaped by the authority of non-marketers, which profoundly and adversely affects it, and taints the possibility for success.

In viewing the techniques of marketing professional services, then, it's important to filter all input through the screen of the limitations of the partnership. If a lawyer or an accountant or a consultant is to succeed, then he or she must function with a professionalism unencumbered by nonprofessional influences. And yet these very professionals tamper with the professionalism of marketers.

This is not a scold, it's a statement of fact in an overwhelming number of firms. It is probably the single greatest deterrent to successful marketing in professional services.

The practitioner must be aware that this attitude toward the marketing professional is counterproductive. The marketer must be aware that the partnership must be dealt with before he or she can function professionally. This is excess baggage.

It manifests itself in specific ways. For example, every professional marketer knows full well about the need for an integrated program. If he or she doesn't know how to do it, there's plenty of help. There are seminars, and courses and *The Marcus Letter* and this book and others as well. There is also the reality that you can't institute an integrated program in a firm whose partners misunderstand and diminish the role of marketing.

What happens in that case is that marketing is reduced to random activities and skills. Brochures that have no relevance to marketing objectives. Public relations that produces only shallow, two-dimensional reputation. Direct mail that produces only pallid results.

Of all we've learned, then, this is most important, because this is the obstacle that must be overcome before marketing can be effective.

## What the Professional Must Know

Inherent in this is that experience has shown that it's not necessary, as was once thought, to make each professional a full-fledged marketing expert. What is necessary is that professionals understand the nature of marketing, as clients must understand what their lawyers or accountants or consultants are saying to them. The professionals need not know how to write a press release, but should understand when one might be warranted. Professionals do have to know, however, how to bring a client into the fold, because no marketer or marketing program can do that.

In the last few years, there's also been a bifurcation of marketing practice. The larger firms, not only more sophisticated and with more money, but as well with a more urgent need, have begun to move toward elaborate and expensive marketing programs. Multi-million dollar budgets are no longer unusual, particularly for the national and international accounting, law, and consulting firms. Major advertising campaigns are mounted, top ten public relations firms are retained, large in-house staffs are developed.

At the same time, the smaller firms, without the large budgets and the marketing staffs, must mount some kind of marketing effort in order to compete. Fortunately, the nature of marketing professional services allows firms of any size to benefit to some degree from marketing activities on any level. Thus, while the larger firm has the luxury of the integrated program that uses all the tools of marketing, from publications to advertising to networking, the smaller firm can benefit from considerably less activity—so long as it's done cleverly and imaginatively.

There are, too, the opportunities to achieve a measure of competitive success without staff marketing professionals, or with the help of outside consultants. The sole practitioner who takes the time to learn some basic skills can write an article, or turn an article into a brochure, or give a speech, or even run a small seminar. While the role of this book is not to turn accountants or lawyers into marketers, the skills necessary to perform marketing tasks are indeed explained in these pages.

## Enhancing the State of the Art

That in essence, is what this book is about. It has two purposes—to enhance the state of the art of professional services marketing by sharing those techniques and skills found to have worked effectively for others; and to make the professionals—the practitioners—better consumers of marketing services. If either is achieved by just one iota, then this book will be deemed successful.

If, during the last few years, a great deal has been learned about what works to market professional services, and what doesn't, we've also begun to get a sense of what is yet to be learned. This is, perhaps, the more valuable lesson.

We know, for example, that we know remarkably little about how and why people buy professional services. And every time we think we know, along comes some failed marketing campaign, or better yet, some focus group, to tell us that we're wrong. And at the same time, we know very little about how to use market research in the first place. This is despite the fact that there are probably more market research firms than any other kind of marketing consultant. The concept of spending money to learn what we think we know already is one that breeds great reticence. Perhaps the fact that marketing is so new to the professions is part of it—the professionals simply don't know the right questions, and you can't do market research without knowing the right questions. The problem is that the research people who should be doing the job seem unable to raise the right questions either, and so they haven't been very successful at selling their services to the professionals.

We do, know, though, that those firms that have spent the money to do sound market research have clearly demonstrated that it's not only valuable, but it offers a vast return on investment. Those firms that have done it maintain that they've saved more than the cost of the research on improved marketing programs.

We don't seem to know much yet about selling—or more to the point, sales training. There is no shortage of sales trainers. They range from some very thoughtful people (some of whom are quoted in the following pages) whose work is based upon extensive research, reinforced by successful experience in actually teaching accountants and lawyers and consultants how to sell, to opportunists who make no distinction between selling vacuums and selling services.

There are several problems here. How do you teach selling to somebody who says, "If I wanted to be a salesman I wouldn't have gone to law school, or accounting school." And the difficulty is that only accountants or lawyers or consultants can get clients—all the tools of marketing can't do it, and nobody has found a way to train professional salespeople to do it.

There are, as well, many intangibles yet to be learned. For example, how do we bridge the gap between the professionalism of the accountant and lawyer and architect and consultant, and that of the marketer?

Why do some things work for some firms and not for others? Why do some small firms grow rapidly and others, spending the same dollars and the same efforts on marketing, stay small?

How do you accommodate the strong cultural differences between the marketer and the professional, so that the professional allows himself or herself to be better served by marketing? In product marketing, this is rarely the problem that it is in professional services marketing.

How do you enable qualified, experienced marketing professionals to function skillfully, professionally, and imaginatively in a context in which the professionalism in marketing is undervalued, or in which, through lack of experience, it's unrecognized?

## Learning from the Past

And perhaps most seriously, where marketing is so little understood, and is accepted almost grudgingly, how do you do research for the future, and gain the experience of ideas and skills, and learn to make those mistakes that teach us how to shape the better path?

This last is the paradox that inhibits professional services marketing. This, in turn, inhibits effective competition, which then inhibits growth for a firm in its own profession.

And if this book can help solve that paradox, it's been more than worth the effort to produce it.

All this and more has happened in just a few short years. And in the dynamic of the world, which refuses to stand still, more is happening to shape the future for professions and those who market professional services. With luck, the next edition of this book will be at least half again as thick as this one.

# Part I

# The Plan

# 1

# Practice Development Strategy

"Marketing," says the conventional wisdom, "is what you do to get clients." Maybe.

You've got a matrimonial law practice. You're full-up. You can't even accept another client, and there's a lineup outside your door.

Or you've got a tax practice that's so overloaded that you drive the temporary agencies nuts every tax season.

If marketing is what you do to get clients, then you don't need marketing, right?

Let's look at it another way.

Assume that you, as either the lawyer or the accountant, were to decide to move to another city. Given the opportunity to start again, you take a pad (legal size, of course) and define the ideal practice you want. Not just a matrimonial or a tax practice, but a practice defined by very specific elements. What kind of clients do you want? What economic parameters? What areas of subspecialties? What kind of clients would you exclude?

In other words, you completely define every aspect of the practice you would like to have, if you could wave a magic wand.

Now compare that with the very busy practice you now have. Are the two the same? No? Then you need marketing. Not for getting new clients—for something else. For defining—or redefining—your practice. There is a profound difference. You get clients by selling. As any professional knows, whether a sole practitioner or a partner in an international firm, you can always get a client if you need one. Perhaps not the client you want, but it's a client.

But you can't always have the practice you want by random client-getting. That can be achieved only by marketing. The difference is that in just getting clients, selling is the beginning and the end. In building a practice, selling is only the end.

## The Urgent Need for Marketing

At least three factors dictate an urgent need to organize and plan the marketing effort.

The first is markedly accelerating competition. And where once it was fought solely on serendipitous reputation, or reputation for performance, or even random socializing, it is now fought with marketing skills. To an increasingly large degree, *the professional firm with the better marketing program is the one that seems most likely to emerge as the most successful.* And as each firm becomes more skilled and aggressive in marketing, it becomes more competitive in the marketplace, and so demands that other firms be competitive as well, if they are to survive.

The second is increasing recognition of the changing economics of a practice. It's gradually dawning on professionals that some aspects of a practice are more profitable than others, and that some aspects cost more to market than others. This means a new view of how to address the market is required. (Budgeting for marketing, under this concept, is discussed in chapter 18.)

The third need for marketing professionalism and strategy is the changing nature of the marketplace itself. The economy is now very much larger and extremely complex, and specialization abounds in every profession. With very rare exceptions, there is rarely, today, a plain lawyer, or a consulting generalist, or a plain and simple accountant—there are negligence lawyers and corporate lawyers and litigators and divorce lawyers. There are auditors and tax experts and computer specialists. This further complicates competition, and dictates the need for not only increased marketing efforts, but for better, more facile marketing strategy.

### Building a Practice

Building a practice begins with planning.

What is the market? What, in the context of what you do, does the market really need? How large is the market, and how does it break down economically? How many people (or companies) are there that really need the kind of service you offer?

Then comes a good look at your own service. How do you relate what you do to what the market needs? This aspect of marketing planning can get very specific. For example, the matrimonial lawyer can think in terms of economic class (accepting any divorce case versus accepting only clients with assets above $500,000, for example), or limiting or excluding cases that involve custody. The tax accountant has an even greater number of options within his or her practice.

Bringing the two together—the market and the service—defines the kind of practice you want to build. It remains only to attack that market appropriately. This means determining the strategy that makes the most effective use of the tools of marketing to achieve your objectives.

Is advertising part of it? How will public relations fit in? What about publications—newsletters, brochures, etc. What's the role of networking? And so on.

It's here that we begin to look at selling. But it's selling against a backdrop of all of the other tools of marketing. It's selling in which the prospects have been developed as part of a plan, and not by random access.

And then, all of the tools must be managed. The public relations and direct mail and networking and other efforts must be put into play, in a proper framework, so that they are effective and relevant to the objectives.

This is marketing. It's how a practice is built, by both sole practitioners and multinational firms. It's how a practice is *shaped*.

That's the difference. Selling gets clients, although not always the ones you want. Marketing builds practices. Good marketing builds the practice you want.

Given the vast array of marketing tools available to professional firms, and the changing nature of the marketplace, how can all these tools best be used to bring the firm and its services most successfully to market?

### Strategy as a Business Decision

The answer, of course, is a plan—a strategy.

It seems to be difficult for professionals to recognize, sometimes, that strategy is a business decision. And as with all business decisions, strategy begins with objectives—where the firm wants to go.

Strategy is rooted, as well, in assessment. Where is the firm now? *What* is the firm now? If the objectives are to move the firm from point A to point B, or to reshape it from X to Y, myriad other questions are raised, foremost of which are the desires of the partnership, and what the partners are willing to do to achieve their objectives.

Strategy, in professional services marketing, is how you define a market, and then how you address that market to win a clientele from it.

Planning the marketing program means deciding how you intend to use the tools of marketing to put the strategy into play.

### Planning

There are, in each profession, legendary practitioners about whom it's said that they can go into a phone booth alone and walk out arm-in-arm with a new client.

Perhaps such instinctive marketing giants do exist, but they are rare, genuinely legendary, and one can hardly build or expand a practice in an orderly manner, in today's competitive environment, with just a few legends. Absent these paragons then, the need for active and aggressive marketing, and particularly marketing planning and strategy, becomes increasingly acute.

For a number of reasons, the concept of planning has never loomed large in the legend of the professional. The manufacturer must plan because his or her future is changed, usually, with new, large capital investments for new plants and machinery and market introductions. The professional expands and changes the future by renting a new office, or by hiring or training someone in a new skill, and then announcing the new facility and capability.

What marketing planning is about—what strategy aims to accomplish—is to organize the *tools* and *skills* of marketing to accomplish the *aims* of marketing. It uses the several tools of marketing to reinforce one another, to allow the marketing effort to move out in a force that accomplishes the marketing aim.

We can see, then, that if competition is increasing, and the market is changing, then classic practice development techniques are no longer sufficient. New techniques must be brought into play, and new strategies must be devised. Otherwise, professional firms that once thrived will languish and be eclipsed. Opportunities for young talent will be foreclosed, and they will look to your competitors for their futures. Your ability to compete will be sharply curtailed.

## The Nature of Professional Services

The response to this new environment lies in the very nature of the professional service. Even within the realm of specialization, service and service concepts can be adjusted to meet the needs of the market. There is the piano player who will play anything you want to hear, so long as you want to hear Melancholy Baby. There is the piano player who sizes up his audience and plays classics for one group and show tunes for another. Both are piano players, but what a difference in the same thing.

The concept of the client (or customer) oriented practice may be a new one to many practitioners, but as a concept, it's old as the hills. And should have been as obvious. It seems so perfectly rational that if you don't offer what the client wants and needs, then the client will go elsewhere.

But perhaps the lack of competition masked that basic reality.

No more. Call it client-oriented, or quality, or any new buzzword you may prefer. The fact is that in a competitive economy, only the client—or customer—oriented practitioner can thrive.

The client orientation for professionals instigates a new perspective on one's own practice. A lawyer who specializes in divorces may be limited by a small, stable, conservative community. Or he or she may perceive that inherent in pursuing his divorce practice are negotiating skills that can serve clients in other ways. Heaven help the accountant, whatever his or her specialty, who doesn't realize the need for computer expertise by virtually all the firm's clients, or his or her role in the entrepreneurial explosion.

Moreover, the nature of professional services is such that there is vast flexibility, even within a specialization and professional and ethical strictures, to adjust the nature of service to the needs of the client. The operating factor is not the limit of the specialization, but the concept of imaginatively expanding the professional capability to serve the dynamic of the client's business. Or to put it more simply, doing what the client needs from you professionally—not what you want to do just because it's what you do best.

That many professionals instinctively understand this can be seen readily by comparing the professional firm of today with those of a decade or so ago. The catalog of accounting firm services today is vast compared with the limited scope of the accountant's activities in the past. And this is true of small firms as well as large. One need only look at the legal or tax and group practices that exist today, some even in department stores, to realize that a great deal has changed in the concept of service. They represent the ideal of understanding the market; understanding the needs for ever-expanding professional services, and adjusting the services to meet those needs.

## Some Considerations and Obstacles

In professional services marketing, more than in any other marketing arena, the marketer proposes and others dispose—and there may not always be a sound rationale for the disposal. This is true for both the professional marketer and the practitioner given the marketing responsibility within a firm. Marketing planning in professional services marketing, then, takes on a somewhat different cast than one finds in the textbook. It would certainly be unfair to discuss marketing planning without a hard and realistic look at some of the obstacles.

The basic marketing textbooks don't include, for example, the structure of the partnership, as opposed to the corporation. They don't include, as well, the problems of dealing with a new discipline—marketing—imposed upon an old one—professional services. Here, the chemistry is strong enough to alter basic molecular structures.

The problems that arise in moving the concept of the total marketing plan to the reality of the professional firm may not be many, but they are sufficient to subvert—or at least thwart—the theory of market planning in professional services.

In a corporation, particularly one that produces a product, marketing usually holds a comfortable and familiar slot. The marketing people are an equal part of management with the administrators and the financial people and the production people. Marketing's contribution is understood, and its practices are not questioned by people who have their own concerns. Because of the corporate structure, the marketing budget doesn't come out of the pockets of individuals. And because products are involved, the movement of products to market is a direct gauge of the efficacy of the marketing operation. In this context, marketing plans have some meaning...some reality...some efficacy.

But what happens in a professional service?

- Because the ability to market competitively is new, there's no tradition for it. Its place in the firm is precarious and unfamiliar. Its language is unfamiliar, its professionalism is alien, its practitioners of another culture. It's understood more in mythology and misconception than in fact.

- The partnership structure really makes a difference. If, in a corporation, the marketing budget comes out of no individual's pocket (shareholders are too far removed from daily management), and the cost of marketing is built into the selling price of the product, in a partnership every marketing dollar comes out of every partner's pocket. And with

7

no tradition of recouping marketing costs through pricing. This means that every partner has an opinion or attitude toward marketing—and every partner's attitude and opinion counts (and is often expressed).

- In a professional firm, the marketer must sell the marketing plan to people who have no way of judging the plan's value, potential, cost, or effectiveness. The marketing professional proposes in marketing terms, but the plan is disposed of in terms frequently inimical to marketing. For the well-trained marketing director new to the culture, this is frequently a high point in culture shock and frustration.

- In a professional firm, expectations for marketing become crucial. If a manufacturing company can expect its marketing efforts to be measurable in units sold, how can a professional firm's program be measured—when there is rarely a one-to-one relationship between efforts and results? If expectations for a program aren't clearly spelled out, there is the greatest likelihood that the results of even the best program will be misjudged. This emphasis on expectations, for every aspect of marketing, is distinctive to marketing professional services.

- There is a very different relationship between the marketing programs of different sizes of professional firms and different sizes of manufacturing firms. More than in most areas of marketing, small professional firms compete on equal footing, in many ways, with large firms.

## Overcoming Obstacles

What does this add up to in developing a marketing plan for a professional firm? Where does the well-trained and well-educated marketing professional depart from the textbooks on marketing planning?

- In marketing professional services, textbook structures don't count—imagination does. The marketing executive for a corporation will be judged by people who know the textbooks; the marketing people for a professional firm will be judged by people who frequently don't. *Look at the problem and the solution—not at the textbook.*

- While it's true that marketing works best in the total context, it won't work at all if a firm doesn't understand the total context. Some of the most successful programs in professional services marketing today are those that go for the win, in terms of the needs and wishes of the partnership, and not for the textbook example. This may mean something like a particularly effective public relations program, and little more. Bad classical marketing, but great pragmatism for the right firm at the right time. It may mean little more than sales training for key partners. Sure, there's a need for marketing backup to selling, but the marketing professional may not be able to get the whole marketing package through the door at once. Learn to think in parts. The success of parts can lead to the opportunity to develop the whole.

- Learn to sell internally. The marketing people at IBM or Xerox don't have to sell what they do to their own firms on a daily basis. In professional services, if the marketing professionals don't sell internally you won't get much chance to sell externally. Keep it simple. If you're in charge of marketing, let 'em know what you're going to do, and what you're doing, and what it means, and what they can expect from it. If you don't have friends in the partnership who understand and support you, you can be a genius, but you won't be there long enough to show it.

- Expectations. Non-marketers, if they don't know what to expect from a marketing effort, will expect the wrong thing. They will expect a newspaper story or a direct mail program to produce clients. They will expect a marketing program to work without their participating in any way. Spell out the expectations, and relate them clearly to the very specific things the partners want from the marketer.

- Marketing professionals tend to want to perform it in terms of what they know. But that works only in a context in which marketing is fully understood. In most professional firms, they may give lip service to the importance of what the marketing professional knows, but they're really interested only in the marketer's producing what they want or think they need. If you have to convert the partners, do it in their terms—not yours as a marketer. The important lesson is that marketers don't get to do what they want to do, and think should be done, until they've succeeded at what the *firm* wants to do, and thinks should be done.

The cold hard fact is that even though every marketing professional is trained to think in terms of the total marketing plan, that plan is a useless document in a hostile or alien land. And unless the firm is truly sophisticated in contemporary professional services marketing, even the sophisticated partner—much less the professional marketing director—is in for a hard time with the classic textbook approach.

## The Options of Strategy

What this leads to, ultimately, is to realize that strategy is really comprised of two elements—choice, and configuration. In marketing, that means a choice from among the many options of tools and strategies, and a choice of many possible configurations of skills applied to meet specific marketing objectives.

The tools of marketing are finite. Advertising, public relations, direct mail, publications, and so forth. But the ways in which the tools can be used are infinite, offering a wide range of choices to allow the marketing program to serve the firm's objectives.

The decision can be made, strategically, to limit the marketing thrust to one or several isolated activities. A newsletter, for example, or a brochure, or a public relations campaign. Unfortunately, this rarely works as an ongoing marketing effort, if for no reason other than that in professional services marketing, activities reinforce and magnify other activities. An ad or direct mail campaign may work to sell a product. In professional services, they only serve to break ground for a personal selling effort.

### The Planning Matrix

Where once the practice could be developed by simply joining the right clubs and giving an occasional speech, today's competition requires more.

Where once there was a clear division of the market between the big firms and the little firms, this too is no longer the case. Big accounting and law firms, with hundreds of partners, now structure themselves to compete against one- and two-partner firms for the small or emerging business. The small practitioner must now market his services just to hold his own. An increasing number of small firms now offer, as boutiques, services that may be national or international. And even the local firm's small local client may be functioning internationally.

Today, in the competitive marketplace, the marketing process is increasingly elaborate and requires strategy and skill. It begins with the conscious decision to grow and compete, departing substantially from serendipity. It moves to developing a plan and a strategy, and then to executing that plan. It includes learning and practicing new skills, and how to manage new skills performed by others.

While there are no planning patterns so universal as to be cast in stone, nor that can serve every business, there are some basic considerations for all firms.

Planning the marketing campaign begins, invariably, with defining the market, because one wouldn't go to market with a product for which there is no demand, or a demand so limited that supplying the product isn't cost-effective. True, demand for products and services can sometimes be created, but only within limits. And only if it can be done on such a large scale as to make the effort worth the price.

And because the needs of the market for professional services are so multifaceted, the professional must understand exactly how those needs are structured, how they vary from one client to another, and how they change. It's very easy to understand that every public corporation needs an auditor or a corporate counsel, but that's rarely sufficient. For example, is an audit a commodity, or can it be developed into a management tool? Is that, in fact, what the client really wants?

Is it sufficient for the attorney to be merely reactive to his client's needs, or should he become more active in his client's business, and contribute to it with new legal services?

What about the small firm and the small client? Is the client happy with just routine accounting services, or is he really longing for help with such aspects of his business as cash management, or computers, or integrating personal estate planning with his business planning? What are the needs for sophisticated consulting or legal services that integrate business and personal structures?

The point is that no practice—or marketing program to grow that practice—can be developed in today's competitive climate if there isn't a clear picture of the needs—the changing and varied needs—of the market place. And that includes those needs that the client company may not itself have perceived.

An intelligently structured campaign should, like legs, be just long enough to reach the ground. It should be structured to meet the needs and desires of *both* your firm and your clients. It is particular and specific and unique to your firm.

If you are by choice a small practitioner, and merely want to maintain a moderate growth, then obviously a campaign for you will encompass deep immersion in very few of the techniques delineated in these pages.

If, on the other hand, you mean to grow and to compete actively, then your campaign must be carefully and elaborately planned.

The techniques presented throughout this book are, essentially, tools. When they are used properly and skillfully, and in conjunction with one another, they can do some powerful building. How each one works, and how they are used in the marketing mix is described further in this chapter.

In all likelihood, most of the skills will be applied by professionals in each marketing discipline. But the plan—the blueprint—must be done with the firm's hand at the helm, no matter how many advertising or public relations or other marketing specialists are brought in.

### Formulating the Plan

Planning the campaign, then, also includes familiarizing key partners with how the tools of marketing work, and what each contributes to the total marketing campaign.

It requires a great deal of introspection, in which the firm asks itself about its own aims and objectives. Merely to want a very large firm, or one that differs substantially from what you have now, is not enough. Partners have to understand what's involved in developing that kind of practice. They have to accurately assess their own skills and preferences, and how those skills and practice relate to the precise needs of the firm's chosen market.

Budget must be understood, not just in terms of what things cost, and how much the firm is prepared to spend, but on the crucial factors of return on investment of the marketing dollar.

Planning should begin with some thoughts on at least the following:

- Do I really understand my market and its needs, or should I consider some formal explorations?

- How well do our skills fit what we perceive our market to want? If new skills are to be added or developed, are we capable of managing them?
- What kind of firm do I have now, and do I want to change its character, size, structure, services, market area? And if I want to change any of these elements, why?
- What are the real skills we have to offer?
- Should the emphasis be solely on maintaining and strengthening the current practice, or do we really want to grow? And if so, how big? Why?
- How much commitment—measured in willingness to participate and in dollars—is available within the firm for marketing efforts?
- Is the commitment sufficiently large to warrant bringing in outside marketing help, or should we limit the effort to what we can do ourselves? And in either event, who's going to take the responsibility for managing the effort?
- If the market warrants it, are we prepared to either add staff, or train people, to better serve market needs? In view of the firm's size, markets, overhead, and the desires of the partners, are we prepared to rethink pricing?

Given the answer to questions such as these, a marketing plan can be developed, incorporating the following elements:

- Market—size and structure
- Objectives—both firm and marketing
- Services and skills to meet the market's needs
- Choice and mix of tools to achieve objectives, and in the framework of the budget.
- Expectations and time frame
- Who is to manage and who is to perform
- Budget
- Structures for monitoring program, and for adjusting firm practices in response to marketing results

In marketing planning, there should be a clear distinction between wishes and reality. It's one thing to wish your firm were considerably larger; it's another thing to be prepared to do what's necessary to make it so.

These are, of course, standard planning elements, and developing a marketing campaign is very much a part of planning. The difference is that here, you're dealing with new and probably unfamiliar elements, including the fact that in most cases you're probably going to have to depend upon the skills of other people—the marketing professionals.

### *The Ingredients of the Plan*

In an article on the marketing program in *The Marcus Report,* August J. Aquila, Ph.D, a Principal in the accounting firm of Friedman, Eisenstein, Raemer & Schwartz and Senior Vice President of Practice Development Institute, and Jodi M. Hier, a Senior Marketing Consultant with PDI, pointed out that there are many ingredients to a successful marketing plan, but the elements that must be added beyond the factors of the plan itself are the ones most often missing—*vision, planning, and implementation. Vision* gives the plan perspective, in terms of the firm's objectives. *Planning* gives the market plan organization and timing. But it's *implementation,* that starts the engine—and keeps it running.

Not surprisingly, implementation is the hardest part of a marketing plan, at least because it involves so many more individuals than the marketing director. A firm may find a comfort factor in having a plan, but there is still a problem in getting partners to apply what they traditionally feel are the more important billable hours to doing something like marketing. And—probably because marketing is still new to the professions—the feeling is that time spent on marketing is not as productive as is billable time. Lost, somehow, is the concept that if partner A spends four billable hours at $150 an hour the value to the firm is $600. But what's the value to the firm of Partner B, who spends four hours helping to implement a marketing program that lands a $10,000 engagement?

Not to be forgotten, Aquila and Hier point out, is that a marketing program is people—not words on a page. The *vision* must be developed and articulated by a *visionary*—someone who can define and describe the firm's goal, and is committed to seeing it realized. It may be the firm's managing partner, or any other influential individual. It's crucial, though, that this person be a leader, capable of leading the firm to accept the vision.

When others in the firm understand the vision, their role in realizing it should be defined. Setting goals—objectives—is crucial to implementing a program. If you don't know where you're going, how can you plan how to get there? And goals must be detailed for each step in the program, as well as for each individual with responsibility under the plan. The goals must be measurable as well, so that the progress and success of the plan can be observed.

## Market Segmentation

Inherent in marketing planning is the growing understanding by professional services marketers of such traditional marketing techniques as *segmentation*—now popularly known as *niche marketing.* In segmentation, we recognize that a particular set of professional skills, whether in law, accounting or consulting, have a special significance to a particular market segment, and so we market to that segment accordingly. For example, The accounting skills used in litigation support systems are distinctive, and can be marketed as a discreet service to law firms. In this case, law firms are defined as the market segment—the *niche.*

13

Another form of market segmentation is by industry. Professionals with a large number of clients in a particular industry have developed a competence in that industry. They've learned the unique industry practices, jargon, and technical terms that allow them to move comfortably in the industry. This capability and competence is especially marketable because it affords the opportunity to make a contribution to a client in that industry that goes well beyond the expertise of the profession itself.

Thinking in terms of market segments also opens avenues of opportunity. A law firm with a general practice in a small city becomes aware of an influx of high tech firms. It occurs to one of the partners that there might be an opportunity for the firm to expand its clientele if it had an intellectual properties practice to address some of the legal problems for these new companies.

Niche marketing, then, is simply, a decision to use a configuration of marketing tools to address a specific target—a niche or slot in the market.

While the current term, niche marketing, is very much in vogue at the moment, it may be seen in better perspective by its more traditional name of market segmentation.

The noted law firm marketing consultants, Gerald Riskin and Patrick McKenna, partners in the Canadian-based international law firm marketing consulting organization, The Edge Group, dealt extensively with the subject in their excellent book, Practice Development (Butterworths Canada Ltd., 1989).

### Choosing a Market Segment

In general, Riskin and McKenna note, markets can be segmented by several different dimensions—by industry, size, revenue, potential, geographic area, behavioral characteristics, or service requirements.

### Evaluation

In considering a niche or specialized practice area, they suggest that you should:

- *Examine the growth rate.* What are the current growth trends for this industry or practice area?

- *Review your knowledge of the niche.* Do we know enough about the technical aspects of this industry or practice area? If not, what more do we need? Where can we get it? For example, can we ascertain what we need to know about representing or working for nursing homes from the nursing home we currently serve? Should we laterally hire a partner who is expert in the area, or an associate who has worked with an expert we cannot or do not wish to hire?

- *Determine potential fees.* What fees can we expect to realize from serving this industry or practice area? Can we anticipate some premium pricing or value billing?

- *Examine the nature of the market/specialization.* What differentiates this specialization from anything else we do? How is this market unique? For example, nursing home owners may prefer less formal settings for meetings, and they may like aggressiveness (they are entrepreneurs), like to talk about fees, and so on.

- *Know the competition.* What other professional firms currently attempt to serve this industry or specialize in this practice area? Who are our potential competitors? What are their strengths and weaknesses? For example, the industry may be presently served by megafirms. A smaller firm might try to show that it can provide more personal attention with the same or better level of expertise.

- *Determine the problems and opportunities.* Can we develop creative solutions to any problems that exist while exploiting the opportunities? For example, the young associate or manager whose spouse is a doctor may be just the right person to put on the team for hospital clients.

- *Determine the marketing effort required.* What level of manpower and resources will it take to enter this niche and to service prospects?

- *Decide what factors would lead to success.* What unique skills and expertise are offered in our service that would entice prospective clients?

For the small firm, evaluation requires considerable personal commitment and time management. A larger firm can form an evaluation team to explore the issues and make recommendations. However orchestrated, these preliminary steps are cost-effective essentials.

Once the evaluation has been completed, what had previously seemed to be a hot new practice area or market niche may appear less attractive, and a seemingly mundane area may generate new interest.

## Choose the Team

Unless you're a sole practitioner, say Riskin and McKenna, you should use a team approach, following a step-by-step process for each practice area or industry being considered.

The team should consist of one or two technically oriented partners who are knowledgeable in the practice area or industry, supported by an assigned staff member, and of a marketing-oriented partner or marketing professional from either the management or the business development section of the firm.

## Perform a Situation Analysis

Having evaluated the niche you've chosen, and determined that you know enough to pursue it, they suggest that you still need more information:

- Are you now generating revenue from this segment? How much?
- Who are your clients now?
- What are your strengths internally? (Be realistic—discount ego statements).
- How large is the specific market in your geographic area? (See chapter 2 for research techniques)
- Who are the potential clients? (Be practical but also creative. If you serve a drug manufacturer, don't overlook pharmacies or individual pharmacists).
- Do you have a full profile on each of your competitors?
- How well are you known or perceived in a particular market?
- What marketing support tools do you currently have? (Do you have professional or support staff with marketing backgrounds? Who could you hire or retain and at what cost?)

Objectives, set by volume of billings or number of new clients, should be realistic, measurable, specific, and clear.

Analysis of the desired market segments, suggest Riskin and McKenna, should include assessing their attractiveness and accessibility. You need to be able to quantify (or make a realistic judgment of) the relative size, purchasing power, potential growth, and expected profitability of the targeted segment.

## Determine Marketing Strategies

And finally, Riskin and McKenna suggest that your marketing strategies fulfill the following criteria:

- They are compatible with the firm's comfort level. With this in mind, should they be highly promotional or based on low-key image building?
- They are ethically acceptable.
- They take financial resources into consideration.
- They have a realistic time frame with reasonable deadlines.

## Niche Marketing as a Strategy

The arguments in favor of niche marketing are overwhelming. It's the rifle shot, compared to the scattershot. There is less that's random. It's economical, because, presumably, you're not wasting ammunition on a large portion of the market that's not for you. And it's not a difficult concept, at first glance, to understand.

These are the advantages, and they're very real. But there are dangers as well.

There is the danger of misdefining the segment, and of miscasting the message to that segment. There's the danger—and a very serious one it is—of becoming so enamored of the niche marketing concept that you ignore the larger canvas of general marketing.

There are, of course, no more inviolate rules in segment or niche marketing than there are in any other aspect of marketing. It's all subject to the skill and imagination of the marketer. But there are some clear guidelines that derive from the mistakes of others.

- Deciding to go for a specific segment is not a lightly taken or arbitrary decision. Does the segment really exist, or are you inventing it to meet the needs of the service you want to sell?

- Do you really have a specific service to offer that niche, or are you forcing a fit?

- How are you defining the niche? It's not as easy as it looks. A niche, we know, should have common characteristics—but which ones? Age? Income? Same industry? Same problems? This is the crucial part, because the common characteristic should relate to the service you want to sell them. If you're selling estate planning, age of the prospective client is an important characteristic. If you're selling cash management services, age may be irrelevant, but size of business can be crucial.

- Given a niche with clearly defined common characteristics that are relevant to the service you want to sell, is there a way to reach that segment directly? Is there a newspaper or other publication that's aimed at—and effectively hits—that niche? If not, you're going to find yourself using general media to reach a specific target, in which case, why bother with niche marketing?

- But sometimes the segment really does exist, and relate well to your service, but there's no specific media that's aimed at that niche. In that case, using general media, can you tailor your marketing material and presentation to that segment? In fact, that may sometimes be more effective than using target media.

- Are you really in a position to deliver to that segment? If you want to sell intellectual property law, it's not enough to know that there's a segment in high tech, which implies frequent innovation and invention. Does it really exist, and are you geared to serve it? High tech may imply innovation, but it may not in fact exist. What's more important is that you may not really be in position, by virtue of staff, to serve that segment. Or serving it properly may simply not be cost effective.

17

- How are you planning to divide your marketing effort among several niches, or among niches and the overall firm itself? What firm marketing activities will be a backup for the niche marketing, or will the niche marketing be the sole effort for the firm (rarely an effective device)?

- How are you going to determine the specific marketing appeal to that niche? Which characteristic is predominant, to the point of dictating the marketing thrust? Which tools will be used to deliver that thrust? Certainly, direct mail becomes an obvious choice because it can be focussed directly to individuals in the segment. But what are your other media choices? And what happens if the direct mail campaign is badly done. Does that destroy your credibility with that target audience?

- Is niche marketing your best alternative? How about target marketing, in which you choose specific potential clients and go after them. Sometimes (depending upon the service you're offering and the potential size of the project you're selling) targeting specific and carefully identified clients can be more cost effective. Even in a well-directed appeal to a segment, you're not going to get everybody in that segment.

- How do you calculate results? As difficult as it is under normal circumstances to relate results to efforts in professional services marketing, it's harder yet to pin results to a specific effort. How, then, do you plan to gauge whether or not your niche marketing efforts are effective—or whether your success might have come just as well through general marketing efforts? In the case of direct mail, there's a measure in the number of opportunities that are produced to make presentations. But for public relations or advertising, it can be difficult. One answer is to use marketing tools specific to a niche, such as direct mail or seminars.

Of course you aim your marketing efforts at an audience most likely to need your services, but that doesn't necessarily constitute a niche. For example, suppose you're a law firm that does general commercial law, trusts and estates, and some SEC work. It can be assumed that each of those three services constitutes a niche, in that each has clearly defined common characteristics. Yet, there are sufficient overlapping characteristics to suggest that a broader appeal might project the capabilities of the firm and its broader spectrum of skills as well, and perhaps more efficiently, than niche marketing.

At the same time, you should consider whether niche marketing should be backed by a broader overall program, in which other aspects of the firm's capabilities are projected.

*Niche marketing,* then, is not always as simple and clear-cut a concept as it appears. In a sense, all of professional services marketing has characteristics of niche marketing, because unlike corporate marketing, it's not effective to simply promote the name of the firm. You do best when you project the firm's capabilities. Those capabilities are best projected through the offices of individuals in the firm.

John Jones, the expert on estates and trusts, writes articles or is quoted on estates and trusts. Sam Smith, an expert on cash flow management, speaks before small business groups on cash flow management. Harry Brown, an expert on personal financial planning, participates in joint ventures with banks on seminars for well-to-do consumers. Is this good general marketing, or is it niche marketing? Does it matter, so long as it's effective?

There are times when segmentation makes sense. If you specialize in pension funds, for example, you know that the people you want to reach are clearly defined—courtesy of ERISA—and the professional service requirements are distinctive. You know there are publications aimed directly at them, and you know the cast of characters. You know your specific capabilities in the field, and you know the specific needs of the target group. Here, the rationale for niche marketing is clear.

But it isn't always so—the rationale isn't always as clear as the drive to try something new to professional services called niche marketing. And if the rational isn't clear, then the niche becomes a crevice.

## Target Marketing

*Target marketing* is yet another sound strategy that works very well for the firm that's fully comfortable with its own competence in specific skills. In *target marketing,* a profile of the firm's ideal client is drawn. This profile may be defined by any number of factors, such as company size, industry, specific problem (e.g. bankruptcy), location, and so forth. Using contemporary sophisticated databases, a list of companies that fit that profile is developed. These become the target companies to which the firm will direct its marketing efforts.

The approach to these targeted companies is sometimes easier to define than are other forms of marketing strategies. Knowing your audience virtually by name means direct mail, seminars, phone contact and followup, and personal selling. It means using brochures to focus on your expertise, and newsletters to maintain a continuity in contact. Each individual company and its officers are a specific target, and you keep hammering at them until they become clients.

## Positioning

*Positioning* is another strategy drawn from traditional marketing. Actually, it's simply a relatively new word for an old and rather obvious marketing practice, in which we attempt to differentiate a product or service by casting it in ways that will have a specifically defined appeal to a specifically defined audience. While it's relatively easy to do in products, it's more difficult to do in services, simply because it's so hard to differentiate one firm's performance of a service from that of another firm's performance of the same service. Still, it can sometimes be done.

19

The small accounting firm that realizes that it can't do audits for the multinational corporation may find a way to focus on its ability to do audits particularly cherished by banks that lend to small companies. That's *positioning*.

There's no great mystery in positioning, nor should it be allowed to become a mystique.

It's certainly reasonable that a market best understands a supplier in terms of a clear definition of the services that supplier provides, and the way in which they're provided. Why not, then, determine how you want your firm, and its services perceived? If that's done in terms of the market you're addressing, then that's your position, and everything you do is cast in the light of that position.

This means understanding the market, or those segments of it that are to become your targets. It means finding ways that *realistically* present your firm, its people, and its capabilities to meet the needs of that market or market segment. A simple example might be to bring an economic orientation to a market that has one eye on international business.

The real danger is to confuse *positioning* with *image*. If you try to generate a position based upon how you want to be perceived, rather than what you really are, then, like image building, you're manipulating symbols to present a picture that isn't real. This rarely works for more than about ten minutes—and then the market sees through it.

If you cast a position for your firm that really distinguishes it from your competitors, then it had better be based on reality. As the old saw goes—what you are speaks so loudly I can't hear what you say you are.

## The Marketing Mix

It's the peculiar nature of professional services marketing that despite the fact that the tools (advertising, public relations, etc.) are the same as those used in all other forms of marketing, they don't always work in quite the same way. It can be very frustrating to someone who has sold millions of dollars in products to find that the same techniques applied to accounting or law or consulting produce not a penny in fee revenues.

Even the jargon of marketing—terms such as *marketing mix, niche marketing*, and *positioning*—take on different meanings. For example, the term *marketing mix*, in product marketing, usually applies to the *four Ps—product, price, place, promotion*. But these *Ps* are totally product oriented, and relate to such aspects of marketing as product inventory, pricing built upon a very different structure than that used for pricing services, a costing and distribution structure totally irrelevant to delivering professional services—a full array of elements that have nothing to do with marketing professional services. Unfortunately, such jargon, perpetrated by academics with little or no hands-on experience, tends to stick to marketing initiates like peanut butter on the roof of the mouth.

A *marketing mix* in professional services marketing, on the other hand, may simply be a convenient way to describe the way in which the tools of marketing play upon—and support—one another in the marketing process.

Marketing in any context is the sum of a great many activities—a thrust of the several marketing tools working together to accomplish specific marketing objectives. And more so in professional services marketing, where, like metric tools in a non-metric context, nothing quite works the way it looks like it was supposed to.

In professional services, more than in any other kind of marketing, it's not advertising alone that works, nor direct mail, nor public relations. Rather, it's a mixture of all tools, working in a balanced relationship. And the mixture may be very different, depending upon the service being marketed and the objectives of the marketing program.

In marketing professional services, the challenge is compounded by the very nature of professional services. Advertising doesn't sell professional services, nor does public relations, nor brochures, nor any other tool. And it's usually the individual who is capable of performing that service.

An intensive advertising campaign can convey some compelling facts about your services, and even generate inquiries. But no ad was ever responsible for a client's signing a contract, without a subsequent personal discussion.

A well-conceived direct mail campaign can make your prospective clients aware of your ability to address a particular problem, but the client will not call you and say "Start tomorrow" without meeting with you, and assuring himself that you really can help him with his specific problems. Nor will any brochure, nor article, nor press release bring you clients. They will only educate your prospective clientele about you and your capabilities, and perhaps lead to direct inquiries. They will convey a great deal of information, leaving you free, in your personal contact, to focus on how your capabilities address his particular problem. (As with most things, there are exceptions, of course. For example, attorneys with national reputations for particular skills—whether their fame is earned or fostered by public relations campaigns—tend to not have to sell their services.)

Yet, these tools of marketing are essential to a marketing program—to helping you meet your own objectives.

### The Role of the Marketing Tools

What role, then, do the tools of marketing play?

They serve to establish a context in which selling can be enhanced. They build reputation and focus a perception of a firm. They develop leads. They pre-sell. They educate the prospective client.

If your marketing efforts were limited solely to selling, then the limits of your efforts would be the number of people you could reach in person, and then could persuade that you can solve their problems more effectively than can any of your competitors. Assuming that you had sufficient contacts to meet a large number of prospective clients, you would be starting from scratch in explaining who you are, what you do, why you do it better, and so forth.

An effective marketing program, using the tools of marketing appropriately, does all that for you on a large scale. Then, when you meet the prospective client that's been produced by the campaign, you don't come as a stranger.

To accomplish this, it's important to know what each of the tools are, how each works, and how to use them, in balance—in a proper mix—to reinforce one another.

Each performs a different role, and each takes on a different quality when used in conjunction with others. Nor are they interchangeable. Advertising will not do what public relations will do, nor is public relations "free advertising." Direct mail will not do what display advertising does, nor is a brochure a substitute for an article about you or by you in a professional journal.

Each of the marketing tools will be discussed in a separate chapter, but for perspective, an overview is useful.

## Advertising

Advertising is a practice and discipline that uses space or air time you purchase in media—print, broadcast, or any other of a number of possibilities—to deliver a message. An ad in a newspaper or magazine, or a message on a pencil or a calendar, or a radio or television commercial, in which the space or time has been paid for and the message supplied by the purchaser, is advertising.

If you've paid for the space, you can use it for any message you wish, as long as it doesn't violate basic laws concerning flagrant misrepresentation, or violate professional canons of ethics.

The major roles of advertising are to persuade and to inform. To be effective, advertising must engender in the reader or listener a desire to do business with you. If it informs, it should do so in a way that fosters a feeling of good will, and even enthusiasm, for what you have to offer. It should persuade the prospective client that you understand and are capable of serving that client's needs or solving his or her problems.

Each of the media used in advertising has a different purpose and value, and makes a different contribution to the marketing mix.

Broadcast media—radio and television (including cable)—are rapidly coming into their own in professional service advertising. At first little used by professionals after the change in the canons of ethics (they were considered too blatant), more and more professionals are learning to use it tastefully, ethically, and effectively.

Broadcast advertising has a very different quality than does print advertising. A reader may choose to overlook or not read a print ad; the listener or viewer has considerably less opportunity to overlook the broadcast ad. True, many people use the commercial as a time to get a fresh drink, but more people don't. One doesn't turn the radio off during a radio commercial.

Credibility and effectiveness in the print ad are a function of the degree of talent of a copywriter. In the broadcast media, that talent is tempered by the ability of the announcer and the effectiveness of the production. The announcer functions as a live and presumably persuasive salesman, whereas in print the copy must speak for itself. The television commercial has the advantage of motion, visualization, and frequently, dramatization.

On the other hand, print media has a staying power not inherent in broadcasting. The broadcast message flees with time. The reader who is interested in any aspect of the print ad can peruse and study it at a leisurely pace. It can even be clipped and saved for future reference.

And so even in advertising, there is a difference in values by media, and therefore a difference in impact.

*Direct Mail.* Direct mail is the form of advertising that has the distinct advantage of bringing the message directly to the individual prospect. In all other forms of advertising, a measure of the advertising dollar is wasted because you pay for readership that includes non-prospects for your service as well as prospects. In direct mail, you have the opportunity to define a universe of prospects—those with characteristics most likely to be amenable to your services—and to write to them directly.

Used correctly, direct mail can be one of the most powerful vehicles for marketing professional services. It allows you to personalize your message, to aim it directly to your prospect, and to talk to more people as individuals than you can possibly meet directly, in person or by phone.

As firms become more familiar with direct mail, it's used increasingly as a precursor to a telephone followup, aimed at getting a face-to-face meeting with a prospect, in order to make a presentation. While all other tools of marketing serve a powerful role in informing and educating and building context, the combination of direct mail and telephone followup is the strongest possible combination to bring the seller and the prospect together.

Direct mail is also a vehicle. It can be simply a personalized letter, or it can carry a brochure, a reprint of an article, a case history, or even a reprint of a print ad.

It's crucial to realize, however, that the limits of all service advertising apply as well to direct mail. The effectiveness of a direct mail letter that sells a product can be measured by the number of order forms that are returned. Rarely can the effectiveness of a mailing for a service be measured in the same way. In marketing professional services, it can inform and persuade and, in some circumstances, invite inquiries. But like any other form of advertising for professional services, it cannot, without followup and personal appearance, be expected to close a sale.

Because it goes directly to an individual whom you've identified as a prospective client, direct mail offers the potential for the best return on investment of all advertising media.

*Telemarketing.* An interesting development, in this context, is the growing use and success of telemarketing—selling by telephone using the cold call, frequently by a professional telemarketer rather than an accountant or a lawyer. Sometimes it's used as a followup to a direct mail campaign.

In the first days since *Bates*, telemarketing was dismissed as being too crass for professional services. However, a growing experience in using it in certain contexts has shown it to be remarkably effective. Nor has there been the negative reaction by prospective clients that had been anticipated for it. For many firms, particularly in accounting and consulting, telemarketing works very well to generate opportunities to sell face-to-face, and has resulted in producing a great many fee dollars.

*Classified Advertising.* Classified advertising is advertising in space specially designated by category, such as *Help Wanted,* or merchandise or services for sale. It's most frequently used by professional firms to advertise for staff. It's sometimes useful, however, to project facts about a firm to a target audience. For example, a display ad in the classified section of a publication, seeking tax accountants for hire, can be used to describe the virtues of the firm. This is useful for enhancing a reputation within the firm's profession.

*Other Advertising Media.* Any medium that can carry your message to a large and defined audience is valid to consider for advertising. There are circumstances, for example, under which billboards can be effective, and in fact, tax, legal, and medical clinics are using them now. They can be used tastefully and ethically, and can be cost effective. Pencils and premiums, as distant an advertising media as they may seem in view of the traditions of professional marketing, are still valid media. Transportation advertising has its uses as well. Yellow page directory advertising is a powerful medium, and is in fact the fourth largest advertising medium—and the fastest growing—in the United States

The point is that no medium should be overlooked, simply because it has never been used before. Professional services advertising has a short history, no tradition, and a future to be determined only by the imagination of marketers.

### Public Relations

The term *public relations* is a broad one, encompassing a great many activities. Publicity, the actual function of developing editorial coverage, is a part of public relations, but by no means the entire public relations function.

Literally, of course, the term means relations with the public—everything you do in dealing with the public. In fact, it's a group of activities designed to enhance the way people think about your firm and know about you. Public relations is the broader technique of creating a firm worthy of being publicized, and developing activities that are newsworthy. Inherent in public relations, as well, are all aspects of your public persona, from the way your phone is answered to your letterhead, to the way your office is decorated—all of which contribute to your reputation and the way in which you are perceived as a professional.

Public relations, and particularly the publicity aspect of it, uses the editorial media to reach its audiences. This can be accomplished by direct contact with the media, or by developing newsworthy devices (seminars, speeches, etc.) that have an inherent news value.

The basic technique of publicity is to cast the story you want to tell in ways that are newsworthy, and then to persuade the news media that the story is of sufficient interest to a broad range of readers. Successful publicity has the advantage of an implied editorial endorsement, because it's assumed that an independent and objective publication has chosen to publish it. It has the disadvantage of lacking control over the way the message appears, as we control the message in advertising. In publicity, we merely propose, others—the editors—dispose.

Publicity, cast as news or information, has no selling power, except under the most serendipitous circumstances.

It's value, however, is immeasurable in terms of its ability to inform, to build reputation, and to enhance credibility. A tax expert who's constantly quoted authoritatively in the business pages develops a reputation that substantially enhances any selling effort. An accounting firm or law firm whose partners are constantly quoted in a context of expertise quickly becomes known by name, and recognized as a source of that expertise.

Unique to the public relations aspect of professional services is the fact that the product is the individual who performs the service. Your firm is represented by every individual, from the senior partner to the lowest ranking associate, who deals with your clientele. Many a client has been lost because a very junior associate has behaved in some deleterious way.

### Printed Material

Material such as brochures and newsletters are standard fare in professional services, and they are a crucial tool of marketing. Unfortunately, they are too frequently used ineffectively. And, as sometimes happens with direct mail, they are too often distributed without a clear view of the recipient. They are, as well, too often used as a sole marketing tool.

Printed material is an important part of the marketing mix, but again, only if used in conjunction with other tools.

### The Classic Practice Development Tools

The traditional practice development tools still have an important place in marketing. Networking, joining organizations, the golf club, seminars, speeches, memos to clients that find their way to non-clients—all are integral to the marketing process.

More business is done, goes the old saw, on the golf course than in the board room. An accountant who volunteers his services as treasurer of an important civic organization is going to be known to a lot of important business people in the community, all of whom will have had the opportunity to see his skills at first hand within a public service context. The lawyer who is active in his local political organization, or runs for office—even against an incumbent running in a safe district—is legitimately exposing his talents and skills, and building a personal reputation.

Nor have there ever been prohibitions against making speeches or appearing on informative panels before business groups, if the subjects were enlightening and educational to the audience. For the more skillful, this has long been a prime means of practice development.

And what about the seminar for clients on the ramifications of a new tax law, sponsored by an accounting or law firm, or even jointly with a bank, in which the panelists were prominent local accountants or lawyers? Only clients could be invited, but if non-clients are invited by clients or friends, new friends could be made. Then there is the memo—or even the newsletter—to clients, on a new law or accounting regulation, that finds its way into the hands of non-clients.

And even though contemporary marketing brings something of a science to those techniques that professionals have instinctively used for so long, these techniques still rely upon the individual practitioner. The professional marketer may program the organizational memberships, or design the seminar, but the professional practitioner has to join the club and participate on the seminar panel.

But now, new elements enter the traditional seminar picture. Non-clients may be invited. Other professionals in the same field are offering seminars on the same subjects. Seminars may be advertised. You can charge admission to seminars you once gave free (which, incidentally, puts you in an entirely different business—the business of selling seminars). Seminars may now be publicized in ways that were not possible before. And because seminars should be part of a total marketing effort, they must be planned differently, as part of a totality rather than as isolated events, if they are to serve a proper marketing function.

Even joining the country club must be seen in a different light. With so many options for marketing a professional service, is the time and effort and money best spent that way than some other way? Are the organizations to which you and your partners belong the best ones in which to be active to meet prospective clients? Are just a few of the partners involved in organizational activity, or is it spread throughout the firm in ways that best serve the firm?

A useful approach is to make a periodic audit of memberships and other activities to evaluate who in the firm is doing what, and whether the time is being most advantageously spent. As in any other marketing effort, community, club, and political activities should be planned.

Another traditional method used in practice development is to broaden the base of business contacts—what is commonly known today as networking. This is simply a function of cultivating business people and others who are prospective clients or patients. Particular emphasis should be placed on the influentials—those members of the business or financial community who may not themselves be prospective clients, but who are in a position to recommend your services. This includes other professionals such as lawyers and accountants, bankers, journalists, political figures, and business people who are prominent in their industry or in the local business community.

It's difficult to say what works best in cultivating business contacts. This is a highly individual activity. Certainly included is being active in those organizations in which influentials and other business contacts are themselves active, whether it be the local Kiwanis or Rotary Club or civic organizations. The business lunch—having lunch periodically with a business contact—is another way in which relationships are developed and maintained. Some people enjoy socializing and are in a position to do so. Networking in this way functions best if there is a sense of mutual interest rather than one-sided pursuit.

Being invited to speak before a number of organizations is very flattering, but are they the right organizations? Are all of those speeches the best use of your time? Or do you choose your targets, and your subjects, and support your speeches, both before and after, with publicity and reprints that turn the speech into a powerful practice development tool?

The traditional practice development tools have always worked very well for those who used them assiduously. They work even better in conjunction with the new tools of marketing.

## Salesmanship

In marketing professional services, no marketing tool actually brings in the client except the selling skills of an individual. All of the other tools may develop reputation and create a desire to do business with you, and even produce inquiries about your service. But only an individual can close the sale.

Other tools enhance the sales effort, and even generate, through reprints, etc., sales aids. But in the final analysis, the personal contact must be made, the presentation, either written or oral, must be made, and the client must be persuaded to sign a contract.

Here too, as in other aspects of professional services marketing, experience has shown that traditional selling skills and techniques that work for product sales don't work for professional services. New techniques have had to be developed, and they will be discussed in chapter 17. But it should be sufficient to note that among the differences are such factors that in selling a product, the product stays behind and the salesperson disappears. In selling a service, the salesperson stays as part of the service. In selling a product, the decision to buy is made on very different grounds than it is for selling a service. Such factors as these and more dictate new approaches to selling skills.

It's important, then, to hone selling skills, and to plan the selling effort.

## Proposals

Proposals, and their associated presentations, have been used in many segments of the profession for so long that only recently have professionals begun to examine the process. The result of a new view is that there's more room for skill, and imagination, and originality, than had ever before been considered.

For many professionals, the whole process evolves beyond the selling stage to proposals—and then bogs down into a process that merely repeats what had been done before. The loser, in the process of mundane proposals and dreary presentations, is not just the proposing firm, but the prospective client as well. That prospect is deprived of the opportunity to see real distinctions, and real values, in the proposing firms.

## Mixing the Marketing Tools

In using the marketing tools, there are several key points that should be kept in mind.

- All marketing tools should be used against a context of the marketing objectives. The best advertising, the most incisive direct mail campaign, are of nothing if they don't further the marketing objectives.
- There is no such thing as a bad ad or a good ad, or a good or bad public relations program. Judgment of each tool's value is always in terms of the degree to which it addresses the marketing objectives.
- The tools themselves are not of the essence—it is the mix that counts. Each has its purpose and its role in the marketing program, and each supports and contributes to the other.
- In choosing the marketing mix, effectiveness is important, but so too is cost-effectiveness. If there is a poor return on investment, in terms of meeting the objectives, then the program is ineffective, no matter how low the cost. Marketing works not by throwing dollars at the problem, but by using skill and thoughtfulness.

Keeping in mind the role that each of the marketing tools plays—the task it performs—the marketing mix is designed to use each tool and technique to support and reinforce the others.

Public relations, for example, builds the reputation, advertising backs the reputation with a selling message for the firm and its capabilities, practice development tools (including printed material and brochures) support the reputation for expertise, direct mail focuses on the prospect and opens the door. All have worked together to build a context that makes it infinitely easier to generate prospects, and against which to sell the prospect.

With a broad array of possibilities, the degree to which each tool is used in the marketing mix is a function of several factors, all of which are flexible:

- *Marketing objectives.* If fast growth is an objective, then all stops come out, with full-scale advertising, public relations, etc. If the objective is simply to build name recognition (particularly after a merger or a name change, for example), then public relations will do it faster and cheaper than advertising.

- *Short-term objective.* Reaching a new market to offer specialized services requires an all-out initial marketing effort, using virtually all tools. Maintaining reputation in that market, once the toe-hold is established, requires a diminished effort. Reaching a market in which each prospect is known or knowable would seem to indicate a heavier direct mail and phone followup campaign.

- *Budget.* Full page ads are very nice, but cost a lot of money. If you're not prepared to invest a large budget, rely more heavily on the less expensive tools.

- *Accessibility to the skill or professionals who have the skill.* If you can't afford to hire a top notch ad agency or public relations firm, don't settle for less than the best you can afford. Scale your program to the limits of the skill. If the talent is available in-house, use it to its limits, but not beyond. Having written for the college paper is a slender experience to bankroll as a copywriter for full page newspaper ads, even for a senior partner.

- *Firm objectives.* If firm objectives call for moderate growth, that hardly warrants large scale investment in expensive media blitzes. If firm objectives call for increasing share of market, then the choice of marketing tools is made accordingly.

Nor is exposure for exposure's sake particularly valuable. The objective, remember, is to serve the needs of the practice, not to build random and irrelevant reputation.

Time frame is also an important consideration. Any marketing program, particularly one embarked upon for the first time, requires time for penetration. The marketplace is noisy, and it takes a great deal of effort to be heard and recognized. But within a given time frame, there has to be careful monitoring, to be sure that if something isn't working, it's clear to you whether the fault is in the tool itself, or your expectations for it.

Expectations are, after all, key to monitoring a marketing program. Assuming a soundly conceived program, with realistic objectives, there should also be realistic expectations for each facet of the effort. If you execute a superbly crafted direct mail campaign, and expect more from it than it is capable of producing, then you are going to be frustrated with even the best results.

The answer, of course, lies in understanding each tool and how it works, and how it contributed to the marketing mix. And that is what the following chapters are about.

## New Services

There are times when exploring the marketplace results in identifying a need for a new service within the context of a profession. New opportunities frequently arise for new configurations of old skills to be put together as "products," and offered to a market as an existing service.

For example, consultants very quickly saw the need for computer training for small businesses. Accountants, particularly in the larger accounting firms, saw the need for more sophisticated services to be offered to small and emerging businesses. The change in the economy and the expansion of the middle class dictated a market need for personal financial planning and management. The need for inexpensive routine legal services for the middle class has bred the highly successful legal clinic.

### *Marketing Concepts*

Developing a new service is ultimately a marketing decision, and invariably functions on marketing concepts. This is why marketing professionals must be involved from inception. The considerations are...

- How is the need for the new service perceived? Does the partnership have a sound notion of the need that's drawn from experience in the practice? Did somebody read an article, and figure it's a good idea? Did somebody conceive the idea, and hope that it can be sold?

  A service, after all, is an answer to a need. If the depth of the need isn't measured, understood or fathomed, then it may be a service nobody needs, in which case, shining as it may be, nobody will buy it.

  *This is one reason, of course, that it's a marketing decision.*

- Did anybody cost it out? It may be easy to figure how much it will cost to deliver the service, but how much will it cost to market it? More significantly, is the market large enough to make it profitable to develop and deliver the service.

  *Again, costing and pricing are marketing decisions.*

- How large is the market? The need may be profound, but only for a small segment of the market. And if you don't know the real size of the market, how do you budget to market and deliver the service?

- Did anybody assess the competitive situation? It's very easy, when you invent something, to think that you're the first person to have thought of it. Or if you know that others are doing it, how deeply have they penetrated the market? What share of market do others have?

  *Again, a marketing decision.*

And so it becomes abundantly clear that new product—new service—development should be primarily a marketing decision. In pure research, applications are developed for which there is no immediately known commercial use. When the first lasers were perfected, some thirty years ago, it was the phenomenon that counted. There were at first no known commercial applications. But few accounting, law, or consulting firms are structured for pure, non-commercial research and development.

## Case Histories

Let's look at two cases—the first hypothetical and the second real—in which marketing-oriented product development worked.

A medium-sized law firm in a small city had a good general practice. One of the partners noted that there seemed to be a growing number of high-tech companies starting up or moving into the area. The partner wondered if the firm couldn't capitalize on this new business growth, perhaps by developing and offering an intellectual properties capability. The firm's marketing director was brought into the discussions at that very early stage, and a decision was made by the firm to pursue the matter.

The marketing director, experienced in law firm marketing and with the full confidence the firm, and using a professional research firm, took the following steps:

- Assessed the actual number of high-tech companies moving into the firm's geographic marketing area.
- Assessed the number of other companies in the area, in any industry, whose processes depended upon patents or copyrights.
- Assessed the nature of patents and copyrights used by the area's companies. Were the preponderance of these intellectual properties new, or were they well established? In other words, was there a body of potential problems or opportunities for protection, franchising, filing, etc.?
- Assessed the number of law firms in the area serving these companies. Were the companies served by local or outside firms? Did any one firm have a lion's share of the market? Were area companies satisfied with the service they were getting?
- Using secondary sources, such as trade association figures, Chamber of Commerce material, census data, etc., assessed the potential area growth of idea-based industry in the area. For example, was the presence of high-tech firms attracting other high-tech firms, or was the growth in the industry coming to an end in the area?

While obviously the available information wasn't perfect, sufficient information was gathered to make the following assessments:

- The real size of the market.
- The nature of work needed by area companies

31

- The growth potential of the market for intellectual properties work, and the rate of growth
- The competitive situation, including share of market

. . . and most important, and ultimately, whether there was indeed a market for intellectual properties work in the area.

It was these market studies that allowed the firm to make an intelligent and educated decision to go into the market. The firm, armed with sound market information, then had to decide how to do it. Hire a specialist? Train somebody internally? Buy an existing firm specializing in intellectual properties?

The point is that they were able to make the decision more wisely because they better understood the potential market, and therefore the potential return on the investment, and therefore the size of the investment that was viable.

While not all risk was eliminated from the decision, a vast amount of it was reduced because they had information on which to base the decision, and not just the intuition of a partner or two.

Given the decision to enter the market, and with a sound assessment of the market, the marketing professional was then able to develop an effective program to enter the market.

Standard techniques were used, but because they were based upon knowledge rather than conjecture, the techniques were more focused and therefore more effective.

For example, public relations consisted mostly of by-line articles by the firm's experts on the more pressing problems in the field, and especially those faced by the area's companies.

Advertising was effective because it addressed specific problems that the firm knew, from its research, existed.

Literature—brochures, newsletters, etc.—was able to address specific problems and to be targeted to local firms.

Direct mail was especially effective, because the firm knew its targets, knew the right people in the companies, knew the specific problems to address.

### An Accounting Example

The same process works as well for an accounting firm.

A partner in a major international accounting firm, working on the accounting problems of major construction projects for large companies, developed an auditing process that preempted classic construction problems. By using the firm's systems and techniques, and instituting them at the earliest possible time in the inception of a project, such problems as cost overruns and time delays could be avoided. There was sufficient history of the success of the technique to warrant its being marketed by the accounting firm. And the size of the market was easy to assess—it included every major plant being planned, every pipeline or refinery, every generator facility.

The problem was not how to determine the market for this new service, but how to design the best marketing approach. It was, after all, a new concept. And it was a high-ticket item, with fees averaging from three-quarters of a million dollars to as much as two million dollars.

A professional market research firm was retained to explore such questions as. . .

- How were new construction projects put together? Who initiated them within a company? How far in advance were they planned? How were they budgeted?

- How were project decisions made? Who did what? Who was involved? What was the hierarchy that most companies used to bring the project to fruition?

- Who made what decisions on purchasing services, and on what basis were those decisions made?

As a result of this research, a number of factors became clear. Or in some cases, where the accounting firm's intuition was at play, elements of that intuition were either confirmed or amended. Among the factors that emerged from the research were . . .

- The decision to develop the project (the plant, the refinery, etc.) were made on a corporate level, usually led by the CEO and approved by the Board.

- In developing the project, three people were usually involved—the CEO for policy; the CFO for the project's financial aspects; the chief engineer (or equivalent) for construction supervision.

- Each had a different agenda for the project. The CEO wanted a cost-effective, trouble-free course of construction. The CFO, aware that no project goes smoothly—weather, labor problems, material shortages, material flow, etc.—knew that all these powerful variables meant that no matter what kind of planning was done, the project would be finished late and with cost overruns. The project engineer is concerned with the flow of the job—keeping it running smoothly, keeping on schedule, keeping costs controlled by planning.

  It was also determined, in this context, that the project engineer was likely to be the most skeptical about the efficacy of outside sources of project control, if only because project control was traditionally the engineer's province.

The importance of this research was that it allowed a marketing program to be developed that was aimed directly at each participant's concern.

The plan was to use direct mail, backed by other marketing techniques, as the major device to move into the selling position. But there was a twist to it.

First, though, were the other marketing techniques.

Because the program was complex, and its concept was new, brochure material had to be developed to make all segments of the target market easily aware and knowledgeable about the program, how it worked, and what its benefits were.

A public relations campaign was developed to be used nationally in appropriate trade and business journals, and locally in the trade and business press in those areas targeted for each sales presentation. This was determined by the location of the target company. It consisted of by-line articles and interviews discussing the problems of project construction, and how the firm's techniques preempted those problems.

Both the literature and reprints of the publicity were used as part of both the direct mail campaign and the selling activity.

But the distinctive element of the program was the direct mail campaign. There were two factors that were decided upon as crucial...

- This was not to be a mass mailing. These projects were each large enough to be known to the industry, and so the approach was tailored to specific companies, and addressed specific projects.
- Not one, but three letters were to be used.
  - A letter to the CEO, written virtually as a personal letter from a firm partner to a CEO, on special monarch-sized stationery, described in just a few paragraphs the nature of the service and its benefits. It included no printed material.
  - A letter to the CFO, outlining the program, stressing the cost savings potential and how they are achieved. This mailing included printed material, to better help the CFO understand how the process could save the company money.
  - A letter to the project engineer, describing the process in greater detail, dwelling on credibility and on how it became *his* tool (and therefore helped him without jeopardizing his expertise or authority), and including literature.

Two other key elements of the program were:

- Each letter advised the others that all three were being written to, so that no one felt that channels were being circumvented.
- While only the one letter went to the CEO, second and third letters were planned and used for the CFO and project engineer should they be warranted by lack of response or inability to reach them by phone. Where three letters were used, the first was soft-sell, the second a little more pressing, and the third a really hard sell.

In sum, the campaign was overwhelmingly successful, producing millions of dollars in fees, and was used for a considerable time after its inception.

## The Smaller Firm

What of the smaller firm, without the resources for expensive professional market research, and large-scale marketing programs?

The same approach works in microcosm. There are ways to fathom the potential market for a new service that don't involve professional market research. The current client base is a gold mine of information. The professional press is another source of information about new services, and how well and deeply they've penetrated the market, and how well the market has accepted them.

For the smaller firm, the investment in a new service, either one developed for the practice or an established service instituted into the practice, is relatively small. The risk in a program of articles for the local press, or in a simple brochure, or in a carefully targeted direct mail campaign, is not that great. And in terms of public relations, even failure means that some positive exposure has been made to the target market.

## New Service as a Marketing Device

The reality is that there are only two reasons for a firm to institute a new service to its clients. One is for the ego of a partner or two, which can be very expensive. The other is as a sound business move.

If the decision to offer a new service is made as a business decision, then it's also a marketing decision, and should be developed in that context before any other.

In developing a new service, then, to be considered are...

- The need for the new service once identified, must be defined as clearly as possible. Where the need is just emerging, the need and the potential market must be defined and carefully assessed.

- The firm's inventory of skills must be surveyed to determine what skills must be brought to bear, who has them, and what additional training may be necessary.

- A dedicated leader to develop a program and staff must be designated, supported, and given the incentives to succeed.

- The service must be developed as a marketable package. It must be clearly defined in terms of the need it's to meet, how it's to be performed and delivered, who is to do it, how much will be charged for it, how it is to be sold, how much of it is to be sold by what date, and so forth.

- A full-scale marketing program, including budget and test markets, must be developed.

Test marketing a new service requires that in addition to the marketing program, there must be some mechanism for reporting market reaction, such as surveys and market research. The pitfall in test marketing is that if too little time, money, and effort are devoted to the test market, the results will be skewed and distorted, leading to the possibility of either losing a major opportunity or investing poorly in an exaggerated opportunity.

When there is a clear picture of the nature of the market for a new service, and of how that service is to be performed, delivered, and marketed, then it can be integrated into the overall marketing program.

### The Small Versus the Larger Firm

There is the question of whether the same techniques that will work for the large firm, with its national reputation and vast resources, as for the small firm, with perhaps two or three partners.

For the small firm seeking to compete with the large firm for national business, the answer is negative, unless the small firm offers a distinctive expertise not readily available elsewhere, or a distinctive advantage that works well on a national or international scale. But for the small firm trying to expand its practice in its own geographic area, the answer is a resounding yes. Any magazine will publish an intelligent article by a lone practitioner as readily as if the article were written by the managing partner of the largest firm in its field in the country. A well-planned direct mail campaign will be as effective for the small firm as it is for the large one. The effort of a small firm to define its market is as important as it is for the large, and will pay off as well in kind.

That is, in fact, yet another unique characteristic of professional services marketing. Virtually every technique works as well for the small firm as for the large one. One reason, of course, is that in both small and large firms, a service is offered and performed by an individual, and so it is presumed that the service offered is deliverable by an individual. This is not the case for a manufacturer who works out of his garage, nor for a bank or an airline. There is indeed very little in professional services marketing, as you will see in following chapters, that is not as potentially effective for a small professional firm as for a large one.

## Strategy Versus Random Marketing

This is a large world, and there are many firms in each profession. Each firm will choose its own approach to developing a practice, or even merely getting clients. If the firm's objectives—even those that are implied or understood without being stated—are met, then that in itself is a strategy. But for the firm that recognizes the changing nature of a new competitive environment, random marketing is a dangerous way to go.

The competitive battle, experience tells us, is won by the better strategist, not the strongest warrior.

# 2

# Analyzing the Market

We're now at a stage in marketing professional services where we begin to understand that research isn't an abstract concept; that knowing your market is a real and crucial part of marketing.

Part of this new attitude derives from the understanding that's grown among professionals and those who market professional services that you've got to know who your real prospective clients are to know how to sell to them. A rational view.

Part of it comes from increasingly realizing that we don't always know what we think we know. In case after case, experienced professionals are discovering—either through practice or research—that their markets aren't always quite what they thought they were.

And part of it comes, as well, from the growing static that fills marketing conferences with words like *niche marketing*, and *positioning*—words and phrases that are easier to say than to understand. Clearly, if you're going to market a service to a specific and carefully defined market segment—a *market niche*, if you will—then you've got to find and understand that group, and fully comprehend what it is they need. And so marketing research finds its respectability among professionals from need and demand, rather than from the pedigree of its birth.

Kenneth Wright, at the time responsible for marketing for Arthur Young and now the national director of marketing for Price Waterhouse, described a successful advertising campaign at Arthur Young that had its roots in a discussion Wright had with a very successful and otherwise knowledgeable partner who insisted he knew what his market wanted of his very specific services. Wright bet his job against a $2,500 focus group fee that the partner didn't know what he thought he knew. The focus group, made up of the partner's clients and prospective clients, perceived the service at 180 degrees from where the partner thought they perceived it. Research has a way of fooling you by substituting facts for myth—or even for conventional wisdom.

How much better can a professional understand his or her market? After all, the nature of professional services is such that the market seems self-defined. People need lawyers because the body of law requires educated and skillful interpretation and advocacy. People need tax specialists because the tax laws are too complex for the untrained, they need accountants because accounting is a technical skill, and they need auditors when the law and the capital markets require independent audits.

While this would seem to be simplistic on the face of it, it really is what most professionals are saying in their approach to their markets. Unanswered are such questions as, "Which services are really needed, and which do I think are needed simply because that's what I have to sell? What aspects of what I have to offer would cause somebody to hire me rather than my competitor, and in what way can I offer them? What value do my clients and prospective clients place on what aspects of my services, and how I deliver those services?"

And most important, "What impels people to buy the services of one firm over another in the first place?"

These are things that every successful product manufacturer knows. The manufacturers also have more than a passing idea of which of their marketing efforts work and why, and what kind of effect their advertising has on the market. Only a very few professional firms—the ones that have spent money on research—know that.

In a society and business world as complex as ours, the market for cash management services may not necessarily be for the individual tax client, nor is the corporation the primary market for the divorce lawyer. And even though the market for the auditor is essentially the 10,000 or so public corporations, or the private company that frequently seeks credit, one can hardly define the market for the small, two-partner general accounting firm as the multinational corporation.

The market for any product or service is defined by needs or wants, and nobody sells anything that the market doesn't need—or can be persuaded that it needs.

But in defining the professional services market, one sees not just a need, but an urgency of need. Urgency of need is perhaps one definition of professional services, and perhaps a strong reason why the professions are so strongly regulated.

Within the broad need, however, is a spectrum and variety. The need for services is varied—more so, perhaps, than for most products, and differs from business to business and from individual to individual. More subtle, and perhaps more important to marketing, is that the way the market needs the service delivered or performed differs substantially from one prospective client to another.

To know how to market, it's urgent, then, to understand the service that's needed, and the way the market wants it personalized and tailored, and the way it's delivered. And it's important to know how the markets' needs really relate to what it is that you can do.

Certainly, the strategic drive toward the segmented market requires more information about that market than can be fathomed by experience or instinct alone. The question inevitably arises, in a segmented market strategy, as to whether all of a firm's markets are segmented, or even more practically, whether there are more or fewer segments that should be considered, either for the same or different appeals. Only astute market research can supply those answers.

## A Case History

There is also much to be learned—some of it surprising—about how best to approach a market. Some time ago, a firm developed a new service for its clients—one that had never been offered before by anyone. Under the direction of superior marketers, the research discovered that in order for the service to be sold successfully, there were not one, but two—and possibly three—target audiences. The first was the technician who had to understand the value of the service and to endorse it to management. The second was the CEO who, because of the high price of the service, had to make the decision to spend the money, even though he or she didn't understand the technical value. The sometimes third was the chief financial officer, who had to vouch for the validity of the potential savings offered by the service.

As a result of that insight developed by research, the marketing program become three separate but inter-related programs, aimed at each of the three target audiences. It was so effective that it produced—and continues to produce—millions of dollars in fees. All for a few thousand dollars of market research.

Fathoming your market, in this context, is so inherent to any marketing effort that it must be done on one level or another, no matter how broad or narrow your marketing plans; no matter whether you are planning a major marketing program or just tuning up a practice you deem to be otherwise satisfactory at the moment.

## Defining a Market

What, in fact, is a market?

One technical definition might be that a market is any single group of potential clients or purchasers of your service that can be reached by a common appeal. Mechanically, it can be defined by common factors, such as income, age, economic status, occupation, social status, and so forth. But for the professional, it goes much beyond that.

There must be the added ingredient of the group's common need for—or advantage in receiving—a specific service that the professional can perform.

The professional has the flexibility to change the scope of his market by changing the scope of his services. An attorney specializing in corporate and SEC law, for example, may determine that there is a potential market in acquisitions, mergers, and takeovers. The expertise may well be within the realm of his or her experience, or at least scope of experience, or he or she may broaden his expertise to expand his market.

A classic example of this exists in the drive of Big Six accounting firms to capture small and emerging businesses as clients. Until relatively recently, smaller firms were not considered cost-effective clients, for either the Big Six accounting firms nor the smaller company. But market saturation in the Fortune 1200, and

39

the reluctance of large companies to change auditors, dictated the need to expand market scope. Ways were found to train specialists and to establish operations, within the Big Six firms, to serve the smaller company cost-effectively. Thus, a new market was opened—one that had not before been feasible or attractive.

Nor is there just one market for any professional, no matter how specialized. For the professional, a market may consist of many specific markets, or segments. But it must be remembered that each market segment must be addressed separately.

Moreover, it must be recognized that several segments may overlap, even though the appeal to each segment may be different. For example, the market segment for a firm's auditing services may consist of the same people that constitute the market segment for cash management services.

The problem of distribution is also distinctive. Among other things, a manufacturer must define his market in terms of his ability to distribute his product. A highly perishable product, for example, can be sold only where it can be delivered cost-effectively within a given time span. Profit margins and transportation costs further decide geographic distribution area.

The geographic boundaries of a professional's market, on the other hand, can be defined by his willingness to travel himself. The small or individual practitioner may have a nationwide practice because of his personal reputation or rare expertise, or he may choose to practice solely in his own home town. This is sometimes determined by the nature of the expertise. The internationally renowned criminal defense attorney may spend half his life on airplanes, although attorneys are licensed by state bar associations and may practice only in those states in which they are licensed. The tax specialist with extraordinary experience in an esoteric field may be in universal demand.

## Market Factors

How, then, is a market defined?

- *By geographic area.* This is defined by each professional in terms of the geographic area he is capable of serving (or willing to serve).
- *By business or industry.* This may be a vertical breakdown (manufacturing, corporations, etc.), or it may break down by industry. Professional practices differ industry by industry. For example, the accounting procedures for the motion picture industry are very different than for a computer company.
- *By size.* Potential clients of a particular size or economic structure.
- *By service need.* This is a function of both perceived need, relative to the professional's capability to perform, and a need that can be generated by marketing. Increasingly, firms are recognizing that the growing variety of services they offer, in each profession, has not only a broader

general market, but a narrower one as well. And increasingly, firms are finding that there is sometimes greater opportunity in reaching out to a market segmented by service need or by industry than by any other characteristic.

- *By function within an organization.* For example, the accounting or MIS or labor law function within a company.

- *Configuration.* A market segment must be configured in a way that it is reachable, by any means of communication, cost-effectively. For example, all companies with pension funds have some common problems, and are reachable through pension publications and other accessible sources.

- *Competition.* There must be a keen awareness of competition. A market in which one or several firms are deeply entrenched must be viewed differently than one in which no firm dominates. Is there a capability to penetrate it? Is it cost-effective to attack a market in which another firm is dominant?

- *Other Factors.* Depending upon the profession, there are myriad other factors that must be considered, including social. An architect who chooses to do public housing, for example, or an attorney specializing in pro bono work, must consider community relations and social factors as part of the market definition. Other factors include any distinctive element that defines your own practice.

Given an understanding of market segments and their parameters, some measure of investigation must be made to clearly define that market. No marketing program can work effectively, and certainly not cost-effectively, without clear definition. To do otherwise is to waste considerable time, effort, and money to reach the wrong people with the wrong message.

## The Target Company

Not to be overlooked, in this context, is the target company.

In some cases, defining specific companies as ideal clients, and then locating and targeting those companies, is an effective marketing approach. Given the definition of the target company, finding companies with those parameters is an important research objective.

## Other Kinds of Research

While the most important form of research that might be undertaken is market research, there are other kinds of research that shouldn't be overlooked.

One frequent use of research is to fathom an attitude toward a firm. How is the firm perceived by its market?

But while this is a pleasant bit of information to have—sometimes comforting to the partners and sometimes not—it's rarely as useful as it might seem to be in the abstract. A professional firm's reputation rarely affects its marketplace in the same way as does the reputation of a corporation. Corporations produce products, which have or have not a sustaining utility or quality. Corporations manufacture, and in doing so, treat the environment ill or well. Corporations do business internationally, and so sometimes find themselves supporting or opposing unpopular governments.

Law, accounting, and public relations firms rarely find themselves in a public context in quite the same way as do corporations. A company may be boycotted for doing business in a country run by a totalitarian government, but who boycotts that firm's accounting or law firm?

While it may be true that a market's attitude toward a law or accounting or consulting firm may not accurately reflect that firm's capability, the reputation to be sought should be for expertise in a particular area. It's difficult to fathom the value of Arthur Young's reputation, a decade or so ago, as "the auditor's auditor"—a description awarded it by other Big Eight firms in a survey taken by *Fortune* magazine. Certainly, it didn't catapult the firm to the top of the Big Eight. The firm's reputation for its work on expatriate taxation, though, when properly marketed, did produce clients.

Market research to determine an attitude toward a firm, then, would seem to be most useful if it's cast in terms of expertise, rather than simple name recognition. It can be terribly expensive—and not particularly useful—to learn how well your firm's name is known, and how it's perceived in general.

On the other hand, research to determine how well a firm's marketing thrust is penetrating the market, and how well it's understood, can be extremely valuable in recasting that thrust for maximum impact.

## Competitive Research

Too little attention is paid to competitive research in the professions.

Considering the cost of entering a market, it makes little sense to enter one without understanding, as fully as possible, what the competitors are doing in the same market. What shall it profit it you to enter a market in which a competitor has a lion's share, without a strategy (and a budget) designed to capture a part of that market? The strategy is very different than one in which there is no serious competition.

Here, too, research plays an important role. Done effectively, it's remarkable how much can be discovered—legally and ethically—about competitors and what they're doing. It's certainly an essential activity as part of any marketing strategy.

## Sources of Information

If there is one word that obtains in market analysis that word is perspective.

At all times, perspective must be sustained in both defining market segments and, as well, in gathering and analyzing market data.

In the enthusiastic drive to gather data, there is too frequently a tendency to overdose—to gather more facts and to correlate more information—than is needed for a marketing program. It's best to start out with a clear view of what you need to know to accomplish specific marketing objectives. This translates into specific questions, which then become the vehicle for defining the outlines of the research project.

There is an important distinction to be made between the words *data* and *information*. Data are isolated raw facts. They mean nothing until integrated and correlated to demonstrate patterns of similarity or common and mutually supported purpose, and blessed with intuition—and then focused toward the specific end of telling you what you want to know. Raw, uncorrelated data leads only to false conclusions.

Then—and then only—is it information.

This point is best illustrated by a statement made by Theodore Levitt, a professor of marketing at the Harvard Graduate School of Business Administration. In his book, *Marketing for Business Growth* (McGraw-Hill, New York, 1974), he says,

> Take the case of the Irish Tourist Board. For years it was enormously successful in building tourist business, congratulating itself for having constantly overfulfilled its objective of generating overseas trade revenue. But the facts were quite the reverse. The Board had targeted high-income, high-spending tourists. When they got to Ireland, they stayed in luxurious, foreign-owned urban hotels, drank imported Scotch whiskey, ate imported beef steak, and rented imported motor cars. Had the target been lower-income tourists, satisfied with staying in less luxurious, domestically-owned hotels, eating in native restaurants, taking trains and buses, and saving by buying picnic lunches of locally grown food at locally owned stores, less might have been spent by each tourist, but Ireland would have earned more.

The point he so aptly demonstrates is that merely accumulating data leads to information that is less productive. It is certainly more time-consuming. It's important to decide, beforehand, what you need to know for your own professional marketing needs, and not be overwhelmed with useless data simply because so much of it is available and it's so easy to assemble.

## Primary and Secondary Research

In the parlance of market research, there are two categories of research—*primary* and *secondary*.

43

*Primary* data is material you gather yourself, or have gathered for you, at first hand. It may be through direct field research, through surveys, interviews or focus groups, or it may be information you ask your own clients.

*Secondary* data is material you glean from existing sources, such as published government census figures or research done by others for other purposes. Of this material there is a plethora, and useful though it may be, it can inundate you if you don't use it selectively and wisely. There is an astonishing amount of information available from government and industry sources, as well as from companies and even the advertising departments of publications. An outstanding source of information is your own professional society, as well as the professional journals in your field. It's useful, therefore, to begin any market research with secondary sources, using primary research to fill in the blanks.

It makes good economic sense to adopt a policy that precludes reinventing the wheel in research. What you should be after is to get your hands on the best, most responsible sources of information and proceed from there.

There are two ways to find secondary data. The first is to do it yourself—hit the libraries, the data banks, and so forth.

The second is to use a reputable and established research firm that specializes in finding data.

Typical of such firms is the internationally recognized *Find/SVP*, located in New York City but with offices throughout the world. *Find/SVP* maintains a large research staff, with access to vast resources that include more than 1,500 databases, 11,000 subject and 10,000 company files, and thousands of periodicals. They work by retainer contract or by project. They also are capable of doing primary research, including competitive intelligence, and they issue several extensive reports each year on a number of subjects.

Using sources such as *Find/SVP* can save vast amounts of time and money, simply because their experts can get to the heart of the information you want infinitely faster than can an inexperienced researcher who must go to many different sources.

### Secondary Sources

By far the best secondary source of facts is the government—federal, state, and local. Another major source, and perhaps the best way to get the government data, is the computer-accessed data base system, such as *Dialog, Lexis/Nexis,* and *Dow Jones.* A great deal of federal and industry data is available from these databases, as well as from libraries or directly from the government. There are now more than 4,400 databases available from 645 online services, and the list is ever growing. (There is a *Directory of Online Databases,* published by Cuadra/Elsevier, NY).

Unfortunately, accessing a database is not always easy, straightforward, or inexpensive. This is another value in using information agencies such as *Find/SVP,* which is the oldest and largest such operation. Others may be found in the *Directory of Fee-Based Information Sources,* published by Burwell Enterprises (Houston, TX).

There are, of course, a great number of data bases available from private sources, such as Dun & Bradstreet and Standard & Poor's. Directories of data sources are available at any public library, but one outstanding directory is *Where to Find Business Information,* edited by David M. Brownstone and Gorton Carruth, published by John Wiley & Sons, NY. It is a compendium of more than 5,000 sources of business information.

For those who have computers, access to data for market (or other) information abounds. Services generally available to the public, such as *Dialog, Lexis/Nexis,* and *Dow Jones News/Retrieval,* offer access to extensive data banks that can be enormously helpful in market delineation, and particularly detailed information about specific companies or industries. Consumer oriented services, such as *Compuserve,* offer less sophisticated sources, but can be useful nevertheless. Given communication capability as part of a personal computer, an initial membership fee is paid ($25 for Dialog, about $75 for Dow Jones) and then hourly charges are billed as the system is used. Among the many data banks available are business news gleaned from business periodicals, regulatory information, company information of such sources as *Standard & Poor's,* and, in the case of *Compuserve,* historical stock market information, *Value Line's* data base, and demographic market information. It can shortcut a great deal of research. Myriad other data bases, some more sophisticated than others, are becoming increasingly available, and at reasonable cost. NEXIS, for example, is a data base that gives you access to the full text of *The New York Times, Washington Post, Newsweek, Forbes, Business Week,* and more than 90 publications and news services. Smaller data bases, more specialized, contain more detailed or technical information. A list of the currently available computer-accessed data bases is included in the appendix.

Perhaps the three most useful sources of demographic and business information are published by the U.S. Department of Commerce. They are *The Statistical Abstract of the United States,* the *County and City Data Book,* and the *Survey of Current Business.*

*The Statistical Abstract* summarizes more than a thousand tables of information compiled by all branches of the U.S. government, including the Census Bureau, and includes a great deal of demographic information broken down by state. It has a footnoted bibliography that gives sources from which the information was derived, so that further delving becomes easily feasible.

The *County and City Data Book* is published every three years and gives even more detailed local information than does the *Abstract.* Its focus is on statistics for all counties of the United States, as well as for cities with a population of more than 25,000.

The *Survey of Current Business* is a monthly publication that contains a great variety of current data and general statistics on all aspects of business. It is particularly valuable in reporting business trends that can help determine the directions in which your market might go.

The U.S.Census Bureau is a treasure trove of information on everything from population to agriculture. While much of the information is abstracted in the *Statistical Abstract*, the basic census material itself is invaluable, even though it's compiled only once every decade. The *Census of Population*, for example, analyzes residents of the United States by age, sex, race, citizenship, education, occupation, employment status, income, and family status—all categorized by state, city, and county, and in large cities, by census tract and city block.

The population census is taken every ten years, of course, but others are taken more frequently. The census of manufacturers and service businesses is taken every five years; others are taken every two years.

The Department of Commerce acts as a clearing house for all government-gathered information. It maintains a large staff of experts, available to the public, in its Washington, D.C. office and in regional offices throughout the country.

Comparable information is available from many state and local governments. Most states have departments of commerce, as do many larger cities, all of which make information readily available. Because their focus is local and regional, the information they provide can be particularly helpful.

In addition to the government and professional societies, a surprising number of other sources are available to professionals. Many universities maintain bureaus of economic research designed to help local business people. Local banks can be helpful, as can be other professionals. Lawyers have information that can help accountants, for example.

As an aid to their own marketing efforts in selling advertising, local and national media do an extensive job of market research and frequently make the information available to prospective advertisers.

## Economic Input

Because the nature of the professional market goes well beyond mere demographics, a great deal of market definition depends upon keeping abreast of current affairs. The financial services revolution, for example, substantially altered the nature of markets for a great many professionals. It developed very quickly, and any professional in a position to serve that market who was not in on it from the beginning has a great deal of catching up to do. The professional who limits his reading to just professional journals, and doesn't pay close attention to economic changes, stands in great danger of missing significant market trends. Sources of this information range from the daily newspapers and *The Wall Street Journal* to the business journals to the economic publications put out by banks.

## Primary Research

Primary research—research you do yourself or have done for you by professional research firms—should follow intensive secondary research in market delineation. In addition to sparing you duplicate effort, it serves to refine and focus information derived from secondary research.

Primary research should begin with an analysis of your own practice. Who are your current clients? What kinds of services do you perform for them and what kinds of services—particularly new services—are they demanding of you? Where do your clients come from? What factors, in a business sense, are common to the largest number of them?

An analysis of your own practice will tell you a great deal about your market as it currently exists. But at the same time, it will tell you a great deal about what you don't know. This, combined with the information derived from secondary research, allows you to move on to the appropriate form of primary research.

While there are many techniques of primary research, it's important to remember that no matter which form you use, whether you do it yourself or retain outside help, you must not abdicate your own intelligence, nor deny your own instincts.

Research is a skill that frequently requires experienced professionals, for both the research itself and the interpretation of the data. Before even the most astute professional market researcher can begin work, there must be a clear statement of research objectives and a complete understanding of how the research is to be used. As in your own practice, the professional market researcher must know what you're trying to achieve if he or she is to function effectively for you.

But while professional research can be extremely helpful, it is only one tool of many. You must supply the judgment that brings all research into focus to help you define your market and, ultimately, your approaches to it.

## Surveys

The major tool in market research is the survey, in which your target audience is asked specific questions, the answers to which can tell you a great deal (but never everything) you want to know.

Surveys are very dangerous. They can be extraordinarily valuable—but they can be diabolically misleading. They can fool you into thinking you know something, only to find, when you bet the farm on it, that you asked the wrong questions, or you asked the right questions in the wrong way, or you asked the right questions of the wrong people.

In other words, really valuable surveys are an art form that must be handled—whether by professional researcher or as a do-it-yourself project—as gingerly as a dish of acid.

Surveys can be simple or complex, depending upon what you're trying to find out. They can be in writing, in person, or by phone. Simple surveys that seek simple factual information—*How much did you spend last year on litigation?*—usually require no great expertise, and can sometimes be done yourself, particularly among your own clients. But accumulating any body of meaningful sophisticated statistical information may require the services of a professional pollster. There are subtleties within subtleties that are part of the realm of professional experience.

Designing a survey begins not with the questions, but with a clear delineation of the information needed. There's a hypnotic fascination with information—a drive to want to learn more and more, so long as you've opened the door to inquiry. Not resisting that siren call can be expensive. It can also lead to accumulating more data than you can use, and to information overload. Handle with care.

A survey works best if it's brief and to the point. Certainly, if you're doing the survey yourself, the fewer the questions the better. For more involved surveys that seek information that is detailed or subtle, or that deals with attitudes, professionalism is dictated if the survey is to be at all productive.

Whether the beneficiary of a survey—the party for whom the survey is being taken—should be identified or not depends upon the purpose of the survey. If clear objectivity is desired, then the beneficiary should be anonymous. But sometimes, a survey can be designed so that is in fact a marketing tool itself. To ask a question such as, *"Do you feel that your tax return has ever been unfairly audited?"* is to imply that the firm asking the question can be specifically helpful with that kind of problem. On the other hand, despite the marketing value of such questions as these, there isn't too much gained in the way of objectivity. It may be a tradeoff between getting information you can use and getting marketing value from the survey.

There are three basic ways to take a survey:

- By mail
- In person
- By telephone

Mail surveys give the respondent the opportunity to answer at leisure, which is both an advantage and a disadvantage. The advantage is that answers may be more thoughtful. The disadvantage is that there is a diminished sense of urgency in returning the questionnaire, which is why percentage of returns on mail questionnaires is usually very low (about 25 percent is considered the average, although if the list is carefully qualified, returns can be as high as 40 percent). There are a great many devices used to motivate people to fill out and return mail questionnaires, such as enclosing a dollar bill or offering to make a contribution to a charity in the respondent's name. But perhaps the most effective motivation lies in the covering letter, which delineates a specific benefit to the respondent, if one can be determined.

Qualifying the list, which is sometimes done by telephone pre-screening, is an important consideration in increasing returns of valid replies. A lot depends, too, on the cover letter. If the letter implies only a one-way benefit to the inquirer, then the rate of return won't be as high as it might be if the recipient perceives a benefit. In many cases, it helps to offer copies of the results of the survey. If that information is perceived to be valuable, the return will improve.

Person-to-person surveys are the most intensive and valuable, but also require the greatest professionalism. Interviewers must be carefully trained to deal with respondents, particularly where the information being sought is complex and therefore, presumably, most valuable. These surveys are obviously relatively expensive, and a great deal of preparation must go into their development. Each interview, remember, is an opportunity to learn a great deal from a respondent, and care should be taken in preparation that the opportunity is not wasted. Surveying, it should be noted, is one of those activities that always seems to be simpler than it really is. There is a great body of experience in the field, and a good professional knows many techniques that increase the value of the interview.

Telephone interviews, while best done by professionals, can still be done by non-professional researchers if the questions are kept simple, and there are not too many of them. But while it's the lowest-cost of the surveys, because it eliminates mailing and higher-priced field surveyors, it's also the least cost-effective. This is because it takes that many more phone calls to qualify interviewees, and to get useful answers, than it does by mail. In the hands of an experienced professional, a telephone interview can elicit a great deal of information, because an experienced interviewer can strive to improve the quality of the response, although telephone surveys do work best when they are objective.

Part of the problem with telephone surveys, aside from getting to the right people on the phone, is that the growth of telemarketing has made many people wary, and indeed weary, of uninvited phone calls. This has increased the difficulty of telephone surveys.

What seems to work best, according to experienced researcher Sam Kingsley of Kingsley Research Associates, is the telephone screening with a mail followup. The screening qualifies the subject, and the mail survey gets the information.

### The Focus Group

A research technique that is being used with increasing effectiveness is the focus group, in which a qualified sample of six or eight people in a target audience are gathered for a group discussion in a controlled environment. Under the direction of a trained leader, the group discusses the research problem, such as an attitude toward a service, or a broader description of service needs. The advantage of the focus group over the straight face-to-face interview is that the group dynamic quickly leads people to be freer and more uninhibited in expressing their opinions. Focus groups are usually held in studios specifically designed with recording devices and one-way mirrors. The one-way mirrors allow the client and the research professional to observe the group at work, and if warranted, to videotape the proceedings for further study and analysis.

Properly done, the focus group contributes a considerable amount of valuable material to the total research study. In a straightforward interview, even in person, people may tend to give answers they feel are appropriate or desirable, rather than those that express their true feelings. The dynamic of the focus group tends to break down that reserve, producing more valuable input to the total research project.

The danger in relying too heavily on focus groups is that under poor direction, one or two participants may tend to dominate or overpower the others in the group, thereby leading their answers. And of course, the sampling must be sound, if six or eight people are to contribute information that may be adequately generalized for an entire market group. The client is never identified. Obviously, to do so would compromise the objectivity of the responses.

As in many aspects of marketing, one tool is not a total marketing program. A focus group, no matter how well done, is not a total research program. As one tool, in conjunction with other research tools, it can make a valuable contribution to understanding.

Focus groups are not inexpensive, and can cost as much as $3-5,000 per group session. Aside from the basic research costs, each participant is usually paid a token sum for his participation, and that may be as much as $50 or $100 per participant. The sum should be enough to make it interesting, but not so much as to color the participant's sense of independence. And because they are so expensive, they should be used wisely.

## The Sample

Professional researchers have complex statistical procedures for determining samples in research that can be accurately projected to determine the knowledge or attitudes of a large whole body of population. For the informal survey, however, the sample need not be scientific, but it must be at least rational if the results are to have any value. Nor is the art of sampling as arcane as many professional researchers would have you believe.

Sam Kingsley points out that the experienced researcher is more concerned with the sample's composition in terms of the subject matter, rather than with a numerical cross section. It's simply a matter of determining the right people to ask the right questions, rather than finding a cold numerical collation or mathematical formula. Quality of the sample, he says, is more important than its size, or even its proportion to the total universe.

### The Informal Sample

In developing a proper sample, don't lose sight of the fact that you are trying to determine those factors about your market that will help you to define and serve it best. You begin the process with a general concept of who your market is and, in terms of your service, the possibilities of what you have to offer.

If, for example, you're trying to determine the specific needs for personal financial planning in your market area, it would be grossly infeasible to survey every one of your prospective clients. There may be hundreds or thousands. Too small a sampling might give you a skewed view of what the market really wants. Short of using the scientific formulae of the professional, you must make an estimate of the cross-section that would really be representative of the entire market. It may be a numerical percentage, or it may be a selection from the total group. For example, five small business owners, five professionals, five executives of large corporations, and so forth. The factors to consider, if you're determining your own sample, are size of the total universe (everybody the sample is supposed to represent), the nature of the information you're seeking, the breakdown of your market by categories that are distinctive, and the depth of the market you feel you must penetrate to get the answers you need.

## Correlating the Information

After having done both primary and secondary research, you will have accumulated a great deal of data. How does it become information you can use?

This is the point at which you go back to your original research objectives, without which you may find yourself overwhelmed by extraneous data. Analyzing data is much like editing copy. A good analyst begins by knowing what to toss out, and how to combine a fact with a fact to see a pattern.

The data must be correlated in terms of what you really have to know to define your market and its needs. You will find considerable extraneous data from both primary and secondary research. You will find data that, in conjunction with data from other sources, will have an altered meaning. But if all of the data is viewed with an eye toward what you really want to know, it should yield significant information.

At the same time, the information must be judged intelligently, and not used without interpretation. For example, the results of a survey on who influences decisions to choose an accounting firm showed that 37 percent of respondents were influenced by lawyers, and 9 percent were influenced by bankers. It would be very simple to assume that lawyers were the prime influentials, and to ignore bankers, but that would be a misreading of the data. The 9 percent of the sample that were influenced by bankers represent a substantial body that cannot be ignored in a marketing program.

And again, your own experience, instincts, and knowledge of your profession are a significant input. As has been noted, even with the best research, you shouldn't abdicate your own intelligence.

## Choosing a Market Research Firm

For some unfathomable reason, there seem to be more market research firms than there are any other form of marketing service. Choosing the right one can be an exercise in fancy footwork.

So many of them seem not to have done their own market research. This manifests itself in their trying to sell their services to professionals in the same way they sell them to manufacturers. They appear to not know the differences between the two kinds of marketing, and they seem unable to understand even the right questions that professionals must ask in order to develop marketing programs.

In looking at a market research firm, then, it's a good idea to know beforehand, as precisely as possible, what information you really need for your marketing program. This should then be developed into a simple RFP—*Request for Proposal*—in which you detail the following information:

- The nature of the information problem you're trying to solve.
- Solid background on your firm, your practice, and your market.
- A description of your marketing program.
- A description of how the requested information is to be used.
- A request for background of the research firm, including personnel, their backgrounds, other clients, other research projects, particularly those comparable to yours.
- A proposal for your project, including approach to be used and its rationale, the people assigned, the time frame, and the cost (including expenses).

While you should be flexible in considering alternate approaches to solving your problem, be sure you buy no research service or project you don't fully understand—and understand particularly in terms of your information needs.

Be wary, too, of research firms that try to sell you marketing services beyond research. Research is not all of marketing, any more than public relations or advertising or direct mail is all of marketing.

There are many different approaches to getting the same data, and many different fee schedules. It's invariably a good idea to interview more than one firm before making a choice. By the third interview, you'll know a great deal about the mechanics of professional research. This will not only help you make a decision, but will save you a great deal of time and money.

And at all times, in all aspects of research, keep your eye on the objectives of the project.

# 3

# Setting Objectives

Setting objectives, even for the smallest firms, is not an abstract exercise.

Absent clear goals, marketing efforts become random, diverse, and expensive. With clearly delineated objectives, marketing programs and marketing activities become relevant and focused. They offer a test—a measure—against which all activities are laid. If a marketing activity doesn't clearly serve to meet a specific objective, it's usually wasteful, inept, and not cost-effective.

Developing a marketing program—or even a simple marketing activity —must necessarily begin, then, with a clear view of objectives; a readily defined understanding of what the firm and its partners want, both in the near and the far term, and what they hope to have the marketing program accomplish. An overriding consideration is your decision as to the nature of your practice. What kind of firm do you want to be? How do you mean the firm to serve the personal and professional needs of you and your partners (and not to be overlooked, your staff)? How do you mean to be perceived by your clientele?

In other words, if you don't know where you're going, how do you know how to get there?

Obviously, defining firm objectives is an essential part of planning for a firm, and as more and more professional service firms are learning, long range planning is as much as anything a marketing function. To reprise a point made elsewhere in this book, how can you plan the future of a firm except in terms of the markets it serves or plans to serve?

In setting your firm's objectives, perspective is important. The large corporation sets objectives of scope and magnitude, and may support those objectives with pages of documentation. The small professional firm is spared the need to go to these lengths; indeed, quite the opposite is necessary. Objectives, clearly defined as they should be, should not be overwhelming. Nor should they be adhered to slavishly. It's often enough to know what you want to do, why you want to do it, and how you plan to get it done.

## Setting Firm Objectives

In formulating firm objectives, it's important to recognize that objectives are a context and a direction, rather than a finite measure. They are not cast in concrete—they are dynamic. Circumstances change, and if the objectives aren't able to be responsive to change, they become unattainable and unrealistic.

And as Gerald A. Riskin and Patrick J. McKenna remind us in their excellent book, *Practice Development*, objectives should be consistent with a firm's comfort level, and should certainly be ethically acceptable to both the firm and the profession practiced by the firm.

Obviously, the basic objective of your firm and your practice is to be profitable. Another objective may be growth—getting more clients and more revenue—although this may not universally be so. A small firm (and particularly a sole practitioner), may feel that it's already at optimum size to satisfy its principals. The objective may be to simply build stability in the client base. But even for this kind of firm, there's always the need to build for the future; to be able to readily replace clients that are lost through attrition.

There's a significant difference, in building a practice, between offering commodity services that are essentially the same as those offered by every other firm in the profession, and offering the value-added service, which is by its nature distinctive and different. The *commodity* is the audit, the will, the installation of a computer system. The *value-added* service is the imaginative inventory control system, the dynamic environmental law practice, the restructuring a firm's management system. The commodity offers stability, but is lower in profit and harder to sell. The value-added service tends to be higher-profile (and therefore easier to sell) and more profitable.

A distinction may be made, in formulating objectives, between retainer clients and project clients. A professional firm may have retainer clients as the largest part of its client base, with only a percentage on a project basis. A law firm that specializes (in real estate law, for example), an accounting firm that does a good bit of consulting work, certainly have different objectives than do their counterparts with stronger retainer client bases. Consultants find the largest part of their practice, for the most part, to be project work, and new projects must be generated constantly, from both existing and new clients. Architectural firms rarely have sustaining clients, although a project for a single client may last for several years. All of these firms have objectives that differ from those with heavy retainer client bases, and they differ from one another.

### Building a Practice

There's a profound difference, too, between getting clients and building a practice. You get clients by selling. As any professional knows, you can almost always get a client if you need one. It may not always be the client you want, but it's a client.

You can't always have the practice you want by random client-getting. That can be achieved only by marketing. The difference is that in just getting clients, selling is the beginning and the end. In building a practice, selling is only the end.

Building a practice begins with planning. What is the market? What, in the context of what you do, do they really need? How large is the market, and how does it break down economically? How many people (or companies) are there that really need the kind of service you want to offer?

Then comes a good look at your own service. What does the market need, in terms of the service you offer? How do you relate what you do to what the market needs? This aspect of marketing planning can get very specific. For example, the matrimonial lawyer can think in terms of economic class (any divorce versus accepting only clients with incomes above $200,000, for example), or limiting or excluding cases that involve custody. The tax accountant has an even greater number of options.

Bringing the two together—the market and the service—defines the kind of practice you want to build. It remains only to attack that market appropriately. This means determining the tools of marketing.

## The Tools

Is advertising part of it? How will public relations fit in? What about publications—newsletters, brochures, etc. What's the role of networking? And so on.

It's here that we begin to look at selling. But it's selling against a backdrop of all of the other tools of marketing. It's selling in which the prospects have been developed as part of a plan, and not by random access.

Last, all of the tools must be managed. The public relations and direct mail and networking and other efforts must be put into play, in a proper framework, so that they are effective and relevant to the objectives.

This is marketing. It's how a practice is built, by both sole practitioners and multinational firms. It's how a practice is *shaped*.

That's the difference. Selling gets clients, although not always the ones you want. Marketing builds practices. Good marketing builds the practice you want.

In determining firm objectives, then, you have to distinguish between getting clients—and building and shaping a practice.

## Expectations

Delineating expectations, as part of defining objectives, serves another purpose, albeit one just as useful.

If the firm doesn't have vast experience in marketing, or in any of its parts, it has no way of knowing what to expect from marketing efforts. Why shouldn't anyone expect a rush of clients, for example, from a single ad—unless that person has been educated very specifically in what an ad can and can't do.

No one should expect anything from a single ad, unless you're selling a car. From a well-developed ad campaign, on the other hand, you can expect:

- Name recognition
- That the serious reader will identify, in the ad, a problem or a need that he or she has.

- That the advertiser has the capability to solve the problem.
- That some action, such as an inquiry, be taken, or that the reader be receptive to a followup call.

This assumes, of course, that the campaign includes advertising that's appropriate to the firm and its services.

There are too many cases of partners expecting that press releases will be printed verbatim, that interviews will be reported accurately, that a three-day sales training course will double the size of the clientele within weeks. This is why expectations must be precisely delineated.

Measuring marketing results is one of the discipline's thorniest problems. There is simply no tangible measure that offers any valuable information that goes beyond the pragmatic or subjective.

A direct mail campaign for a product can be measured by the volume of checks that come in by return mail. But direct mail serves a different purpose in the professions. The best that can be expected of it is to serve as a red carpet to develop a personal meeting. It does it by pre-selling; by educating; by whetting the appetite for a solution to a problem that the letter has identified and perhaps exacerbated. But don't expect anybody to call and say "I liked your letter. Start Monday."

To do a direct mail campaign without spelling out expectations is to subject oneself to unwarranted frustration. To do a direct mail campaign without delineating objectives is to offer the potential failure in an otherwise excellent campaign.

In other words, the expectations are tempered by the quality of the way in which the medium is used. Poor advertising, poor public relations, poor direct mail—all mean sharply diminished performance. To ask more than the medium is capable of producing, or that level of quality can deliver, is a vast self-deception.

### Specific Factors

In defining firm or practice objectives, some specific factors must be considered:

*Firm Environment.* Nothing—not even profitability—is more important than the kind of firm you are or want to be. Without a firm environment that's satisfying and fulfilling to its partners and staff, there will be no growth or profitability.

*Size.* Businesses usually don't grow substantially by accident. It's almost invariably a conscious decision by its partners or owners, who then take steps to implement that decision. However, some professional firms may feel that they want to limit their growth, fully cognizant of the implications of growing, and of managing a large firm. Growth alone may not be of the essence—even a firm that chooses to stay at its current size must make that a conscious decision. But it should face the fact that in order to contain growth, it must take steps to sustain its size; it must perform marketing functions to overcome loss by attrition.

*Profitability.* Profitability, of course, is as much a function of margins as it is of volume, and so it's useful to know your costs as precisely as possible—a particularly difficult task in a professional firm. It becomes, as well, a function of the kind of service you're offering, and the kind of market you want to reach. Corporate work, for example, usually has higher margins than working for not-for-profit organizations.

*Time Frame.* The ability of a car to accelerate—to go from zero to a hundred miles an hour—is measured in seconds. The ability of a firm to meet its firm objectives is measured in a larger time frame. But two things are necessary. First there must be a time frame for the objectives to be met, and second, that time frame must be realistic.

It can, however be flexible. It can allow, for example, five years for the firm to double in size, if that's what it wants, but only two years to expand its market geographically.

*Pricing.* Pricing is as much an element of marketing as is advertising or promotion. Aside from the fact that it affects revenues and profitability, it also affects positioning. The classic question is, do I charge less and go for volume, or do I charge more and go for a more affluent clientele? This is a function of conscious choice, although, often, the choice is dictated by such other factors as access to affluent clients, the ability to supply the kind of service needed, or in some cases, simply the ability to ask for and sustain a high fee schedule.

Not to be overlooked is that in today's competitive climate, pricing has become a tool of marketing, in ways that it had not been before. As in other forms of marketing, pricing is now being set by competition, where before it had been relatively arbitrary.

*Market.* There are three aspects of a market that must be considered—its size, its needs, and its location—and all three must be viewed carefully in formulating objectives. How large a market can you realistically serve? What are the parameters of the market's needs that you're prepared to serve effectively? What geographical limitations are realistic?

*Share of market.* When a firm is in a rapidly growing market, or functioning in an era of rapid growth, share of market is not significant. Growth will come with the market. But when that market or industry slows its growth, and competition for existing business is the only possibility for growth, then share of market is crucial. If the only way to grow is to capture your competitor's clients, then obviously, your share of market grows as your competitor's diminishes.

Share of market is an equally important consideration in an industrially mature market area, where industry is either stagnating or declining, and where a substantial part of a practice is in the mature industry.

Still, within those strictures that dictate strong competition or static markets, growth can come by offering new services to existing clients, or by offering new services to clients of other firms. If market share is meaningful, it's measured not only in terms of the total practice, but for specific services as well. A major accounting firm, for example, may be only the fifth largest firm in town, but it may have 70 percent of the market in small business services.

And of course, the two classic approaches to increasing market share are price cutting, which is now more complex than merely lowering prices, and is therefore fraught with danger, and improved marketing efforts, which is infinitely preferable.

*Service concept.* As a professional service, your relations with your clients dictate that they are served personally. But even within that function, there are degrees and options. A law firm may decide to give impersonal service to each client, particularly those not on retainer, or it may decide to devote a considerable amount of time and effort to client relations. A practice in any profession may be a 9-to-5 operation, or it may express a willingness to function around the clock, from both office and home, for its clients. One major accounting firm opened a second office in the Wall Street area of New York, ostensibly to serve the needs of its financial clients (and to expand its financial clientele). Another accounting firm opened a branch office in suburban Dallas, to better serve the growing number of smaller businesses located there. The service option, of course, is the firm's, but it should be made a specific choice. If it's not, if it's arrived at arbitrarily, it sends a diverse message to clients, and is counterproductive to a firm's growth and success.

Objectives, then, should be realistic, as should be expectations for achieving them, or else they become wishes that will remain unfulfilled. If the aim is for growth that's greater than is realistically achievable, or for penetrating a market strongly overwhelmed by a competitor, and the expectations for achieving those aims are not substantiated by the elements, then obviously failure is in the offing.

It's always wise, also, to consider those elements that are beyond individual control. One can't control, for example, the national economy, which can throw the best formulated objectives awry. An entire legal practice can be created or destroyed by a legislative change. An accounting practice can be made or broken by a new tax law, or a new FASB change. Opportunities for professionals are generated or obliterated regularly. This is why objectives are never more than guidelines that serve to define a course of action, whether in marketing or otherwise.

There's always the danger, too, of successfully achieving marketing objectives too soon, and thereby outrunning your ability to serve a new or growing clientele. It makes little sense to do a successful job of increasing your tax business if you can't find a sufficient number of tax specialists to serve your new clientele.

### The Mission Statement

Increasingly popular among marketing oriented firms is *the mission statement,* which purports to tell the world what the firm's role in life is.

What's wrong with that? Why not tell the business world, and particularly your clients and prospective clients, that you have a purpose beyond simply doing what they think they're paying you to do? Nothing's wrong with the mission statement, if it clarifies an aim and a purpose that's rooted in reality. And certainly, mission statements used internally to let the firm's people know what the firm stands for can be valuable.

The problem is that most mission statements tend to be banners, flaunted to the outside world, painted in bright colors, designed to attract attention, but rooted in no known reality.

Let's go back to first principles. What a firm is really saying is, "These are our firm objectives. We state them so that you may understand how our firm can serve your firm."

Essentially, this makes sense. Professional firms have nothing to sell but services, and nothing to project their abilities with but service concepts. If you can't say, "We do better audits," or "We do better briefs," you somehow have to persuade clients and prospects that you're more dedicated to serving their needs than are your competitors.

One way to do this is to state your own firm objectives. "Our goal is to serve our clients in the best context and performance of our profession."

But in the drive to bring a marketing orientation to a firm, the straightforward statement of objectives took a wrong turn. The objectives have too often become a *mission*, and the statement of objectives have became a *mission statement*, appearing ubiquitously in annual reports, press releases, brochures, and so forth, giving an almost religious fervor to objectives. Here it moved from a valid statement of dedication to a gimmick. And that's how audiences perceive some of those more glorious mission statements.

If your mission is to solve client problems, that can be a different story. But not necessarily a better one. It doesn't matter who you are, you can't solve every problem. One of the things we really have learned in marketing professional services is that we sell better when we address specific problems, and then show how we can solve them. Unfortunately, mission statements tend to be too broad to cover that.

The mission statement may work, then, when it transmits to the audience a genuine and believable objective—one to which the client or prospective client can relate. If it's any less than that, if it appears to be merely self-serving, you can depend upon the mission statement working against you.

## Formulating Marketing Objectives

If the marketing program is to be relevant, marketing objectives must stem from, and serve, firm objectives. There are so many options and variables among marketing tools that without defined marketing objectives there's no way to rationally use these tools to optimum value.

The primary objectives of a marketing program can have rather specific goals. For example:

- To change the structure of the clientele and the nature of the firm
- To get new clients
- To strengthen relationships with existing clients
- To sell new services to existing clients, as well as to new clients
- To enter a new market for a specific service
- To introduce a new service
- To broaden a geographic base
- To change a perception of a firm by its market

...and so on.

But within the context of these goals, the key elements to examine in setting marketing objectives are:

*Publics.* In every marketing program, the target audience must be clearly defined. The universe for every professional must be realistically defined by the service offered, or planned to be offered, as well as by the needs of the market. Obviously, the accountant who specializes in tax work is not looking at the same public as the accountant who specializes in preparing financial statements for companies seeking financing.

Actually, in any market there are several publics. There are existing clients, whose needs for service must be constantly addressed, as must be their needs for new services. There are the prospective clients, who constitute as many publics as there are services you can perform for them. Your firm may serve one public with corporate services, another in the same market group with financial services, and a third in the same market with personal financial services. The three groups may be contiguous, but each may still be separate and distinct.

Defining a target audience is a function of determining those universal characteristics of the target group to which your services are most profitably addressed. The universal characteristics must include the ability to reach them in a uniform and economical way. For example, the best way to reach small businesses as a target audience is through such defined publications as *INC* magazine.

*Client Perception.* How do you want to be perceived by your clientele?

While the answer to that question is crucial to the marketing plan, it should be remembered that marketing alone cannot develop *images*—a perception that belies reality. No marketing program can convey an image of high service at low cost if, in fact, you are not *performing* high service at low cost. The acoustics of the marketplace are extraordinary, and what you are speaks so loudly that people can't hear what you say you are.

In developing client perception as an objective, there must first be a clear look at the reality of your firm and its practice. If your objective is to change the way you're perceived, then you must first change what's necessary to make the way you want to be perceived a reality. Then, and only then, can you expect a marketing program to project those elements that will contribute to a realistic perception of your firm, and to a reputation that serves your marketing goals.

*Time Frame.* A practical and realistic time frame in which to achieve specific goals is essential to establishing marketing objectives. Marketing must be given a reasonable time to work. And yet, if it's not working within a reasonable time, this should be recognized in time to make adjustments. Unreasonable expectations are a clear danger, in terms of both results and time frame. Marketing professional services has a longer time frame than does product marketing. A retailer placing an ad knows his results almost immediately, by the number of people who come into the store. In professional services, the results are felt not when the brochure or direct mail piece goes out, or the release is printed, or the ad is run, but when the contract is signed.

*Revenues and Return on Investment.* Presumably, the objective is to increase revenues by increasing the clientele or the services to existing clients. But at what cost? In designing a marketing program, the cost of achieving a revenues goal—the return on investment—is a primary factor. Merely to set an arbitrary figure or percentage increase is insufficient, without asking pertinent questions about what must be spent to achieve that goal. Nor is the expenditure in marketing dollars alone. The increased revenue, presumably from increased volume, must be serviced. Will new staff have to be added? How much will new staff add to overhead, in both salaries and support costs—space, secretarial and clerical help, support services, and so forth?

Thus, in setting a goal for increased revenues, the size of the investment to achieve that increase must be calculated, and from that must be determined the goal for return on that investment.

It must also be recognized, in this context, that in marketing, there is no one-to-one relationship between efforts and results. An ad that costs a hundred dollars cannot be expected to produce two hundred dollars in revenue the week after it's run. Marketing has a dynamic, particularly if it's successful. A well-run campaign increases in effectiveness as it continues, and as the effectiveness increases, so does the return on investment. For example, an accounting firm may identify a need for a new service to banks. The firm must spend a certain amount of money to develop that service, and then to make it known to its prospective clientele. At the beginning, it's talking to a market that may be as unaware of the firm as it is of the service. But after a period of sustained marketing effort, the market is educated, and it takes less to sell more.

It should be noted, however, that the converse is not necessarily true. If the effort is diminished, there is no sustaining recollection by the market. Other competitors move in, and the value of the earlier efforts are lost. It's like a hoop. As long as you keep hitting it with a stick, it keeps rolling, picking up momentum. But when you stop hitting the hoop, it eventually runs down and falls over. It doesn't matter how far it's rolled or where it's been. It's down and out.

At the beginning of a marketing campaign, the return on the investment is smaller. But if the investment and the effort is sustained, the penetration of the effort is greater for the same dollar, and so the return on investment is greater.

*Budget.* There are a number of techniques for determining budgets. But it's not a simple process, and requires a great deal of consideration. And again, it should be remembered that in budgeting, effectiveness—and therefore return on investment—will increase as the marketing program gains in penetration. The budgeting process is discussed in greater detail in chapter 18.

*Share of Market.* If share of market is a significant element in your growth or competitive picture, then it must be generally quantified, and marketing plans must reflect the competitive values in your efforts.

### Realities to Consider

In formulating objectives, there are some basic realities to consider, such as . . .

- How realistic are the objectives? Can they be achieved as marketing objectives? Is the market really there for what you want to offer? Can the firm really deliver what it plans to market?

- Does the firm really understand the cost of meeting those marketing objectives, in terms of staff? Dollars available? Professional staff time? Risk of failing in any particular marketing effort or activity?

- Has the firm realistically assessed its commitment to marketing, in terms of supporting the creative effort, the staff, and the program?

Not facing these realities, and not understanding what's involved in moving into the marketing arena, can be wasteful and expensive.

When the marketing objectives are clear, then there can be a clear view of the program itself. Only then can there be valid assessment of the marketing mix—those several tools of marketing that, together, move the program forward, and the blueprint to accomplish it.

# Part II

# Advertising

# 4

# What Advertising Is

The funny thing is that everybody thought that the *Bates* decision, which struck down the canons of ethics prohibiting frank marketing, was about advertising. And then, for many years since then, and for most firms, advertising has been the least used of all marketing tools.

Probably the least understood, too.

Now, as marketers and their firms become more sophisticated, and as budgets become more realistic and substantive, advertising is increasingly becoming part of the marketing mix.

In fact, in just the past few years, remarkable strides have been made in advertising professional services. What was once a mystique to most advertising executives is now becoming clearly understood. A Rubicon has been crossed.

Everyone knows what product advertising is, of course—we see it all the time. But at the beginning, nobody knew what it was in terms of professional services, nor how it would work. And most significantly, nobody seemed to know what advertising could be expected to do for a professional service.

Even the advertising people were wary. Good product advertising produces sales, and sales (over a period of time) are measurable in relation to the advertising dollars spent. The success of an ad announcing the availability of a product is easily measured by the volume of the products sold. The success of a campaign for a new product is measurable by sales, and perhaps by the share of the market it captures.

But will "X" dollars in advertising produce "X" dollars in revenue from new clients? Unfortunately, there was at first no experience to supply the answer. And so the first advertising for professionals was all test and conjecture.

Other problems surfaced. The changes in the canons of ethics allowed advertising, but still let stand prohibitions against the kinds of claims that are standard in product and nonprofessional service advertising. An accounting firm still can't say, "We balance books better"; a law firm can't say, "We do better divorces"; a medical clinic can't say, "We cure illness faster"—unless they can prove it, which is not likely. There are still residual professional codes, in some states, with odd prohibitions, that will no doubt continue to fall. These prohibitions fall either by mutual consent or, as in the case of aspects of direct mail, by U.S. Supreme Court fiat *(Shapero vs. Kentucky Bar, 1988)*. Almost universally, however, professional ethical codes preclude any claims of superior ability to perform the professional tasks that are not readily provable, and these prohibitions are likely to stand for the foreseeable future.

But if you can't prove your services are better than your competitor's, how can you use advertising to distinguish your firm's services from those of a competitor, or make the kinds of claims that persuade buyers? What, then, is the role of advertising in professional services?

What have we learned about advertising in professional services? What works and what doesn't?

At the heart of understanding advertising for professional services is the reality that advertising works somewhat differently for professional services than it does for products.

There are no rules, of course. Advertising is a function of thoughtfulness and imagination, as much as of its technical skills. In that context, to say that something works or doesn't work *absolutely* is foolish. There are too many examples of classic rules being broken successfully.

Slowly, and after spending many thousands of dollars, many professional marketers began to feel that the ability to advertise was less of a marketing advantage than they had at first thought. Moreover, it became clear that the techniques of advertising that had been so successful in selling products didn't quite work in the same way for professional services. Still, there is more than sufficient success, particularly in the last few years, to consider advertising a major tool in marketing. Even smaller firms are coming to find that this is so.

## Product Versus Service Advertising

Where is the difference?

Why does it matter?

It matters, of course, because if you don't know the difference, you're not likely to use advertising effectively. The difference between the two strongly affects the techniques.

At the same time, the more adventurous and sophisticated professional services marketers have learned how to bring the two closer together; how to make what works for product advertising work as well, with subtle changes, for professional services advertising. There have indeed been breakthroughs.

By definition, advertising is the marketing tool that uses purchased space (or time) to deliver a specific and focused message. It has the *advantage* of allowing us to say precisely what we want to say to a generally defined audience. It has the *disadvantage* of a credibility that's limited by the fact that readers understand that it's our space, our dollar, and our subjective claim. It has the additional liability of competition for attention in a clutter of other advertising.

Product advertising, for example, can persuade people to go to a supermarket and choose one brand of toothpaste rather than another. It can make distinctions—and comparisons—between two brands of the same product. It can build desire for a product where no desire existed before. It can educate and inform about a products advantages, and the advantages of one brand over another.

But can you imagine an ad campaign that persuades someone who doesn't need an audit to get one? Can you imagine an ad campaign for a matrimonial attorney that's so persuasive that it convinces a happily married man or woman to get a divorce?

In the commodity aspects of professional services—the audit, the divorce, the data information system—there's no foundation for building desire, and even less basis for making a distinction between one firm and another when both perform the same service. In this kind of commodity advertising lies the greatest challenge—making that distinction.

In the value-added aspects of professional services, however—the long-range tax planning, the litigation, the solution to a dynamic management problem—advertising finds its greatest potential. Here, the latitude to explain, to distinguish, to sell, affords the imaginative marketer new opportunity.

After all, people *buy* what they need. They are sold what they can be persuaded they need.

People buy an audit or a will because they need it.

But a company may not feel it needs the services of an environmental law firm, until it sees that firm's advertising, in which the potential legal penalties are described in a way that threatens the company. They are then persuaded they need something they hadn't realized they needed. And they are likely to go to the advertiser who told them about it.

And while the advertising campaign for most products is designed to get the consumer, on his or her own, to choose one product over another, the advertising campaign for a professional service can't sell a law or accounting or consulting firm in quite the same way. It can only provide information about a service the reader may not have known about, and generate a favorable context for a lawyer or an accountant or a consultant to sell the service. *This is perhaps the most crucial distinction between product and services advertising.* It colors that nature of the advertising.

The harsh reality is that advertising may sell products of itself—may move products off the shelf. But only the professional who performs the service is able to close the sale.

Increasingly, the techniques of advertising the non-commodity service are improving, and are carrying more and more of the burden of selling. *But they have not yet gotten to the point of the final sale,* which must still be made by an individual practitioner.

## Corporate Advertising

The surprising change of recent experience is that corporate advertising—what used to be called *institutional* or *image* advertising—is being used with increasing success in professional services. Part of this is a function of skill and imagination. Another part is that professional firms are learning more about the subtleties of marketing, as they pertain to objectives.

If the objective is to build a long term name recognition, as is often done with a corporation, then corporate advertising tends not to work, unless other marketing factors are brought into play. Name recognition and reputation alone seem to have a shorter shelf life, and to be more fragile, in professional services than in products.

But if the objectives are more focused, it often works. For example, the earlier Arthur Young "We take business seriously" campaign did indeed work to convey project Arthur Young's position of being an enthusiastic participant in its clients' businesses.

The traditional techniques of advertising that continue to be effective, are, for the most part, those that are predicated upon sound rules of copy, layout, media, frequency, and so forth. In that respect, a good ad is still a good ad.

But it's the strategic differences between the product and professional services advertising that are even more significant than are the similarities.

There is still the problem, in advertising the commodity-like services of a professional firm, of how to distinguish one firm from another, particularly in corporate advertising. When all firms in the same profession perform the same services, and where the distinctions between firms reside primarily in the ability of individuals who perform those services, it takes extraordinary skill to project that subtle distinction with credibility. All auditing firms do audits under the same basic principals. Under very few circumstances are there distinctions in the audit process that can be projected, one firm from another, in an advertising statement that's acceptable under the canons of ethics. Can an SEC attorney say he writes better prospectuses? Only if the claim can be proven. In fact, that's why adjectives that are at the heart of most advertising—*better...stronger...creamier...healthier*—have so little currency in advertising professional services. They can't be proven.

There are other problems.

You can sell a diamond ring with a picture of the ring, but how do you photograph a professional service? How do you capture the idea behind the service?

In firms with offices in several cities, national advertising is too often precluded because the firm's capabilities differ from one city to another.

Advertising for professional services, then, has had to start, in many ways, from the beginning. It has had to develop an entirely new body of skills built upon elements of old and tested skills.

In the first years after the *Bates* decision these distinctions between product and professional services advertising weren't recognized. As a result, most early professional services advertising was a pale imitation of product advertising. Early ads suffered from restrictions that produced ads in which what can be said for one firm can be said for any other in the same profession. One need only have changed the name of the firm in the ad, and not the message, and truth would not suffer. This put a burden on all parts of marketing, since advertising will not carry the same weight as it does in product advertising.

Some approaches have emerged, and have proven successful. They will be dealt with in the next chapter.

## Why Advertise?

Increasingly, advertising is finding a firmer footing in the marketing mix. There is indeed a growing sophistication, and a growing understanding that advertising contributes something to the growth of their practice. In this, advertisers are not wrong.

## The Role in the Marketing Mix

Despite all of these strictures and obstacles, advertising has an important role in the marketing mix:

- It can help sell some services
- It helps to establish a professional presence
- It clearly delineates a firm's attitude toward the way its services are delivered
- It helps increase market penetration
- It enhances and supports a position in the market
- It helps define and project specific marketing objectives, based on a realistic perception of your firm and its services.
- It helps to define a new service, in the context of the problems it solves
- It affords the opportunity to be persuasive, even within the limited context of professional advertising
- It can focus on a problem, and define how your service can help to resolve that problem for a prospective client
- It reinforces, and is reinforced by, the sound public relations program designed to build and enhance reputation, to inform, and to focus an accurate perception of your firm and its services.

Most of all, it functions well in conjunction with all other marketing efforts, such as public relations, direct mail and personal selling. It builds a foundation that can enhance the more active marketing functions.

With direct mail as a door opener, advertising serves as a pre-selling device; it sells your firm, so that you are free to sell your services.

And in the cold call, it helps take the chill off of ignorance about who you are and what you can do.

In the broader campaign, then, advertising's role in the marketing mix is consequential.

## What Advertising Can Do

What, then, can you expect advertising to accomplish? At least the following:

- To spread word of your existence, and to broadcast the name of your firm and the nature of the services you perform
- To convey a favorable impression of the kind and quality of your services, and the way in which you perform those services
- To develop a need for your firm's services by appealing to either the intellect or the emotions.
- To build a favorable context in which you can use other marketing devices and methods to urge and inspire people to take action in retaining your services.
- To announce or define a specific service you perform within the context of your profession.
- To strengthen internal pride and morale, by demonstrating to staff a visible, concerted effort to project the firm and its strengths to the public

Advertising, then, has four major purposes:

- To inform, and to reinforce that information
- To create an umbrella of favorable attitude toward you and your firm
- To either generate action, or to allow for a more favorable context in which other action may comfortably take place, that sets the stage for selling
- To focus internal priorities and appropriate actions

## What Advertising Can't Do

To understand its effectiveness, it's equally important to know what advertising can't do. For example:
- Not everyone who reads your ad is in the mood to be persuaded by its most logical or emotional appeals at any given moment.
- Advertising, with the exception of direct mail, can never limit itself to precisely the audience you want, and so a measure of it — and a measure of its cost — is always wasted. You may safely assume that by advertising in a journal for naval engineers, your ad will be read by people who are primarily naval engineers. But not all of them are in a position to buy nor to influence buying decisions. Under the best of

circumstances, there is a great deal of slippage in reaching an audience, and certainly in the cost of reaching that audience.

- No ad can work entirely on its own and out of the context of a larger program. No matter how startling, exciting, new or valuable the service you offer in your ad, each ad fights other ads and editorial copy for attention, credibility and persuasiveness. The degree to which any advertising works is in proportion to a larger marketing effort.

- It can't supply complete objectivity or credibility. It's your space or time and your message, and readers know it. Readers also know that because you say something doesn't necessarily make it and so, and so all ads are read with a measure of skepticism.

- No ad can close a sale for you, particularly in professional services. The best that can happen is that an ad inspires your prospective client to inquire further of you, or even to send for a descriptive brochure, but that's not the same thing as making a sale or signing a contract.

## What Works?

Kenneth Wright, perhaps the most successful user of advertising in professional services, puts at the forefront the concept that advertising without clear objectives can be pointless. Moreover, he notes, it's impossible to judge the efficacy of any campaign except in terms of those objectives.

How do you judge a campaign that's designed to change attitudes about the firm, rather than to sell the firm's services, he asks, without understanding the objectives of the campaign?

When he was head of marketing and advertising for Arthur Young, the (then) Big Eight accounting firm (before its merger to form Ernst & Whinney), he had ample opportunity to develop these concepts. The positioning program Wright initiated for Arthur Young, and the advertising to support his positioning, was a case in point. A corporate program designed to enhance the name and reputation of the firm, and to position it in its marketplace, the campaign was overwhelmingly successful. And vital to that success was the impact internally. According to Wright, "It served as a powerful internal force to make the partnership and the staff, throughout the country, enthusiastic about aggressively marketing the firm's services. It was worth every penny of the national campaign, just to have integrated the marketing process into the partnership."

Probably no campaign in professional services advertising, incidentally, made greater use of market research than did this one. Focus groups and other aspects of primary research were used beforehand, from which was developed the campaign's theme, "We take business personally." Frequent and periodic surveys monitored its effects on target audiences all along the way. It was a classic example of the best use of both advertising and research done thus far in the professions. It also contributed substantially to what we now know about advertising in this area.

In the total context of the past decade's experience, what have we learned that we didn't know before for sure? We've learned that . . .

- Advertising a single service in a single market works very well. It works particularly well if the ads address a single problem, rather than attempt to address several problems with several services.

  The principle is simple. When a major accounting firm decided to open a suburban branch office to serve emerging business, the local ad campaign addressed a single small business problem in each ad in the campaign. The ads were measurably successful—more than 500 coupons were returned, requesting further information.

- Concentrating on the problem, rather than the solution, seems to be sure fire. "We can handle your estate" is what we want to sell, but it may not be what you want to buy. "Not having a will can be the most expensive way to save money. We can help you save money the inexpensive way—with a sound will," goes to the problem first, and then the solution. Properly done, this approach is very powerful.

- Trying to sell a local service nationally can be ineffective. First, not every geographic area may see the problem in the same way, and so the ad is perceived differently in each locale. And it's not likely that every office of your firm can offer the same quality of service in every discipline in every office.

- *Image,* or *corporate,* advertising works for services in the same way that it works for products. When IBM says, "Trust us, we make good computers," that's corporate advertising. It sells the company itself — not product features. Professional service firms can do the same thing. They can enhance what prospects believe about them and the services they offer.

  As a bonus, if your objective were to build a more positive internal attitude toward marketing the firm's services, the corporate campaign will help do that as well.

  In this context, Arthur Young's campaign worked because it sold an *idea*—the attitude toward serving its business clients that was the firm's guiding force. And it did so in a context that implied—*implied,* not stated—that this service concept was distinctive to AY.

- Trying to make advertising carry the load of the entire marketing program is usually ineffective and expensive. Today, advertising should be part of the large mix of marketing tools. It can help define the firm and its services to a large audience, and engender a favorable attitude about the firm. It can, in many ways, describe capabilities favorably. Supported by other marketing efforts, it can be a major marketing tool. But it can't do the whole job by itself.

- Advertising without a clear picture of objectives and expectations can be a disaster. If you advertise expecting your phone to ring off the hook, but your ads are designed to change attitudes, you've got a losing proposition going in. If you put a coupon in your ad, and don't follow up on the leads the coupon returns bring you, then you're wasting your time. But if you want to develop inquiries for your solution to a particular problem, and your ads are geared to developing inquiries, then you have a right to expect that the ads will produce inquiries. The expectations are clear and realistic, the ads are designed to meet the expectation, and the ads are well and professionally done. That adds up to success.

- How do you distinguish your service from those of your competitors? One way is to describe your service enthusiastically, as if you're the only one to do it. It doesn't matter if others do it as well—your great description of the service, and the problems it solves, position you effectively, and give you something to sell against. And if you're the first, than your firm will be the one identified with the service. Everybody else will be an imitator. It really works that way. Just look at the Arthur Young campaign.

  Increased name identification in the professions, we've learned, has very little staying power. The finest reputation, with the broadest name recognition, is like a hoop. So long as you keep beating it with a stick, the hoop keeps rolling. When you stop using the stick, the hoop falls over, and the great distance it's covered is quickly forgotten.

  This means, of course, that if your objective for advertising is to build name recognition, be prepared to spend a great deal of money—and to continue to spend it. It will work fine—until you stop.

  And then, if all you've got is name recognition. And if you haven't changed people's attitudes about your firm or its services, then it's been an expensive and wasteful exercise.

### Advertising and the Small Firm

Does advertising work for the small firm? Of course it does, in most cases in the same way it works for the large firm. But it works only when...

- There's a clear objective
- It's part of a larger mix of marketing tools
- It addresses a specific problem
- It offers a specific service
- It describes the problem clearly, and describes the service as if it were unique (without saying so, of course)

75

Then it works.

Can corporate marketing work for the small firm? Possibly, if it's well conceived and executed, has a clear objective, and is backed by a larger marketing program.

If you have no total marketing program, of which advertising is just one part, and if your objectives in advertising are not clear, then you're not ready to advertise.

And if you can't back up the promise of your ad, in terms of delivering the service, or following up to sell what you're advertising, then advertising is not for you.

But if your advertising is correctly perceived, and conceived, and done professionally and well, it can be an effective marketing tool.

Within the context of advertising there are several different categories that are distinctive. Each is different from the others, and each has its place in the total marketing mix.

## Categories of Advertising

Essentially, advertising breaks down into several major categories.

*Corporate advertising,* sometimes (unfortunately) called *image advertising,* is advertising designed to enhance the reputation of a firm. For example, a law firm ad shows a picture of the scales of justice. The headline and copy say that you need a good law firm to balance all of the forces that can tilt those scales against you, and that this is a good law firm. This is corporate advertising. It's not trying to sell or promote any specific service or capability. Rather, the firm is attempting to generate good will through its broader message...to project an identity for itself.

In a sense, all good advertising—and most marketing activities—should have some corporate overtones, in that no matter how specific the service described, the general feeling should be favorable towards the advertiser—the firm that's sponsoring the ad.

Corporate advertising for professional services can be useful, but has some very strong potential for danger. It's too easy to expect too much of it; to expect that the favorable impression it means to convey translates quickly into new business. In this context, it won't be successful. It can certainly be a poor investment if it's used for the wrong reasons, such as supporting the ego of the partnership, or for simple name recognition, or doesn't make a credible claim.

*Service advertising* is display or promotional advertising in which a particular service or capability is described in a selling context. These are highly focused ads that describe a particular service to a clearly defined audience. This is the kind of advertising that would be used by the consultant who specializes in computerizing an office, or the accountant who specializes in addressing the problems of emerging business, to sell these services.

76

In fact, the ad limited to one particular service appears to have greater impact than the ad that attempts to sell many services at one time. For example, an accounting firm may have a broad spectrum of capabilities, but its advertising is more likely to be effective if each ad campaign addresses only one such service, such as tax preparation, or estate planning, or offers the solution to only one kind of problem to be solved by these services.

*Direct mail,* in which, to sell a service, letters (with or without enclosures) are sent directly to a carefully predetermined list of prospective clients. It's a particularly effective form of advertising in professional services because it is so precisely and directly delivers a specific message to a carefully defined audience. It can address a specific problem, and it can be used as a door opener to develop the opportunity to sell a prospective client personally. Like other forms of service advertising, however, and unlike product direct mail, it cannot be expected to produce clients by return mail.

The use of the computer, and the growing sophistication in developing data basis that and isolate target markets by the most keenly defined parameters, have brought a new dimension to direct mail—and perhaps to all of marketing. The ability to define a market with such fine gradation puts a new facility to target marketing. It has become more accurate, and more effective, thereby tilting more and more advertising to the individual and the individual company, rather than to the broader market.

*Tombstone ads* are the simple, straightforward announcements, originally used by brokerage firms to offer new issues of securities for sale. Eventually, they came to be used by all professional firms to announce major personnel changes, such as new partners, a significant event such as a merger (or the firm's role in a merger between two clients), an acquisition, or a new office. It may be simply a calling card (a simple ad that states only name, address and profession) to establish your name and presence.

While the tombstone may seem to be mundane and routine, it nevertheless has a place in the marketing mix simply because it's one more technique that supplies visibility and an impression to be conveyed to your perspective clientele.

*Classified advertising.* For many years, both here and abroad, when other advertising was prohibited, classified "Help Wanted" advertising was used as a frank marketing tool. A display ad in the "Help Wanted" section that was ostensibly placed to recruit personnel served as a marvelous vehicle for describing the features and benefits of a firm. Until very recently, when the rules prohibiting advertising changed in Great Britain, it was considered a primary form of advertising for both the accounting and legal professions. It was assumed that prospective clients read those sections, as did prospective employees.

*Yellow Page advertising* is yet another form of advertising that is now universally accepted by professionals. The small, tasteful display ad in the Yellow Pages can be both ethical and effective, even though it must be devoid of the kind of selling message used for products.

It should be remembered that Yellow Page advertising has a life of a full year between issues of the directory, so that anything that's said in the Yellow Page ad must apply at least until the next issue.

Because Yellow Page ads are usually small, considerable skill must be used to get a logo or effective message into the limited space. Layout, use of logo, and type selection are all important, and it must be remembered that your ad competes with others in the same profession on the same page.

In larger cities you may want to consider advertising, or at least being listed, in several different categories. For example am accounting firm can be listed under Accounting, Consulting, and Tax Services.

*Billboards* and other forms of advertising, all of which were considered far fetched for professionals just a few years ago, are now commonly used. While reaction to their use has been mixed, and a number of problems that spring from inexperience have surfaced, billboards, car cards, posters, etc. are all now very much in the realm of professional services advertising, and must be considered for any marketing plan.

### Broadcast Advertising

Radio and Television—the broadcast media—are an entirely different advertising structure.

As in print media, the audience is definable. You need only look, for example, at the successful use of radio and television by the major computer and business machines manufacturers to know that radio can reach a business audience. Several of the law clinics throughout the country are already using broadcast media successfully. Tax preparers are experienced broadcast advertisers, and recently, accounting consultants have begun to use this means extensively.

Obviously, then, broadcast advertising generally has its values as part of the marketing mix. It's useful to:

- Build reputation and to penetrate deeply into a market.
- Sell a specific service.
- Expand a market by reaching new people, or to move into a new market position.
- Visualize a concept through television.
- Dramatize a concept.

As part of a larger marketing and advertising program, broadcast advertising should work well for all professional services if it's used with the following in mind:

- As in all advertising, it should have a specific theme and be part of an overall program

78

- Its objectives should be understood. For example, a print ad can tell a complicated story about your service because if the reader can be made to become absorbed in the ad, he or she will take the time to read it. A broadcast message is fleeting, and will be lost on the listener if the message is too complicated.

- The value of repetition in the broadcast media, particularly in radio, can be extensive in building name, reputation, and recognition.

- Even though the primary advantage of television is to demonstrate, and it's difficult to demonstrate service, television can be effective. Henry Bloch successfully appears on television on behalf of his own company, H & R Block, to sell tax services. As the head of his own company, he projects a quality of credibility—his personal reputation is on the line. And as a result of repetition and ubiquitous appearance, Bloch is himself a celebrity, and commands attention.

Each of the broadcast media has some rather distinctive advantages of its own. For example, in television:

- Television reaches more households in any given moment than does any other medium. About 80 percent of all adults are believed to see television at some time during the day and 95 percent during the average week.

- The diversity of television programming makes it possible to pinpoint a market somewhat more specifically than in newspapers. Programs are aimed quite specifically at defined audiences, as are magazines. Newspapers are aimed at a more broadly defined audience.

- Television is extensively and carefully researched, which means that a great deal is known about the target audience.

- Television has presence. It can demonstrate, it can illustrate in a way that no other medium can.

- Television rivets attention. When your commercial is on it's not competing against editorial matter or other commercials for attention.

Radio, as well, has its advantages and disadvantages. For example:

- It tends to be a more intimate medium, in that the announcer appears to be talking to the listener as an individual.

- As in television, although to a lesser degree, there is focus. While your commercial is being read or played, there is no competition with other commercials or editorial. It is, however, less riveting than television, and listeners can be doing other things, such as driving, at the same time.

- Radio sells *ideas* well, and most services are ideas that are often difficult to demonstrate with a picture. With no picture, radio then has a significant advantage.

- Radio programming tends to be more clearly delineated and focused on particular markets. Thus, you can choose the kind of audience you want through the programming (radio news, classical music, popular music, talk shows, and so forth).

- As a media buy, radio is the most flexible of all the media. You can buy a single spot or a series covering any period of time. You can move in and out of radio as your needs require.

- Radio production is relatively inexpensive and can be as simple (a single sheet of paper with a 30 second spot announcement to be read by an announcer) or as complex (an elaborate dramatization) as you want. It's a convincing medium that reaches a lot of people at very low cost.

And of course there are disadvantages as well in the broadcast media. In actual outlay of dollars, television is usually the most expensive of all media (although it may be more cost efficient in terms of viewers reached and impact). All broadcast media is limited by time constraints. Local television, and sometimes local radio, can sometimes be subject to clutter—a lot of commercials back to back.

Radio is limited by its reliance upon the spoken word for visualization. It can be heard but not seen (which may also be an advantage). And while you can buy one or two spots, the repetition needed for impact requires many more.

But in the final analysis, more and more professional services are turning to radio and television, for its very specific advertising advantages.

There are, of course, other forms of advertising, such as billboards and calling card ads. But these forms of advertising will be spoken of in another context.

## The Elements of an Ad

Producing a good ad, in any medium, is a combination of skill and art. There are indeed some basic rules. But as successful abstract painting frequently succeeds because of the ways in which it deviates from the rules, so does successful advertising succeed in altering rules through flair and imagination. Originality opens new paths and accomplishes new success.

Nevertheless, there are basic elements that are part of all good advertising, and that tend to produce good ads:

- *The objective.* A favorite game in any profession is to look at the ads of other firms in your profession and to find fault with them. The problem with that is that you rarely know the objectives of a campaign. If the objectives are clearly stated, and the ad is written to those objectives, then the judgment of the efficacy of the ad must be made not on its aesthetics, but in terms of the objectives.

- *Theme.* An ad must say something. Its story line, no matter how many or how few words are used, must go someplace very specific. The theme of an ad is its basic line of attack. No matter what kind of ad, in any medium, it should be consistent in all its elements In developing a theme, the basic question used to test an ad is "What do I want the reader to know or to feel after reading (or hearing) this ad?" If that question can be answered clearly, and the ad is responsive to the answer, then it is more likely to be successful.

  An ad with no theme, on the other hand, tends to become diffuse, and fails to make its point. It lacks unity and won't hold a reader's attention, much less serve any marketing objectives.

- *The headline.* The purpose of a headline (in print ads) is to capture the reader's attention by saying something meaningful or involving. The headline must be relevant to the rest of the ad—to its theme and text. Merely to capture someone's attention and then not follow through with a consistent selling message destroys the value of the ad.

- *Copy.* The copy is the text of the ad and usually contains the selling message. Copy, as everybody knows, should be simple, terse, clear, concise, and credible. It should say as much as possible in as few words as possible. But that's as far as the rules go. Any copy that captures the reader's attention and imagination, and moves the reader in ways that fulfill the objective of the ad, is great copy no matter how it's written.

- *The layout* is the position of the various elements within the print ad. The way the elements are laid out should attract the reader, be appealing, and contribute to the reader's becoming absorbed in the ad's message. No matter how little copy or illustration you put in an ad, the words or the picture still have to be carefully sized to fit the space, the typeface must be selected, and it must all be laid out effectively in a defined space. A well-designed ad is easy to read, focuses the reader's eye where you want it, is easy to digest and to understand, and from a reader's point of view makes the whole process of dealing with an ad painless and even enjoyable. A poorly designed ad, on the other hand, with the wrong (or too many) typefaces, or an illustration that overwhelms the copy, can be a disaster, destroying the effectiveness of what might otherwise be superb.

- *Logo and Identification.* While it seems obvious that the firm name and address should be present, there is a clear advantage in using a logo to build a visible and readily identifiable identity for your firm. A logo (short for *logotype*) is a design factor that may use any of several design elements, including a distinctive typeface.

- *Media.* Media are the vehicles in which the ad is placed—newspapers, magazines, radio, television, billboards, etc. Media should be appropriate to the prospective clientele. As you will see in chapter 8, selecting media in which to place ads is a highly refined technique. It's important to note here, however, that an ad should at least be designed to keep a medium's audience in mind. Nothing is sillier than seeing an ad written for one audience appear in a publication clearly subscribed to by a very different audience.

- *Placement.* While it's not always possible to indicate where in a publication your ad will appear, to the extent that it is it should be considered. If you're practicing sports medicine, you may want an ad to appear in the sports section. If you're practicing corporate law, the sports section may be precisely where you don't want your ad. In broadcast advertising, placement is a function of where in a program your ad fits.

- *Production* is the physical preparation of the ad. It should be meticulous and professional.

The success of any ad campaign is more than the clever headline or the catchy illustration. It is, rather, the sum total of the effectiveness of all of these elements.

But most significantly the effectiveness of any advertising depends upon its ability to fit consistently into the total marketing program, and to carry its weight as an element of that program.

# 5

# Advertising Strategy

It's like little kids coming out to play after being locked in the house by a three-day snow storm.

At the time of the *Bates* decision in 1977, there was no professional alive who could remember when advertising, or any other form of frank marketing, was allowed. And for the first five years or so after *Bates*, only a few accountants and lawyers ventured out into the competitive world.

But as they saw that nobody was wilting from it, and that clients weren't criticizing or pulling back from those who advertised or marketed discreetly and intelligently, more and more professionals sallied forth into this brave new world of marketing.

And not just the tort lawyers and the legal clinics and the tax clinics. By the early 1980s, nice, big respectable firms were doing it. And then smaller accounting and law firms and consultants.

A good thing, too, because only by trial and error did we learn what would work and what wouldn't.

## Effective Advertising

What indeed have we learned about what really works? Certainly, not as much as we know about product or nonprofessional advertising, but still, much more than we knew a few years ago. And more than enough to begin to use advertising with confidence. The evidence is still coming in, but it's coming in fast.

We know, with certainty, that because advertising can't sell professional services the way it sells products, ads work best as part of a larger marketing program. Whereas in many cases an ad campaign may sell a product off a retailer's shelf—if the product is sufficiently unique and offers important benefits—people rarely buy a professional service from an ad or ad campaign. People rarely see an ad for a professional firm, and call up and say, "I like your ad—start tomorrow."

On the other hand a campaign devoted to describing a service that addresses a particular business or legal problem seems to capture the attention of prospective clients. And if the campaign consists of a series of ads that are integrated, the corporate advertising effect seems to take over in a most positive way. An example is a series of ads in which each ad addresses an aspect of small business management. By the end of the campaign, the consciousness of the prospective clientele is well penetrated, and there is an impression that the firm has an expertise worth listening to.

There are some other basic strategies that have demonstrated a measure of effectiveness:

- It is absolutely crucial that all advertising must be cast in terms of the clients' needs—not the firm's wishes. There is a strong tendency to want to advertise what you want to sell, not what the client wants to buy. And despite the fact that this is a classic advertising theorem, even the most creative advertising agencies still make this mistake (possibly because touting the product on its own merits sometimes works so well in product advertising). The idea is, "This is your problem, and we understand it, and we can solve it." The other way, "We do tax returns," just doesn't seem to make an impression. Of course you know how to do tax returns, or file briefs, or do audits. So does every other accounting and law firm.

- Market research can make a vast difference. How can you advertise that you know how to solve a client's problem if you don't know what the client perceives to be a problem? How can you know how best to position your firm if you don't have a good idea of how your market perceives your firm?

- Except in those instances where corporate advertising is indicated, keep each ad as tightly focused on a single service as possible. With the ethical limits on characterizing the quality of your service, the broader the focus on the services you offer, the more likely the ad is to be diverse, bland, and ineffective.

- A strategy that has demonstrated effectiveness in its impact is based on timing. If by offering a service, or defining it in a new way, you can imply that you are the first to offer it, then you have a strong chance to beat the competition. The competition must then face the possibility of being perceived as an imitator or a follower in the marketplace rather than a leader. This is a bit of slight of hand discussed further in chapter 7.

- Sound basic advertising principles work—or at least, nothing works in their absence. Advertising must still be well-conceived and executed. Objectives must be clearly delineated, campaigns must be well-planned, ads must be well-planned and designed, media must be intelligently chosen.

- Ads compete for attention against other ads. Print ads do not stand alone. They are surrounded by other ads, sometimes for your competition, as well as by editorial matter. Each element of an ad is important. Superb copy in a poor layout or with a badly conceived headline is wasted. A magnificent ad set in unreadable typeface or running in the wrong medium can be a total disaster.

- Repetition is a crucial element in all advertising. The reader of display advertising is a random reader, and is rarely searching the pages of a newspaper or magazine looking for your ad. Repetition is necessary to ingrain your name and message in his mind. Moreover, advertising for professional services is very often for the future—the casual reader may not be looking for a doctor or a lawyer or a consultant at the time he reads the ad, and so the ad's message must have staying power. The ad must offer the kind of recognition that stays in the mind for that time in the future when the doctor or lawyer or accountant is needed, or when you make direct contact with him in some other context. We know as well that no one absorbs or retains the contents of a single ad. Research has shown that it takes at least three ads to make an impression on a reader. Repetition, then, becomes extremely important, and if it can't be built into an ad campaign, then advertising of any magnitude should not be considered at all.

- It takes a lot of words to describe a service. And while the fewer words the better, this should not, on the other hand, breed a fear of text. If the ad is addressing a prospective client's problems, and offering him a solution to his problem, large blocks of text will be read and understood.

- The basic media rules still apply. Newspapers do what newspapers do, broadcasting the same, and so forth. The rules of media haven't changed, and each requires its own advertising approach. At the same time, there is no medium that hasn't demonstrated some value for some aspect of professional advertising, including billboards, transportation advertising, and even premiums. All media should be considered in planning a campaign.

- Advertising seems to work best, even for a national firm, when the ads are localized. They work even better if there's a clear understanding of the distinct nature of a local community's business practices. In Dallas, for example, research showed that the drive for success, among smaller business, is unique. A successful business person may be an absolute newcomer to the community, but he'll be more readily accepted than an unsuccessful old timer. Knowing this contributed to the success of one firm's ad campaign.

We know that the call to action inherent in most good advertising must most frequently be supported by an outreach by the professional. Nobody every hired a professional by coupon. In one of the greatest fiascoes of contemporary professional services advertising, an overwhelmingly successful ad campaign for a firm resulted in an extraordinary inundation of returned coupons—*not one of which was followed up*. Thousands of dollars in advertising went down the drain, along with the firm's reputation.

Indeed, the impression made by professional service advertising is fragile. This may be because it's so difficult to make the distinction between two firms' ability to perform the same basic service. Thus, selling efforts must be made while the iron is hot, because the iron cools off quickly. And keeping it hot without striking can be tremendously expensive.

But beyond that, your ads must distinctly recognize the unique nature of professional services marketing, and your creativity (and, of course, that of your agency) must reflect that. Advertising strategy is limited not so much by rules, and certainly not by experience, but rather, by sheer imagination.

### Strategy for the Smaller Firm

It's all well and good for the larger firm to speak in terms of advertising, particularly in the context of a full-scale marketing program. But what can the smaller firm do with advertising?

A great deal.

Certainly, the firm offering a special service that solves a particular problem has a lot to say in an ad, and experience is showing that on a direct response to advertising, the smaller firm is outperforming the larger firm.

The law firm that specializes in estate problems for the small business owner is appealing directly to a defined audience with an easily identifiable problem. The accounting firm specializing in cash flow problems for retailers faces the same potential.

This doesn't even begin to address the tort lawyers, the legal clinics, and the tax preparers, for whom advertising is a prime source of business.

Consider, too, that even the national firm must advertise solely on a local level, simply because few services are supplied nationally. From that point of view, the national firm, in each city, becomes a local firm, against whom the small local firm is competing. It tends to level the playing field.

This distinction, however, is beginning to change, as national firms realize that they can deliver any service of the firm to the clients of any office of the firm, even if that capability isn't resident locally. The response of the local firm, then, must be in more effective marketing; in choosing targets and the services offered them more carefully.

Corporate advertising for the smaller firm works well in addressing specific problems in perception. For example, if your firm is particularly strong in an industry or service, and you want to project that expertise, an ad campaign in that context can help accomplish it.

## Who Does It

Experience dictates that professionals who are new to advertising, or who feel that their firms are too small to involve outside agencies, should accept the fact that ads should be professionally written. There is simply too large a body of experience in designing advertising, even though not necessarily for professional services, for the inexperienced ad designer or writer to know how to do it instinctively. An amateurish ad for a professional firm is worse than no ad at all.

Successful advertising always looks easier than it really is—and the better the job the more effortless it looks. Just as the professional accountant, doctor, or lawyer knows his or her skills, so too does the marketing professional.

At the same time, in all advertising there must be a strong collaborative effort between the client and his marketing services.

Professional services advertising is relatively new, and you're unlikely to find many agencies that have ever worked for a firm like yours (a situation that's rapidly changing). Here, your constant and patient input is crucial.

And the fact that advertising for professional services is so new too frequently means that even the best advertising professional is not always aware of some of the problems in advertising professional services. For example, most advertising professionals are trained to talk about product advantages, which too frequently don't exist on a tangible basis in professional services. Thus, the collaboration between client and agency must be greater than in any other kind of advertising.

In the collaborative effort between the client and the agency, the client's role is clear-cut:

- You must be absolutely open in describing your service to your agency. They must be made to understand, as clearly as possible, what you do, who you do it for, the kinds of problems you address for clients, the kinds of solutions you bring to those problems, the nature of your practice and your overall service concepts.

- The agency must be made to understand the dynamics of professional services, in which (unlike product marketing) there is a human relationship involved between the supplier of the service and the client. It's this dynamic, more than even the service offered, that must be sold.

- You must be sure that your agency recognizes and understands the ethical constraints in your profession, including, if applicable, state and local regulations. While the laws and regulations regarding these ethical constraints are diminishing, what remains is still murky and in many areas untested. It's important that your agency understand that they exist.

  On the other hand, to restrain a creative agency out of a residual anxiety about how your market will accept your advertising can be self-defeating. Taste is difficult to define, but squeamishness in the face of

87

advertising experience is difficult to justify in today's competitive arena. This, by the way, is one reason that research will often tell you unexpected facts.

- Most professional services are partnerships. To subject your advertising agency to the full force of constant criticism and oversight by all of your partners is to court disaster. Designate one partner to take the responsibility of dealing with the agency. But channel through your marketing director. When it comes to advertising, everybody is an expert and everybody has an opinion. What is most dangerous is that not everybody recognizes the professionalism in marketing, and from this springs subversion of good marketing. The ideal solution, of course, is to have a knowledgeable and well-trained marketing professional on staff.

There is a new breed of marketing professional emerging. These specialists are marketers who have come to know and understand the nature of their firm's profession, and how to best apply sound marketing principles to professional service marketing.

Not only do these marketing professionals bring great skill to the firms they serve, but they act as translators between the firm's professionals and the outside agencies. The savings on wear and tear is tremendous. More significantly, the quality of the marketing that results is superior.

## Ethics

Despite the new ability of professionals to advertise, both common law and ethical codes still apply. In some cases the ethical codes are governed by state bodies or professional societies, and should be carefully observed. In all cases overall ethical considerations are extremely important if advertising is not to be counterproductive. The clients of any profession expect ethical behavior of professionals.

Obviously, the overall ethical constraint against lying or misrepresenting applies. There are also a number of laws pertaining to advertising generally, covering such practices as misrepresentation, offering merchandise or service that don't exist, or that can't be delivered within a reasonable amount of time, and so forth.

But beyond that it would simply be taken amiss to advertise in any way that would be unethical within a profession in other contexts. This might include promising results in areas that are beyond your control—winning a case, curing an illness, even saving money on a tax return. And even if you could deliver on these promises, to make them so subverts professionalism as to strain credibility and to be counterproductive—much less to risk the wrath of professional bodies.

The imaginative boundaries allow more than enough room to advertise and market within ethical considerations.

Ultimately, the question of ethics in the professions, and certainly in marketing in the professions, is a function of good business. What we perceive to be honest and ethical is invariably what works best in a business climate. The obverse, on the other hand, results invariably in distrust, failure of reputation, and economic disaster.

In marketing, as in everything else, judgment in the area of ethics evolves to a business decision.

## Measuring Results

There are some technical methods that can be used to help judge advertising. For example, surveys can be taken both before and after a campaign to determine such factors as:

- *Name recognition.* How many people knew and recognized your firm's name before and after the ad campaign?
- *Attitudes.* What was the perception of your firm before and after the ad campaign?
- *Penetration.* How many people actually saw the ad and remember it?
- *Communication and readability.* How many people read and understood the ads and retained an understanding of what it is you have to offer.

Surveys of this kind can and should be taken professionally if the size of the advertising program warrants it. In a smaller campaign, however, simple surveys can be designed with a sample of very few people to give you a sense of the answers to these questions.

Focus groups, in which a cross section of individuals representing a target audience discuss specific aspects of a service or a firm, are especially useful. These sessions are recorded and observed through one-way glass. Professionally done, they bring a dimension of information to a research project that tell more than surveys about attitudes.

In-depth research, in which intensive individual interviews are held with a carefully selected group of clients or prospective clients, can be a powerful source of information.

In fact, you'll get plenty of feedback about your advertising—from clients, friends, and even competitors. If the campaign has any impact, positive or negative, you'll hear about it. The information may not be scientific, but it will contribute to your own reaction.

Judging the effectiveness of an ad or an ad campaign is primarily a function of understanding at the outset what you expect that campaign to accomplish and then judging whether that mission has been fulfilled. Presumably, your expectations will have been realistically and clearly delineated. Unrealistic expectations can sink the followup of an otherwise successful campaign, and warp your valid judgment of it.

But ultimately, a successful ad is one that meets its objectives, no matter what they are.

But within that context, a successful ad will . . .

- Be seen and read, or heard and listened to
- Make its points clearly and quickly, with nothing obscure
- Relate and be responsive to the needs of the prospective client who reads it
- Cause or contribute to a change in knowledge, in attitude, in proclivity (no matter how subtle), or to action, if appropriate. But if the reader is totally untouched, unchanged, then the ad is a failure

For the smaller firm, another aspect of context is the locality. Advertising works differently in an arena of heavy competition than it does when competition is lighter. When there is little competition, there is less need to distinguish your firm from others, and a greater need to project the value to the prospective clients of the services you're offering.

Nothing so much as advertising points to the fact that marketing is a structure, in which each part of the structure depends upon the others for substance and support. Advertising may sell products by itself (but rarely does), but it will virtually never sell professional services by itself except in the odd and random case of a unique and specific service.

There comes to mind the case of a legal or a tax clinic. There, the service is virtually a product, because there is implied virtually no variable of performance. A will is a will, and a form 1040 is a form 1040. It's also the price that's selling.

The same kind of exception exists in the peculiar case of personal injury law, where what's being sold is the promise (always implied, never stated) of big bucks at the end. This, too, moves advertising into the product realm.

We're back to rules, and why they don't hold universally. What we've learned thus far is that some techniques in advertising seem to work and some don't. We've learned that advertising is the most complex of all marketing tools, because it responds least of all of them to rules. It's still a product of the human brain, which means that skill and imagination count far more than do rules.

# 6

# Direct Mail

Direct mail's ability to contribute to selling professional services is extraordinary. When it's properly used, direct mail fills a role that can, in most circumstances, make it the most universally effective of all professional service marketing tools. The emphasis, of course, is on *properly used*.

It has an exceptional track record as a primary tool for developing personal selling opportunities, and substantially increasing their number and effectiveness. It's highly flexible, and can focus on any or all of several aspects of a professional service's capabilities. Its ability to address the problems that a professional service might solve is singular. The ability to go directly to a target market, virtually prospect by prospect, is unparalleled.

And it works exceedingly well to support other marketing efforts.

The one thing it can't do is get clients.

If you understand that, and understand that the major objective of direct mail is to get you the opportunity to meet with, and to personally sell, a prospect, then you have the potential to use direct mail as a powerful marketing tool.

## The Difference between Mass and Direct Mail

If you send out 20,000 letters offering a desk clock, and the list is carefully chosen to include people who can afford to buy clocks, and who've bought desk items in that price category before, and the selling material is good, then you can count on getting back about a thousand orders with checks. Five percent.

Easy. There's nothing personal between you and the individual who buys your clock. He doesn't expect to see you again. He likes the clock and wants it. When it comes, he has the clock and you go away.

Now, why shouldn't that work the same way in professional services?

If you send out 20,000 letters to a carefully selected list of small business owners, people who use or need the services of a lawyer or an accountant, and offer your services, why can't you, too, anticipate that you'd get a thousand new clients? Or even a thousand opportunities to discuss ways in which you can serve them?

Because people don't buy professional services the way they buy products. And that's why you'd be wasting your money using direct mail with the same matrix you'd use for selling a product. Here's what happens. . .

- The detachment in selling a product, in which the product stays and the seller goes, doesn't exist in professional services marketing. The person who does the selling in professional services marketing stays after the sale is made.

- Not every company, or individual, regardless of the numbers or the profile on paper, is the right client. No matter how hungry you are for clients, there are still those prospective clients you want to screen—be it for financial reasons, or personalities, or the nature of the business, or the kinds of problems.

- This is a problem with mass marketing—no choice of who buys your product. But with products, it doesn't matter. With services it does. *Controlling the nature of your clientele is extremely important in a successful practice. And so it's important in professional services marketing.*

- Direct mail may sell a product—even to someone who doesn't really need it—by virtue of appeal or impulse. Everybody who needs an accountant probably has one, and except for those with attorneys on retainer, anybody who might need a lawyer at one time or another may not need one at the time you send your letter. That means that your description of what you have to offer must be sufficiently focussed and intriguing, by virtue of the problems you offer to solve, to pique interest in you and your firm. *This does not constitute a sale, however, which can come only through further discussion and personal contact.*

- There are more broad general categories of those who buy products than there are of those who buy professional services. The category of people who buy cat books is very large and homogeneous. They may, as individuals, differ in many different ways—but in their affinity for cats they're the same. The people who use professional services almost always include much smaller groups with more specific needs for aspects of those services.

   For example, all Americans and all companies must pay taxes. But within those very large categories, specific tax problems, or compliance needs, or tax planning objectives, tend to be more distinctive, and of concern to smaller groups of companies or individuals.

   *This is a crucial factor in marketing. It means that the target market for a very specific service is relatively narrow. It also means that the opportunity to sell to that smaller group improves the ability to sell successfully.*

## The Advantages of Direct Mail

The rationale for direct mail is deceptively simple. I know the that nature of what you do can be enhanced by the nature of what I do. If I want to write you a

92

personal letter to persuade you of that, and that I understand the nature of a particular problem you may have, and that I have the solution, then I have an extraordinary opportunity to get your attention. But if "you" are a potential client, then there are many more of "you" than there are of me. When I mail that letter to a number of people, and it's properly personalized, and cast and presented in a way to increase the likelihood that "you" will actually read it, then the effect of the relationship established is the same as if I were to send "you" the one personal letter.

Properly done, then, direct mail has significant and clearly discernible advantages:

- It allows the target audience to be carefully defined and selected. Unlike display advertising, where the limit is the broad demographic base of a publication's readers, direct mail allows you to select and define your target audience to the tightest possible parameters.

- It aims a highly personal and individualized appeal or sales message to a carefully defined audience. It functions as if you were writing an individual letter to an individual, even though it's a mailing to many people.

- It has the flexibility to deal with complex or technical problems and solutions.

- It's useful in reaching both large and small audiences. If the letter is perceived as a personal letter from you to the recipient it makes no difference how large your audience is. It's particularly effective in pre-selling a service and a service organization, particularly to people who don't know you or your service.

- It can sum up in a very few words a specific problem faced by the prospective client and, in a very few words, explain why your service can help solve that problem.

- It's *relatively* inexpensive and cost-effective, in terms of return on investment. With a highly focused message to a clearly defined audience, the likelihood of getting a broader return is greater than in other more diverse advertising. It's timing can be carefully controlled. You can send out letters at any time that's to your advantage, and you can time the letters to your ability to follow up.

- It eliminates cold calls by serving as an introductory device.

Clearly, then, there are profound advantages to direct mail in selling professional services.

## When Direct Mail Is Indicated

As with any marketing tool, direct mail won't be effective without a clear rationale within the marketing program. It's important to distinguish those factors that are most conducive to using direct mail effectively and those that dictate when it's not practical.

Essentially, direct mail is used when a specific service is best sold directly to a specific individual or company; when it's the first step in directly selling to an individual, the second step of which is the actual face-to-face selling effort.

Direct mail doesn't sell firms—it sells services.

It's particularly useful in selling a single service as a solution to a specific problem. It's even more effective if the problem or the solution is complex or technical. For example, if you have a system to help small companies manage surplus cash, then direct mail is a natural. You know the problem, you have the solution, you know your target audience.

In an era of sophisticated computers and other technical devices, in which target and segment marketing are emerging as most potent, effective, and cost-effective approaches to moving products and services to a market, direct mail stands out as the preeminent marketing tool for professionals. It's significant that there are today marketing specialists who believe that the time is near when every soap manufacturer will know and approach every individual buyer by name. Professional services marketing has already crossed that bridge.

Direct mail should be used, then, when there is:

- *A clearly defined market,* in terms of the need for the service you're offering, and your ability to reach that market effectively and efficiently (usually by choosing the right mailing lists).

- *A clearly delineated product or service,* particularly in your defining both a specific problem and your service to solve that problem.

- *The capability to follow up on mailings,* in terms of direct contact and selling. No one sees an ad or gets a letter and decides to retain you. The best that can be expected is that it will help develop a personal selling opportunity. Therefore direct mail should be used only when there exists the capability to follow up on mailings to develop a selling situation.

- *A service or a concept* you want to sell to a defined market.

- *A distinction between national and practice office capabilities.* In a multi-office operation, the distinction should be made, as in print advertising, between the ability to perform a service nationally and to perform it on an office-by-office basis. Direct mail works best locally, not nationally.

94

When these factors are not favorable, then using direct mail may well be contraindicated.

## Elements of a Successful Program

Perhaps one of the disadvantages of direct mail is that it appears so easy to use that it's often misused. "After all," you might say to yourself, "I've been writing letters to prospects for all these years."

In fact, the professionalism involved in using direct mail effectively goes well beyond merely writing a letter.

Experience tells us that at least the following elements comprise a successful direct mail campaign:

- The marketing objective for the program must be stated and understood. A program begins not with the letter, but with the marketing objective. What do you want the campaign to accomplish?

- There must be an integrated relationship between the direct mail program and other marketing efforts. Direct mail rarely stands on its own. If it's not integrated with other marketing efforts, the likelihood of its success is substantially diminished.

- The target market must be defined, identified, and readily accessible, with up-to-date and accurate mailing lists available

- The selling message must be sharply delineated. Writing the selling message in the letter may ultimately be an art form that depends upon the skill of the writer, but before it demands art, it demands technical marketing skill.

- The service being sold must be defined in terms of the audience's specific needs, and presented in terms of advantages to the prospect. It's not a question of what you want to sell, but rather what the prospect wants to buy.

- Each direct mail program must be tailored to the specific service being sold and to the specific audience. There is no such thing as a standard program, or a standard letter, or to sell your firm generally.

- If you're trying to get clients for your firm generally (no specific service), the campaign must still be cast in terms of either a specific service, or a distinct and definable advantage you offer.

- The mailing package must be carefully designed, including the letters and enclosures. Each envelope that goes out has a great many options in what it can contain—the letter, brochures, reprints of articles, and so forth. Each element is as important as the others, and all elements must support and complement one another.

- The timing of the mailing must be meticulous, in terms of the ability to follow up, the spacing between letters in a multiletter campaign, the timing of a market's needs, and so forth.

- There must be assiduous followup. Again, a letter doesn't sell—people do. A campaign comprised of the most effective letter and mailing material will accomplish nothing if there isn't followup to the prospect to establish a meeting and to make a presentation to close the sale.

A direct mail campaign is just that—a campaign. It's not just shooting some letters in the mail.

## Expectations

Without clearly understanding what you may rationally expect from direct mail there's a danger that a successful campaign—one in which exceptional entree is gained into the potential market—may be perceived as a failure. This is why the results of direct mail must be judged differently for professional services than for products.

There's often a tendency to think of its potential in the same context as in selling products. A direct mail campaign to sell books, for example, can be expected to sell a number of books in proportion to the number of letters sent out. Numbers like 2 percent or 5 percent return are usually heard.

In professional services, however, because the role of direct mail is to presell—to develop the opportunity to sell in person—there is no direct sales return. Nobody receives a letter and sends a check, as in product sales. Nobody responds to a letter by calling and retaining the firm (although there is sometimes an inquiry).

Therefore, the measure of success in direct mail resides in the degree to which the individual professional is able to make a personal presentation.

In a successful and well-run direct mail program, phone followup may result in from 10 to 50 percent acceptance of offers to make a personal sales presentation, depending upon the service offered and the target audience.

Planning the direct mail campaign begins, as you might expect, with a clear understanding of the campaign's objectives. Beyond getting an appointment to sell your service, and informing the prospect of the nature of your firm and service, the best approach to determining your objective is to clarify the problem that the service you're offering is capable of solving.

## The Program

No direct mail campaign should be started without a carefully delineated program to give it form and direction. The program should include at least the following elements:

- *The problem.* This should be a statement of the problem faced by the market—its needs, as seen in terms of the firm's ability to meet those needs and to solve the problem. This is a crucial element of a direct mail program—that it stress the needs of the prospective client rather than focus on the service you have to offer.

  Choose the problem you're going to address. Here, less is more. You may be capable of solving a hundred problems for companies of many sizes in a broad range of industries, but don't bite off too much in each mailing.

- *The strategy.* Each campaign should have a distinctive strategy that relates the campaign to the overall marketing objectives, and that addresses the configuration of the specific market. For example, a campaign may recognize that the decision maker is the chief executive officer, and that he or she must be the recipient of the letter. The campaign strategy must be designed to present the letter in a way that increases the likelihood of its being read. At the same time, another campaign strategy may dictate that the letter be aimed at a lower echelon decision maker, in which case the strategy for reaching the executive is different. In some cases, you've got to sell more than one person in a company. In any event, this strategy must be detailed.

- *The letters.* A decision must be made about the number of letters, the style and tone of writing, the copy platform, and the balance in each letter between the clarification of the problem and the statement of your ability to solve the problem. Examples of tone might be senior executive talking to senior executive; formal versus informal; technical or lay terms.

- *The timing.* How often will the letters go out, how many go out at each mailing, when the letters go out, the amount of time between letters.

- *The list.* A complete description of the mailing list, its composition and its source should be included. In choosing the target list, pick a small segment of companies, in one or several industries, that seem susceptible to a common problem.

- *Collateral material.* Reprints, brochures, etc., and how they're used

- *Tactics.* This is the plan for the campaign itself. Should it be tested? In how many cities? How many letters in the initial mailings and in each batch? Should separate but simultaneous letters be sent to influentials and decision makers? Who signs? Who copes with responses? If the strategy you choose works on the smaller list, you can expand it. If it doesn't, you can change it for the next group, with very little lost. If, on the other hands, your strategy is wrong in a mass mailing, you've spent a lot of money for no good reason.

- *The phone followup.* Who does it, and who says what.

- *The appointment.* Given a successful followup, who goes and what's said?

- *Telemarketing and its relationship to direct mail.* Is it used simply to qualify the prospect? Is it to be used as a selling effort in conjunction with direct mail?

All of these elements must be measured and balanced against one another.

Is this the only way to go? Of course not. This is one way that's proven to work. In this relatively new arena, we know what doesn't work, but we only know some of what does work.

## Strategy

One successful campaign for a consulting firm began by understanding that fluctuating interest rates created a problem of great magnitude for banks, and had a strong potential for adversely affecting their profitability. The banks' problem was to keep track of portfolios with loans with mixed interest rates and differing maturities. Many banks were not able to constantly monitor and control their mixture. The service the consultant had to offer was a system to monitor and control these diverse portfolios.

Moreover, the consultant was aware that the problem was most prevalent in medium-sized banks, which, in fact, tended to be unaware that the problem existed until it was too late.

Thus, the primary objective of the program was to make the target audience—medium-sized banks—aware of the serious problem, and to make them aware that the consultant had a solution. A second objective was to generate a context of receptivity that offered the opportunity to sell the consulting service. A third objective was to develop inquiries, if possible. And ultimately, the objective is to get the opportunity to sell the service in person.

It was determined that the decision maker for retaining the consultant was the bank's chief executive officer. This might not have been the case with larger banks, where responsibilities are more diversely spread among a larger management group.

The decision to write directly to the chief executive officer dictated both the strategy and the tone of the letter. The strategy was that a series of letters were to be sent, alerting the bank's officers to the problem, advising that a solution existed in the consultant's service, and soliciting a direct response for further followup. (Despite the fact that each letter was to be followed by a phone call.)

Two letters were planned, with a third to be used if needed.

## Why More Than One Letter

In most programs, more than one letter is necessary for at least the following reasons:

- Despite the highly personalized nature of a letter, it's still a direct mail piece, and one of many to arrive every day. While the well-designed letter and package enhances readership, it must be assumed that readership of the first letter is at least cursory. However there is frequently a subliminal retention of the firm name and logo, which makes the second letter more acceptable because it comes from a source that the reader now recognizes or finds familiar.

- In many cases the letter is coming from a source unknown to the recipient. Credibility and knowledge doesn't begin to build until the second letter.

    If the second letter doesn't do its job, a third letter affords you little risk in using a stronger sell. After all, if the prospective client hasn't demonstrated interest after two letters, you have nothing to lose by pushing a little harder.

In a situation like this, the first letter should focus heavily on the problem itself and the dangers inherent in not recognizing it. The letter then indicates that there is a solution to the problem, and that the consulting firm writing the letter offers that solution.

In the campaign to the banks, the brochure describing the services was not included with the first letter. To do so would be to divert the focus away from the problem, and by telegraphing the message, diminish the urgency of the personal call. Your prospect can then say, "I've read your brochure and know what you want to tell me. There's no need for me to meet with you to hear it again."

The second letter, on the other hand, indicates the problem, but focuses heavily on the solution and the firm's ability to help.

The third letter, should it be needed, is more balanced between the problem and the solution than were the first two, and is a much harder sell. In this case, the brochure may be included.

Considering the problem and the target audience, the tone of the letters was that of senior executives talking to senior executives. The letter was written on the finest stationary that the firm has, with the first letter no more than one page. In its delineation of the problem it was quietly alarming, offering the solution in the broadest terms as a comfort factor, and soliciting an inquiry.

The first two letters were spaced three weeks apart.

Because the campaign was for a firm with offices in several cities, the campaign was tested in two cities, each of which was selected because of its ability to control the followup. Initial mailings were in batches of fifty, so that the responses may be coped with effectively. The signer of each letter was the person who will be in the best position to deal directly with each response.

The campaign was a rousing success, with more than 50 percent of the addressees allowing the sales presentation to be heard, and a large portion of that number buying the service. And even those prospects that didn't accept the opportunity for a presentation, were aware that the firm offered the service.

## *The Three-Person Campaign*

There are times when a campaign is best directed at three people in a company at once.

In a campaign to sell a high-priced specialized auditing service to corporations embarking on major construction projects, research determined that three people were involved in the decision—the chief executive officer, who had to understand and approve major expenditures; the chief financial officer, who was obviously involved in the problems of saving or spending money; and the chief engineer responsible for the actual construction. The CEO and CFO could say yea or nay on expenditures, but were not expert on construction. The engineer was expert on construction, but had no authority to spend large sums of money on his own.

A letter to each, tailored to the specific problem and office, turned out to be overwhelmingly successful. Each was informed that the others were being written to, so that everyone was in the same loop.

Similarly, a maintenance management service that had traditionally been sold to plant maintenance managers faced difficulties because the roles of plant executives had changed over the years. There was a declining number of executives with the title of maintenance manager, and the role had been variously reassigned. The problem was solved with a three-person direct mail campaign to the CEO, the CFO, and the plant manager. This way, the message got to the right person. The campaign was overwhelmingly successful.

This is the fun of direct mail marketing—finding ways to change the rules in order to get the job done.

## Writing the Copy

While the general rules of copywriting will be discussed in the next chapter, direct mail for professional services has a distinctive body of elements that do and don't work, as well as a number of elements that have not yet been tested. Unfortunately, writing a direct mail letter is a combination of art, experience, skill, and luck—probably in that order.

There are no hard and fast rules, but we do know some things that work and don't work in letters for most campaigns.

- Letters that start off with "we," and then go on to describe your firm, tend not to work. Who you are and what you have to offer is your concern—not the potential buyer's. The potential buyer is intrigued only by his perception that you understand and can help him serve his needs.

- Self-serving descriptions, and adjectives that try to tell the readers how they should perceive you, are turn-offs. "We give better service," for example, is a road sign to the waste basket. What's the obverse—"We give lousy service?" As the old saying goes, what you are speaks so loud that I can't hear what you say you are.

100

- Letters that start off with a question can be a trap. "Do you have a problem with...?" means that if the reader doesn't know that he or she has that problem, there's no reason to read beyond that point. (On the other hand, "Do you know that you may be paying taxes you don't have to pay?" can work. You have to be careful about hard and fast rules.)

- Letters that deal with more than one problem tend to fall on deaf ears.

- Letters that include brochures or other literature tend not to work for a simple reason—they tell your whole story to readers, who then feel that there's no reason to meet with you. That deprives you of the important opportunity to make a strong personal presentation, predicated on an analysis of the prospect's specific problems and needs. Brochures and literature are for leaving behind after you've met with the prospect. One possible exception might be reprints of articles that support your description of the seriousness of the problem, or that enhance your reputation. And these should rarely be used in a first mailing.

- Absolutely crucial is to understand that while you may get an occasional response that says, "I like your letter—let's start on Monday," *the aim of the exercise is solely to get an appointment to make a presentation—not to make the sale.* To expect anything other than that from direct mail in professional services is to doom yourself to expensive failure.

- What seems to get better readership is the letter written on Monarch-size letterhead. It looks more like a personal letter, or one from a CEO to a CEO.

- One approach that almost invariably works is to open with a strong—and startling, if possible—statement of a specific problem. It should be said in a way to get to the very heart of what your research says really bothers your target. For example, a tremendously successful letter for a consulting firm selling maintenance system services began, "Do you know what portion of the more than one billion dollars in wasted maintenance dollars is yours?" Another sentence expanded the theme, bringing the terror of it even closer to home.

  The second paragraph simply said, "We can help you, as we've helped dozens of other companies like yours, in your industry."

  The third paragraph described the firm, and why it was qualified to help. No self-serving adjectives. Just the facts.

  The fourth and last paragraph requested an appointment to discuss ways in which "we can help you."

That letter was extraordinarily successful.

Some of the other devices, such as multicolored letters, jazzy headlines, and extremely strong claims tend to be counterproductive, in that they're considerably less than the public expects from professionals. They diminish credibility, with exceptions dictated by both the material and the audience to whom the campaign is addressed.

At the same time, there are some devices that can be used that have the appearance of simply making the letter and its point more readable. For example, the indented paragraph. Underscored words to make a point. The headline-like sentence before the salutation. These are some of the devices that, if tastefully used, strengthen the letter without diminishing the appearance of professionalism.

As you'll see in the chapter on copywriting, there are really very few rules that are so hard and fast that they can't be broken or bent experimentally.

If there is such a thing as a hard and fast rule, it is that the letter must focus on the prospect's problem, and not on your service. And there can be exceptions to even that rule. Can you imagine a reader not reading through a letter that begins, "I have found the cure for the common cold."?

But unless you have indeed found the cure for the common cold, the letter must be cast primarily in terms of the prospect's needs and anxieties as a lead-in to the solution you have to offer. Thus, the first paragraph should get directly to the heart of the matter in delineating the problem in its most dire form. And it should be done in a way that doesn't state the obvious, merely as a platform for your argument.

For example:

"Everybody has a problem in choosing the right computer to solve small business accounting problems," is merely a statement of an obvious fact. Very dull.

"When you know that choosing the wrong computer can be more expensive than choosing no computer at all, then you understand the high cost of being confused." This is a statement of fact that's designed to hit a nerve and to generate anxiety, without dwelling on the obvious.

And the second paragraph should say, "Our firm can help."

. In writing a direct mail letter the questions that should be foremost in your mind are:

- Who am I writing to?
- What do I want him or her to know, think, or feel after reading the letter?
- What do I want them to do after they have read the letter?
- Are there any questions that go unanswered, except those that I mean to have go unanswered?
- And then comes the first crucial question before writing—"What is the most startling, riveting, attention-getting thing I can say in the first sentence?"

The answer to these questions dictate the nature of the letter, its copy platform, its tone, and its content.

Aside from the emotional appeal of the first paragraph, and the beginning of the sell in the second paragraph, the subsequent paragraphs should succinctly describe the service being offered, your qualifications to perform that service, and a call to action—even if you plan to call.

## Mailing Lists

Whom the Gods would drive mad, they first put in charge of mailing lists.

Mailing lists are indeed the bane of everybody's existence. Deceptively simple at first glance, they are in fact extraordinarily complex—more so, if they are to be at all useful. They must be targeted to specific audiences, they must be kept up-to-date (which can be a horror in industries where personnel changes constantly, such as the press), and they must be fed, cared for, and managed like a pet dog.

Every professional firm maintains lists. Every partner in each firm maintains his or her own lists. They are lists of clients, prospective clients, suppliers, influentials, and the press—lists of everyone they've met on planes and at parties, and lists of names that seem to have appeared from nowhere. These lists grow like weeds. But they are now crucial to any professional firm and its people. They're absolutely essential to the simplest control of client relationships, as well as for the most sophisticated marketing program.

If direct mail is to be properly used in marketing professional services, the chances are that none of the lists will be extensive. Few professional services do national mailings, and so most lists are either regional or limited to a specific industry. Very large lists, such as might be used to sell a product nationally, are simply not rational. And certainly, no list should be larger than one's ability to follow up after a mailing. The lists, then, should be qualified not only by a mailing or list house, but by your own sense of where your potential clientele lies. In fact, if you've been in practice for any length of time, the chances are that you already have a mailing list of current, former, and potential clients. This list, if accurate, should take precedence over any purchased mailing list.

### The Cost of Mailing

The continually growing cost of a single piece of first class mail—including addressing, stuffing, printing enclosures, postage, and the time in managing the process—dictates that mailing lists be as accurate as humanly possible (a process than can be helped by, but not done by, computers). The cost of doing otherwise, whether it results in mailing to the wrong address, or misspelling a client's name, can be disastrously high.

A mailing list is more than a collection of names and addresses. Mailings must be tailored to reach specific groups with specific messages, and so must be structured accordingly. A list of clients, for example, is different from a list of prospective clients. But a list of clients is also a list of prospective clients for a new service you have to offer.

A list, then, is a dynamic picture of audience segments that are relevant to your practice. And sometimes lists overlap one another, based upon how each is to be used.

### In-House or External?

Lists can be maintained in-house, or can be acquired from mailing list houses. There are advantages and disadvantages in both.

With increasingly sophisticated (but relatively easy to use) software and hardware now available, bringing lists in-house offers such advantages as better responsiveness and shorter turn-arounds, better control, and a greater tendency to use the list for targeted mailing campaigns. You may also be able to more efficiently link other internal mailing and list systems.

Outside list bureaus' services may also include labeling, stuffing, and mailing. They offer the advantage of greater facility and convenience, the benefits of information derived from their serving many customers (change of address, etc.), and the ability to track costs precisely. On the other hand, you own only those lists you supply to them, and so you can rarely control their lists.

Mailing list brokers, who can be found in the Yellow Pages in any major city, seem able to supply rather precise lists in every category except the one you want, which means that to get any advantage from a list house, you have to define your needs accurately. A good list house will usually qualify its list (purge it of out-of-date names and addresses), charging more for guaranteed up-to-date lists.

It might be useful to understand where mailing houses get their lists.

The sources range from subscriber lists of specific magazines to extensive research (by the better and larger mailing list houses). Mailing lists made up of publication subscriber lists are useful only if the publication that served as a source rather precisely covers your potential clientele. This is not often likely to be the case, however, under most circumstances. Other mailing lists may be derived from successful mailings of other vendors.

For example, you can buy a list of purchasers of books by direct mail, drawn from those who have purchased books by mail in the past. How, on the other hand, can you get a qualified list of prospective accounting or legal clients without very carefully describing your own criteria for clientele?

In fact, you don't really buy a list—you rent it. Reusing a list, particularly if it's more than a few weeks old, is a poor idea because in most cases many of the names on that list will have become obsolete, even in that brief period of time.

A qualified list, guaranteed to be up-to-date and with a very high percentage of accuracy, is worth the price. Inaccurate lists are expensive, and mean wasted postage and production costs. The larger the list, of course, the less likely it is to be accurate, since people move, change their circumstances or interests, change their jobs, and so forth.

## Factors in Choosing a List Control System

Marketing computer consultant Tim Powell, of Find/SVP, writing in *The Marcus Report*, suggests several factors to be considered in developing or reviewing a list control system:

- *Specific list functions required.* How is the list to be used, and does the list program support those uses? Features you should consider are:

  ° Does it support a full identifier scheme? Each entry should at least include fields (spaces) for individual name and salutation; individual title and function; company name; company industry; phone number; and complete mailing address. Other fields should be available, if they're useful to you.

  ° Does it support merge and purge, allowing separate lists to be integrated and duplicates eliminated? How are duplicates handled? Can match codes (the long number-letter combinations on your mailing label that serve to control the list and avoid duplications) be included?

  ° What kind of outputs are provided? These could include mailing labels; customized form letters; reports; and gross statistics. Can they be tailored to meet your specific needs?

  ° Does it provide necessary external linkages? This could include export to MailMerge files for use with word processors, and the ability to convert to and from other data formats (Lotus 1-2-3 or dBase, for example).

  ° What kind of record selection is possible? For example, can you generate form letters and mailing labels for only those clients and prospects in a particular industry?

  ° What kinds of sorts can be done? Mail pre-sorted by zip code, for example, can be sent less expensively than unsorted mail.

  ° Does it allow for sample mailings? This allows you to mail to a random sample and evaluate the results before investing in a full-scale mailing.

- *List size.* A 40 megabyte hard disk can handle more than 100,000 entries.

- *Costs.* Generally, service bureaus charge for each of their services, with additional charges accruing for each operation performed. Get a written bid based on your detailed specifications. If you're considering taking part of the function in-house, don't forget to add back the costs of those functions that you will still contract out (for example, letter shop).

- *Human resources.* The people and expertise to complete the job accurately and on time must be available.

- *Nature of input/output.* How many additions and changes to, and deletions from, the list are made over a typical time cycle? Is the input centralized or decentralized? Are external lists being folded in?

- *Institutional imperatives.* Are there existing internal lists that must be compatible? Are interfaces required to other internal systems?

- *Control issues.* Is direct access to the system required? By whom, how often, and for what purposes? What kind of security must be provided?

## Management Issues

Regardless of the tools you use to manage your mailing lists, Powell suggest that the key factors include:

- *Maintenance.* Every list must be constantly maintained to control quality and costs. Duplicates and non-current names must be eliminated, titles and locations must be kept current, and accuracy must be sustained.

  There are several methods. One is a self-addressed reply card (preferably postage-free) included with a publication to indicate changes of address or title. A self-addressed postcard to gather updated or corrected information is useful. This is usually done on a revolving basis, using a different portion of the list each time.

  Another effective method is to have the practitioners themselves periodically review and update their own lists.

- *Practitioners' access.* How are the practice professionals going to be able to access the mailing data for their clients? Will they have direct on-line access, either dial-up or through a network? Will they receive hard copy periodically? Will they receive diskettes to be used locally?

- *List audits.* Don't assume that the list is getting your message to your target audience effectively and efficiently. Test samples of your list periodically to verify that the mailings are in fact being received.

- *Prospect lists.* One method is to purchase a list, either from a mailing list vendor or directly from a publication or membership organization. Another is through research, either on-line from a business database, or from business directories. A third is through prospecting—drawing names from such sources as information requests that come to the company, or from business cards gathered at trade shows.

- *Coordination among practices.* In firms where practice areas maintain their own mailing lists, coordinating mailings to a particular individual may be difficult. This may work against the marketer's having an appropriate mix of materials delivered to the target on a regular basis.

- *Prioritizing.* Priorities on mailing lists change, and must be constantly re-examined, a task that practitioners may be reluctant to address. Remind them of the adverse effects on recipients of misspellings, duplicates, or inappropriately targeted mailings.

Ultimately, all direct mail is as much an art form as it is a collection of techniques and skills. No aspect of it requires more skill—or is more of an art—than managing mailing lists.

## Assembling the Package

There is always a question as to what goes into the envelope in a mailing. The answer depends upon what you are trying to sell, to whom you're trying to sell it, and the strategy you've chosen.

If you mean to personalize the mailing so that letter is you speaking to each prospective client as an individual, the chances are that the less you enclose the better. Quite the opposite is true in mass direct mail campaigns for products.

For example, if you're writing to describe a rather specific service to the chief executive of a corporation, then you want it to look as much like a personal letter as possible. You'll use monarch size stationary, the letters will look as if they're individually typed, and there will be no enclosure—at least in the first mailing. The enclosures—the brochures, the reprints of articles, etc.— should in most cases be saved for the second or third mailing. It should be assumed that the first mailing sparked the interest, the second mailing will have a higher readership, and the third mailing is hard sell.

The letter and the brochures and other enclosures should complement one another, and no piece should be expected to do the job of another. The letter is the sales message, the brochure is the description of the service, the reprint of the article or clipping is the support. This is where the emphasis should be. The letter may describe the service, and the brochure may have some sell in it, but focus on each piece's primary job.

If each piece of the package is seen in this way, then judging what goes into each mailing is a function of what you want each mailing to accomplish.

It's important, then, to tailor the package to do only the job it's supposed to do.

## Timing and Followup

The timing for a mailing is dictated by two factors:

- The ability to followup.
- External circumstances.

The external circumstances would be those that might normally limit attempting to sell a specific service at an unpropitious time. For example, just as you would sell a tax service within a reasonable proximity of tax filing time, you might not sell a hay fever test in mid-winter.

The ability to follow up is yet a different matter. It's a function of your ability to schedule phone or personal visit followups within two weeks after the letter has gone out. In a multiletter campaign this should be a minimum of two weeks and a maximum of four weeks between letters, to allow for a continuum of impact.

### The Telephone and Direct Mail

In direct mail for products, you send out the letter and wait for the checks. In direct mail for professional services, you're after an appointment. This means that direct mail rarely should be trusted to work on it's own. You can test it, to see how many people call you back. Some will, but most won't.

That's why you have to follow up each letter with a phone call. "I wrote you last week about accounting or legal or business problems you may be facing. When can we get together to discuss ways in which we might be able to help. Is next Tuesday at 10 good for you?" In some cases, the phone followup can be done by a well-prepared and skilled telemarketer, who can arrange appointments for you or somebody in your firm. But the phone followup is crucial, *even if you say, in your letter, "call me for details."*

In the phone followup, it's extremely important that you (or whoever is on the phone) not get sucked into a potential selling situation. That must be done in person. The objective of the phone followup is solely and simply to arrange an appointment. Any questions should be deferred with a statement such as, *"Well, that's what I want to discuss with you. I think I can give you a better answer after we've taken a few minutes for me to better understand your needs. Is Tuesday at 10 good for you?"*

Because the letter is a precursor to an appointment, you have another reason why mass mailings don't work. *You can't send out more letters than you can follow up on within a week after the mailing.*

## Measuring Results

Among the advantages of direct mail is the ability to test aspects of it inexpensively. In print advertising, only those advertisers with large budgets can afford to try several different approaches, in different media. A direct mail campaign, however, can be tested in several ways:

- Different letters can be sent to different segments of the mailing list.
- Separate mailing lists can be tested with one letter.
- Different packages (one with, one without a brochure) can be tested.

You should remember, when testing a direct mail campaign, to keep careful records so that you can score results and use them for subsequent campaigns.

Ultimately, the best test of results is the response you get to phone followups. If the campaign has been done properly, and is effective (see chapter 17), a significant number of phone calls should demonstrate recognition of your firm, recall of the letter, and the willingness to meet with you personally for further discussions that can lead to closing the sale.

For moving your service directly to the potential client, direct mail, properly conceived and executed, is an unparalleled marketing tool.

# 7

# Copy, Design, and Production

Essentially, an ad is a vehicle for a message.

And while a number of elements contribute to presenting that message, and controlling its quality, the burden is usually carried primarily by *copy*—the words—the text.

In advertising copy, it's amazing what works and what doesn't work.

While a great deal is known about what works in ad copy, even more isn't known. And what makes it difficult for the uninitiated is that what you may judge to be great copy because of the sheer poetry, imagery, sound, and lyricism, may be lousy for accomplishing the mission of the ad.

To try to define the art of copywriting is as futile as trying to define the art of how to paint like Michelangelo. Nevertheless, there are the *mechanics* of copy, a view of which can help to understand what it is and how it functions to do its job.

And whether you do it yourself (which is difficult for the inexperienced non-professional copywriter) or you must judge the work of those who do it in your behalf, the guidelines and limitations of copy should be clearly understood. They should be understood even if they are to be honored in the breach. There are indeed ways to break the rules. But the best abstract artists, who know better how to abstract because they are fine realistic artists, know which rules should be violated, so that it can be done with control, skill, and aesthetic strength. It's likely that those who know the rules best are those who break the rules best.

In fact, copy rules are far from decisive. When David Ogilvy was told that copy should be short and terse, because nobody reads more than a few words of an ad, he wrote the classic, "At 60 miles an hour the only sound you hear is the clock." It was a full page of text, describing the features of the Rolls Royce. It sold cars.

But in an imitative world, a great many ad people imitated not the selling aspects of the ad, but its length. We were then treated to a bunch of long text ads, most of which sold nothing. Some ad people simply didn't understand. Or couldn't write like David Ogilvy.

Perhaps the hardest thing for people who are not marketers to understand is that the process is a function of not only training, but skill, intelligence, and imagination—all of which are what we usually mean when we use the peculiar word "creative."

## *The Limits of Copywriting*

The mechanical limits of copywriting are essentially the limits of the medium. You can't write 10 minutes of copy for a 30-second radio spot. The mechanics of writing for one medium are too infrequently translatable into another medium. You can't put 50 words of copy on a billboard alongside a high speed highway and expect the message to be read.

And yet there are times when originality, imagination, and skill dictate that all rules be violated. Fifty or 100 words on that billboard may be just the ticket if the headline is something like, "There are not enough words to describe ... "

## The Objectives of the Ad

Writing advertising copy begins, as you might expect, with defining objectives—of the campaign, of the marketing program, of the specific ad. These objectives will be unique to you and your firm, to each campaign, and to each ad. They dictate that the copy—as well as all other elements of the ad—are focused and relevant.

## Elements of a Good Ad

Generations of copywriters have found that the elements that constitute a good ad include at least the following:

- *Attention.* In the clamor and clutter of sight and sound, and the competition for the reader's eye, ear, and heart, it's imperative that you compete successfully for attention. If you can't capture your reader's attention then your copy may offer the formula to transmute base metal into gold, and no one will notice. There should be some element in the ad—whether it's the headline or the illustration or the layout—that attracts the eye or ear and arouses sufficient interest to warrant attending to the message. And the copy itself must sustain that attention.

- *Promise of Benefit.* There must be an element in the ad that promises the reader or the listener some benefit that will accrue from accepting the ad's premises. (In the subtlety of advertising, this may not always be obvious. The benefit may be one of being comfortable with a concept or a problem, rather than the solution to the problem itself).

- *Credibility.* The premises of the ad must be believable, and credible within a context that the reader can understand. To speak the truth is not sufficient; it must be believable as the truth. This is not straightforward as it sounds. To borrow an example from product advertising, Exxon advertised that it put a tiger in your tank. Literally? Of course not. But the strength and vigor and energy of a tiger was clearly implied—and believed. Credibility is sometimes for a metaphor, and not necessarily a factual statement.

- *Persuasiveness.* The ad should be persuasive and reasonable in its selling message. It should sell the need for the service you offer, and project your service as superior. And if that need isn't immediately apparent, it should generate the need. It should be noted here that this is more often accomplished in the premise of the ad than with words that are persuasive. For example, a case history that the reader can relate to is more persuasive than just words that are meant to persuade.

- *Interest.* Once you've captured the reader's attention you've got to say something to sustain his or her interest. If this isn't accomplished, then once again, your message will not be heard. Dull is dead.

- *Desire.* The ad must generate a desire to accept what you have to say about what you have to offer; to want to do business with you. It must generate a favorable atmosphere in which you can function to sell your service. In product advertising, this can be done with words or pictures. In professional services advertising, it's done by describing a service in ways that make the benefits of the service appealing and useful.

- *Action.* Basically, the ultimate aim of an ad is to generate action on the part of the reader or listener; to cause him to want to do something that you want him to do, such as buy your product or service. But as we've seen, the nature of professional services marketing precludes that, beyond generating an inquiry. Even in those situations in which an ad might inspire an ultimate action (for a specialized service, for example), there is almost invariably an inquiry and discussion before the decision is made to become a client. But even a call to be aware of something is an important call to action.

It can be said that an effective ad is one that achieves a preconceived objective. It's difficult to judge an ad on the basis of it's ability to generate inquiries if the objective of the ad is to enhance name recognition. In marketing, serendipity counts for a lot, but you can't build a career on it.

## The Foundation for Copy

Experienced copywriters know that ads work best when they're predicated on two factors:

- *Know your prospect.* Understand not only who your prospect is, but what his or her needs are. Do you know what kind of service your prospective clientele really wants, and what kind of problems they'll depend upon your service to resolve? If you don't understand your prospects, and can think only in term of what you do and what you have to sell, then it becomes impossible to develop an ad or an advertising program that will effectively reach them.

- *Know your service.* You know, of course, what you do and how you do it. But in an ad, the way you present what you do must be in terms of your prospective clients' needs, not your needs. The important distinction is to know your service in terms of what the prospective client is willing to buy, not what you're offering to sell. This is what research is about—to tell you that you don't always know what you think you know about your audience.

Even within the context of professional limitations there are differences in the way you and your competitors perform the same services. These are differences in approach to a problem, in organization, in service concept. Nothing must be taken for granted in analyzing just who you are and what you do. The view of how your way of doing things differs from the ways of others must be realistic.

Here, there comes into play a catalog of who you really are and how you function as a professional. What's unique about what you do, or about the way you do things that aren't of themselves unique? What are your strengths and weaknesses? What can you realistically offer your prospects, and where are your shortfalls? What are the physical dimensions of your capabilities in terms of service, personnel, technical skill and so forth?

In other words, what is your service really about, beyond the mere definition of your profession?

The problem, of course, is how these differences can be projected.

In good copywriting the clearest answers to these questions will produce the most effective ads.

## Copy Structure

Although there may be deviation for sound reason, ad copy usually consists of a headline, text, and signature.

### The Headline

The basic purpose of a headline is to attract attention and to bring the reader to the ad. It usually accomplishes this by promising, by imparting news, by direct address, or by being clever or funny. It's usually in larger type, designed to jump out of the page to catch the reader's eye and interest. If the headline is the device your ad uses for this purpose (it could just as well be the illustration), then it must have power. If its purpose is to promise, then the promise must be made clear. If the purpose is to be clever or funny, then clever or funny it had better be (although not to the degree that it veers from the ad's main point). A headline that offers nothing to the reader in terms of either benefit or interest may effectively mask the cleverest ad, and one that's offering the most useful service.

## The Text

It's extremely important that the text should spring from the headline, and follow through the promise it offers. It should explain and clarify the facts and claims. And no matter how long or short the text, it should be a logical progression of ideas. It should cover all of the points you mean to cover and exclude no information of importance.

Copy can be either factual or emotional. It can appeal to the intellect and reason, or it can appeal to the emotions. It can do both, of course, but the choice and effort should be knowledgeable and conscious—you should know why you're doing it.

## The Illustration

There are many problems in the relatively new field of advertising for professionals, but none is more trying than illustration. How do you illustrate an accountant or a lawyer or a consultant at work—and do it interestingly.

The irony is that in most advertising research, it's quickly determined that most readers' eyes are caught first by the illustration. The answer may lie in context—showing the professional in the client's plant—or in symbolism—an abacus imposed on a computer. A major challenge.

## Call for Action

The text should lead naturally to a call for action. What precisely do you want your reader to do? Call now? File for future reference? Send in a coupon? Send for a brochure? Remember something? Experienced copywriters know that the call for action works. It's not so much that when readers are told to do something they do it. It's that when they're not told to do something they're less likely to do it. It's assumed, of course, that there will be someone to take the call and to mail out requested literature.

## Logo, Signature, and Slogan

The copy usually ends with a logo and a signature for identification and impression, and sometimes also a slogan.

Slogans in advertising professional service must be used very cautiously.

A slogan is a battle cry, and is in fact derived from the Gaelic words that mean battle cry. It's usually a simple statement that, in contemporary marketing and

**115**

advertising, is used to drive a position. It acts as shorthand to sum up the firm's position—to keep it in the forefront of the reader's consciousness. When a slogan is repeated over and over again, it gains currency, and therefore marketing strength.

The danger in relying on slogans in professional service advertising is that it if the slogan can't be backed by reality—if the firm can't deliver what the slogan promises, the acoustics of the marketplace have a way of reverberating that fact to the outer boundaries of the market.

There is a danger, as well, of trying to use a fine-sounding statement as a slogan, simply because it is fine-sounding. This in no way helps the ad, the ad campaign, or the firm.

A slogan should be used only when there's a clear view of what it's supposed to accomplish.

## The Copy Platform

In facing the prospect of writing copy for an ad, the professional copywriter must develop a concept, sometimes called the copy platform, which is a clear statement of the copy objectives, focus, and approach. This is an attempt to articulate, as clearly and as simply as possible, what the copy shall say and how it shall say it. Shall it be extensive or brief? What tone shall it take? Shall it be breezy and light, or formal? What message shall it try to convey? What is the rationale behind the approach?

The purpose of this copy platform, which should be articulated on paper, is to serve as a guide to actually writing the copy. Many copywriters use it to present to their clients for a clear understanding of how the ad will come out.

### Research

Larger firms can frequently afford the benefits of market research prior to developing an advertising campaign. Smaller firms that try extensive ad campaigns can't afford not to partake of market research. Advertising without it almost invariably wastes money.

The positioning program that Kenneth Wright, then National Director of Marketing Development, initiated for Arthur Young, the Big Eight accounting firm (before its merger to form Ernst & Whinney) was a case in point. The positioning program included a corporate advertising program designed to position Arthur Young in its marketplace, and to enhance the name and reputation of the firm. The campaign was overwhelmingly successful. But the campaign's greatest success was internal. According to Wright, "It served as a powerful internal force to make the partnership and the staff, throughout the country, enthusiastic about aggressively marketing the firm's services. It was worth every penny of the national campaign, just to help integrate the marketing process into the partnership."

But probably no campaign in professional services advertising made greater use of market research than did this one. Qualitative depth interviews and other aspects of primary research were used beforehand, from which was developed the positioning concept of "Personal Involvement." Frequent and periodic surveys monitored its effects on target audiences all along the way. It was a classic example of the best use of both advertising and research done thus far in the professions. It also contributed substantially to what we now know about advertising in this area. Wright, who is now National Director of Marketing for Price Waterhouse, believes that market research was instrumental in putting the campaign on target.

"In this context," says Wright, " Arthur Young's campaign worked because it sold an *idea*—the attitude toward serving its business clients that was the firm's guiding force. And it did so in a context that implied—*implied*, not stated—that this service concept was distinctive to AY."

## Positioning

Positioning, in professional services, is a function of relating the firm to the marketplace in terms of the firm's greatest strengths. Those strengths, however, must match the market's greatest needs.

Too often, the concept of position is confused with the rubric of image, in which it's inferred that symbols can be manipulated to present a firm to its market in a favorable light. The problem is that the banner of symbols is transparent, readily showing the reality of what's behind the banner. A firm must position itself to its markets on the foundation of strengths that are real, not simply wished for. If you position your firm as completely service oriented, then you had better be service oriented—or the market will discard you faster than you can believe possible.

Even in the smallest firm a position shouldn't be arbitrarily chosen, but should spring from research, no matter how simple or basic. How does the market perceive you in terms of your service? Capabilities? Strengths and weaknesses?

What does the market really want from a firm such as yours? Attentiveness? A range of services? Participation on a management level? Aggressiveness in searching out and solving problems?

If your strengths coincide with the market needs, then that's your best position. If not, either change your strengths or change your position.

And when you've chosen a position, use every marketing tool at your command to flog it to the market. Then, and only then, does positioning have meaning.

## Presenting the Position

Having determined a position, it then becomes the basis for the entire campaign and as the thrust for the copy. It's then supported in every aspect of the ad, including the illustration, design and layout, and the selection of the media.

But in a context in which so many professional services are indistinguishable one from another, how can a position be projected?

There are several possibilities:

- Presenting material in an original way. A classic example is the Arthur Young advertising campaign, "We take your business personally." Here the layout, copy theme, and subject matter is done so originally and with such enthusiasm that despite the fact that it makes no overt distinction between its service and that of its competitors, the personality of the firm is crystallized and conveyed as unique.

- The configuration of services, in which several different aspects of classic service are presented in ways that appear to be unique.

- The unique presentation of a single aspect of service, in which one aspect of the service is described as if it were developed yesterday. It's presented as if no other firm has it, without actually saying that. "Now you can have accounting records that comply with all regulations" says one thing. "Now you can have instant information about your own company's performance—using your own data!" says something else.

- The new service, in which a new approach to solving a problem, or a new solution to an old problem, is presented for the first time. The first firm to announce it effectively wins the field, and all others subsequently offering the same service are perceived as merely followers. The fresher the view you take of your own services and how you perform them, the more likely you are to successfully project a valid and useful position.

# Writing the Copy

The artistry of advertising lies in the ability to manipulate symbols and ideas in order to inform and persuade people. As in any art form, there are no rules that can guide you in doing this, except to list those factors that seem to work most consistently. And yet, some of the most successful ads are those that violate the rules. In all likelihood, the rules are best violated when they are best understood.

It should be noted here that writing advertising copy is very different from writing promotional copy. In advertising copy, every word counts, and must do a job, in helping to develop either an emotional or an intellectual appeal. It tends to focus on a single idea—a single point that must be made to persuade the reader. Promotional writing has much more latitude. It flows differently, and contributes to moving the idea without the conciseness and—often—the shorthand of advertising writing. The ability to write one well doesn't automatically mean that there's the ability to write the other.

Two universally accepted axioms are that an ad must be simple (although the Ogilvy Rolls Royce ad mentioned earlier was not), and it must look and sound as if it's worth paying attention to (as the Ogilvy ad certainly was). And obviously, it must be complete—it must contain all the information you want to convey. These axioms—if indeed they are axioms—spring from the fact that few ads are successful when these rules are ignored. Beyond that, clarity is essential. No matter how an ad is written it must be understood and easy to read.

It should be grammatical—despite the fact that there are many examples of successful advertising that are clearly ungrammatical. A breach of grammatical rules, however, should be deliberate, and designed to serve a specific purpose. The rules of grammar are not arbitrary, nor are they inflexible. But the purpose of the rules of grammar is consistency, understanding, and clarity. Unless there is a conscious reason to do otherwise, the copy should be consistent, understandable, and clear. Or grammatically sound, if you will.

There are some other guidelines that professional copywriters also find useful:

- *Talk to the reader, the listener, or the viewer.* Don't announce, don't preach. And don't get carried away by words and lose sight of the message.

- *Write short sentences,* with easy and familiar words. You want the reader or listener to do the least possible work to get your message. Even when you're talking to very bright people, communication of ideas, not language manipulation, is the point. (But don't patronize and don't talk down).

- *Don't waste words.* Whether you use three or a thousand words make sure each is exactly the one you need. Make sure each word is exactly the right one to convey your meaning.

- *Try to avoid being formal.* You're talking to people as people. You're not writing an insurance contract for lawyers. An ad is information and persuasion. It's unfettered communication, and the less bound it is by formality, the more likely it is to communicate.

- *Use the present tense and the active voice* ("All professional copywriters have extensive experience in preparing material," rather than " ...extensive experience in the preparation of material."). If you do want a formal style it should be deliberate, and you should have a clear idea of why you are using it.

- *Punctuate correctly.* Punctuate to help the reader, and not merely to follow specific rules. The less punctuation the better, within the bounds of clarity, but don't be afraid to use it if it helps the flow of an idea. Don't be afraid to use contractions and personal pronouns, just as you would in chatting informally with a prospect. After all, that's what you're trying to accomplish in your ad.

- *Watch out for cliches.* They turn some people off. More significantly, people don't hear them as they pass automatically through the mind, and the point you're trying to make is lost. (Again, unless you're doing it deliberately.) Try to use bright, cheerful language that keeps the reader alert and maintains attention. To be enthusiastic and exciting is to be well along on the way to being interesting.

Writing is not manipulating words—it's expressing ideas. Words, grammar, and punctuation are merely the tools and devices we use to express ideas most clearly. To think of copy as a configuration of words is the same as thinking of a symphony as a configuration of notes.

Why do ads that seem well written sometimes not work? Because they miss these points of advertising. Because they attempt to merely translate somebody's idea of persuasive talk into the ad medium, which can sometimes be like wearing a tuxedo to the gym.

And because somebody didn't recognize that the art of advertising copywriting is not the art of literary or professional or promotional writing. Different medium, different art form.

## Copywriting for Other Media

While these rules and concepts apply generally to all copywriting, obviously different media have different copywriting requirements.

A print ad may successfully consist of little more than a solid block of copy with perhaps as many as 1,000 words. A billboard, on the other hand, allows you only five or six words to tell the entire story. Nevertheless, these five or six words should follow the same basic concepts of all copywriting, in terms of objectives and so forth. They should begin with a specific thought, which then becomes words, and not with just an arbitrary choice of words that might be clever. They should be consistent with the thrust of the total campaign. Billboards seem to offer a greater temptation to be cute or funny than do other media. There is nothing wrong with that, unless the funny line is neither funny nor relevant to the point you are trying to make.

The strictures of broadcast copy stem from the fact that the words are heard rather than read. The added element is, of course, the speaker. If the copy is to be dramatized, then the rules of dialogue and drama weigh more heavily than if the copy is merely to be read. There is a vast difference in the skills necessary to write copy to be spoken, and copy to be read. Timing, phrasing, punctuation, all tend to be different from one medium to the next. For example, the experienced radio writer tends to stay away from longer words that might work well in print, and from words that are difficult to pronounce or that have too many "S" sounds. Rarely does a print ad read consistently well on radio.

Copy for direct mail is a lot more personal in its appeal and should be written as if it were an individual talking to an individual.

## Ad Design and Layout

The cohesive force that makes a print ad work—that pulls together all of the elements of copy and illustration in a way that attracts the reader—is the design. The elements are laid out in a total configuration to make the ad stand out in a busy page, and engage the reader's attention. In designing an ad, the art director is concerned with three basic things that make the ad work as a sum of its parts:

- *A sense of unity.* The art director tries to see the ad as a totality, rather than as a mere collection of individual parts. To an experienced and competent art director, an ad is not a headline plus an illustration plus copy. It's a total unit that achieves the complete visual effect to fulfill the ad's objective. Everything must relate to everything else—the headline to the copy, and the illustration to the total ad.

- *Balance.* The elements of an ad should be balanced, both in the proportion of each element in relation to all the other elements, and in their location in the space. An ad in which elements are out of proportion to one another is as awkward and unattractive as might be an elephant's head on a giraffe's body. Typefaces of the wrong size, or that don't complement one another, or that give the wrong graphic feeling to the message, can make the reader grossly uncomfortable, and destroy the best written ad. The balance can be formal, in which every element is centered in relation to the others, or it can be deliberately informal. To the art director, each form has its purpose in conveying a mood, a feeling, an attitude.

- *Flow.* The reader's eye must be attracted to the ad, and then flow logically from the headline to the text to the signature and logo. This makes the ad more effective by making it more compelling, more readable and, in a sense, more hospitable.

A well-designed ad, one that succeeds in these three elements, functions better in achieving its objective, and competes successfully against other ads and editorial material on the same page.

## The Design Elements of an Ad

There are ads without headlines and ads without illustration and even ads without text. But the various elements that an art director might have to put in juxtaposition with one another in designing an ad include:

- *The headline* The headline, usually in a larger or different typeface than the text, sends out a signal to the reader that says something particularly interesting or attractive. Visually, it supplies the emphasis and the drama.

- *Subheads.* Usually in a smaller typeface than the headline (but still different or larger than the text), they're sometimes used to expand or clarify the message of the headline. Subheads also help the reader to skim the ad, the better to decide whether the ad is worth reading.

- *The body copy.* This is the text of the ad.

- *The illustration.* It could be either a photograph or a drawing—or even a painting.

- *The caption.* Sometimes used to describe an illustration, and separate from the body copy.

- *The logo.* This is the distinct design, emblem or typeface that identifies the advertiser, and is sometimes different from the signature.

- *The signature.* This is the name of the advertiser, the subject of the ad, the company that's sending the message.

Naturally, few ads contain all of these elements at one time. Some ads use no illustrations and some use no headlines. But no matter which of the elements are used in any ad, the art director must lay them out effectively.

Even an ad that consists of only a few words poses a design problem. What typeface should be used? How large should the type be? Where in the space should the words be placed? A glance at any magazine, much less a book of typefaces, tells you that there are hundreds of different typefaces, and many sizes in each face. The art director knows that each face has its different values and uses. Some faces are more dramatic, some more subtle and flowery. Some shout, others whisper. Some are official looking, and others are more informal or humorous. Some are great for headlines but difficult to read in smaller sizes when used in text. Art directors also know that in typography, less is more. Too many typefaces in one ad spoil the look and values of the ad.

In a display ad, there's no right or correct way to design an ad in which you're looking for a particular feeling. Some ways work better than others. But the wrong layout, the wrong balance, the wrong typeface—any of these can spoil an otherwise excellent ad in which the headline is brilliant and the copy superb.

## Producing the Ad

Ad design usually begins before the copy is written, and uses the same concepts and objectives as copywriting does as a point of departure. An ad is conceived in its totality, so that design and copy complement one another. Design and copy must be coordinated so that the art director understands how much space is needed for copy, and the copywriter understands how much space he has for copy. If the type is smaller, there is room for more words, and so the copywriter must know the size type to be used. If the copy is written first, or must contain a specific amount of information, the art director knows how much space he must allow for it.

After the ad is conceived, the art director usually does a rough sketch—called a thumbnail sketch—indicating the approximate size of each element in proportion to the others, and where it will go in the space. When the sketch is approved, preparation of the final ad begins.

The copywriter works on the copy. If a drawing is to be used, an artist must be set to work. If it's to be a photograph, the photographer must be assigned. If stock art or photos—art already done and available for reproduction—are to be used, then files must be searched to find the right material.

When all of the elements are approved, the art director does a comprehensive layout—called a *comp*—in which a drawing of the ad is done that's as close to the finished ad as possible. A rough sketch of the art or photograph is used, the headline is hand lettered, and the body text is indicated with straight lines. This enables everybody to get a good idea of how the final ad will look. It also serves as a guide to the technician who will put the finished ad together.

In the meantime, the other elements are completed. The copy is written and approved, final illustrations purchased and so forth.

In the days before computer typesetting and Desktop Publishing, the process was arduous. The type had to ordered, usually from an independent typesetting firm. All of the elements except photographs were then pasted down in place on a special piece of cardboard, using the comp as a guide. This is called a *mechanical*. It's this board that's photographed to make the plate used to print the ad. Photography is keyed in to indicate location, but shot separately because it must be screened—photographed through a screen that reproduces it in dots rather than in a continuous gray scale.

While there may still be artists and art studios working that way today, most of this work is done—from typesetting to layout to producing the camera-ready mechanical—by computer. It's faster, cheaper, and requires fewer skills of the computer operator. It also reduces the costs of changes in both layout and copy.

When the mechanical is ready, it's either sent directly to the publication, or a special photo is taken of it for the publication, depending upon the physical requirements of the medium.

## Who Does the Design?

Because of the technical skills involved, a measure of experience, as well as talent, is needed to perform the task of the art director. The art director may work for your agency, for your firm, or for an independent art studio. In some cases, the publication itself will supply design and layout help, but this should be accepted with some caution. Few publications—newspapers or magazines—maintain sophisticated design staffs for their advertisers, and so you're not likely to get the best work. And if you let the publication set the type, you're limited to the typefaces the publication has available, which is usually not a wide variety.

With Desktop Publishing, which is done on the ordinary computer but can produce professional quality work, there's a tendency to feel that a competent computer operator can handle design. Nothing is further from the truth.

There is very little money to be saved by using less than professional ad design services, since a poorly designed ad can negate the best advertising concept. At the same time, learning the elements of ad design is important to the advertiser, to judge the quality of his own advertising.

## Print Production

While most of the functions of production in a print ad are performed by technicians, the successful planning of an ad can very well depend upon your understanding the mechanics of the production process. If you understand the process, then you understand the creative routes that must be taken, and the options you have for designing a better ad.

### Typography

At the heart of both the design and production process is typography. The evolution of typefaces since the ancient Chinese invented movable type centuries ago has resulted in a complex art form. The vast array of typefaces available today offers a variety of values in readability, mood, and pure aesthetics. The variety of techniques available for setting type has, in recent years, undergone a revolution that's resulted in new, better, and cheaper techniques.

Some typefaces are new and modern, and new ones are constantly being redesigned. Others are as old as printing itself, and are still in use. Each face has its best uses and purposes, from the simulated handlettering style of the Middle Ages, to the old style Roman letters with their classic, formal but highly readable look, or the contemporary faces, with their crisp and futuristic look. In some typefaces the letters are graceful, with varying thicknesses in the lines of the letter, and ornamental *serifs*—short lines at the ends of each letter. Others, without the serifs (called *sans serif*) are more contemporary, and sometimes look like block printing. Each face has its own look, its own feel And each purpose has its own most effective typefaces. The boldfaces—in which a letter in a typeface has heavier lines—seem to work best in the larger sizes, and are most frequently used for headlines. The same typeface, in a smaller size, may or may not work for body text. It can be Roman, a name which can be applied to any typeface in its normal fashion, or italic, which means that the letters are slanted slightly for emphasis, as the word *italic* is in this sentence.

All the letters of a style are called a font, which includes all of its sizes, bold, italicized and Roman, and numerals and punctuation. Typefaces of one font can be mixed with faces of another in the same ad, but some faces complement one another and others clash.

The measure of type size is a point. There are 72 points to the inch, which means that a 72-point letter is one inch high. Typefaces up to 18 points are usually used for text. The smallest type size commonly used is 6-point, too small for body text, but sometimes useful for picture captions. The most common sizes for the text of ads are 8-, 10- and 12-point. In these sizes, text is easier to read without distracting from the message the text is trying to convey. This book, for example, is set in 10-point type. Type that's 24 points or larger is called display type.

The spacing between lines also affects readability, and therefore the choice of type size. The spacing, called leading, is also measured in points. This book, set in 10-point type, has 2 point spacing between lines. Printers refer to it as 10/12 or 10 on 12.

The width of lines of type is measured in picas. There are six picas to the inch. The lines of this page are set 30 picas wide. Picas are also sometimes called ems. A half pica is an en. When all the lines of a body of copy are even to the margins on both sides, they are called justified. When they are on just one side, they are called (depending on the even side) flush left, ragged right, or flush right, ragged left.

In newspaper advertising, and in some magazines, the height of the ad on a page is measured not in inches, but in agate lines. There are 14 agate lines to the inch.

## How Type Is Set

For centuries the only way to set type was by hand, one letter at a time. This is called foundry type, and is used today only for very special and rare fonts.

With the invention of Linotype, type was set by huge machines, with a keyboard like a typewriter. When a key for a letter is pressed, a brass matrix for that letter slides into a holder. When a complete line has been set, hot molten lead is forced into the matrices, and a line of type is cast. Machine type set this way is known as *hot type*.

Today's technology, both in typesetting and printing, has made hot type almost obsolete. Most type is set by computer photo composition, called *cold type* or by Desktop Publishing. By simply changing a computer disc, the computer can set thousands of different fonts.

Today, with so much writing being done on word processors, type is frequently set by taking the writer's own data disk, with the text corrected and formatted, and feeding the data directly to the typesetting or desktop publishing computer. This saves the considerable time and expense needed to re-key a manuscript on the typesetting machine. This book is set in exactly that way, from the author's computer disks.

Because any kind of cold type can be photographed for printing, it can also be set on a typewriter. The wide range of typefaces available on typewriters that use interchangeable fonts makes it relatively inexpensive, although not as versatile as computer type.

## *Printing*

There are three basic methods of printing. Letterpress is the oldest method, requiring either hand set or hot type. It goes back to Gutenberg and the ancient Chinese. The type is locked into a metal form, and mounted on the press. The type is then inked and impressed on the paper. In larger plants, where whole pages are printed, such as newspapers, a more advanced form is used. The entire page of type is pressed into a fiber matrix, hot metal is poured into the matrix, and the entire page is cast as one form. This is used primarily on rotary presses where the single form is curved to fit a roller. A rotary press that prints from a continuous roll of paper is called a web press. A rotary press can also be fed a single sheet at a time. A flat bed press, in which type is set in a flat form, is sheet fed one sheet at a time.

Most printing today is done by offset lithography. The matter to be printed is photographed on a photo-sensitized metal plate. When the plate is developed, a barely perceptible raised surface remains for the matter to be printed. On the press, which is rotary (either sheetfed or web), the plate is treated with a chemical. When the plate is inked, only the raised surface accepts the ink, which is then transferred to the paper. Because offset lithography uses cold type, it is considerably less expensive and more efficient than letterpress. Today, even major newspaper are printed by offset lithography, and it's rapidly replacing all other printing methods. Color printing is done by making separate plates, one for each of the three primary colors (cyan, magenta, and yellow and one for black). Each plate is printed separately, either in individual press runs or, on larger three-color presses, with one roller for each color. As each color is printed, it either stands separately if the color is needed in its basic form, or is overprinted to blend the various shades (blue and yellow in various combinations of intensity, for example, make different shades of green). The printing technician must be sure that the paper passes through the press in exactly the right place, so that all colors register exactly where they're supposed to be.

Almost all advertising is supplied to the printer in camera-ready form. This can be either the pasted-up mechanical, or a fine quality image made by computer. In offset lithography, the mechanical or computer generated image is photographed directly onto the litho plate. In letterpress, it's photographed on a plate to make photoengraving.

The two main types of photoengraving are line and halftone.

Line plates can be used only for drawings or other illustrations that use solid lines or masses, but with no shades of gray. Photographs and paintings, however, have a spectrum of shades, and must be engraved by the halftone process.

The halftone process uses dots in clusters on the printing surface. The more dots—called screening—per square inch, the darker the area will print. A photograph or painting to be printed consists of a combination of dots in different densities for the different shades, which gives the impression of the finished photograph. In color printing, the density of dots on the different color plates makes it possible to combine them, in the final printing, to give the various shades of color.

These dots are achieved by photographing the original artwork through a screen made up of a crosshatch of some 50 to 150 hairlines per square inch. This forms little windows—from 2,500 to 25,000 of them—through which the light passes. The greater the number of hairlines per square inch, the more dots the plate will have, and the finer will be the finished picture. Newspapers tend to use a courser screen because newsprint absorbs ink more quickly, and finer dots would tend to blur. The better papers, sometimes coated with a material (usually a clay) to make them harder on the surface (and glossier), absorb less ink, and can take finer dots. this is why artwork in magazines or on coated stock looks better than in newspapers.

The screens are standardized. Newspapers, for example, usually use a 65 screen (65 dots to the square inch), and magazines usually use a 120 screen.

These basic processes are used in the production of virtually all advertising, whether it's in newspapers, magazines, poster billboards, brochures, or handbills. The advertiser who understands the process invariably finds that it's easier to design ads, to judge ads designed by others, and to schedule their production.

127

# 8

# Media

The choice of vehicles to carry your advertising to the public—the media—is extensive. That means that with so many options available to you, the media you choose must be thoughtfully considered. Each medium has its advantages and disadvantages, measured in terms of circulation, readership, audience, effectiveness and cost.

The selection of media is made simple in only one way. The media, in their eagerness to sell space or time, supply a great deal of demographic information to the prospective advertiser.

Your primary objective in selecting media is to get your message to the largest possible audience of prospective customers and clients, as effectively as possible, at the lowest cost that brings you the best return on your advertising dollar.

In the last statement, the effective factor is *return on the advertising dollar*, not lowest cost. In buying media, cheap can be expensive, if your ad isn't seen by the very people you most want to reach.

The first measure—but not necessarily the last—used by media buyers is *Cost per thousand (CPM)*, which is the cost of delivering one thousand impressions within a defined population group. In technical terms—of which there are many in media analysis—its the media cost (in dollars) divided by gross target impressions (in thousands).

Selecting media, then, is a function of more than buying space and time. As in every other phase of marketing, your choice of media must be predicated on the marketing objectives. And as in all other aspects of marketing, media choice is always a mix—a balance of many factors to reach the appropriate, as well as the larger, audience; the cost-effective smaller but more select audience; the audience most responsive to your own position in the marketplace.

As in copywriting, there are rules. But as in copywriting, few of the rules are inviolable. For example, what rule of cost-effectiveness can preclude the wisdom of buying an ad in a fraternal organization's journal that reaches very few people, but gives you more than your money's worth in good will?

## The Rules of Media Buying

Buying media, today, has become a combination of science and art. With the advances made in statistical analysis and audience measurement, the calculations in analyzing the marketing power of media have become highly technical and complex.

In putting together a media plan, then, the choices in even a small campaign can be extensive, and therefore difficult. And if the campaign warrants more than one medium, it can move into a fairly technical realm.

Without attempting to evaluate the technical aspects or the statistical criteria of media buying, it's useful to understand some of the pertinent factors used to evaluate media...

*Circulation.* Circulation is the number of copies of a publication that reaches the public. In the broadcast media, it is the number of viewers or listeners at any given moment. Publications may be sold or given away free. They may be sold on newsstands, by subscription, or delivered door to door. They may be distributed free at supermarkets or shopping centers. Circulation figures must be supplied by the publication. Circulation figures for most newspapers and magazines are audited and certified by newspaper and magazine trade associations.

But even audited circulation figures must be taken with a grain of salt, since it's impossible to know that every copy of a publication that leaves the printing plant will land in the hands of a reader. Mail subscription figures are perhaps the most accurate, and most newspapers and magazines accept and credit returns of unsold copies from newsstand dealers. But still there's a lot of slippage. In a media plan, circulation is important—but of itself it's the least important of all the elements. It's the context of a number of factors that qualify the usefulness of a circulation figure.

*Audience.* Audience is more important than circulation, because who reads the publication is more important than *how many people read it. Business Week* magazine is a powerful advertising medium, with a huge circulation. You would hardly use it to sell the services of a local accounting firm or a small local civil law practice. The audience of a publication is its *demographics*—the educational and economic levels of its readers, their ages, their locations, their purchasing habits, and so forth, which are what's important. While no medium (with the possible exception of direct mail) can define its audience precisely, each medium is directed at a specific and clearly defined group. It accomplishes this by controlling its editorial matter, or in the case of broadcast media, its programming. In New York City, for example, *The New York Times* is read by people who generally have a higher income and higher levels of education. *The Times* is read by white collar workers, professionals and government and industry leaders. But it's also read by students and academics, who have less purchasing power. *The Daily News,* on the other hand, has a much wider circulation, but is read predominantly by blue collar workers and people with generally lower income. *The New York Post* is read mostly by middle income groups.

*The Times,* because of its higher income readers, is the preferred medium for most professional services advertising. But the *Post* and the *News* also reach an audience that might be appropriate for mass-market legal and medical clinics, or tax services. All three have reasonably large circulation, but in choosing one over the other as an advertising medium, the distinction is clearly in terms of audience, not circulation.

*Readership.* A newspaper or magazine that enters a household is counted as one unit of circulation. But the publication may be read by two or more people in that household, each of whom is a potential consumer. A magazine in a dentist's office may be one unit of circulation, but may be read by fifty people. Thus, circulation is tempered by readers per copy, and a publication with a small circulation may have a large number of readers per copy. It's also possible that, in terms of advertising readership, a publication with a large circulation might have a small ad readership. This is why most larger magazines and newspapers, and such organizations as the Newspaper Advertising Bureau, conduct frequent readership surveys. One word of caution. All advertising research—readership, audience and circulation—should be viewed skeptically. While it may be scientific, it's usually weighted to favor the publication that supplies it.

*Cost and return on investment.* There is a distinct difference between cost and return on investment. Simply put, a $100 ad that nobody sees is no bargain. A $1,000 ad that produces leads that result in $10,000 worth of sales is a profitable investment. There is no such thing as good, cheap advertising, if low cost buys you a low return. In budgeting for a media plan, then, cost must be seen in terms of effectiveness.

*Size and frequency of the ad.* Size is important in print advertising because your ad competes with others on a page. But size can sometimes be tempered by frequency. And there's a trade-off between the cost of the larger ad and frequency in the smaller ad. For example, an eighth or a quarter-page ad that appears in the same space regularly for a long period may have an equal or greater impact than might a larger ad that appears only occasionally. Even a calling card-sized ad that becomes a fixture in the same space for a long time has the power to fix name identity and to keep the name in mind. And repetition, remember, is crucial to effective advertising.

*Frequency of publication.* Newspapers come out daily. Magazines can be weekly, semiweekly, biweekly, monthly, and even annually. Some community newspapers are weekly. There is a close relationship between a publication's frequency and its audience, dictated by the frequency with which each publication feels it must deliver its editorial content to its readers. Sometimes an annual reaches a specific and clearly defined audience that may be in the very market you want to reach, and annuals tend to have staying power; they're usually kept and referred to frequently.

Newspapers and other publications frequently have special feature days. For example, Thursday has traditionally been the day that newspapers feature food and recipes editorially, with heavy food advertising. Some papers feature real estate advertising one day a week and extensive business news coverage on another. Circulation and readership tend to be higher for the audiences targeted on those days.

In the context of these guidelines, media should be bought by the advertiser, not sold by media salespeople. Each media salesperson who calls on you will be persuasive, and armed with data about his publication. But the judgment to buy should be made in the total context of a media plan that meets your marketing objectives.

## The Media

Each medium has its purpose, its audience and readership, its place in the marketing mix. Within each category of media, each publication or broadcast vehicle has its own elements of value and disadvantage, and is competitive with others in its category. This competitiveness is an advantage to the advertiser, of course, because it keeps each vehicle working to improve itself—its circulation, audience, editorial content, and so forth. And the competition frequently takes the form of keeping you better informed about the nature of the market, as each develops more information about itself to use for its own sales efforts.

Here are some of the values, advantages and disadvantages of each medium:

### Newspapers

There is virtually no community in the United States that isn't served by a newspaper of some kind, and perhaps three-quarters of all adults read newspapers. Their journalistic quality ranges from the meticulous professionalism of the influential big city papers, such as *The New York Times* or *The Washington Post*, to the sometimes (but not always) casualness of small town weeklies. Unique are the *Wall Street Journal*, *The New York Times* (National Edition), *The Washington Post*, and *USA Today*, which are the country's only national newspapers, and testimony to the efficacy of electronics and contemporary computer technology. You can buy regional editions of the national papers, which is useful and saves money.

Because the editorial content of newspapers—news—concerns nearly every resident in a paper's market area, newspapers are widely read by people of all ages, economic status, and education. In communities served by more than one daily paper, there's usually a distinction among the several competitors. Each one takes a position in the market —*The New York Times* reaches for the more affluent and better educated reader while the *New York News* is written for the less well-educated and less affluent reader. There is occasionally a distinction, other than the currency of that day's news, between morning and evening papers. In a community in which there are a great many commuters, for example, the morning paper might tend to feature advertising of items and services for which the breadwinner makes the buying decision, and evening papers might focus on advertising food and furniture for which the buying decision is made by the housewife. Not a hard and fast rule, but one you might look for in your own community.

Except for classified advertising, which is sold by the line, most newspaper advertising is sold by the agate line or the fraction of a page (quarter-page, half-page, two-thirds page, etc.). Newspaper advertising costs are usually in proportion to the circulation and audience, with the major city daily papers charging considerably more than the weekly community paper. Rates are frequently calculated on the basis of cost (dollars) per thousand readers, although other calculations may also be used.

The disadvantage of advertising in daily newspapers, in addition to the cost, is that advertising readership is usually a small proportion of circulation. Of the readers of 100,000 copies of a newspaper, for example, only a small portion—perhaps .1 percent—may be prospective buyers or sellers of your service, but that .1 percent may be a vast potential market for you. That's what research is about. Moreover, newspaper advertising competes with other ads and editorial material on the same page. Any one ad can be overlooked or only glanced at by the very people you want to reach.

Two ways to overcome this are by repetition—running the ad or the campaign on a consistent, frequent basis—and ad positioning. Many newspapers and magazines will, for a premium, place your ad in a specific part of the newspaper. This may be in the business or financial section, a special real estate section (which is sometimes sold at a discount rather than a premium), or in the sports section (a favorite for cars, for example), on the first page of the second section (wider readership) or opposite the editorial page (also wider readership).

Though suburban and community weekly newspapers usually charge considerably less for advertising, they are still valuable advertising media. Their editorial material is generally local in nature, and geared to community interests. Advertisers are usually local stores and services, although some weeklies have a large enough audience to garner some national advertising. The advantage in advertising a community or suburban weekly is that it's easier to judge the demographics of its readership, since you can easily come to know the community.

## Magazines

National magazines reach a national audience, and the cost of advertising in them is proportionately high. Only the professional with offices throughout the country, or a valid national market, should consider national magazines an effective medium. But many national magazines sell regional editions, some of which break down to fairly small areas. You can buy *Time, Newsweek* or *Business Week,* for example, for just New York City, or the executive, edition. This allows you the prestige of the major national publication to reach a specific market area at a comparatively reasonable price.

For most professionals, however, the city or local magazine affords the prestige and access to specialized market of magazines at a cost-effective price.

Not all cities or regions have local magazines, of course, but their number is increasing. Almost all major cities—New York, Chicago, Philadelphia, Albuquerque, San Francisco, Dallas—have publications that range from fair to superb. Their markets are clearly defined geographically, as well as by audience. Most local magazines are editorially slanted toward a more chic and affluent audience—some, in fact, are particularly trendy.

## Direct Mail

While the structure of direct mail is obviously different than for publications, direct mail is nevertheless a medium. It's discussed in great detail in chapter 6.

## Radio

Radio, as was noted, has the advantage of knowing a great deal about its audience by virtue of each station's specific programming. You might then consider that a classical music station, AM or FM, is likely to appeal to a better educated—and therefore probably a more affluent—audience. The size of the audience may be smaller, but with its demographics more easily definable, it might give a better return on investment. A rock and roll station, on the other hand, would have an audience of predominantly teen-agers, hardly a market for professionals. Other types of stations feature talk, easy listening, and heavy metal rock.

The entire country is covered by radio, with few areas reached by fewer than five or six stations. The more powerful the station, the more expensive the time. And the more people it may reach outside your market area. Most radio stations, however, have useful information available to advertisers about their audiences and their markets. If a market is clearly delineated, the relatively high cost of radio (as compared to newspapers or magazines) still gives a good return on investment. And the cost of production for local radio can be reasonable.

## Television

Television coverage is geographically as broad as is radio, although there are not as many stations. And unlike radio, television programming aimed at different audiences changes from program to program, rather than from station to station.

Television time costs considerably more than local radio, even on a local basis—perhaps as much as five or six times as much. For the professional who can afford it, though, it can be a very effective medium.

The growing cable television industry may ultimately make television advertising more feasible for the professional firm. It's more localized, its audience is more readily identifiable (from subscriber lists), and its advertising more localized. Currently, only a percentage of the country—but growing rapidly—is covered by cable television that accepts advertising, but this situation is improving.

## Other Media

It's been said that any public place that can sustain an ad is a viable medium. One wag even suggested selling advertising space on the tails of attractive dogs.

The number of vehicles for advertising is infinite. Penny savers, the free publications distributed by supermarkets and shopping centers, proliferate. They vary in quality and distribution, and so are hard to categorize in terms of price and value as advertising media. Special publications, such as the journals of church and fraternal organization, offer opportunities for reaching clearly defined audiences, even as the act of buying an ad in them is an act of good will. In fact, every firm that has any outreach program should build in a program of good will advertising. Trade journals can be useful to reach a particular profession or industry—engineers, doctors and so forth.

National Public Radio now offers the opportunity to support their programming with contributions, in return for which the mention on air is often the equivalent of an ad. This can be a particularly useful and cost effective kind of advertising.

But no matter what the medium, the same factors apply for judging the appropriateness of the medium within the framework of your objectives and your budget.

## How Advertising Is Bought

Almost all media supply rate cards, indicating the purchase arrangements, costs, production limitations, and deadlines.

*Standard Rate and Data Services, Inc.*, simplifies the job for larger advertisers by publishing directories for all major media categories that contain standardized media rates and other information in an exceptionally useful form. They are comprehensive and up-to-date, providing information for media buyers, production people, and others in advertising.

Display advertising is somewhat complicated. The rate card lists the costs by agate line or fraction of the page, with discounts for the same ad repeated or for multiple space buys for a campaign. Production limitations usually allow a great deal of latitude, because most display ads are supplied camera-ready. There are extra charges for different production options. Deadlines for display ads are frequently longer than for classified, because larger space has to be set aside. Costs for publication-set ads are usually clearly spelled out.

Classified advertising is perhaps the simplest of the major media. The classified ad is almost invariably sold by the line, and the advertiser is limited to the typeface and style of the publication. Logos, for example, are rarely accepted by daily newspapers. Type sizes are usually limited to a body type size, a headline size and occasionally a boldface. Deadlines are usually pretty tight—two or three days in most cases, and Thursday for Sunday's papers. Usually, discounts are available for multiple insertions of the same ad.

All print and broadcast media buys are discounted 15 percent to accredited agencies or to individual advertisers who make prior arrangements. Rate cards also spell out guarantees for mistakes in publication costs, for special positions or edition, and terms for prompt or delayed payment.

## How Radio and TV Are Sold

Television is sold by network, by region of the network, and a spot basis or locally. Spot television means selecting key markets and purchasing the time for individuals through station representatives. There are innumerable purchase options.

Time on an individual television station is usually sold in 10-, 20-, 30- and 60-second spots. The 60-second commercial allows time for a miniature dramatization. The 10-second spot allows time for little more than a quick message and identification.

Television rates are usually based on time classification, with class A time—from 7:30 to 11:00 PM—the most expensive; and class B time—all other times, less so. Local stations may, for example, have a finer breakdown depending upon their market and sell accordingly.

Every station has its own rate practices, all of which are quoted on a rate card supplied by the station. *Standard Rate and Data Services*, the media buying publication, publishes the rate cards for all media, including radio and television.

Radio, too, is sold on local and spot basis. Prime time for radio is usually automobile drive time, which would be 6:00 to 10:00 AM and 3:00 to 7:00 PM. This is when most people are listening. Daytime rates from 10:00 AM to 3:00 PM are usually lower and evenings from 7:00 PM to midnight, which is television prime time, is lower still.

Broadcast media is becoming increasingly popular in professional service advertising, because of it's ability to focus a message to a carefully defined audience.

## Who Buys Media

Buying a classified or a single display ad requires no special skill, and you can easily do it yourself. And while buying display advertising sometimes requires a measure of paperwork to clarify terms, positions, etc., it isn't too much of a burden.

Buying space and time for a full campaign, on the other hand, can be a little difficult, and requires some specialized skill. Large buys, for example, can be negotiated, particularly if an agency buys a lot of space from a publication for several clients. Instructing the publication on complex scheduling and production techniques, and following up, can be a full-time job.

In radio and television, some agencies specialize in bartering goods and services for radio and television. While it's difficult to consider how professional services can be bartered within an ethical context, the bartering agencies can often make time buys at bargain rates. But these are complex arrangements that should be done by professionals.

The media staff of an agency usually includes traffic experts, who are trained in the techniques of scheduling and guiding advertising from the advertiser to the media.

The complexity of media buying is a function of the schedule and the number of media involved, as well as the number of different ads involved in the campaign. To the experienced media buyer, however, a great many complex activities become almost routine.

Media planning, however, requires a full understanding of the objectives of the marketing program, of the campaign, and of the ad. It requires knowing target markets, and the options available to you for reaching them.

But whether you do it yourself or use a professional media specialist, you don't abrogate your responsibility to keep the plan and all its elements within the framework of your own objectives.

# 9

# The Advertising Agency

There are, as you've seen, a great number of skills and techniques involved in putting together even the simplest ad. The ad that you write yourself requires knowledge of many things that go beyond your own profession, and the fact that you may be able to write and place your own advertising is testimony not to the simplicity of the process, but to your own capabilities.

But for the larger campaign, particularly one that uses several media, a great many skills and specialties are required. The coordination and teamwork required is extensive, whether that team consists of one multitalented person or an individual professional for each skill.

## The Full Service Agency

While titles change, and responsibilities shift in any agency, a fully staffed, full-service advertising agency may, then, include a team made people with either the following titles or comparable responsibilities:

- Management supervisor
- Account supervisor
- Account executive
- Creative director
- Research director
- Copywriter
- Art director
- Media buyer
- Production director
- Traffic director
- Art buyer
- Agency administration
- Administrative personnel

If you write, produce, and place your own ads, you are all these people rolled into one. If you use a one-person agency, that person must either have all these skills, or subcontract those he doesn't have. In a larger agency, at least one person, a specialist, performs each of these tasks, all of which you should understand.

One significant caveat.

Advertising, perhaps more than any other marketing discipline, is like electrical contracting. If you don't know what you're doing, and you make mistakes, the mistakes can be profoundly damaging and expensive.

The best insurance, then, whether you do your advertising in-house or use an agency, is to have a strong and qualified professional marketing director on staff—one who speaks the language of the advertising professional, and who is wise in the ways of both the profession and the firm's partnership.

## The Agency Structure

In a full-service agency, fully staffed, each person functions in a particular way.

- *The account personnel.* The people responsible for the day-by-day operation of your account may not be specialists in any of the creative or production skills, but they must be thoroughly familiar with how each skill is performed, and how it contributes to the finished ad. The account supervisors, or the account executives who report to them, must also be marketing specialists, and more significantly, strategists. They must understand your business and its objectives. The account people must be experts in costs and budgeting. And ultimately, they must be able to communicate your marketing program to the various specialists who will implement it.

   In some agencies, a marketing specialist helps in developing the overview; in others the account supervisor or the account executive performs that function. Your account executive, or the person with that responsibility by any title, is your direct link to your advertising agency.

- *The creative director.* The creative director, usually a heavily experienced copywriter or an art director, is responsible for designing and creating the thrust for the campaign. The creative director is the conceptualizer, and usually contributes as well to the marketing strategy. He or she visualizes and articulates the best approaches and techniques to be used by the specialists in developing the campaign and its individual ads. And perhaps the creative director's most important role is to maintain creative quality control in all areas. In most agencies, nothing leaves the place without the approval of the creative director.

- *The copywriter.* In larger agencies, the copywriters may specialize in different media and sometimes in different industries. In most agencies, the copywriter is the real creative force.

140

- *The art director.* The art director is trained in the visual aspects of advertising—its design, layout, typography, and illustration. Art directors may also specialize by media. The television art director is concerned with the visualization of the TV commercial—the scenery, costumes, camera angles, and in color television, the color balance. The print art director and his staff are also responsible for buying the typography and illustrations, and pasting it up for the camera-ready mechanical.

- *The research director.* The research director is responsible for every aspect of marketing research, from defining the target audience and its demographics, to evaluating readership of ads. The research director and his or her staff supply the basic material that allows the account personnel and the creative director to function intelligently and relevantly to your needs.

- *The media buyer.* The media buyer is responsible for understanding the options among all media, and the effectiveness of each medium that might possibly be used in your campaign. This means knowing circulations, audiences, rates, timetables, and production schedules and limitations. The media buyer must also be experienced in negotiating with media sales representatives for schedules, rates, and positions and must monitor the delivery and appearance of the ad.

- *The traffic specialist.* In a busy agency, or in a large campaign, a great many elements must be coordinated. This is the job of the traffic coordinator. Schedules must be adhered to so that all of the elements of the ad—design, copy, layout, typography, etc.—are delivered at the appropriate time, and that the ad is ready for the publication or broadcast station on the proper schedule.

- *The production director.* The production specialist is responsible for the physical production of the ad, from typesetting to printing in print advertising; from filming and recording to reproduction of tapes and film in broadcasting.

- *Administrative personnel.* An advertising agency is a business. Its personnel must be managed, it must bill its clients, it must pay its own bills. It must keep track of its suppliers, including media, and pay them. The larger the agency, the more elaborate the administrative staff and its organization.

- *Other specialists.* Larger agencies will include staff specialists in other areas, such as promotion or public relations. Some agencies specialize in specific media or industries. An agency that specializes in direct mail, or classified advertising, must have specialists in those fields. Agencies that specialize in specific industries need other specialists as well. For example, a fashion agency might have fashion coordinators on staff. A retail agency might have specialists in merchandising.

Should you choose to use an advertising agency, the options of specialties and specialists are numerous. This makes it easier for you to choose the agency that can best serve your needs.

## Agency Compensation

The commission system of agency compensation seems to have grown up with the advertising industry and was an integral part of it. Originally, this system was quite simple. The media discounted the cost of the advertising space to the agency by 15 percent. The agency billed the client at the full rate, and the 15 percent became its commission.

While this system is still used to some extent, the growth of advertising, the increase in the variety of media, and the elaborate techniques of advertising have resulted in developing new compensation structures.

The straight agency commission, in its traditional form, is still used by some agencies, with commissions varying according to discounts given by different media. Outdoor advertising operators, for example, usually discount 16 2/3 percent to advertising agencies. These commissions rates are often negotiable, both with the media and with the client. Agencies now pass along the cost of production plus a service charge of 17.65 percent (which is actually 15 percent of the gross cost of production). This arrangement is made by prior agreement with the client.

More in vogue now is direct fee compensation, rather than commission. This change came about because many agencies and clients found that the amount of time and effort it takes to service two different accounts that bill the same amount is not always the same for each account. Some accounts require more time and effort than others. Under the direct fee structure, the agency usually predicates its fee on a formula based on its own cost for overhead, etc., plus a fair profit margin. These fees are then negotiated with clients. Agencies on a fee structure usually bill the clients separately for production costs and expenses, adding the 17.65 percent markup.

The many services supplied by the modern full service agency go so far beyond just placing advertising that there are fewer and fewer campaigns that continue to warrant the straight commission basis, and it seems just a matter of time before the straight commission basis is replaced completely by the direct fee.

## House Agencies and In-House Capability

The traditional advertising agency structure today has many variations, including house agencies and in-house capabilities for larger companies.

Some large advertisers maintain subsidiary house agencies as full service profit centers owned by, and servicing, only themselves. They have only their parent company as a client. Possibly a valid concept only where there's a great volume of advertising, the house agency has both advantages and disadvantages. The 15 percent media discount pays for the operation of the agency, and sometimes even shows a profit that can be passed on to the parent company. There is complete control of the agency's personnel and complete focus on the advertiser's problems. Agency personnel have the opportunity to become totally immersed in the advertiser's products or services and markets, without the distraction of other clients. On the other hand, there is the lack of input that comes from working on a variety of other products and services. There's also the tendency for the house agency to become immersed in the advertiser's management structure, which usually results in the agency's being unable to attract the best talent and to compete effectively in the marketplace of ideas.

For many professionals who've tried it, there is the painful realization that retaining an outside advertising agency doesn't guarantee positive results or satisfaction. The decision to bring advertising in-house is a function of the firm's personality, its services, its physical capabilities, and its intellectual and financial resources.

At the base of the decision is an understanding of what you expect advertising to do for you. In a firm for whom service is a form of product, such as a Jacoby & Meyers, or an H. & R. Block, or a personal injury law practitioner, advertising's role is to bring in clients—just as advertising sells products. These firms' services are designed to function in volume, and good advertising shows a hefty return. Because few of their clients are ever on retainer, the mill must be constantly fed.

This is very different from the services offered by most law, accounting, or consulting firms, which use advertising to build a bridge to the future, and require more support from other marketing efforts.

### *Running an In-House Agency*

Running an in-house agency is more than simply sending advertising insertion orders to the media. It has to be run as a business. While you may hire an experienced advertising manager to supervise your advertising operations, you'll still have to oversee and manage the function, set up books, monitor efforts and expenses, and hire and fire staff. An advertising agency—even an in-house one—is a profit-making—or at least, profit center—business whose tangible service is advertising—creating it, producing it, selling it to your client, and placing it.

Whether you expect advertising to build a volume business for you, or to develop a backdrop for other marketing efforts, whether it's done by an outside or an in-house agency, there is a basic advertising process that requires skills and facilities in the four general areas of research, creative process and function, account management, and media.

There is also the pure business of advertising—costs, salaries, employee benefits, and so forth.

## The Business of Advertising

All advertising activity generally falls into these four areas, no matter who does it. Each of the functions is performed by specialists—creative people are rarely account managers or media specialists, for example—and talent in each specialty is rarely interchangeable. If you're thinking of bringing advertising in-house, these are the things you must be prepared to staff and pay and for.

Other questions should be addressed:

- *How well-integrated is your total marketing plan?* What else is in your marketing plan? Public relations? Direct mail? Seminars? Publications? What portion of your total plan will be advertising? Will you have just a few small ads, or a campaign? Do you envision elaborate illustrated ads, or smaller, simple calling cards, in which only your name and address, and the fact that you're a law firm, appear?

- *How much do you plan to budget for advertising and other marketing activities?* Are your plans realistic in terms of your budget limitations? In the light of everything involved in advertising and marketing, how committed are you to spending the dollars involved in producing a high-level program?

- *How committed are you to marketing?* There's no question that you or your partners are going to have to get involved, even though you're not marketing professionals. Marketing professionals know marketing, but without experience and input, they don't necessarily know law, accounting, or consulting—they have to depend upon professional input for that. It takes time and commitment.

- *What are your firm objectives?* Do you want to be big? Do you want to expand your market? Do you want to expand your services? Do you have the capacity to handle new business generated by marketing, or are you prepared to develop that capacity?

The answers to these questions are crucial to making the judgment about whether to go outside to a full-service agency, or to try to do it in-house. If your plan is to do a few small ads, hiring a staff is not practical. If, on the other hand, you anticipate major campaigns, thinking through these factors is important.

There is no simple answer to the in-house decision, but looking at the advantages and disadvantages on both sides can be helpful in making the decision. For example:

- *Knowledge of the firm's services and profession.* Obviously, the in-house agency has the opportunity to gain a deeper knowledge of the firm's services, its profession, and it markets. It has, as well, access to the partners and what they're working on, on a day-by-day basis. The outside agency is less likely to understand any of this, without a deep orientation. And given the unique characteristics of marketing a professional service, unless the agency has served other firms in your profession there's a lot for them to learn.

On the other hand, the outside agency is in the advertising business and you are not. You may staff your in-house agency with talented and experienced people, but the outside agency is in the business full time, and serves a variety of clients—which gives it a diversity of experience and skill that may serve you well.

- *Objectivity.* Sometimes, the staff of an in-house agency finds itself in a political position that defeats its objectivity. This is particularly true in a partnership, where every partner may have input and a measure of authority. Decisions can be made to satisfy a partner's ego, or his or her misconception of what good advertising is. The problem is that advertising is a craft that in many respects looks easier than it is. The notion that any bright person can do it, without too much training, experience or talent, can create political situations and second-guessing that can destroy the effectiveness of an in-house agency. While it's true that an outside agency can be susceptible to the same kind of political pressures, a successful agency—and why deal with any other kind—tends to be insulated by its own financial stability and the need to preserve its reputation by doing objectively good advertising.

- *Cost control.* The in-house agency may be in the better position to keep control over most advertising costs, such as production and creative fees, because it has only one client to follow. It also has a better fix on the cost of partners' time. But it may not have the perspective to spend money effectively. Nor is the in-house agency as readily able to absorb the cost of ineffective advertising, and testing for it, as can an outside agency. And because it requires a smaller staff, overhead costs can be lower, but it doesn't usually do as well in tracking the hidden costs of overhead, such as rent, salary allocation in shared services, etc. The outside agency can give you a budget that contains your costs on everything but coordinating with your staff. The good agency may also be more experienced at budget planning, and with its volume buys, may be able to keep your media costs down. Still, the outside agency may not be as inspired to keep costs down as is the in-house agency.

- *Creativity.* Your in-house staff may include the most creative people around, which is good, but may go stale by working for just one client, which can be bad. The outside agency, presumably has talented people too, plus the energizing experience of facing a new creative challenge almost daily. And of course, the larger the agency, the more creative people available to address a problem.

- *Speed and service.* A well-run in-house agency can usually turn work around fast, and with less red tape. It can however, move too fast, allowing too little time for evaluation and judgment. An outside agency can help its client remain on target and organized, and still turn work around quickly because they have experience and skill in doing it.

- *Staff.* In-house employees tend to be loyal and enthusiastic, and to have the firm's interest at heart, while agencies offset that with their ability to attract a strong pool of talented people, whose loyalty is to their talent. Firm employees, with only one client, tend to become jaded, and to lose objectivity, while agency people, with several clients, have variety and objectivity. But of course, if you're at the wrong agency, there is always the danger that other more exciting (or profitable) clients may preempt attention and care.

In the final analysis, all the foregoing taken into consideration, an in-house agency's potential strengths are:

- It can afford a better integrated marketing program, with greater tie-in to other aspects of marketing.
- It may give the firm direct access to the people who plan and implement the advertising, with no red tape. This, of course, can be a disadvantage as well—if access becomes interference. In-house people, with daily access to the professional staff, may have a better grasp of your firm's services and personality.
- Budgets are more likely to be tied to marketing goals, rather than to an agency's own concerns with its revenues, percentages, or returns.

Going to an agency also has advantages as well. For example:

- An agency can afford to hire and sustain better talent, who see both a faster career growth path and the opportunity to work on many different things. *This alone can be a crucial difference,* if creative advertising is of the essence for the firm.
- An agency has an experience and perspective of many different clients, which can broaden its scope of marketing and creativity.
- It's easier to hire an agency, based on it's track record, than to hire people in the several disciplines of advertising, particularly if you're not experienced in hiring advertising people. Then, maintaining staff productivity becomes the agency's problem—not the partners'.

For most, it's not an easy decision. But knowing the pros and cons of each alternative can sometimes reduce the burden of a difficult choice.

To take advantage of the 15 percent agency commissions on media placements you must prove that your agency offers legitimate advertising services. This may require setting up a legally recognized independent organization, or giving a name to the department or group that will function as the agency. The structure is not as important as being able to demonstrate that the entity doing the advertising is separate and clearly established, and that your firm is credit worthy.

## The Agency Services

Your in-house agency will have to perform exactly the same services for you that an outside agency would, and so there's no better way to establish a sound operation than to model your agency on an outside agency of comparable size and capability. This means the ability to function in at least the following areas . . .

- *Creative.* At a full-service agency, this aspect of the operation would comprise more than one-third of your payroll costs—and even more than that if the agency has creative superstars. The staff required would be experienced and proven copy writers, design and layout artists, and radio and television producers. Because these are creative people, you have a few concerns. Are you hiring genuinely creative people? How do you judge their work? How do you integrate them into your firm's culture?

- *Research.* This function can take 10-15 percent of the payroll costs, depending upon the extent to which you use research. Research people have very different temperament and training than do creative people. They must be equipped with computers and access to databases, and frequently supplemented with outside services for surveys and interviews.

- *Media.* This department usually takes about 10 percent of the payroll. The media buyer is a specialist in media costs and requirements, and is capable of negotiating space purchases at favorable prices.

- *Account Management.* In a full service agency, this area can take as much as 30 percent of the payroll, and somewhat less in an in-house agency.

Other functions include a traffic department to keep track of the flow of all elements of ads; a legal department to advise on media and advertising regulations, and to review the legality of copy; and a finance operation to control the financial and business aspects of the agency. These functions take up the remainder of the payroll in an agency.

## Alternate Approaches

There are a number of alternative approaches to structuring your in-house agency:

- *Full Service In-House.* Some in-house agencies handle the full spectrum of advertising needs. They conduct their own analyses, create their own advertising plans, write, produce, and appear in their own commercials, buy media time, and track advertising effectiveness. Some agencies even conduct market research programs. They are fully staffed with everything from an account manager to copy writers to TV producers.

  This would seem to be practical, however, only for a very large firm that does a great deal of advertising throughout the country, such as a large chain of legal clinics. It requires vast expenditures of money for people, and the payback can come only from the rebates on the 15 percent commissions on vast advertising budgets.

- Using Outside Services. Some in-house managers oversee their firm's advertising efforts, and contract with outside agencies, consultants or freelancers to handle specific jobs. At Jacoby & Meyers, for example, the marketing director wrote and supervised the implementation of the plan, but hired outside services, such as a media buying service and a Yellow Pages placement service, to execute aspects of it. One of the Jacoby & Meyers partners generally wrote the commercial scripts, and the marketing director would hire a production company to produce the commercials. Except for the very lucky, or very talented, this can be a dangerous path.

- Joint venture with independent agencies. Many small agencies—there are more than 8,000 agencies of all sizes in the United States—offer a flexible variety of working arrangements and payment terms. This is a feasible approach for the smaller firm, with a moderate advertising budget. In addition to the standard 15 percent fee structure, or a month-to-month retainer, there are:

  ° *Special Projects.* An agency can be hired to help create and implement a special campaign, on clearly defined projects. You may want hire an agency to test direct mail, for example, on a flat fee basis, with a mark-up for expenses, or at an hourly fee, with a limit based upon an estimate of the number of hours required.

  ° *Straight Fee Arrangement.* If an agency works on a full fee basis, it will credit all commissions (such as the 15 percent media discount) to the client. The agency will estimate their costs in advance, and then add a percentage as a service fee. All purchases made for the client, such as typography, printing, television studio costs, etc. are then billed to the client at cost (or net).

  ° *Combination Fee/Commission.* If agency costs are below what the commission would be, the agency and client sometimes agree to split the remaining commission. If the agency expenses exceed the commission, the agency costs and profits are covered in a straight fee arrangement.

For example, let's assume that you purchase large amounts of media, but produce new ads only occasionally. The agency may agree to split or reduce the commission, as long as they are guaranteed a given amount of income. Should their costs increase, as when new commercials are needed, the advertiser pays the difference to guarantee the fees.

An in-house arrangement can work if you've got a rare marketing director and unusually talented and motivated employees. But recognize that it requires tremendous commitment, time, and energy from very valuable and busy members of your firm.

The in-house concept has sustained in recent years as independent groups known as boutiques came into existence. The boutique uses the talent of creative specialists in small firms that specialize in only one or two aspects of advertising, such as copy or art. This has been further enhanced by the growth of modular system in full service agencies, in which individual services such as copy, art, or media buying may be purchased separately from other agency services. An in-house advertising staff can frequently produce high-quality advertising by judiciously using independent outside services to supplement its own capabilities.

There has also been substantial growth in independent media services, which do in media buying what the boutique does in the creative field. While they function in all media, they're of greatest value in television and radio, where buys can be more complex than in print media. Their growth in recent years is predicated on the fact that the media have become more aware that advertising space and time are ephemeral. When they're not used, they can't be recaptured—they're lost forever. Thus, the media are frequently willing to make arrangements with these media services that go beyond the standard rate card. So many of these deals are possible that it takes an independent organization to keep track of them, and thus serve both the media and the advertiser.

The independent media service functions as an intermediary between the agency or advertiser and the media. It does media planning, scheduling, negotiating, buying, and monitoring. These companies save both time and money for both the small advertiser and the larger company, and can supply a great deal of valuable expertise at reasonable rates. There tends to be no standard method of compensation for their service, and arrangements differ for each deal. Sometimes it's a straight media commission, sometimes a fee based on total billing, and sometimes a fee based on the amount of money the service saves the advertiser.

## Selecting an Agency

Finding an agency need not be difficult, even if you're located in a smaller community in which there are few choices. There's no rule that says that your agency has to be right in your own community, although that's certainly preferable. Finding the *right* agency, and qualifying it, can be difficult if you don't have marketing background and experience in the selection process.

If your marketing plans, and the size of your budget, warrant it, an out-of-town agency may work as well for you as can a local one, particularly if the quality of the out-of-town firm is superior. Lists of accredited agencies (accredited by the media, and therefore entitled to media discount) are readily available from regional or national advertising trade associations, or from the Yellow Pages.

Selecting an agency, on the other hand, requires some thought and foresight. First, advertising professional services with any degree of sophistication is relatively new, and few traditional agencies without actual professional services experience can be expected to understand it without extensive orientation. And second, as a professional, you perform a service. An advertising agency also performs a service. You understand the service concept. On the one hand, you know how difficult it is to forecast how a service will perform for you. On the other hand, this knowledge should make it relatively simple for you to understand the agency's service concept, and to judge its ability to develop and produce your marketing program.

Prior to asking agencies to make presentations to you, it may be useful to spend some time with each of the candidates explaining your agency and your profession, including some of the ethical strictures. It will save a considerable amount of time, because the more the agency knows about you, the more likely that it will zero in on what you really need.

### Factors in Agency Selection

Beyond this, there are a number of specific things you should look for in selecting an agency:

*Creativity.* What's your own impression of the work it's done for other clients? And not just the ads, but the full range of marketing services? How effective has the work been? Can you get references from other clients that attest to the fact that the agency's work produces results that are equal to the creativity, or does the agency just produce prize-winning ads that don't really sell?

*Reputation.* An agency's reputation can be checked by discussing it with media representatives in your market area, or with other of the agency's clients. Certainly, any reputable agency would be delighted to give you references and a list of its clients. Reputation should be based upon service, creativity, and integrity.

*The agency's client list.* The list should include a large number of clients whose advertising budgets are in the same range as yours. That can be more important than their having other clients in similar fields. If you're the small client in a shop with large clients, are you likely to get as much attention as the larger clients do, or be assigned superior account or creative personnel? If your budget is twice as large as your, or a fraction as large, your account may be out of the agency's realm of capability.

*Range of services.* Does the agency have the capability to perform the services you need for your advertising and marketing program? If the capability is not on staff, which are the outside services it uses, and what's their quality of work?

And even more important, what's your feeling about the way it understands your problems and marketing needs? What sorts of questions does it ask you? Are they routine, or searching? Simply because an agency has been successful in a campaign for one kind of product or service doesn't mean that it can grasp and understand your objectives, and successfully translate them into a great campaign for you.

Of course, the really crucial question is whether the same team that produced the great ads they've just shown you will be the one that works for you.

*Service.* Who's going to service your account? How much of his or her time will you have available to you? Do you personally like the account executive, and are you impressed by him or her in your initial conversation? Advertising is not only a creative business it's a personal business, and you have to work well with the person handling your account.

*Fee arrangements.* Are the fees reasonable for the service the agency says it can offer you, or are they too high or too low? Are they realistic in terms of your own budget?

## The Chinese Wall

When an accounting or a law or consulting firm takes several clients in the same industry, it's a marketing device that projects an expertise in that industry. It's good marketing.

But it's often felt that a public relations, marketing, or advertising agency can't take competing firms as clients, even when different account teams work on different clients. It's sometimes thought to be unethical and unsound business for the agency to accept competitive clients and for the firm to hire an agency that has competitive clients.

To cast rules like this in stone may well take rigidity too far. The spectrum of considerations a decision like this depends on is very large.

Consider, for a moment, what the accounting and law firms do. First, they recognize that specific industries have singular bodies of specific guidelines, practices, jargon, rules and regulations, accounting practices, and nuances. There is a distinct advantage to having a law or accounting firm with expertise in your industry. It enhances the wisdom of the professional services offered.

But if you ask an accountant or a lawyer why his or her firm wouldn't hire an agency that has other law or accounting firms as clients, you'll be told something about competitive secrets. Or, "If they have a marketing or public relations idea, how do we know that they'll apply it to us, rather than to the firm's other client?" Or, "How do we know if we can trust them with our firm's secrets?"

151

Are we assuming, then, that only accountants and lawyers and consultants can be relied upon to have a Chinese wall that separates one client's interests from another? Is this rational?

Granted, there is a canon of ethics-defined code of confidentiality that governs the professions, and that therefore exudes confidence to companies that their secrets will be respected. Is the feeling that marketing and its parts are too fragile—its people too unprofessional—to understand the Chinese wall and the meaning of confidentiality?

We know better, don't we? We know that it's the firm, not the profession, that builds Chinese walls. Accountants and lawyers and consultants, with their canons of ethics, do have more of a stricture, and therefore more to lose if they violate client confidentiality, than do marketers. Marketers, lacking this ethical strictures, have nothing to lose but their clients.

Violating client confidence is not just—or even merely—unethical. It's dumb. Every profession has dumb people, and no dumb accountant or lawyer or marketer should be hired. But because Chinese walls are a function of sound business, and not arbitrary ethical structures, the choice of sharing confidential information with a client or an agency should be made on the basis of the individuals involved, not the profession.

It's true that some agencies feel that their clients are more comfortable with a non-competitive policy, that they can concentrate better on solving the client's problems without diluting efforts, that there's enough anxiety about marketing for lawyers and accountants without adding the additional worry of confidentiality or dilution of creative efforts. It's the agency's choice, and if they're comfortable with it, then that's their policy. It's the client's choice to accept or not accept that policy.

But the paradox is that the people in a superior agency, like accounting or law firms with industry expertise, have a singular and superior expertise in marketing professional services. When the personalities are mature, and have the kind of integrity that can build better Chinese walls between clients of the same profession, the agency is actually depriving professional firms of potentially superior marketing support.

Marketing professional services is, after all, a distinctive and unique form of marketing. It's also, as is all of marketing, an art form, and there are very few artists. Unfortunately, there are more professional firms that need this expertise than there are experts to go around. Extending trust to a marketing firm that they will serve each client well, and confidentially, and with energy and artistry, can often be a wiser policy than one based upon suspicion.

There's another aspect to consider. Some marketing consulting firms, which are no different in practice than are any other kind of consulting firms, can serve the needs of competing clients because they don't actually perform the marketing function. They address each client's marketing problems, within the context of each client's own structures, objectives, and marketing programs. And while it's true that they are privy to each client's secrets, they have track records of integrity, so that no question is ever raised about breaches of confidentiality. They are good business people, and are recognized for it.

And there's the crux of the Chinese wall, and the essence of real service. Not arbitrary ethical codes, but rather, a sense of good business and sound judgment. Respecting confidentiality, and producing the best for each client, is good business and sound judgment. Nobody should work with or for anybody who doesn't have a dynamic sense of both.

In the final analysis, the best evaluation of an agency comes, unfortunately, only after an expenditure of time and money. Does it get results for you or not? An agency must be allowed a reasonable time to prove itself, and the time should be agreed upon at the outset. If after that time you feel that the agency hasn't worked for you, then don't hesitate to change. It's no reflection on either you or the agency. Sometimes a perfectly good agency can't perform as well for you as it has for other of its clients. There's no onus in facing the fact if everybody's been given a fair chance to perform. A fair chance means as well, that you've been cooperative with the agency.

# Part III

# Public Relations

# 10

# Public Relations

Public relations is one of those peculiar terms that everybody knows, everybody uses, and everybody can define. But no two people seem to define it in the same way, much less practice it within the context of its fullest value.

Certainly, it falls prey to considerable misconception and mythology. For example, public relations is too often confused with publicity, which is just one of many tools of public relations.

The term *public relations* is perhaps best understood if the words are taken literally. Public relations is the way you meet and deal with the public, and in turn, how you are perceived by the public. The public, of course, is your clientele and prospective clientele.

But all that is just common sense and common courtesy. Certainly, public relations is more than that. It is indeed publicity. It's also those positive activities that function in your behalf, such as issues programs and community relations. It's also the quality of your service—how well you meet the needs of your clients. It's damage control and crisis management.

And so while public relations is the benign and vague concept of doing nice things so that people will have a favorable impression of you, it's also a large body of positive activities that function in your behalf in a business context.

Too often, public relations is seen simply as a manipulative discipline, sometimes with sinister overtones. True, public relations is indeed sometimes used that way. But rarely successfully, since that's not it's value or purpose. And that means that concepts of ethics are very much part of the concern of public relations. More of ethics in a moment.

## Image

The word *image*—another myth—comes to mind.

There is no concept in marketing more misconstrued, more misused, more deleterious to ultimate marketing achievement, than the concept of *image*. It implies that facts or symbols can be manipulated to offer a representation of a company or an individual that's in any way different from reality. It implies as well that reality doesn't matter, if an image can be conjured uPthat suits the purposes of the vendor.

The concept of *image* in the context of marketing was put forth many years ago by public relations pioneer Edward Bernays, in a book on public relations. He spoke of it as the perception the public has of a company—a view that engenders an attitude toward that company. *Image* very quickly became a hot word—one of those easily used bits of jargon.

Unfortunately, when it's used that way, it makes it difficult to bring non-marketers to the same plane of understanding with the marketers in professional services.

Design firms tend to be flagrant offenders, particularly when they suggest that the way your company is represented graphically—your *image*—is a valid picture of what your company really is. A book, they are saying, is judged by its cover.

There's no question that a well-designed book jacket will better attract a buyer's eye than a dull one. But will it foretell what's in the book? Does anybody seriously believe that it will?

The attractiveness engenders a predilection toward that book, perhaps, but it very quickly mitigates by the reality of the book itself. That's what's so silly about the notion that a corporate graphics program offers much more than instant identification and a primary attractiveness.

Truth told, facts and symbols are not often successfully manipulated, and misrepresentation to the public rarely works in the marketplace. The acoustics of the business world are much too good to allow flagrant misrepresentation to pervade over any extended period of time. In the real world, this concept of image very quickly falls apart.

The danger of the concept of *image* lies in the notion that if your firm is badly flawed or incompetent in some way, you can submerge that fact with public relations or marketing. There are responsible people who really believe that a good public relations campaign will present a firm as it wants to be seen, and not as it really is.

So long as this nonsense is believed, lawyers and accountants and consultants will expect their marketers to absolve them of the need to improve, or to change to meet the real needs of the marketplace. Rather, the marketers will be expected to manipulate symbols to give the appearance of being virtuous—to present the shining *image* of goodness and light.

On the other hand, if the reality of your firm is reasonably favorable, that reality can frequently be focused and projected in ways that clarify a perception of the best of your firm, and that enhances your reputation as a superior practitioner. If this is what's meant by *image,* then the word is used well.

And so the concept of *image* is not merely a matter of toying with a word. It's a matter of understanding how the concept subverts the opportunity to do the right thing; to be the good firm rather than to simply appear to be the good firm.

And if the word *image* is indeed appropriately used, then public relations is the discipline that focuses on the reality, sharpens the perception, and enhances the reputation.

## *Public Relations and Advertising*

Public relations is the discipline, as well, that generates an atmosphere in which more people want to do more business with you.

Thus, by affording the public the opportunity to think well of you, thereby making the market more receptive to your sales efforts, public relations enhances your selling effort.

Like advertising, public relations can't of itself sell professional services. It's activities serve to educate your prospective clientele about who you are, what you do and how you do it. These activities may even generate inquiries. Public relations can enhance your relations with existing clients by projecting an attitude of service, and a willingness to serve—if indeed that attitude and willingness exist—that adds enthusiasm to the idea of doing business with you. But, as with most other marketing tools, it can't close a sale.

Public relations considerations dictate how you do what you do. This includes every aspect of your public persona, from the way your office is decorated to the way your letterhead looks, to the way you and your staff dress; the way you structure and conduct client meetings and client communications; the visible aspects of the way you manage your firm. In sum, the way you do business. It's this projection of the reality of a sound firm that builds credibility for everything you do or say, in either a professional or a frank marketing context.

In essence, then, effective public relations resides in the classic observation that what you are speaks so loudly that people can't hear what you say you are. The most effective public relations program projects the best of what you are.

## Role in the Marketing Mix

In the marketing mix—the balance of all marketing tools used in competition with one another—the major and overriding role of public relations is primarily to build and strengthen reputation within the context of professional expertise and business relationships, and to enhance perception of a firm's skills and abilities.

A secondary value addresses important human concerns. Is the company a good one to do business with? Is it (or rather, are its people) cooperative, service oriented, and client-concerned? Are community relations good and are they a good corporate citizen?

Public relations uses publicity through the media to reach its audiences, both by direct contact and through activities such as seminars, speeches, etc. that generate newsworthy exposure. The basic technique of publicity is to cast the story in ways that are newsworthy, and then to persuade editors that the story is newsworthy for their readers. Publicity may have the advantage of an implied editorial endorsement, as well as ubiquitousness. But is also has the disadvantage of lack of total control. You propose and others—the editors—dispose.

Advertising works only when there are advertisements. Public relations' many facets, beginning with an attitude about service that's ingrained in a practice, work constantly. Public relations works, even without publicity, on a day-to-day basis, with positive effects that compound.

Although strategy differs in each case, ideally an ongoing and persistent public relations program would be used to generate a broad-based knowledge of a firm and its skills and to build credibility. Advertising would be used to focus the message and to add selling strength. Direct mail would be used to bring the firm closest to the sale, which ultimately must be consummated by an individual.

Public relations supports and extends the value of advertising in several specific ways. It should be made clear, however, that public relations is not free advertising, even though it may use publicity that results in telling a great deal about your company through the editorial pages of a publication.

Public relations, with its ability to build and strengthen credibility, is particularly important to professional services marketing. In an arena in which product distinctions can't be made, credibility for any of a firm's marketing messages takes on an increased value in enhancing reputation.

When a public relations program succeeds in developing a favorable attitude towards your firm, it makes your advertising and sales claims more credible, because successful publicity efforts have the added advantage of the implied editorial objective support; the third person endorsement of the publication, which appears to be saying, objectively, that because you are newsworthy, you are to be viewed favorably.

When your public relations efforts succeed, then they succeed on all fronts—improved client relations, improved perception of your abilities, enhanced reputation, and a broader base of understanding of what you do and how well you do it.

## Elements of Public Relations

Public relations functions, essentially, in several basic areas:

*Attitude and basic service concept.* How do you perceive and project your own role in serving your clients? To what extent will you extend yourself in their behalf? How significant is it for you to deal with your audience—your clients and potential clients—in ways that exude a willingness to serve in their behalf, rather than to perform what you do in ways that serve only your convenience? Do you consciously favor quality over expedience?

That aspect of public relations that projects the concept of service, and delineates your firm as one that is substantial, is an ongoing and never-ceasing affair. It should be a constant in any business.

But public relations is more than just an attitude of *niceness*, or even of service. It must function in a realistic context of sound business practice and genuine excellence. News of poor practice or business techniques will travel farther and faster than you can possibly offset with any kind of publicity campaign or manipulative *image*.

At the same time, the good things you do, the services you perform and the way you perform them, those activities that contribute to the very reputation you'd like to have, all travel well. And while everyone makes a mistake from time to time or makes an enemy, or mishandles a situation, the balance sheet also travels.

*Publicity.* This is the communications function in public relations. It's the skill —and sometimes the art—of communicating to the public, through news media and other devices, those factors that focus attention on you, your firm, your expertise and skills, your service concept—all those elements that ultimately enhance your reputation as a superior performer and outstanding service organization.

In a highly competitive marketing situation, publicity should also be ongoing. In publicizing a professional service it's never sufficient merely to expose the name. The essence of publicity, in this context, is to project expertise.

But publicity, and reputation, are very much like a hoop. As long as you keep beating a hoop with a stick it keeps rolling. The minute you stop, it falls over. So it is with reputation. The effort must be sustained.

Being publicity-minded doesn't mean being brash or unduly forward. Rather, it means being thoroughly professional in the sense of being a reliable source of expertise for the business press.

At the same time if public relations is to function effectively as part of the total marketing mix, and if it is to contribute to meeting marketing objectives, then the publicity program must be designed with the marketing mix in mind.

*Newsmaking events.* Frequently, a good measure of public relations consists of activities you generate to focus attention on the firm, its members, and its expertise. In many cases, it will serve as a basis for most of the publicity you garner.

A seminar for clients and prospective clients serves a valid purpose in marketing. But when that seminar deals with a subject in a way that's new or unique, it serves as a basis for publicity—for making news. When a new approach to solving a problem—a new audit technique, a new computer control system, a new legal service—is developed and presented to the public, this is a newsmaking event that's been generated in a way that affords special attention and news coverage. Speeches, and even participation in trade shows and conventions, serve in the same way.

The range of newsmaking events is limited only by the imagination. Special studies, seminars, community service—all these and more can be invented legitimately to serve as newsmaking events.

*The Issues Program.* A newsmaking event of great magnitude can be the issues program, in which the firm chooses an issue of importance to the business community it serves, and builds a public relations program around it. More than a one-time event, an issues program should be chosen to sustain for a period of time, and should therefore be based on an issue that will sustain interest, attention, and importance for a period of time.

The objectives of an issue program are:

- To associate the firm with an attitude toward—or a position on—the issue that redounds to the benefit of the firm.
- To develop programs around the issue that result in generating favorable publicity, and positive public relations, for the firm.

The issues program should be supported with a series of events and activities that generate publicity. But they should also contribute to favorable public relations by making an important contribution.

This is accomplished with:

- Position papers
- Seminars
- Speeches
- Study grants to universities and other professionals
- Press conferences
- Press releases

Issues programs of magnitude must be carefully managed and coordinated. An issues manager is usually assigned to follow the issue itself, and to monitor new developments and new thinking in an issue that can be incorporated into the firm's issues program.

In some cases, the results of an issues program produce sufficient information to warrant publishing a book on the subject—one more element of positive public relations.

*Quality.* Quality of service is indeed a public relations device, albeit a peculiar one. *Quality*, of course, is one of those words that means different things to different people. Here, we mean a consistently high level of performance in meeting the needs of the client.

Certainly, there's a value in a reputation for quality, although it's hard to discern or quantify. And certainly, a reputation for lack of quality, or for poor quality, is plainly destructive. The question is, though, how valuable is quality as a marketing tool?

The answer is that it's valuable, but it won't work of itself. The better mousetrap theory, in today's market, doesn't work at all.

In the professions, quality is assumed to be a given, and so you get bad marks for poor service, and not much credit for good service and good work.

Excepted in all this, of course, is extraordinary quality—the brilliant lawyer or accountant whose work is highly visible, for example. But here, the emphasis may well be on the *visible*, and not the *brilliant*. The really superior firm, with a really superior group of partners and staff, will not attract clients except as that brilliance is made visible, and is marketed.

But high quality of itself, the better mousetrap, will not alter the frequency with which the path to its door is trodden. In today's competitive arena, marketing is fought on other planes, unfortunately.

*Professional relations.* There are few industries that serve their members so well in public relations as do professional societies. Lawyers, doctors, accountants—all owe a large measure of the favorable public view towards their professions to the public relations efforts of their societies. The tangible value to professionals of this achievement is a public perception of probity, ethical behavior, reliability, and integrity. That is pure money in the bank to any professional.

At the same time, good public relations demands that a professional comply with the ethics of his or her profession. Ethical codes remain a major factor in sustaining the somewhat elevated view of the professions, and good public relations demands the public perception of ethical behavior, as well as the reality of it.

*Ethics.* In fact, concepts of ethics, both in the professions and in public relations, are crucial—not alone because they are practical and philosophical aspects of human behavior. And if one is to relate to the public, ethics—or at least those aspects of behavior and demeanor that are usually held in the purview of ethics—are much of the essence.

One would do well, in this context, to understand the meaning of the word *ethics,* and its relation to *morality.* They are two different things—and neither is handed down from Parnassus.

*Ethics* are those aspects of behavior that a specific group agrees to accept for the mutual good of that segment of society. The problem is that circumstances change in our lives, and what's mutually good at one time may not be so at another. And even ethical codes can be immoral, at least in the sense that they sometimes spill over to unduly restrain others from serving the common good, for the benefit of the few. The ethical codes of professional associations, such as the bar, medical, and accounting societies, and even PRSA (Public Relations Society of America), have frequently been accused of that. That's why the US Supreme Court, in *Bates vs. The State Bar of Arizona* (1977), struck down the restrictions in canons of ethics against frank marketing. It was, they noted, restraint of trade.

And the word *ethics* is also used by people who really mean *honesty.*

*Morality* is an ethical position that's been crystallized. And while there are moral positions that are likely to be universally accepted, such as those in the Ten Commandments, moral positions change as well. Morality, as anybody over twenty years old can testify, changes with the times, so it's hardly absolute.

What is unethical and immoral and certainly undemocratic is to deny access to expression, or even advocacy, to unpopular ideas, or to those who espouse ideas or concepts we oppose—and to try to justify that denial in the guise of ethics or morality. That's not democratic—that's totalitarian. It's also stupid.

In that abstract arena of human behavior, in which we use the term *ethics* to mean a mode of behavior that is above reproach (a misinterpretation, by the foregoing definition), *ethics* might well be considered in terms of a definition by Peter Drucker. Ethics, he says, is behaving equally towards everybody. In fact, the real question of behavior is not primarily a philosophical one. Simply put, certain kinds of behavior are simply good business; certain kinds of behavior are bad business. If one misrepresents to a client, is that poor ethics, or poor business behavior?

The essence of good public relations, then, is to behave honestly, with integrity, and with a view to the consequences of that behavior. Given this approach, you don't have to think much about ethics until next Sunday—and maybe not even then.

*Community relations.* Long a cornerstone of professional practice development, serving the community is still a crucial part of marketing professional services. The public expects the professional, in his exalted stature, to be a pillar of the community. This, of course, has public relations overtones. It also gets clients.

As with all aspects of marketing a professional service, public relations does not function in the abstract. No agency, no matter how effective, can perform the public relations function without the total participation of the people in your firm who perform that service.

## Crisis Management

A firm crisis that's enacted in the public spotlight is a public relations problem.

There are two key factors that often mark the difference between a crisis and a disaster—advance planning and effective communications.

No firm is immune to a crisis of public nature. Good planning, and good public relations, make the difference between crisis solved and crisis turned into disaster. Sometimes, unfortunately, the crisis, unanticipated and without a plan, turns into disaster even though, on the surface, it appears that the right steps have been taken.

A few simple steps, well planned and well organized, can take a crisis and turn it into a weapon in behalf of the company.

Says Dorf & Stanton's Alex Stanton, writing in *The Marcus Report*, "The most important first step, of course, is to designate a crisis management team. This team should not be arbitrarily selected, but rather should be comprised of a small group of quick decision makers who represent all key functions of the firm. They should be cool-headed people who operate well under pressure, and are fully familiar with the crisis plan."

Crisis team members, he says, should be accessible to one another on a 24-hour basis with either a wallet-sized telephone list or beepers. Their task, as team members, is to assume that a crisis will come.

## *Job One—Assess Severity*

And when crisis does come, the most critical job of the crisis team is to realistically define its scope and severity. All future decisions and judgments will flow from this assessment, so it's important to accurately estimate the severity of the situation as it unfolds.

"The crisis team," says Stanton, "is both a decision-making and fact-finding body, and because it must be constantly and immediately exposed to all new information, it should meet to review the situation with frequent 30 to 60 minute sessions throughout the crises. In the intervening times, team members should be gathering vital information in their areas of responsibility."

The crisis team must also quickly identify the key target audiences affected by the crisis, to establish who needs to know what information. The best approach is to establish an order of priority for disseminating the news, and to determine who in the company is in the best position to communicate with each key audience.

"We counsel clients to use a cascading notification system," says Stanton, "in which the most important audiences hear first, and the least important last. Ideally, this system should be spelled out in detail in the crisis plan, because it relies on key people in the organization, including those not on the team, to pass along information to others who need to know. If you rely on a small crisis team to do all the communicating while it also manages the crisis, key audiences will not be notified, or will hear about the crisis, probably inaccurately, from other sources.

It's also vital that you move quickly so that key audiences hear about the crisis first-hand from you. A system to monitor their reaction to the initial information should be established, so that you can respond quickly to any new developments.

## *Quick, Open and Honest*

When the extent of the crisis and the information to be disseminated is determined, it's important to tell your story as quickly, openly, and honestly as possible within the confines of prudence. "In our experience," says Stanton, "many firms either under-communicate or over-communicate their messages, but without professional help, very few strike the right balance between the two."

Some firms don't begin to communicate until the crisis has engulfed them, which can make the corporation seem ill-managed or unfeeling.

Other firms, fearing the unknown and under pressure to say something, release unverified information and speculate on the causes and outside effects of the crisis. One health care institution found itself constantly back-peddling after a junior staff person revealed inaccurate information to the press in the first hours of a patient crisis.

It's important not to place blame for the crisis on any particular situation, individual, or outside party. The key audiences are far less concerned with assigning blame than with the company's ability to address solutions to the problem.

Another caution. When key audiences are forgotten in the havoc created by a crisis, it can derail even the best laid plan. It's amazing that firm managers think nothing of discussing a crisis situation with the media before communicating to one of the most important audiences of all—their employees. Employees should never be the last to know, since they will often be the first to get a phone call from the press or the public asking what's going on. Receptionists, security guards, and telephone operators can often be the front line in dealing with callers. It's critical that they be briefed within the context of their responsibilities.

It's also important to recognize that every employee, at all levels, who is properly informed and armed with the correct messages can be a significant soldier in your communications army. And they must all be told the same story. Inconsistency can be fatal to a crisis management effort.

### Proper Role of Attorney

In every instance, a legal adviser will be an important member of your crisis team. Your firm counsel or outside attorney should be consulted on a continuing basis regarding the legal implications of the crisis and proposed response actions. However, firm executives should not be afraid to move boldly and against the counsel of their attorney when the situation warrants. Without denigrating the significant role of legal counsel, it's important to recognize two things—law, not communication, is the expertise of the attorney; and the final responsibility for actions resides not with the attorney or the communications expert, but with management.

Ultimately, management has responsibility to preserve the reputation of the firm and its special relationship with clients. Often, attorneys will seek to limit liability by releasing as little information as possible and moving more slowly than the situation demands, which is not always the right decision for the firm.

One of the housekeeping details often forgotten in the midst of a crisis is to record events as the crisis proceeds. This can be invaluable in telling your side of the story, should you ultimately have to. It's equally important to issue a final statement when the crisis has subsided, citing measures being taken to avoid repeat occurrences.

### Effective Media Relations

Today, no crisis can be successfully managed without effective media relations. The fundamental mistrust of the media that persists in many professional firms is most often responsible for the lack of effective media interface during a crisis. There are some basic guidelines we follow in helping clients handle crisis situations with the media:

- Establish a single designated spokesperson who has had media training and is kept well informed. This spokesperson, ideally a crisis team member, must fully understand—and be able to articulate—the firm's position.

- Develop a press statement and a tough internal question-and-answer document before speaking to the media. The press statement establishes the key facts that have surfaced, as well as the company position. The Q&A anticipates press behavior, and asks all the questions you can foresee, including those you hope the media will never ask. It allows the best answers possible under the circumstances to be developed thoughtfully, rather than under fire.

- As new facts become available, the information originally conveyed to the press must be updated. The media will be trying to find source information as energetically as you are, which may be inaccurate and fuel the fire of the crisis, so it's important to stay one step ahead. Make new information available on a continuing basis, so the media won't feel compelled to find sources their own,

- Once the crisis starts, it's important to be as accessible to the media as humanly possible. Under pressure to file stories and scoop competitive news outlets, reporters will go elsewhere to get their information if they can't get it from you.

- Avoid "no comment" at all costs. It doesn't cut mustard with the media, and it just raises suspicions that facts are being hidden. If you can't discuss something, explain why. Don't be afraid to say, "I don't know, but I'll get back to you as soon as possible." Then fulfill that commitment.

- Seriously consider reporting your own bad news. While the pros and cons, and legal requirements, of this strategy must be weighed in each situation, it's rare that withholding information pays off in a crisis. By allowing the media to uncover information you might otherwise have revealed on your own, you lose the opportunity to position the crisis to your advantage, and to show that you have the situation under control. The information almost always surfaces anyway, and often at a far more disadvantageous juncture in the crisis than it might have been had you controlled the release.

The three key words in effectively managing any crisis are *communicate, communicate, communicate.* "The firm that plans ahead for the crisis that hasn't happened yet," Stanton says, "and communicates effectively to all key audiences before, during and after the crisis, will fare well under even the most trying circumstances."

## Objectives

The objectives of a public relations program, and particularly one that relies heavily on publicity dictate the nature of the program and the techniques that are to be used. Generally, a public relations program should build a structured capability that would:

- Expose and project the firm's capabilities, and those of the people who comprise the base of the firm's expertise, to its target audience—in a context of a consistently high level of quality.

- Focus on the firm's greatest strengths and capabilities.

- Develop activities that increase exposure.

- Compete successfully for exposure against the public relations activities of the firm's competitors.

- Give a measure of feedback on how the firm is being perceived by its target audiences.

- Develop editorial reprints that inform and magnify the implied editorial endorsement.

The mechanics for achieving this are dictated by the nature of the profession and the firm itself. The broad range of the firm's activities, and their predominantly technical nature, frequently dictate a strong in-house capability. Even with a good external agency, the program must be driven internally, because it would be exceedingly difficult and expensive to expect an outside firm to be fully aware of even a fraction of the public relations possibilities of the activities generated by a professional firm on a day-to-day basis. Nor could they have the technical understanding of these activities without expensive and time-consuming participation by the firm's professionals.

Of all marketing activities, public relations is the one that requires the most consistent attention. Your firm and its people, after all, are constantly in the eyes of your clients, and should be for prospective clients as well. Even if you don't have an active publicity program, all other aspects of public relations—the way you deal with and present yourself to the public—are as crucial to developing your practice as are your technical skills.

No one marketing tool of itself comprises a program, but of all of them, public relations can supply the greatest mileage for the marketing dollar.

# 11

# Publicity Techniques

Of all of the parts of public relations, publicity is the most ubiquitous. It's techniques are also the most complex, and use a great many skills, including those of journalism, writing, and communicating internally and externally. It requires judgment and the ability to think originally.

Publicity is frequently referred to as media relations, because it involves so many aspects of dealing with individuals in both print and broadcast media. Like advertising and direct mail, publicity—or media relations—is a full specialty.

Public relations, as we've seen, is the sum of a great many factors designed to give your public—your markets—an impression about you and your company that's favorable, informed, and conducive to doing more business with you. It's an ongoing attitude that should pervade every aspect of your business.

But doing the right thing, doing interesting and newsworthy things, is only part of the effort. The other part is to communicate what you're doing to your target audience. This must be done in a way that not only informs, but enhances your reputation as well. You want to be known, of course, but primarily for those things that will directly or ultimately help your business.

The technique for doing this—the tool of public relations that makes this happen—is called publicity.

Unlike advertising, in which you purchase the space for your message, publicity depends upon a presumably objective third person—the editor—who is more concerned with meeting the needs of his publication than with meeting your needs to inform. If the editorial thrust of a publication is not successful in consistently meeting the needs of its readers, it will lose circulation, diminish its value as an advertising medium, and go out of business. This is as true of the smallest community newspaper as it is of *The New York Times* or *The Washington Post*. It's as true of the smallest and most remote radio and television station as it is of the largest network.

Publicity, then, must be structured to meet the editorial needs of a publication or the broadcast media. The person to be persuaded, in the first instance, is the editor, not the ultimate reader.

## What Is News?

Unfortunately, the definition of *news* is not absolute.

In any newspaper, or any newscast, all news is relative. It's more than just the report of an event or an activity that's never been publicly reported before. Each day, editors of the largest and smallest newspapers and broadcast news centers must review all reported events and make a subjective judgment as to which of those events will concern or interest their readers sufficiently to warrant the allocation of rare and precious space or air time. On any given day, the news of a major airplane disaster will garner more editorial interest than the news of a major urban redevelopment plan. The urban plan, in turn, may preempt in importance the announcement of a company's decision to build a $5 million plant in the community. And this, in turn, will preempt the news of plans to build a 200-home development of middle-income homes. Lower down on the list would be an announcement of the appointment of a new partner of an accounting firm. Yet, sometimes, if not very much has happened that day, (or if it's precisely the kind of information for which the publication is read), the new partner news may be the most exciting thing the newspaper has to report.

Even feature material—general background or general interest stories, or service stories such as new techniques in estate planning or how to read a contract—has its editorial stringencies. Even the feature story must have its news hook—a focal point of immediate interest that serves as a fresh basis for writing about a familiar subject.

Moreover, every segment of the press, even broadcast news, has its own target audiences, and therefore its own point of view. The big city newspaper usually focuses on international and national domestic news, with local or regional news relegated to a secondary position, except for matters of citywide significance. The community newspaper focuses entirely upon news of interest to the community, which means news about the community.

Television news as well is targeted to a clearly defined audience. Some stations position their newscasts to reach a mass audience that's more interested in sensationalism than in politics. Others focus more heavily on government and national news. Some publications are large enough to be departmentalized, so that financial or economic news becomes the province of the business or financial editor. Only occasionally is financial news considered by news editors to be of sufficient interest to the larger audience to be put in the general news section. Other newspapers make no distinction of news by industry, and a business story will compete for space with a school budget story. Sometimes the accounting or legal story is considered to be business news, and falls under that editor's province, and sometimes it's considered to be of interest only to other accountants and lawyers, and so is relegated to the back pages.

## Competition for Space

Newspapers and magazines have limited space and broadcast news has a finite amount of time. Each day an editor must make fast decisions about the priorities of what news should be given that precious space and time, and how much of that space and time should be devoted to each news item. Any information you have that you believe to be newsworthy, then, must compete against all the other news about which the editor must make a judgment for the next edition.

And so the basic techniques of publicity are designed to help you compete successfully for the editor's attention, and to win a judgment in your favor in the competition for space and time.

Even in the smallest newspapers, news is categorized, with an editor assigned to each category. For example, a major city newspaper may have a separate staff for international news, another for national domestic news, another just to cover the activities of the federal government. Other departments might include city news, business and finance, real estate, sports, automotive, art, theater, music, women's interest, foods, etc. The smallest community newspaper, with a staff of only three or four people, may categorize news by special interest, such as city-wide news that affects the community, school news, real estate news, sports, news of people, and so forth.

## The Media

The media for disseminating news, and particularly news that serves your market, are not confined to just your local newspaper. You have at least the following options:

- *Daily newspaper.* Every community is served by at least one, and usually several, newspapers. Larger cities may have two or more competing daily newspapers, and sometimes a morning and an evening paper. Smaller cities and towns usually have a daily paper for the city, and in some cases a county or area-wide paper. In many cases, smaller communities are served by both a local paper and the newspaper from the nearest major city. Many communities are served by local papers, most of which are published weekly. Because newspapers have the broadest news coverage they are the prime outlet for distribution of publicity material.

    Recently, media coverage of the professions has proliferated in two ways—increasing coverage of news from professional service firms, pertaining to technical material, and increasing coverage of the professions and the firms themselves. More newspapers have assigned the professions to reporters as a beat, and the media is seeing, publishing, and broadcasting news in what the professions themselves are doing.

- *Radio.* Most radio news is limited to small segments of time during the course of the day. This means that except for the all-news stations, most stations will be concerned primarily with news of broader interest to most of its listeners. From your point of view, the only news of your profession that might concern a radio station is either a professional story of such magnitude that it affects the whole community or feature material that might interest a larger audience. Smaller radio stations, however, frequently pride themselves on local coverage and could very well be interested in direct, on-the spot coverage of an interesting event that you might stage or sponsor, such as a seminar.

- *Television.* Television stations, except for the smaller ones and cable TV, usually devote remarkably little time to business and professional news in proportion to the total broadcast day—and particularly to news of activities that concern what they perceive to be a small portion of their total audience. Some stations might pick up events or feature material that would add a human interest or informative angle to a newscast, but in all cases that would depend entirely upon how heavy the news day has been. If it could be measured statistically, television as a publicity outlet for most business or professional news ranks a poor third after newspapers and radio.

  This appears to be changing, as more stations increase their business news coverage. This is particularly true of the cable news stations, such as CNN (Cable News Network) and FNN (Financial News Network). The number of financial and business channels and programs is growing, and their coverage is now extensive.

- *Trade Journals.* Most trade journals rely heavily on publicity sources for news. This in no way demeans trade journals—they simply tend to be short of staff, and must look to the companies and firms in the industries they serve to supply news. If the readers of a journal in a particular industry are in any way a part of your potential market, trade journals can be an excellent publicity outlet. A typical news story might address legal or accounting techniques that particularly concern the chemical industry, for example. This might be of interest to the chemical trade press. Trade journals number in the thousands, with some industries being served by several publications. These journals are listed in several directories (see Appendix).

- *Magazines.* There are two general categories of consumer magazines that you might consider—city or regional magazines and national magazines. City magazines, and particularly the growing number of them that are devoted to local business, are a natural outlet for feature material because of their geographic distribution and their editorial slant. The narrower the geographic distribution, the greater the likelihood that the editors will be interested in news and feature material from a local source. Most of the city magazines are fairly sophisticated, however, and are not often concerned with the kind of routine information in which people might be interested as members of a small community. Yet, these publications offer the opportunity for general feature material, citing you as a source, on subjects that spring from your expertise, and that affect or interest the general public. This might include, for example, how to choose a tax specialist, how to get a mortgage, and so forth. National consumer magazines, on the other hand, including news magazines such as *Time* and *Newsweek*, are not interested in any but the most unusual news that a professional might generate in the normal course of affairs. But the size of a professional firm's operation doesn't preclude considering opportunities to submit articles under your own name to appropriate consumer magazines, even though the distribution is far afield from his market. In this case, it's the reprint that counts. An article on "Five Ways to Finance a Home in a Tight Money Market" under your byline in *Family Circle* makes you a national authority. And reprints of it are better (and cheaper) than any brochure.

- *Penny savers and shoppers.* There are literally thousands of such publications distributed throughout the country at shopping centers, supermarkets, and sometimes door-to-door, that include editorial material as well as advertising. The editorial material is usually chatty and loaded with items of interest to community residents. They are a natural outlet for publicity to a very local community.

- *Other media.* Other vehicles for publicity consist of any media distributed to the public. This includes the house organs and newsletters of other companies (and even their bulletin boards), the journals of fraternal or church organizations and even the ads of other companies. When IBM runs an advertising campaign for its personal computers, using a small professional office as an illustration of the kind of business that can use the computer, it's an ad for IBM but publicity for the professional.

## Dealing with the Media

It's a primary rule in publicity that before you consider publicity in any medium you should spend time acquainting yourself with it. Each publication has its own editorial requirements and point of view, and you should look at several recent issues to try to fathom exactly what kinds of news or feature material each publication uses. *Harper's* or *Atlantic Monthly* are not likely to use news of four new partners, and in fact neither of those magazines uses news at all. Some daily newspapers publish a great deal of information about individual professional activities, and others publish news of only major consequence, such as a merger. If you sent a photograph to *The Wall Street Journal* to accompany a story you'd be wasting your time—*The Wall Street Journal* doesn't print photographs in its news pages. Knowing a publication's requirements is crucial.

A second major rule is that with rare exceptions, there is a high, thick wall between a publication's advertising and editorial departments, and if that wall is sometimes breached, it's never through an open door. Few consequential publications, and certainly none of any editorial quality, will make a regular practice of *quid pro quo* publicity in exchange for advertising. The fact that you're a major advertiser in any publication doesn't entitle you to breach the editorial independence of the paper except on the merit of your news or feature material alone. While it's true that advertisers sometimes have greater access to editorial pages than do nonadvertisers, any publication that allows its advertising department to influence its editorial department would rapidly lose its readers and its credibility with its audience. And since the value of editorial publicity is the implied editorial third person independent endorsement, using advertising clout for editorial space can be self-defeating. Even in the smaller publications such as some community newspapers, penny savers and so forth, where the practice of catering to advertisers is fairly common, the news should still be capable of standing on its own. Poor publicity is not better than no publicity at all.

## The News Categories

Within the media structure, there are several news categories that offer publicity opportunities for the professional; that serve as a framework for the strategies for publicity for a professional firm:

- *Straight news.* In the course of your daily activities any number of things might happen—or be made to happen—that are sufficiently different, and sufficiently out of the ordinary, to warrant interest by the readers and listeners of the news media. Certainly, if you win a landmark case in the Supreme Court, or merge your practice with a big national firm, that might well be news for the local paper as well as other media, and might well be considered newsworthy by local media. Depending upon the size of your firm and the size of the community in which it functions, some personnel news can be newsworthy as well. If you're the largest firm in town in your profession, and you've made one of your associates a partner, editors might like to know about it. If you're a small firm and just added two new associates, editors of publications covering your market area might well consider that important enough to publish. By reading the local media carefully—the media that service your market area—you can get a fair idea of the kinds of activities and events that might warrant publication.

- *Manufacturing newsworthy events.* With the absolute caveat that no attempt should ever be made to lie to or mislead a publication—it can ruin your chances for ever being successful in publicity—you can do a great many things to develop or manufacture newsworthy activities. Speeches and seminars are primary. Sponsoring community events often serve well. But publicity is more successful with ingenuity. For example, surveys (of which more further in this chapter) of attitudes or preferences within your expertise—attitudes toward a particular law, or high-rise vs. low-rise buildings—all of these are likely to interest editors. If they are well done, and well presented to the press, they will be reported.

But this kind of information must be assembled and presented to them. This is manufacturing a newsworthy event in the same way that having your staff dress in period costumes to commemorate a holiday might attract the attention of the local press. Again, this is a function of understanding the media that serves your area.

- *Feature material.* Newspapers aren't run on news alone. They have an educational function as well. The service article on how to get the most from a legal clinic, or how to chose an architect for a store front, or when it's safe to throw away old financial records, is as important to a newspaper as is the front page. This is feature material. It's the kind of story that serves as the backbone of most professional service publicity. As a professional, you're in a marvelous position to use your expertise to develop these very features.

- *By-line articles.* Magazines, Sunday supplements, and sometimes newspapers, and certainly trade and industry publications, are delighted to consider articles written by outsiders who have expertise. Local media are constantly looking for service material to help their readers function as better consumers, and their business readers to function as better business people. This would include articles on any appropriate subject in which you have expertise and authority.

## The Editors

The person responsible for selecting and publishing or broadcasting news is an *editor.* Some editors are giants of intellectual and journalistic perspicacity; others are not. Some are skilled and knowledgeable in the professions they cover; others are remarkably unsophisticated in those areas. But regardless of the publication, or the editor's professional capabilities, every editor has the same responsibility— to find news or feature material to meet the publication's readers' (or listeners') needs in terms of editorial position, to prepare it for publication within the context of style and format, and to publish it. This must be done with fresh material every day or week or month, depending upon the frequency of the publication. He or she may be the editor responsible for the entire publication or for just a department of it. Editors are aided in their task by *reporters*—journalists who are trained to gather news and write it in the publication's style. Sometimes editors do both editing and reporting.

In publicity, the important thing to remember is that the editor's responsibility is to give his or her readers what they want to read. What is consistent with the editor's needs is not always consistent with yours. The techniques of publicity are designed to make your needs consistent with the editor's.

## Delivering Publicity

Given an understanding of the media, and of the quality of newsworthy or feature material, it must be delivered to the publication in a way that's acceptable to editors; that's most likely to succeed in garnering the publicity. There are several specific techniques for accomplishing this.

### Direct Contact

The simplest way to deal with the press is by contacting the appropriate editor of a publication and discussing the story with him. Experienced publicity people know that the order of accomplishing this is:

- *Make sure you know what your story is.* Get it clear in your mind, read the publication, and be sure that your format for presenting the story on paper is consistent with the publication's own techniques for reporting similar stories.
- *Choose the media.* Not every story is for every publication. The news of a merger between two small firms is of interest only to those publications that serve the community involved. Unlike the news of a merger of two large national firms, it's not a national story. Winning a landmark decision, on the other hand, can be of interest to even the largest newspaper. Know your media so that you can determine what story is right for what publication.
- *Find the right editor.* In a small community weekly it's easy—there's usually only one editor. At a larger newspaper there are many editors covering different departments. If your local papers have editors covering your profession, you should make it a point to know who they are and to meet them and to let them know you. This is best done, however, by having a story for them on first contact. Your story may be a business story, in which case you'll want the business editor. It may be the kind of feature that should go to an appropriate features editor. The simplest way to find the right editor is to call the publication and ask for the name of the editor who covers the kind of story you have.
- *Contact the editor.* Start with a phone call, remembering that editors are tremendously busy people. They are constantly facing deadlines and are besieged by people like you who have story ideas for them. Introduce yourself, explain that you have a story, tell the gist of the story in as few words as possible and ask to come to see the editor. He will tell you very quickly whether the story's of any interest and whether it warrants further discussion. It may be a news item the editor can take over the phone or, if it isn't an absolutely timely story that will be stale news within 24 hours, he may ask you to send it in writing. In that

case, deliver it by hand, trusting the mail only for stories that will be as newsworthy a week from now as they are today. If the editor is interested in the story, you'll be asked to come down to the publication and discuss it, or if it's big news, the editor may assign someone to come to the site of the story to cover it. Ultimately, you'll want to establish a personal relationship with as many editors as possible. If an editor thinks that you have a large enough story or, more important, that you might be a fairly consistent source of news, he'll be delighted to accept an invitation from you for lunch or a drink after work. Most editors are professionals and build personal relationships slowly. They are not swayed by gifts or elaborate presentations. Just the story will do. Then you're doing your job and he's doing his.

Does a personal relationship with an editor make a difference? Only in that you're more likely to get a hearing for a story you have for the publication. Few editors will allow a personal relationship to affect their judgment of what's acceptable to their publication, nor is the friendliest editor likely to print a story as a favor to you that's not consistent with the editorial needs of his paper. Remember the competition for news space is extraordinarily keen. Editors receive five or ten times as much news as they can possibly print, and so the form of presentation of news to a publication is extremely important. It must attract attention for its essential news value in the shortest possible time. To ask a journalist to give you valuable space because of friendship rather than because of the quality of the news is to take unfair advantage of the friendship and jeopardize his position on the publication.

## The News Release

The news release is the standard form for distributing news to the media. The form of news releases is deceptively simple. Properly done, it looks easy.

In fact, it's not simple at all. It's a complex form of journalism, in which the news release writer competes directly with the professional journalist, and other news release writers, for scarce space or broadcast time. It competes, as well, with every other news release issued at the same time, and it competes in an arena in which the initial recipient, the editor, is not particularly receptive.

The physical form should be that which is accepted and traditional in most newspaper city newsrooms. It should be remembered that most city newsrooms receive hundreds—sometimes thousands—of releases every day. The editors charged with going over those releases grumble over the volume they receive, and invariably most releases end up in the wastebasket. They appreciate, however, those releases that are professionally prepared and which make their arduous job simpler.

Succeeding with news releases lies, primarily in understanding the journalistic process. There are some basic rules:

- *Printed news release letterhead.* The subject of the printed release head versus the blank sheet of paper is a matter of more debate than one would find at a philosophers' convention. Obviously, there's an element of silliness in the printed head that has the big words "NEWS FROM XYZ, CPAs" and then reports that John Jones has just joined the firm as a junior accountant. This is hardly earthshaking news for a paper the size of, say, *The New York Times*. The printed news release letterhead, on the other hand, is valuable if you're dealing with editors who have come to know you as a regular source of information. Printed letterheads are also acceptable from public relations firms that are well known by publications, and particularly if they're known to send news with a high percentage of acceptability.

  If you choose to use a printed letterhead, then every release must have at its top the date and the words, "FOR IMMEDIATE RELEASE," unless it's an advance story where the information is not to be released until a later date; in that case the line should read, "FOR RELEASE [date]." If a printed release head is not used, then the same statement goes at the top, but so too does the name, address and telephone number of the source of the news, including the name of the particular person to be contacted if more information is required. In any event, the release should be written (typed, of course, on one side of the paper only.)

  With the increased use of computers and laser printers, there is a growing tendency, incidentally, to produce news releases with a typeface similar to that used in printing. The result is a news release that looks more like an ad than like a news story. If you accept the fact that a news release works best when it's cast in the same format as is used in the newsroom, it would appear that the laser-printed release that looks as if it's typeset and printed is counter-productive.

- *The Headline.* Newspapers write their own headlines. Furthermore, the headline is never written—except perhaps in the smallest newspapers—by the person who writes the story itself. The purpose of a headline in a news release is to summarize the meat of the story, so that the editor can quickly determine whether the story warrants further attention. It should consist of no more than two lines, stating briefly and succinctly what the release is about—for example, "NEW AUDIT APPROACH SERVES NON-PUBLIC COMPANIES" The headline should be centered, all in capital letters, at the head of the release.

- *The Dateline.* Following the format used by virtually all daily newspapers, the first words of the release should be the dateline. This means the city or origin of the story and the date the release is issued: "Detroit, July 10 . . ."

- *The Text.* All releases should be double spaced with paragraphs indented and wide margins. This makes it easier for the editor to read, to mark up and to indicate notes in the margin.

## Writing the News Release

As for the writing, old myths die hard, and one of the most persistent is that newspaper articles—and therefore news releases—must start with the traditional five W's—who, what, when, where, and why—as elements for the lead of the story. The myth also says that news releases are edited from the bottom up, particularly when it comes to cutting for space, and therefore the least important information goes at the end.

You have but to read any good daily newspaper to know that papers are run on journalistic practice, not myths. In today's fast-paced journalism, the lead paragraph contains the most terse, exciting summary of the crucial heart of the story. It gets to the point of the release as quickly as possible. A good technique is to cover up everything but the first line or two of a release and try to see it with the editor's eye, since that's about as far as an editor will read before he decides whether the rest of the release is worth reading. Do those two lines impart something that is genuinely news? Do they get to the heart of the matter? The name of the company is not news—the facts are. The best possible first sentence might read, "The first building taller than ten stories to be built in Linwood is to be designed by Smith & Dale, local area architects, it was announced here today by..."

Each subsequent paragraph should cover a point of the story in descending order of importance—the lead paragraph with the primary news, the second paragraph with the next item of importance and so on. If it's appropriate, the mechanical facts—where and when, etc.—should be noted early in the story. Every topic of the story should be given its own paragraph for simple editing. Both for style and because so many newspapers now write and edit by computer, stories are no longer edited to fit the available space by cutting from the bottom. They are edited for style throughout the entire release, Writing paragraphs in descending order of importance, however, is frequently done for interest.

The text itself should be written in the journalistic style of the largest and best newspaper in your area, no matter what publication it's to be sent to. It should be written in simple English, grammatically correct, in the active—not passive—voice, and shouldn't read like a legal contract. Its job is to communicate—to impart news.

A news release should be straightforward and should not in any way editorialize. Opinions, projections, and other subjective points of view should not be reported as facts. They should either be put in quotes or otherwise attributed to a partner by name.

The last paragraph of the release should be a simple, one or two-line statement describing the company's business.

End the release with the traditional ending mark—the three number symbols—###. The old telegrapher's ending mark—30—is quaint, but has long since gone out of style and is infrequently used today.

Releases should rarely be more than one page long. If they are longer, then at the bottom of each page type the word "MORE," with a dash on each side, and at the top of subsequent pages should be a key word identifying the story ("NEW AUDIT TECHNIQUE") and the name of the issuing company, followed by the page number.

### Distributing the News Release

Releases sent to the press should be addressed to a specific editor by name only when you are sure that the editor to whom the release is addressed is, in fact, the appropriate person, that he is still employed at that publication in that capacity, and that he will be at his desk on the day the release will be received. Otherwise, it should be addressed to a departmental editor—Business Editor, Metropolitan News Editor, etc. If it's important to get the release into the hands of a specific editor at a specific time, it should not be mailed, it should be sent by messenger and followed up with a phone call to make sure that it's not stalled at the reception desk. If it's just a general release, designed for no specific editor, it should be addressed to the City Desk, a newspaper term for the editor who covers general news.

Except under extreme circumstances, it's bad form to call a newspaper to find out why your release wasn't printed. The chances are that it wasn't run because the editor didn't think it was important enough to print in his limited space, in relation to other information received that day. No newspaper is required to print any news, no matter how important it is to the firm, and pestering an editor will only incur animosity and risk that subsequent releases will find their way directly to the wastebasket. It is, however, appropriate to phone ahead, talk to the particular editor and advise him that the release is on the way. In view of the large number of releases received every day, if the news is important enough the editor will appreciate it and watch for it. It will not, however, guarantee that he will print it. There are times when it seems obvious that a release should have been printed and wasn't. It would be surprising, for example, if the announcement of a major event were not published in a local paper. Under these circumstances, it's perfectly appropriate to phone the editor—not to ask why the release wasn't printed, but merely to confirm that the release was received. Frequently the editor will appreciate it if he has reason to believe that news he should have received never reached him.

Radio and television should not be overlooked in a distribution of news releases. Many stations carry some business news, although considerably less than most newspapers. The measure is the importance of the news to the largest number of viewers or listeners. The newspaper reader disinterested in business or real estate can turn the page, the listener cannot. This is why radio and television editors choose only major items for their newscasts. In most cases it's pointless to send routine releases to radio or television stations. If, on the other hand, there is a reason to believe that something is particularly newsworthy, the station's news editor should be dealt with in exactly the same way as the newspaper editor.

## Feature Material

The approach to developing feature materially is generally different than it is for the straight news announcement. In feature development, you're usually addressing a subject in an explanatory way, and not in the terse, straightforward news release style. Nevertheless, the lead paragraph should be exciting and to the point, and preferably based on a news hook.

For example, "The new law that changed banking regulations, passed last week, can profoundly affect the smallest depositor, if he or she isn't paying attention to his account." It would then go on to explain the law, how it affects depositors, and what can be done to minimize the affect and increase the opportunity. As a professional, and an expert, your contribution enhances your authority, and your reputation.

In approaching this kind of press coverage there are several basic guidelines that are important. They apply whether the story is generated by you or by an outside public relations consultant:

- In a feature story it's even more important than in a news story that the target publication must be clearly understood. Several issues of the publication should be studied to determine the kind of material it uses, its style, its editorial viewpoint, and its apparent taboos. Any attempt to try to convince a publication to print a story that's not in keeping with its general editorial policy is not only a waste of time but could lead to a singularly adverse reaction by the editors to you, your firm, or your public relations consultant.

- Even a feature article must have a newsworthy point of view. Sometimes this is a hook—an event or activity that serves as a focal point for the story, an indication that the timing for the story is appropriate. Or it can be an angle that is at least unusual and perhaps unique, such as your new approach to financing a small business, or little used techniques of estate planning for individuals in lower income brackets. Developing feature material usually requires a measure of skill, if not artfulness. When a man murders his wife, it takes no public relations skill to get his name in the paper. The skill is in fathoming the unusual in an otherwise usual story, and projecting it as the basis for a feature article.

Approaching the publication requires some relatively simple procedures:

- Once a target publication has been selected and its editorial policies analyzed, the story is developed specifically for that publication. The same general story may function for several different publications, but each approach must still be tailored.

- Don't try to sell the same story to two competing publications at the same time. If both accept it you're in trouble for the future. Approach publications with feature stories one at a time.

- Find the proper editor, either by reading the masthead or by calling the publication and inquiring.

- Write a letter to the editor describing the story. In some cases the letter may be preceded by a phone call or even a meeting with the editor. Almost invariably, and with very few exceptions, the story will ultimately have to be presented to the publication in written form. Sometimes the letter presenting the story can be prepared before the first contact. Sometimes, if a discussion with the editor beforehand is feasible, the letter should be written only after the meeting and should be patterned on the guidelines set forth by the editor. Naturally, the letter should be brief and to the point, starting with the basic premise of the story, followed by a statement of fact to support that premise. It should indicate the availability of the people involved, and of the graphic or visual material, if appropriate, that's available or can be made available to supplement the story.

- A few days after the letter has been sent it's appropriate to follow up with a phone call to determine the editor's interest, to answer questions he might have and to make arrangements for whatever interviews or further discussions are necessary.

Feature stories are a major tool of any publicity program. They can be the core of a program for professional services. No opportunity to develop a feature story should be allowed to pass without some attempt to sell it.

## Major News Coverage

Major news can sometimes be treated somewhat differently than routine releases. If the news is of sufficient consequence to warrant greater attention than just routine release—dealing with a new national tax law, for example—there are other techniques that can be used.

*The national campaign.* Frequently, it's possible to anticipate national coverage of a major event in ways that redound to the credit of an individual firm, whether the firm is national or local. For example, if an event of national magnitude, such as the passage of a new law that affects a great many people nationally, is about to occur, the press will be seeking a source of expertise to help report it clearly to readers. By anticipating this, and through careful planning, becoming that source, there's an opportunity for grand scale publicity.

Given a reasonable lead time (two or three days or more), and a fair certainty of the event's taking place, at least the following steps should be taken:

- Garner all of the expertise you can marshal. For example, how is the law likely to read? How is it to be administered? what does it mean in terms of the Man in the Street? What are it's subtleties? What are its weaknesses and strengths?

- Organize all of the experts in your firm. If you have more than one office, identify a lead expert in each office. If you are a one-office firm, who are the experts in your office? These people become your spokespeople.

- Prepare your material, which should include ...

  - A news release
  - A position paper
  - A summary sheet (brief) about your firm, its expertise in the area, and why it's an appropriate source of information on the subject
  - A brief—*brief*—cover note (press advisory), explaining that the law is about to be passed, that it will affect a great many of the publication's readers, and that you're offering the enclosed to help the reporters in their coverage. Indicate that your firm and "the following list of people (with phone numbers)" are available for further information.

- A day or two before the expected passage, call key people in the press, remind them of the imminence of the law's passage, and offer to meet with them for a pre-passage press briefing. If you have more than one office, have a designated spokesman do this in every city where you have an office.

- Coordinate this effort with (if appropriate) both internal and external public relations staff, with each staff person assigned a different group of editors and publications. They will make the pre-passage calls.

- With all press materials prepared, the coordinated staff moves out the material to the press—by wire, by phone, and in person or by messenger—the very instant the bill is passed.

- After the material has gone out, and allowing time for it to have been received and digested, followup key editors by phone, offering your services.

Timing is crucial, simply because your competitors will be doing the same things—and the first with the best wins. And, experience has shown, wins big.

## News and How to Make It

In publicity, as in most other aspects of marketing, the strategy for a successful program for professional firms is somewhat different than it is for product or non-professional service campaigns.

### Projecting Expertise

In the early days of publicity, when it was low-down press agentry and not high-blown public relations, the idea was to get your client's name in the paper. Often. In any context. Just spell it right.

In the early days of marketing professional services, it became clear that merely to get your firm's name in the paper, in any context, didn't help much. Ego, maybe, but nothing more. A new approach to publicity had to be developed.

What worked, and is still an integral part of publicity for professional firms, was to get individual firm members' names quoted in a context of expertise. *"You can save a million dollars on taxes,"* according to John Smith of Bigeight & Co, *"by..."* Or, *"The party liable for your accident may be the person you'd least expect it to be..."* according to Harry Writ, of Writ & Writ.

This, in conjunction with such valuable activities as by-line articles and interviews on consequential subjects, has been at the heart of the professional services public relations program for quite a few years. Some firms developed it to an art, and could produce clippings in multiples of their competitors'. Soon, the competition for space was fought with clippings. Who got quoted more in *The Wall Street Journal?* Or *Business Week?* Or *The New York Times?*

But is this still the way to go? Is more still better?

For more effective coverage, probably not. In the early days, when few firms were doing any sophisticated public relations, the firms that could play the numbers game skillfully generated very high visibility. But ultimately, a few interesting facts emerged:

- Any name recognition generated by repeated mentions quickly faded when the mentions diminished for any reason. The staying power of name recognition built by these quickie mentions was very short-lived.

- As more sophisticated marketing techniques were brought into play, publicity became part of the overall program, and not necessarily the spearhead. While publicity is invaluable, the numbers game seems to contribute very little to the overall program.

- How do you convert those mentions, however many, into sales? True, reputation is important, and particularly the reputation for expertise. But it won't stand on its own, without moving people into a sales configuration.

- There got to be an easy tendency to rely on volume of mentions, rather than *quality* of mentions. This meant that a lot of effort was going into irrelevant publicity.
- As everybody learned the technique, everybody was getting into print, and nobody was distinguished. What had been exclusive became a mob scene, diluting the value of each mention for each firm.

An important element of publicity, in professional services marketing, is leadership. When you can't lead the pack, and are merely one of them, you're accomplishing little to enhance or establish your reputation.

More, then, is not necessarily better. Better is better. Less publicity, but each placement more relevant to the firm's marketing needs. Fewer clippings, but each with more impact to the firm's reputation for expertise.

In corporate or product publicity, merely getting the firm mentioned can be sufficient. In accounting or law or consulting, the problem is not just name recognition, but distinguishing one firm from another. This seems to be best accomplished by focusing on a firm's expertise in specific areas. And because expertise in professional services is resident primarily in individuals, getting individuals identified in the press is crucial.

In fact, this is fortunate, because the thrust of business news relies on expert support. The tax columnist in *The Wall Street Journal* couldn't do his column on taxes in any readable fashion if all he did was repeat government releases on tax rulings. He depends upon tax experts from accounting and law firms to point out loopholes, anomalies, and pitfalls, which is why so many of his items quote an individual. Articles on personal finance, or small business, rarely give advice or direction without quoting an authority.

## Getting Quoted

In developing a program to get partners quoted in the press, there may be many approaches, but what seems to work best is . . .

- Organize the program by service. Tax, consulting, audit, emerging business, and so forth. No firm is expert on everything across the board, and to try to present an entire firm in this way is like getting six people abreast through a narrow door at one time.
- Read the press you want to reach carefully to see who gets quoted, on what, and how. You can be imaginative in many ways, but you're not going to change the way the press works. Don't waste time on unlikely targets.
- Pick the individuals in the firm. (Or rather, have them designated by the firm). While everybody in the tax department deserves to be quoted, only those experts on particular aspects of taxation will indeed

be quoted. For example, there may be an expert on state and local taxes, one on repatriation, one on sales tax, and so forth.

- Don't overload. No matter how good you are, or how good your experts are, you can get only so much in print at one time.

- An important caution. Most by-line writers depend upon a few experts, and are frequently reluctant to go beyond them. If the reporter writing the regular tax column for the local newspaper needs a supporting quote or an interpretation, he or she knows specific individuals who can be depended upon to come up with an answer and a good quote in a quick phone call. Why should the reporter go beyond the established and reliable? This means that you've got to develop a solid relationship with that reporter. This is done by classic public relations devices—sending a series of short, terse releases with eminently usable quotes, or setting up an interview with a solid news hook to establish a relationship. It may take a while. Be patient.

- If you're a sole practitioner, or in a very small firm, you may find that a personal note to an editor works better than a release—if you're saying things that are useful to the publication. Certainly, a correspondence, rather than impersonal news releases, can establish valuable relationships.

- It's important to be sure that your partners understand the kind of thing that's wanted of them. Make them part of the effort to find quotable stuff—the ammunition for the campaign.

- Demonstrating expertise also includes by-line articles in trade journals or even the local press. The trade press article not only displays the expertise, and gives you a reprint to use for direct marketing, but serves as a basis for a news release to the national press. *"Most entrepreneurs lose money by not integrating personal and business financial planning, according to John Smith, a partner in the accounting firm. . . ."*

- Look to current events for opportunities for interviews and other press coverage. When an important new tax law was about to be passed, a major national accounting firm anticipated it by priming the partners in all offices on how to deal with the press; preparing news releases that interpret the law; assigning every available marketing person inside the firm and in the outside agency to a specific segment of the press; sending a letter to every appropriate editor advising that the local firm expert (name and phone number included) was available to help editors in their coverage. The minute the bill was passed—literally—it was all unleashed, by phone, by wire, by messenger. The result was that in city after city, as well as nationally, the press quoted the firm's experts twice as often as those of any other firm. A survey by the clipping service of all other Big Eight firms showed that the firm with the program was quoted at least twice as often, and in more major publications, than any other firm.

Does it all work? Absolutely. Given enough appearances in the press, a strong picture is developed of a firm's expertise in a specific area. The high visibility has impact that implies that the expertise is here—look no farther. With marketing followup, the effort pays off in marketing results. And it's a strategy open to the smallest, as well as the largest, practitioner.

And even if the primary objective is to enhance name recognition, it's still best done within the context of projecting expertise.

## The Survey

A poll or survey is frequently a useful way to get publicity.

There is something compelling and intriguing about surveys. Look at how they've taken over election reporting. There is now more coverage of polls and surveys that show how the people plan to vote, or how they view a candidate, than there is of what the candidates stand for.

But like so many valid marketing or publicity devices, there's an easy tendency to fall into the trap of thinking that any casually done survey will work.

Simply because a good survey gets space or air time doesn't mean that a bad survey will too. Assuming that the subject of the survey is interesting, it's the validity and credibility of the survey that get's the space, in most cases—not the survey itself.

A survey need not be elaborate or expensive. Its questions should be simple, and shouldn't cover too many areas. Silly questions may get space, but they get space because they're silly, and not because anybody takes them—or the surveyor—seriously.

The audience surveyed should be appropriate as well. Asking a hundred hot dog vendors the criteria they use for picking an accountant is silly; asking the same group how they feel about a new local tax law is virtually guaranteed space in a local paper.

Robert Hilliard, a leading public relations expert in professional services, developed the survey to an art form when he was at a Big Eight accounting firm. The firm ran a seminar series in a number of different areas. Each seminar was attended by fifty to a hundred people, each of whom was asked a single relevant question. The results of the survey were then publicized, with remarkably valuable results.

### The Index

In the same general category as the survey is the index, in which information developed by a firm on a regular and periodic basis is used to calculate an index.

Some years ago, Arthur Young & Company, then a Big Eight firm, took certain of its executive search placement results, calculated by the same criteria each quarter, and developed them into an index. By tracking this information and reporting it with a consistent formula, the index gradually took on a prestige and substance, and was duly reported by the major press each quarter.

It was not so much the validity of the underlying information that mattered as did the consistency. If the index was up or down in any period, that showed a valid trend that was more important than the underlying information.

In indexes, then, consistency and publicity matter a great deal.

## The Issues Campaign

The issues program described in the last chapter can generate a great deal of publicity, but only if it's properly managed.

Issues management, which is a specialty within public relations, considers the role of major issues in public and business life. This includes how these issues affect constituencies, and the role that individuals or companies can play in either swaying positions in the issues or educating the public about them.

For the professional, they offer a singularly prestigious opportunity for public exposure under the best possible circumstances.

While the techniques of full scale issue management are extensive, and require considerable professional skill to execute successfully, there are several considerations that can be examined:

- Is the selected issue of sufficient magnitude to concern a large enough audience to warrant a substantial effort? And is that magnitude sufficient to have a longevity that will allow you to make an impact before the matter is resolved or becomes passe?

- Is the issue relevant to your profession? For example, air pollution may be a matter dear to your heart, but not exactly relevant to your accounting practice. If you head an environmental law practice, however, it's an issue to consider.

- Is your expertise sufficient to give you credibility on the issue?

- Are you prepared to commit the time and dollars necessary for an investment in a professional issues program?

Do you have the staff, internal or external, to run the program? This includes researching the issue and constantly updating the research, developing your position, developing the platforms, preparing the material (speeches, articles, news releases, panels, etc.), and publicizing your activities in behalf of the issues.

Given a favorable answer to these questions, an issues program might serve your purposes very well.

## *The News Conference*

The old-fashioned press conference—or news conference, as it's now called out of consideration for the broadcast media—for routine news has gone out of style. Newspaper people are too busy to spend several hours away from their desks to attend a news conference. They get particularly disturbed—and appropriately so—if they're invited to a news conference and are led to believe that the news they will be given is of greater importance than it actually is. The fact that they're wined and dined is not of the essence. There's no law that says a journalist who accepts your hospitality has to print your story. Journalists are further annoyed at being invited to a news conference to be given news that can just as easily be covered by a news release or even a telephone interview.

A news conference should be called only when:

- The news is monumental
- There's some clear reason, such as demonstration or the need for an elaborate explanation, why the news cannot be covered by a news release
- Full understanding of the news requires questioning and elaborate answers

If a news conference is warranted, there are some basic procedures to be followed:

*The Invitation.* Unless it's a fast-breaking story, the invitation should be sent out several days to a week in advance of the event. It should state the purpose of the conference, and give the time and the place. It should indicate available facilities and accommodations for microphones and television cameras. If there are specific visual aspects to the story, they should be indicated, and a separate invitation should be sent to the photo desk of the publication, if there is one. If the news is important and urgent enough, send your invitations by telegram or night letter, but certainly not a week before the event. The urgency of the news implied by the telegram is defeated by the time lag. It's a good idea to telephone the invitees on the morning of the conference to remind them and to verify their attendance.

*The Place.* The place should always be appropriate to the event. If it's a major announcement about your firm, then it should be at your office if possible. The next best choice is a private room at a restaurant or club. (Obviously, a public table in a restaurant is an inappropriate place to hold a news conference). The room should be large enough to hold everybody comfortably, but not so large that the crowd seems dwarfed and the room seems empty. Set up the room well beforehand to assure that all speakers can be easily seen and heard, and that all graphic material is easily presented. Set up the room, as well, to accommodate television cameras and microphones.

*The Time.* The time for a news conference is determined by newspaper and TV station deadlines (most radio stations don't face deadline problems. They can

189

broadcast news almost immediately). The best time for a news conference is late morning, noon, or very early afternoon. News announced at a 10:00 A.M. news conference will make both the afternoon and next morning papers, and the 6 P.M. radio and television news. If it's a major story, the afternoon papers, which in most cities are not as widely read as the morning papers, will preempt the story, which will not please the morning papers. Be sure that everyone has time to hear the news and to write about it before deadline. Journalists still go back to their offices and pound typewriters or word processors. Only in the movies do they rush to the phones to call the city room.

*Press Kit.* A complete press kit should be prepared for every newsperson attending. This should consist of a basic release, a background sheet on the company, any financial or other background material, 8" x 10" glossy photos captioned with a half sheet attached at the bottom and any other pertinent material such as brochures or descriptive literature. Half sheet captions on photos should be headed exactly as are news releases so that if the caption is detached from the photo the information is complete. The photo should also be identified on the back with a label, for the same reason. Do not write directly on the back of a photo since it will mar the surface of the photo on the other side. Make the press kit as complete as possible, but don't overload it with so much material that a reporter can't find the facts for all the paper.

*The Presentation.* The presentation itself should be short, simple and to the point. While there's a great temptation to dramatize, few journalists are impressed by this. The drama should come from the material, which should be simple, to the point and graphically illustrated. It should take no longer than thirty or forty minutes to present, and time should be allowed for questioning. Immediately following the news conference, representatives for the company involved should be prepared to spend a few minutes to answer any reporters' questions. Some should be available by phone for the remainder of the day to answer any question that may occur to a reporter back at his desk writing the story.

### The Video Release

Growing in popularity are video releases, which are really news releases on video tape. They are usually made and distributed by production companies that specialize in them.

The purpose is to supply an interesting video story to television stations that might otherwise not cover an event.

If the right story is used—which is rare and difficult in professional services, since there is little that can be dynamically and graphically represented—a one or two minute tape can sometimes garner great exposure on TV news stations.

## The Interview

One of the advantages of being known to publications as a good news source is that you're frequently called upon to comment on, or contribute to, stories of interest to the publication's readers. In fact, becoming a major source of expertise in your field is a primary public relations objective. For example, if a newspaper, on its own, plans to do a story on a new tax law, and the writer knows you and you've established a sound relationship, he or she is more likely to call on you (rather than your competitor) to express your point of view, or to give technical help.

The relationship is important because journalists tend to depend upon sources they know, trust, and can be relied upon to deliver clear and useful information at deadline time. This relationship takes time to build, but it's worth it. It's done by consistently supplying useful material to the writer. After a reasonable period, the writer comes to know the contributor, and the relationship is established.

Another situation in which you might be interviewed is one in which the contact has been generated by you or your public relations staff. Here, it's presumed that you're on solid footing. You've been briefed, or at least had time to think out what you're going to say, and you've had time to anticipate questions and to frame answers.

While there's no way that every possibility in a press contact can be anticipated, there are some basic elements that can be prepared.

You should know, first, that being interviewed by the press, even with a single question, takes you behind the scenes of the journalistic process. While normally all you see of it is the polished result, you rarely get to understand the process. Some basics:

- Except on small weekly papers, the reporter you talk to is only one link in a chain. He or she usually reports to an editor, who may in turn be responsible to a managing editor. This means that the story the reporter writes passes through a number of hands, and may not be the story that gets printed. And it's presumed that you know, by now, that the person who writes the headline may not even know the reporter. The headline writer works from final text.

- The crucial fact here is that the reporter is not likely (with exceptions) to be expert in the subject you're talking about. The reporter also lacks your emotional concern with it. Tomorrow he or she will be covering something very different. And the farther up the editorial chain the copy gets, the less the knowledge or concern about the subject. It's just not as important to the reporter as it is to you.

- Reporters have time constraints that may conflict with yours. They're usually on a deadline. This can make them more curt than you would like them to be.

What this all boils down to is that these are facts to be kept in mind during an interview. How to handle it, then?

- *Be well briefed, if possible.* This may mean rereading a few memos, or, in the case of a major interview, building a briefing book with the help of others in other departments, and learning its contents.

- *Anticipate questions.* Not just the easy ones, but the tough ones, too. In an in-depth interview, you're not likely to anticipate all the questions, but the more the better. Try to avoid curves.

- *Get the answers down very carefully.* This is where that "I was mis-quoted" syndrome is avoided. The less you have to say on the wing, the better you're going to like the way the story comes out.

- Rehearse. Unless you're a former Secretary of State, with experience in being interviewed almost daily, the more you rehearse the fewer mistakes you're going to make.

- List the key points you want to make, in order of importance. You may not get to make them all, nor will you be assured that they all get printed, but that list of points is the spine of the successful interview.

For a successful interview, everything depends upon this list of points, because if you're careful, and skillful, you can lead the interview. How? By crafting your answers so that those points are made, *even, sometimes, if they are not directly responsive to the question.*

How does it work?

Question:     Do you plan to open other offices?

Answer:       Yes. *(Responsive to the question. Then add:)* We'll use two criteria to select sites— economic and market needs for our specialized services

Keep it up, and you'll be very subtly running the interview. And if you're calm and friendly and cooperative, and the reporter brings no inherent hostility, and his or her editor doesn't cut or rewrite it, the story will come out the way you want it to.

## The Crisis Call

The real problem comes when there is a fast-breaking and controversial news situation, and you're unprepared for the call or the questions. Or when there is the loaded press inquiry. "We hear one of your clients is going to jail. Do you have any comment?" It can be a naked feeling.

When you're the victim of adverse news—a problem not always restricted to the larger practitioner—the situation is particularly sensitive. It can happen to anyone. If a newspaper reporter who knows you calls before the story breaks to get your side of it, you should, of course, think carefully before you answer. But at the same time, those experienced in situations of this kind know that it's better to simply state facts, never deal in personalities, and try not to be defensive. Controversy on even the most routine subject is more newsworthy than straightforward reporting on noncontroversial news of greater importance. Reporters seem to have an instinctive tendency to ask the kinds of questions that breed and inflame the controversy. With that thought in mind, think carefully.

The problem is that in most businesses, the frequently onerous role of dealing with the press is usually left to the public relations staff. Not so in professional services. The phone call can come to anybody, and frequently does.

Those inquiries from the press that are client-related (or may relate to the client of another firm), or involve your firm, are particularly taxing. They may be controversial, and are potentially hostile. In those cases, a reporter is merely doing a job when he or she tries to solicit a controversial statement on a matter, or to badger you into saying more than is appropriate.

While it's difficult to make hard and fast rules about dealing with the press beyond the normal professional considerations and bounds of confidentiality of client matters, there are a few guidelines you may find helpful in dealing with press inquiries.

The objective should be to remain politely aloof and uninvolved, without fostering animosity with a member of the press with whom you might want to deal in your own behalf sometime in the future. The following hints may be useful:

- If it's a matter in which you might anticipate a press inquiry, your position should be drawn beforehand. It should be written and distributed to key people in your office who might get a call from the press. Preferably, in such matters, specific spokesman should be designated, and appropriate personnel should be advised that all calls on that matter should be given to the designated spokesman.

- Because people not used to dealing with the press are frequently surprised when they see that statements made in all innocence look very different in print than they did when they were spoken, there is an advantage in writing out a position beforehand. If a call is not anticipated, always think of how you can minimize your comments, and how your words will look out of context in hard type.

  The shock is when that nice, rational remark you made—you know, the witty one—shows up in print. "I was misquoted."

  Maybe, but probably not. This is the point at which you learn that how it sounds isn't necessarily how it reads. Gone from the printed words are the inflections, the half-smile, the arched eyebrow that gave the spin to the words. What's left, in cold type, can be harsh, possibly out of context, and a distortion of what you really meant to say.

And this assumes both the good will and the skill of the reporter, which can sometimes be more a presumption than an assumption.

- Usually, it's not advisable to give a press a statement "off the record." While a journalist may respect your request, he's not going to like you for it unless it serves as legitimate background for him to understand something that you can say on the record. Journalists, remember, make their living on what they can print—not what they *can't* print.

- There is nothing more challenging to a reporter than to hear someone say "no comment." It's a red flag. On the other hand, if you were to smile, and say in a friendly way, "I'd like to help you, but you know it would be a violation of professional ethics (or client confidentiality) for me to discuss that with you," you're asking him to understand that you'd really like to help him, but you can't for reasons beyond your control.

  And again, as you'll see further in this chapter, there are exceptions.

- It helps to keep people informed—and to have them keep you informed—of potential situations where the press may be involved. If everyone is alert to potential danger and there's preparation beforehand, then the likelihood of being misquoted—or worse, being quoted accurately in a misstatement—diminishes substantially.

It's all very well to try to reduce press relations to rules, but press relations is real life, and life doesn't work that way. Press relations is also judgment and making tough decisions, including whose advise to take on how to deal with the press. Being calm helps, and so does being rational and thoughtful.

Sometimes, in press relations, being able to walk on water helps, too. But we can't have everything. We can only try.

If you find yourself in such a situation and have no opportunity to present your side before the story appears in print, your best tack is to calmly call the editor and ask him for the opportunity to present your side. This may require a letter to the editor, which should be carefully, carefully prepared. And this assumes, of course, that the editor wants to hear and print your side of the story.

### Relating to Journalists

While it seems obvious that your relationships with the media are enhanced by being cooperative, you needn't abdicate your own intelligence. Good media relations doesn't always mean cooperating with the media.

Are there ever times to tell the press to go away and leave you alone? Maybe.

On the face of it, the press seems to have all the power. They speak to a lot more people than you do, and they do it with what the general public accepts, usually unquestioningly and not always with good reason, as objectivity.

Virtually every company, and every marketing or public relations executive, has a story of being trashed by the press—sometimes despite following all the rules and cooperating extensively.

But then, there are stories of companies that refused to deal with segments of the press, and are still around. Mobil refused to talk to Wall Street Journal reporters for years. There is no empty crater where Mobil once was; they still thrive.

There may indeed be times, then, when being cooperative with the press is not the best thing you can do for your firm.

If you're dealing with a hostile reporter or publication, and believe you're in a no-win situation, you may have more to gain than to lose by refusing to cooperate.

If you're dealing with a publication whose editor thinks that his publication is more important than it really is, and you know you're not going to get a fair shake anyway, why waste your time?

If you're asked to comment about a competitor, or about a situation in your industry to which you're ancillary, and there's any chance that your comment may be misinterpreted or even misreported, here, the straightforward "no comment" is warranted.

There are many comparable situations, but they all add up to one thing—blind obedience to all rules, particularly the rules of marketing, doesn't always make sense.

The rules of media relations aside, the governing factor should be the well-being of your firm. There are values to public relations, obviously, and there times when, despite the negative aspect of the story, you have an obligation to tell your side. But not always, and not universally.

Frequently, the press will trash a firm. A few years ago, a major public relations firm took a beating on the front page of a major newspaper. Conventional wisdom at the time was that because of the story and the place in which it appeared, the firm was through.

It didn't happen that way. After a flurry of trade discussion, and possibly the loss of a potential client or two (no current clients were lost), the firm continued to thrive. Why? Because one story, positive or negative, doesn't have much effect. Only an ongoing campaign, positive or negative, has sustaining results.

So if you know that you're going to take a beating no matter what you say or do, or if you know that the reporter is unlettered or unknowledgeable in the subject and is only passing through the beat, or if you know that commenting is going to get you involved in something that may turn out to be flat, stale, and unprofitable to you, then tell the press, politely but firmly, that you won't cooperate.

If you know that a reporter is misrepresenting to you what he's writing, in order to get your participation in a story that you might otherwise be reticent about, or if that reporter has done that to you in the past, you're perfectly right to decline.

In fact, participating in a roundup story should be done cautiously anyway, with you asking the reporter as many questions as he or she asks you. And if you do consider participating, take notes of what you're being told about the nature of the story. You may want to complain later.

The press has an inalienable right to pursue. They don't have an inalienable right to catch. There's a difference between being firm in declining and being rude. Rudeness is somebody else's game. Declining firmly and politely may very well be the way for you to win your game.

### When Publicity Goes Wrong

What happens when you do it all right—when you follow every rule of media relations to the letter—and it still comes out all wrong. Does that mean that the process is wrong, or that the journalists haven't been controlled properly? Can journalists, in fact, be controlled by process.

Probably not. For all that the myth about that elusive *spin control* implies, when it comes to the media, we propose—but others dispose. Thus it was, and thus it always shall be, so long as we have a free press.

Sometimes, despite all of the public relations professionalism, and despite all the cooperation we may offer the press, the story comes out badly. Disaster, dispensed in the aura of a supposedly objective press, doesn't merely strike, it reverberates.

The picture you so carefully and accurately painted is distorted, the wrong people are quoted and the right people are not, the facts are warped and bent beyond recognition, and the whole piece reads as if it were written by your most malicious competitor. Certainly, it will be relished by your every detractor.

### The Experts' Advice

Beyond the first scream of outrage, what can you do? Or more significantly, what has been done most effectively by others who have lived through it—and survived?

Perhaps the hardest factor of a negative story to deal with is that most people who are not professional marketers tend to overreact. At one extreme is incredible upset and anger; at the other is casual disdain that says, "so what, no one will believe it." Neither extreme is warranted nor accurate.

The most useful course, then, is to do nothing until you've recovered from your anger. Even doing the right thing in the wrong frame of mind can perpetuate, not cure, the damage. So . . .

- Don't act precipitously. Think of every action in terms of possible reaction. What seems like a good idea at the moment may be a backfire next week.
- After you've gotten over the emotional impact and the anger, don't think vindictively. You may have to live with that publication again someday, and vindictiveness in any event is not profitable.

- Assess real—not assumed or presumed—damage. That's where you've got to focus your attention. Much assumed damage at first light disappears when the sun comes up. What's left is damage you can deal with.

It's this last point that's crucial to successfully limiting the damage of bad press. Too often, the defense is predicated on imagined damage, in which case the reaction is an overreaction, and causes more damage than the original article.

Experts rarely concern themselves with why it happened. Unless libel is involved, it doesn't really matter. The reporter could have functioned out of ignorance or laziness. Reporters are people, and are not immune to such foibles as preconceived notions that can subvert the professionalism of even the most experienced journalist. There may have been an adverse chemical reaction to somebody in your firm, or a fight at home that morning. It fact, it really doesn't matter, because the reason for an adverse story is rarely an element that can be dealt with in damage control.

There are some specific questions to be addressed:

- What does the article *really* say? is it bad because it's wrong—or because it's right?

- Is the article distorted because the facts are wrong, or because they are put in a wrong context that distorts the facts? What is the real damage? Is it libelous? Misleading enough to cause real business damage? Or just embarrassing?

- Consider the publication. Is it widely read, or will people you care about never see it? (Consider that under certain circumstances, your competitor may want to make a point by sending a reprint of the article, along with a favorable one about himself from the same publication). What's the publication's reputation for credibility?

- Is the potential damage internal as well as external? Sometimes an unfavorable article can hurt internal morale more than it affects an external perception of the firm.

## The Impact Fades Quickly

Staying power is an important consideration. How long after publication will the story, or at least it's negative aura, linger? Depending upon the publication and the nature of the story, considerably less time than you think. As one experienced marketer put it, the impact fades quickly, but the impression can linger.

Some time ago, a major professional firm was savaged in the press for nepotism. The impact was shocking. In fact, the firm not only lost very little business, but continued to grow. Did the story, on the other hand, contribute to competitive defeats? Hard to say. An impression may have lingered in a prospective client's mind, and contributed to other negatives. But ultimately, the damage was nowhere equal to the impact and shock of the article's first appearance.

### Responding to the Damage

Assessing the damage accurately allows you to choose the appropriate response. There are, in fact, a number of inappropriate responses. You can:

- Sue, but only if there is real libel and real—and demonstrable—damage. There rarely is.
- Get on the phone and scream at the editor. Good for your spleen, lousy for your future with at least that segment of the press. And you'll never win.
- Write a nasty letter to the publisher. Only slightly better than screaming, but with the same results.

On the other hand, there are some positive things that can be done:

- Avoid defensiveness. Plan positively.
- Warn people. If you know an article is going to appear that might be unfavorable, alert your own people, so that it doesn't come as a surprise.
- Have a plan and a policy, preferably before you need it. This should cover how to deal with the press, who does it and who doesn't how to deal with client reactions, how to deal with internal reactions. It should cover how calls are handled, who responds and who routes calls to whom, what to say to clients and who says it, and so forth.
- A letter to the editor is important, if only to go on record. But it should be positive, non-vitriolic, and deal only with the facts. It should not sound petulant or defensive.
- Deal with the real damage. If the real damage is in specific markets, mount a positive public relations campaign aimed specifically at those markets. If the damage is internal, try to assess the root causes for the negative reaction. It would take a powerful article in a powerful journal to demoralize a firm that's otherwise sound and comfortable with itself.
- Consider how a competitor might use the piece, even within the bounds of propriety. It could be, for example, reprints to a particular market. Offset this with positive publicity to the same market.

No story is so bad that it should warrant extreme reaction. No publication that's still publishing is so devoid of credibility that some readers won't accept what they read. The role of the professional trained and experienced marketer is to maintain perspective, to assess the damage appropriately, and to see that the response is equal to—but does not exceed—the damage.

If bad press meant nothing, then neither would good press, and we know that consistently good press means a great deal. But one story—good or bad—rarely has sufficient impact to seriously aid or damage a company (although a negative story is more titillating than a positive one). Most positive public relations is a consistent series of positive articles, interviews, and news stories. If a negative press consists of more than one story, then the problem is usually not the press— its the subject of the stories.

The perspective of the bad story, then, requires dealing with it as an anomaly. This means dealing with it as a calm and rational business decision. And no business decision, in any context, is ever a sound one if it isn't arrived at rationally and professionally.

## Merchandising Publicity

Since you can't always assume that everybody you wanted to see or hear your story was reading the paper on the day it appeared or was broadcast, you should arrange for reprints of the publication or transcripts of the broadcast. With permission from the publication or broadcasting station, which is usually readily granted, you take the story from the paper or a typed version of the transcript and turn it into an inexpensive brochure. This allows you to paste it up as a continuous story and to add your own editorial comment. The reprint is then distributed in exactly the same way as you would distribute any brochure.

In fact, the reprint, as you've seen, can be more valuable than the original story, because it allows you all of the advantages of the original appearance, plus the opportunity to repackage it to your advantage. It then becomes a superb direct mail piece.

## Cost

In budgeting a publicity program, whether you're doing it yourself or using outside counsel, costs are somewhat different than they are for advertising. Agency fees aside, the major costs are for reproduction and mailing of releases, photography, messenger services, subscriptions to appropriate publications, and the cost of any special events you may develop for publicity purposes. If your program is large enough and you have reason to believe that your publicity is appearing in a number of different places beyond those of your immediate and daily reach, you can retain one of several clipping services to be found in the Yellow Pages in most big cities. Clipping services charge a flat monthly fee plus a small charge for each clipping they find and send you.

Publicity is an important part of any marketing effort because it complements advertising and promotion, and extends and enhances the selling aspects of advertising and the attention and traffic-building effects of promotion. Given a reasonable amount of time, the success of a publicity program may be measured by both the amount and quality of press coverage you receive and the general feeling you have that it's advancing your marketing efforts in terms of recognition, reputation, and support.

# 12

# Speeches and Seminars

Well before the changes in the canons of ethics, speeches and seminars were among the few promotional devices not prohibited, and so they were crucial to effective practice development. Despite their clear promotional aspects, speeches and seminars can be construed as proffering a public service, in that they use the platform to impart knowledge. That they also enhance one's reputation, build prestige, and expose one's self to prospective clients, seemed irrelevant to ethical concerns. Speeches and seminars perform a useful service.

It behooves the professional, then, to pursue these activities assiduously, and to do them meticulously, with every aspect of marketing value extruded from them.

## Speeches

People who've achieved some prominence or visibility for their expertise and authority are frequently invited to address audiences. These audiences may range from highly visible national organizations, where press coverage is extensive, to small local groups. Except for a very few prominent professionals, these invitations are usually serendipitous, and are most often random. The superstars—highly visible politicians, TV-nurtured personalities, best-selling authors—are all in another category. With the help of agents and lecture bureaus, they command high fees.

But in a marketing context, it becomes necessary to develop these opportunities. The value of the exposure to a defined audience, and the opportunity to enhance reputation, shouldn't be left to chance. And the opportunity to extend each speech with reprints, and to adapt the speech into an article, magnifies many times the basic value of each speech. It's a prime practice development tool, and should be assiduously pursued by both large and small firms.

In fact, the sole practitioner is on a par with the partner of the largest firm, when it comes to speaking engagements, assuming that each has relevant expertise.

## Planning a Speech Program

Like all things that seem random, an effective speaking program doesn't happen by itself. Speech making, particularly as part of a marketing program, requires planning.

It begins with specific objectives, derived from the answers to these questions:

- Who are your target audiences?
- What do you want them to know, think, or feel as a result of a speech or series of speeches?
- How will this speech program be integrated into the overall marketing program, and be both supported on its own and used to support other activities?
- What are the specific topics to be presented, and for what clearly defined purpose?
- Who in your firm is going to participate in the program?
- What is their long-term availability for speaking engagements?
- Who is going to write the speeches?
- What kind of support (reprints, articles, publicity, etc.) will be given and who is to do it?

The answers to these questions are an important guide to focusing efforts, and avoiding wasted time and money. For example, if the objective is to build relationships to the banking community, then you know precisely which organizations to court, who is to speak, and how to select topics.

### Finding the Platforms and Forums

Platforms and forums for speeches include any organization that holds meetings and uses outside speakers—a wide, wide world. There are, in fact, so many platforms and forums that the appetite for speakers is voracious.

Major platforms, offering national exposure, exist in several large cities, and range from The Economics Club of Detroit to college campus-based organizations. These platforms, obviously, seek people of national stature, or experts on subjects of national interest.

Many local organizations in larger cities, such as chambers of commerce, rotary clubs, etc., are also of sufficient stature to be considered national. Other national platforms include trade associations at annual or more frequent meetings.

But virtually every city or town, regardless of size, has local organizations that can serve as platforms for the professional. The size of your firm, and the size of your community, offer no obstacles to this kind of exposure.

In developing a speaking program, two key points to remember are that most organizations plan their programs well in advance—sometimes six months to a year ahead; and in selecting platforms, you must become familiar with the organization's interests and their recent speakers and topics.

A valuable tool in developing any speaking program is the directory of trade associations, called *National Trade and Professional Associations of the United States* (Columbia Books, Washington, DC).

Keep in mind, in choosing platforms, that while a platform is important and lends context and perhaps prestige to the speech, the reprint is even more important. The reprint, too, benefits from the prestige of the platform. No matter how prestigious the platform, or how large the audience, it will never equal in size the number of people that the reprint will reach. And as part of a larger program, the public relations and article follow-up offer a value that multiplies the value of the original speech.

## Who Participates?

Every individual in a firm who is capable of imparting expertise, and who is not pathologically shy, should be part of a speaking program. Obviously, a very junior associate is not likely to be accepted as a speaker on a national platform, nor is a very senior partner going to spend too much time addressing an obscure organization without a profound reason to do so. With careful planning, however, topics and platforms can be developed for every member of your firm who has any ability to participate in the program.

## Selecting the Topics

Selecting the topic for a speaking program goes beyond a simple catalog of your expertise. What's the information that your audience may want to hear? The keen competition for some of the more popular platforms is won by your ability to persuade a program chairman that what you have to say is precisely what his group wants to hear or needs to know, whether your subject is technical or a partisan point of view on a currently popular topic.

Topics, then, must be current, significant to the audience, and cast in a mode that makes a clear contribution to the group you plan to address.

## Soliciting an Invitation

In developing a speech program, don't lose sight of the competitive aspects of it, particularly in making your availability known. Many other people, including your competitors, are trying to get the same speaking engagement. Once you've identified the platforms you want to be invited to, soliciting a speaking platform requires its own marketing program. Take these steps:

- When the topic is chosen, a description of it should be written, cast in terms of the perceived needs of the prospective audience.

203

- A letter should go to the program chairman of each organization describing the speech, the key points you intend to cover, and the advantages to the audience. For major platforms, this can sometimes be preceded with a phone inquiry.
- A brief description of the speaker, his qualifications, and his experience as a speaker should be included. In describing the qualifications, emphasis should be on the expertise most pertinent to the topic.
- Three or four weeks after the letter of inquiry has been sent to the program chairman, there should be a follow-up telephone call, if no reply has been forthcoming.
- Availability within a time frame of six months to a year should be clearly stated.
- A description of the firm should be included.
- A modicum of substantiating material should be included (reprints of articles by the speaker, descriptive material about the firm, etc.).

## *Writing the Speech*

Writing a speech, as is the case with any writing, is an art form within the context of a formal structure. And with any art form, there are more rules promulgated by non-artists than can possibly be calculated. There are many schools of thought about whether a speech should be fully written out, or whether an outline and notes are sufficient. This, of course, depends upon the speaker and his or her experience. Some speakers are sufficiently talented to give a superb extemporaneous presentation; others are more comfortable with a fully prepared speech. In fact, one does not preclude the other. For the speaker who prefers to be extemporaneous, or to speak from an outline and notes, the fully written speech isn't a waste. It's reprintable, and can be distributed even if it isn't read verbatim. It also helps even the most experienced speaker to organize thoughts.

And even the most experienced and talented speaker will sometimes find it to his advantage to use a professional speechwriter. Not only is time-saving a factor, but with the right speechwriter, objectivity and input can be tremendously useful.

In working with a professional speechwriter, there'll be long discussions of the topic and points of view. If you're working with a speechwriter for the first time, he wants to learn not only what you want to say, but what you want to emphasize, the points you want to cover, the points you particularly want to avoid, your speech rhythms and patterns, and your personality in regard to the material. Any professional speechwriter will take a speech through several drafts, the first of which may be so far afield as to be discouraging. Don't be discouraged. Until something is on paper for you to react to, it's almost impossible for a speechwriter to track your thinking with you. Frequently, ideas that you've articulated in a conversation take on a different cast when viewed on paper. Ideas on paper will generate other ideas leading to subsequent drafts. It may take many drafts before the final draft, which you must then polish to match your own style, pacing, phrasing, language, and so forth. If you prefer to speak from notes, the notes can be abstracted from this final draft.

In writing your own speech, there are a few pointers to keep in mind:

- Talk to the paper. You're not writing a contract.

- Talk to an individual. Visualize a single member of the audience, and talk to him as you would in a conversation.

- Outline your thoughts. Whether you use the formal outline structure you learned in school, or simply scratch a few ideas down on the back of an old envelope, blocking out the ideas helps organize your thoughts and saves time.

- A strong opening is important. This doesn't necessarily mean the standard but trite, "Funny thing happened to me on the way to the theater ..." opening joke. Unless you're genuinely funny, and unless the story serves a specific purpose relative to your material, stay away from it. But a startling or an interesting opening is extremely important, gets the audience's attention, and sets the mood and the pace for the rest of the speech.

- Stick to the point. Keep in mind the objective of the speech and what you're trying to accomplish. What is it you want the audience to know, think, or feel after they've heard your speech? Keep it simple and logical in progressing from one idea to the next.

- Edit, edit, edit. Professional writers often allow a day or so to pass before editing a draft. It brings a fresh perspective to the material.

- When you think you have it, let it sit for a few days, and then read it aloud. It is, after all, a speech and not an article. Frequently, beautifully written prose reads well on paper but doesn't speak well as a speech. If it doesn't make you self-conscious, you may want to record your reading and listen to the speech yourself.

## Delivering the Speech

Some people make speeches regularly, and do them well. They're a pleasure to listen to. Some people make speeches as if there were a gun to their heads. Some people make rules about how to make speeches, and the trouble with that is that few rules (about anything, in fact) work well universally.

The one rule about speech making that does work, though, is to understand who you are in regards to speechifying, and what works for you. And then stick to that.

Speaking styles, like so many other things, have fads. A current fad is to steer away from the typed speech and to work from note cards. If you can do it, fine.

But if you can't, why add feelings of inadequacy to the anxiety of making speeches?

There are several ways to deliver a speech, and some are great for some people and bad for others. Ultimately, you've got to choose the technique that works best for you, and not be forced into somebody else's idea of what's right.

For example, how many times have you been told that you shouldn't make a speech without visual aids? Nonsense. Visual aids can be useful in some contexts. They can be so distracting, in others, that they destroy the effectiveness of the speech. Everybody's watching the pictures and nobody's listening to what the speaker has to say. Of course, if what you have to say is less important than the numbers on the screen, then you should know that too.

The rules aren't wrong, by the way. It's the insistence that they're the only rules that work that's wrong. For example . . .

- Unless you're a trained and experienced speaker, don't use a typed speech—use 3 x 5 cards with notes.

The idea is to be spontaneous, and if you look and sound like you're reading, you're likely to be dull. And some people *are* dull when they read. They make a great speech sound like an insurance contract. Speaking from notes or an outline is supposed to be answer.

But suppose that between inexperience and stage fright those notes on a subject on which you're a leading expert suddenly become incomprehensible. Wouldn't it be nice, to keep those beads of sweat on your forehead from blinding you, if you could reach into your pocket and pull out a well-written, clearly stated speech? For some people, the notes are great. They can appear to be spontaneous. But if you're not one of those people, read from the page, and practice looking up occasionally. You'll be better off.

Some people, in fact, can indeed speak extemporaneously, and be lucid and coherent and interesting. But it's a talent, or it can be learned only with extensive training and experience.

Another rule . . .

- Make eye contact, do it frequently with somebody in the audience. Somebody differently each time, presumably.

Making eye contact is the result, not the process. The process is that you're not preaching—you're talking to people. If you grasp that concept, you'll make eye contact regularly. That's the way it works, not the other way around. People who have no trouble speaking to individuals can come close to heart attacks when they're up on a platform.

But if you can see the entire audience, in your mind, as one individual, and talk to—even with—but not *at*—that individual, then you're going to be heard and understood. And eye contact becomes a natural, not artificial, thing to do.

Which brings up another point. What a speech is about is not a performance by an individual, but an individual's imparting information to (or trying to persuade) a group of people. While this is the simplest and most obvious point about speechifying, it's the one that most often gets lost. It's like those golf teaching programs that talk about your swing and your grip, and somehow forget to tell you what the game's really about.

Do you remember Professor Harold Hill in *The Music Man?* In the end, he taught the kids to play the instruments he sold them by getting them to think the tunes, not by learning the notes and the scales. While that may have been an amusing fancy, it does indeed work for the inexperienced public speaker.

The rules aren't as important as your learning to tell me, as clearly, forcefully and persuasively as possible, what it is you wanted to say. And do it your way. Look at me, as you would if we were alone in a living room, and tell me. You've done it a million times before.

If you do it that way from the platform, you'll be great.

And if you're concentrating on talking to me, and not on making a speech, then you won't have to worry about those other problems, such as where to stand, and what to do with your hands. It won't matter, because I'll be *listening* to you—not *watching* you.

Some more rules.

- Start out with a joke.

Not if you don't normally tell jokes. How'd you like to start a twenty minute stint of being exposed on a platform, after your first joke left 'em stony-faced? That could create a lot of sweat on a cold day.

The chances are the audience didn't come to hear jokes. They came to hear you share your expertise with them. They all have television sets at home for entertainment. If you want to warm up an audience, tell them the facts you want them to know and that they came to hear. Don't be a showman if you've never gotten a laugh at a party without putting the lamp shade on your head.

On the other hand, if you're pretty good at story telling, and the funny story you start out with makes a strong point to get into the real substance of your speech, then by all means tell a joke. It'll work for you.

Yet another rule.

- Rehearse.

This one makes sense, for most people.

The excitement of the moment doesn't improve your performance, it impedes it, if you're not well rehearsed. Nor does rehearsing diminish your spontaneity. What it does is make you so familiar with your material that it removes the material itself from the path of your conveying it. It builds spontaneity. It also allows

207

you to focus on the clarity of your presentation; to strengthen the emphasis on the important points, and on the pacing and other niceties.

Rehearse in front of friends or relatives, not a mirror (which is more distracting than helpful). A video camera is even better, because then you can see yourself in action. A tape recorder can be helpful too, if you can accommodate to the fact that your voice on a recording is as others hear it, not as you hear yourself when you speak.

As for visual aids, they can be useful if they're used properly, and if you're comfortable with them. For example, if you're explaining some complex numbers or relationships, it's useful to have the picture (or diagram or charts) up on the screen. If it's so complex that you have to build the elements piece by piece, then the overhead projector is useful. But using the overhead projector, which obscures the speaker, when a slide projector in the back of the room will do the job better, is an impediment, not a help.

One way to think about visuals is to go back to the concept of one on one in a living room. If you're explaining something to me, and you need a picture or a chart to make it clearer, then use the same visuals in a speech. If you don't need it in a living room, you don't need it in a hall.

There is cause to wonder if the exhortation to use visuals hasn't been promulgated by people who are bored by speeches. The idea is that looking at pictures in a dark room is better than listening to—and looking at—a boring speaker. The problem is that when the speech is good, visuals don't always make it better. When it's bad, visuals don't save it. When a visual helps to illustrate a point, and not obscure it, then it's useful.

And the idea that people remember facts better when they see a picture than when they hear it is a myth. If it's true, send a brochure and don't make a speech. Sometimes, though, people *understand* facts better when they're visualized than when they're heard. Some people, that is. Different people respond in different ways to the same stimuli. And that's the trouble with rules.

Beyond rules, there are a few tricks that experienced speakers have learned:

- Unless you're an actor, speak naturally and let the material carry the drama.

- Stand comfortably at the rostrum. Take your time. Take a few breaths before starting. Look out at the audience and establish eye contact, so that you're talking to friends, not strangers. If you're not an experienced speaker, you may want to practice by yourself in front of a microphone in an empty hall. Facing an audience is no time to get used to hearing your voice get back at you from a loudspeaker for the first time.

- If eye contact is important to you, choose an individual in each part of the audience, and speak to those individuals as you would to a small group seated around a table.

- Don't be in awe of a large audience. Speak to them as if they were one person to whom you speak earnestly and sincerely, with eye contact.
- And again, take your time.

If you're truly self-conscious or uneasy about speech making, it's well worth taking a course or some professional training.

Too many people who know something that other people would benefit knowing are constrained by the fear of public speaking. Too many people are impeded in learning to speak in public by rules that are too general. If you've got something to say that would benefit others, then please, learn to speak in public. Your way. There's just too little shared wisdom in the world.

## Publicizing and Merchandising a Speech

If the value of the speech is to go beyond its presentation to a limited audience, it must be publicized and merchandised.

A speech can be publicized both before and after it's given. Depending upon the topic and its importance, a press release describing the forthcoming speech may very well be in order, distributed to the appropriate media. And certainly, after the speech is given a press release focusing on its subject should be distributed. It's good practice to coordinate with the organization sponsoring your speech, to be assured of no conflict or violation of organizational taboos regarding press coverage. If the speech is sufficiently important, and the audience of sufficient consequence, the press should be invited with the first press release. Copies of the speech, if appropriate, should be made available to the press to accompany the second press release. If the appearance is of sufficient consequence, advance copies of the speech should be distributed with the proper embargo limitations (see chapter 11).

Every speech should be reviewed to determine whether it can be easily rewritten into an article. A copy of the speech should also be sent to the magazine, *Vital Speeches* (Southold, NY), which regularly prints speeches that the editors feel may be of interest to a broader audience.

Reprints of the speech, distributed by mail, multiply many fold the value of any speaking engagement. As part of the speaking program, a mailing list should be developed and a structure for distributing speech reprints should be established so that there is immediate follow-up. Reprints of speeches are also useful as part of publications packages for clients and prospective clients.

## Fitting the Speech to the Marketing Program

While no single marketing activity can carry an entire marketing program, nor can function to its maximum effectiveness on its own, there's no question that making speeches is a powerful marketing tool.

Extending a speech with reprints, articles, and publicity substantially enhances its effectiveness.

But integrated with other marketing activities, speechmaking becomes a consequential and dynamic factor. Reprints supply direct mail; publicity enhances visibility in a context of expertise; the very fact of the platform adds prestige and focus to the expertise displayed in the speech itself.

At the same time, working from the center of a marketing program gives a speech a focus; a specific task to perform in moving toward marketing objectives.

Alone, then, speechmaking is a sound marketing tool. As part of a program and overall plan, it's exceptionally powerful.

## Seminars

One of the significant differences between a seminar program and a speech program is that in running a seminar program, you have complete control over the context, the audience, the subject matter, and the conditions under which the presentations are made.

While seminars are ostensibly for the purpose of educating clients, which in fact they do, they serve an even more important purpose in practice development. They afford the opportunity to display the firm's capabilities to both clients and prospective clients, and they can be a focal point for both press coverage and reprintable material. Seminars, with all their advantages, can be done as easily by sole practitioners as by larger firms.

Seminars have been a practice development tool for many years—well before *Bates*—and so professionals are experienced in running them. But it should be remembered that no two seminars—even on the same topic with the same panel—are alike in terms of timing, place, depth of subject material, mixture of clients and nonclients, and so forth. No matter how many seminars you've done, the next one is different.

### The Value of Seminars

Organizing a seminar begins with a defined objective and ends with a carefully structured followup. Running a seminar means considerably more than merely assembling a panel to hold forth on a subject of particular interest to the panelists, and then inviting people to come and listen.

In fact a seminar is:

- An opportunity to fulfill an obligation to clients, and to make them better clients, by imparting knowledge and information that they'll find useful.

- An opportunity to reach out to the business community to project expertise, to both clients and nonclients, to engender their perception of that expertise and enhance your reputation as a leader in your field, in a context that can result in turning nonclients into clients.
- An opportunity to display to clients the breadth of your firm's capabilities, beyond the individual partner and staff that serves each client, or the specific project under contract.
- An opportunity to develop and cement relationships, and to establish contacts, with nonclients who might become prospective clients, and with those who influence their decisions in changing professionals.

## Formulating Objectives

Planning a seminar should begin with the answers to the following questions:

- What is the purpose of the seminar? To merely impart new information? To cement relations to clients? To expose clients to a broader base of your firm's people? To develop relationships with nonclients and influentials as prospective clients?
- Who is the target audience?
- What is it you want people to know, think or feel as a result of the seminar?
- How will the seminar be followed up for best marketing advantage?

A major consideration is whether the seminar is to be free to invited guests or one in which admission is to be charged. A seminar to which you charge admission becomes a distinct and separate marketing problem.

If the seminar is to be successful it must ultimately be cast in terms of what the audience wants and needs, and not simply what you want to impart. A seminar solely for clients may address some rather specific material that you know to be of concern to them. A seminar for nonclients can be broader, and include more material on more subjects. A seminar designed for nonclients may even warrant an outside speaker—somebody with reputation and expertise—to serve as an attraction.

The subject matter for a seminar should be clearly defined, well-focused and not too diverse. Don't attempt to cover too broad a spectrum of a topic in a seminar that will last only half a day or a full day, and don't confuse a seminar with a course.

It should be remembered that for an attendee at a seminar there is an investment of time, and the return on that investment is information. Even though a seminar may not be comprehensive on a subject, it should still include sufficient material to make the attendee feel that his valuable time has been well spent.

## The Panelists

Choosing a panel for a seminar is a function of the objectives as well as the material to be imparted. Rarely in a seminar that's shorter than a full day is there time for more than four speakers, each covering an aspect of the subject, plus one person to act as mediator to introduce the program, introduce the speakers and to handle questions.

In a seminar that goes through lunch, a luncheon speaker may be appropriate, and preferably should not be one of the panelists. It could be a distinguished individual from outside the firm, or a ranking nonparticipant, such as the firm's managing partner or national director. The luncheon speech ideally should be an overview—broader in its perspective than any of the presentations by the panel.

The panelists' expertise and credentials should be sufficiently strong to serve as an attraction.

Each panelist's material should be prepared in much the same way as for a speech. And questions should be anticipated to the fullest degree possible, with answers prepared beforehand. This is to avoid surprises from tough questions.

## Target Audience

Assuming that you know who you want to come to the seminar (clients, prospective clients, lawyers, bankers, etc.) you've got two major primary tasks—specifically identifying the targets, and finding the lists.

If you're aiming at clients, then it's assumed you've got those lists. Each of the partners may have lists of the particular clients they want to invite, as well as lists of prospects, lawyers, bankers, accountants, etc..

Beyond that, you may have to go to secondary sources, such as mailing list houses.

Getting lists together early is important, because it tells you how many invitations to print, which tells you about both cost and timing. It also tells you how large a room to get.

## Controlling Costs and Mechanics

The mechanics of a seminar are relatively simple, but yet beset with details that can easily go awry. The success of a seminar may reside in how well those details are managed and anticipated. Setup of the room. The moderator. Seating. Catering. Lunch or post-seminar cocktail party. Giveaways (both information packets and premiums, if you choose). Pads and pencils. Publicity. Audio visual facilities. Sound system. Photographer. Taping or stenographic coverage. Panelists name signs. Name tags for participants. Registration desk and attendant. Message center structure. And many, many more.

These details can also be a focal point for breaking the budget. Stratospheric postage charges. Unanticipated rush charges from the printer. Unexpected expense charges from guest speakers. They can all add up to more than you budgeted for.

What makes it worse is that you probably made a deliberate attempt to cut down costs by not charging for the seminar, by inviting fewer attendees, by choosing a cheaper site, or by inviting local speakers. But somehow, even these measures don't always work to keep you in budget.

How can these budget busters be avoided?

The obvious answer, of course, is planning. Particularly useful here is a flow chart, which would allow you to see some of the potential cost dangers. More of flow charts in a moment.

At the base of most seminar problems is the lack of a dedicated individual to be responsible for the seminar—whether it be a staff person with meetings as a full-time responsibility, a professional program planner, or an individual with other responsibilities who is detached from those responsibilities just to run the seminar. Assigning an individual to the project can be the largest step towards cost cutting and a successful seminar you can make, because the greatest waste comes from late charges—rushes, overtime, lack of options in site selection, etc.— that result from inattention to details and timing.

Budget busting also arises when the person in charge has too little authority, and must coordinate diverse opinions on every aspect of the seminar, from program to site. It's useful, then, to have responsibility assigned to a partner who has the authority to make decisions without the need for constant consultation or the danger of second guessing.

## The Flow Chart

The secret weapon of good meeting planners, on the other hand, is the flow chart. Activities interrelate and can cost more if not coordinated, and money is wasted when the timing of activities is allowed to slide. Other factors, not properly anticipated, can cause terminal seminar failure as well. These elements can best be tracked with flow charts, not checklists.

Flow charts can be done by hand, or on a computer, using such standard software as Symantec's *Timeline, The Harvard Total Project Manager,* or *Microsoft Project For Windows.*

Each element must include the item, the timing (including both deadline and how much time is needed to accomplish the task), and the person responsible.

It's useful to give each major participant in the seminar a copy of the entire flow chart. Cooperation and timeliness is more likely if people realize that others depend upon the timely fulfillment of their responsibilities.

Does this seem to be an elaborate approach to the simple seminar? It isn't, really. Not when you consider that it does two important things.

It guarantees an efficiently run seminar, and it closes up the holes through which leak money—often in large amounts.

The flow chart not only shows timing on each activity, it also shows interrelationships. For example, you can't send out the invitations until they're printed. You can't order participant kits until you know how many people are coming.

The flow chart, then, isn't simply a linear listing of activities and timetables. It's got overlapping activities and interdependencies. It also has the name of each individual responsible for each activity, which means that it serves as a management tool as well.

Assuming a clear understanding of the objectives of the seminar—who you're talking to and what you want them to know, think, or feel after the seminar is over—and that you understand what the subject matter is to be, at least the following general categories must be covered in the planning flow chart:

- Target audience
- Site
- Panel
- The seminar itself
- Followup

All of these are cost factors; all have different time frames; all are subject to increased cost if not ready on time.

## The Mechanics

In preparing for a seminar, the following mechanics must be considered:

- *Site selection.* Site selection depends upon a number of different factors—geographic convenience, budget, size of audience, available services (catering, audio visuals, etc.), appearances, and post seminar plans (cocktail party, dinner, etc.). All of these bring their own cost factors, and each can affect costs. For example, the closer you get to the chosen date, the fewer available sites. By being late you could wind up having to pay more for a site because the lesser priced options are no longer available. Site selection, then, appears fairly early in the flow chart, except that it's subject to the size of the mailing lists and some semblance of understanding of how many people are coming.

  In selecting a site for the seminar, its always useful to choose a location that's not only convenient and sufficiently prestigious to be appropriate to the occasion, but if possible, one that's frequently used for similar activities. Absent that, you stand a strong possibility of working with a hotel with inexperienced help and lack of appropriate facilities. If you're working with a new site, it should be very carefully checked beforehand for all amenities, including audiovisual capabilities (slides, films, etc.).

214

- *Panel.* If your panel is to consist of only your own partners, then you've got less to worry about than if you import an expert or a name. Transportation, out-of-pocket, and food go with the expert, as sometimes does honorarium.

  And from each panelist—who must be invited early enough for a response, which must arrive early enough to include in the printed material promoting the event, or to find a replacement if the invitee can't make it—must come biographical material and a summary of his or her presentation. For publicity or followup purposes you may want more—a photo, a copy of the speech, etc. If the information comes late, it holds up the printing of the invitational material and the seminar packets, which may mean rush costs in printing.

  That means that the panel also appears several times in the flow chart, related to other elements.

- *Date.* There are two primary considerations in planning the time of a seminar—allowing yourself enough lead time to develop the seminar and to get out the invitations, and potential conflicts. As a general rule you should allow at least six to eight weeks prior to the seminar for the first invitations to go out. Add to that any preparation time that's needed for the seminar itself and for clearing schedules of panelists and participants.

- *Invitations.* First invitations should go out six to eight weeks prior to the seminar and should be carefully written in terms of the advantages to the attendees. It should be remembered that even free seminars are competitive with other seminars on the same subject, and even more significantly, for the attention and time of very busy executives. And as with all direct mail, it can't be assumed that every piece of mail you send out will be read and digested by the recipient.

  An invitation letter should, where possible, be individually addressed and personalized. Great care and emphasis should be placed in the first paragraph to state the problem clearly and urgently, as a context for which the seminar offers a solution. *The invitation to the seminar doesn't come in the first paragraph—it comes after the problem has been stated.*

  Invitations should have a response mechanism, such as a phone number or post card, and arrangements should be made to deal with responses in an organized manner. Not everyone who accepts on the first invitation will actually attend, and so follow-up becomes necessary. This may be done by mail or by phone call, usually three weeks prior to the seminar, depending upon the response of the first invitation. If response to the first invitation is not satisfactory, a second letter should go out. If attendance and response require it, a follow-up phone call two or three days before the seminar to those who indicated that they would attend can be a helpful reminder.

- *Mailing lists.* Mailing lists of existing clients are relatively easy. Mailing lists of nonclients can be considerably more difficult. Presumably every firm has a list of prospects, as well as contacts with those who influence prospects. Beyond that, there are many sources of mailing lists that can be used. The best, of course, is a mailing list developed out of your own marketing program, in which you've identified and targeted specific companies as prospective clients, and specific influentials. Mailing lists can also be purchased from reliable mailing list brokers.

- *Site preparation.* In selecting and preparing a site for a seminar you might consider the following points:

  ° Room size should be smaller (slightly,) rather than larger. Fifty people in a room for 200 looks like a small group. Eighty people in room for 75 looks like an enthusiastic crowd.

  ° Some rooms, even with sound systems, have poor acoustics making it difficult for people in parts of the room to hear the speaker.

  ° The sound system should be checked to see that it's adequate to the size of the room.

  ° Check the walls. You don't want to share your meeting with the meeting next door, nor for them to share yours.

  ° Decide whether you want tables or not, and how they should be set up . Classroom-style? U-Shape?

  ° Check the chairs and make sure they're comfortable. If you're not using tables, chairs should preferably be set up in semi-circles rather than straight rows.

  ° Lobby signs and signs outside the room are necessary to help people locate the seminar.

  ° Amenities should be attended to, such as water pitchers and glasses for both speakers and the audience, plenty of ashtrays (you should consider smoking and no-smoking sections), and microphones for questions from the floor.

  ° Be sure that the hotel supplies adequate audio visual equipment to meet your needs, including maintenance and spare bulbs for projectors. If possible check their equipment beforehand.

  ° If meals are to be served, check menus beforehand, and if possible, try to see (or even eat) a sample meal. Know precisely what you're getting.

  ° Tell the hotel that you expect twenty percent fewer people than you really do, and then get the real capacity of the room after the price has been quoted. Check penalty arrangements and deposits required.

° If there is to be a cocktail hour, be sure to understand beforehand exactly how beverages are to be served.

° Arrange for a sufficient number of registration tables at the entrance to the seminar room, preferably just outside. Determine beforehand how many people you're going to need to man those tables to help you register attendees, the form of registration you're going to use, and the number and kind of badges you're going to need.

° If press is attending, arrange for press facilities, such as seating, phones, typewriters or word processing, faxes, a press room, etc. If broadcast media is expected, be sure to have setups for them, including room in the aisles for cameras.

° Not only should the site be inspected before you sign the contract, it should also be inspected on the date of the seminar, in time to make any corrections if arrangements have not been properly made.

• In negotiating for a site it's useful to remember that prices aren't fixed in stone. They are frequently negotiable, particularly if the hotel isn't busy. You should always make a counteroffer. A hotel room is a perishable commodity; they can't inventory yesterday's empty room, which is why most hotels will negotiate unless there's really competition for the space.

• Regardless of the subject matter of a seminar, there should always be a kit of materials for each participant. This might include:

° A seminar program.

° Appropriate brochures.

° Biographies of the panelists.

° Descriptive material about the firm.

° Useful background material on the subject, including a position paper if pertinent.

° Reprints of articles by the participants.

° Blank pads and pencils.

It may be useful to hold something back from these packages that can be sent out on a follow-up. However, given a choice between inadequate materials and the need for follow-up, the option should include the materials in the seminar packet. There are other techniques to use in following up.

If the preparations for a seminar have been made adequately, then the seminar itself should be an anticlimax except for the presentations. The person responsible for the seminar should get to the site as early as possible and review the checklist to make sure that everything is in working order and that all arrangements have been made properly. He or she should review the audiovisual and sound materials and equipment. Recheck, also, with the banquet department to make sure that feeding arrangements are fully understood and will be followed, and that cocktail arrangements are understood and in place. Panelists should arrive early enough to have a dry run, to check and become comfortable with the room and the sound system, and to check details such as panelists' nameplates (which should, if possible, be large enough to be seen from the back of the room).

## Giving the Seminar

Preparing and rehearsing for the seminar cannot be a casual event. While it's assumed that each panelist who participates is an expert in his field, and even that he or she is extensively experienced, a seminar is still an ensemble function.

In planning a seminar a segment of the topic is assigned to each participant. However, it should be the responsibility of each participant to make clear to the others on the panel precisely what areas he or she is going to cover. Of course, one way to do this is to write the speeches beforehand and circulate them among other panelists. Written copies of the speech are useful in several additional ways—they may be reprinted, they may be adopted as articles, they may serve as a background piece to help the press develop interviews.

However, many people prefer to speak from notes and outlines rather than from prepared speeches. Where this is the case the notes must be discussed among the participants to avoid duplication and to enhance coordination. And as with a speech, individual rehearsal, as well as group rehearsal, is extremely important. It will improve the presentation of each individual performance and sharpen and help with the timing of the ensemble performance. It also gives you the opportunity to test and time your presentation with any audio visual material.

## The Panel Chairman

The meeting leader or chairman has four major responsibilities:

- To introduce the seminar and each of the speakers.
- To chair the question period and direct the questions to the appropriate panelists.
- To keep the seminar moving, well-paced, and focused.
- To sum up at the end

While the chairman may not be one of the panelists, it's his or her opening remarks that set the context of the seminar. They should consist of a brief welcome and introduction of each of the panelists, including background (with focus on

218

the expertise on the subject) and a very brief summary of the context of the material for the panel.

During the question and answer period the chairman selects the questions from the audience, and if they are not addressed to a specific panelist, he directs them. In this context, it's also the chairman's role to be alert and evenhanded in choosing questioners from across the room, to keep the questions focused, and to keep the answers relevant. During the questions and answer period the chairman should not be passive, but active in directing the questions and answers.

At the end of the seminar, the chairman should sum up the points made as briefly and succinctly as possible, thank those who attended, and make other announcements about follow-up or mechanics. The success or failure of a seminar depends as frequently upon the skill of the chairman as it does on the subject matter being imparted.

## Press Coverage

Seminars frequently offer an exceptional opportunity for press coverage.

Certainly, a news release should be distributed to announce the seminar, particularly if it's open to the broader business community. A decision should be made as to whether the press should be invited.

Press should not be invited unless there's a clear feeling that material will be discussed that's newsworthy or of interest to the press (see chapter 11).

For press coverage the following steps should be taken:

- A press kit should be prepared that includes:
  - A basic press release about the seminar and its topic
  - Biographical material on the speakers
  - Individual press releases, if appropriate, on each of the speaker's topics
  - A general background and fact sheet about the topics—any pertinent material about your firm
- About a week prior to the seminar a basic news release should be sent to the appropriate segment of the press including an invitation to attend. For broadcast media, include a description of available radio and TV facilities
- The day before the seminar the press should be called, not to see whether they got the release, but to reaffirm the invitation.
- If the subject warrants it, an attempt should be made to arrange for an interview of participants
- Should any members of the press attend, they should be recognized at the door, greeted by a responsible person from your firm, and given a

press kit as well as other seminar material. Interviews following the seminar should be arranged as expeditiously as possible.

If the press is not interested in attending, a copy of the press kit and the seminar material should be sent to the appropriate reporters immediately following the seminar.

## Followup

In any seminar attended by a nonclient, the effort is totally wasted if there isn't an immediate and appropriate follow-up.

Attendance at a seminar of itself implies an interest in the subject. Certainly, each person who attends should be registered, even if it's simply signing a log. This facilitates post-seminar mailings, letters, and phone followup.

The details of followup should be planned, including press followup, distributing attendance lists to partners, determining the followup process, what's done by mail and what by phone and who does it, and so forth. If this is not planned at the very beginning of the process, it can cost more to set up at the last minute. These elements should be included in the flow chart.

Because the most important part of any seminar may be the cocktail party afterwards—that's where the networking is done—details must be as carefully structured as for the seminar itself. This is the occasion in which the expertise that's been projected by the seminar is turned into contact. If your firm is large enough, nonparticipating partners and others should be invited, with each assigned to cultivate prospective clients individually. The seminar may attract nonclients, but they don't really become prospects until the contact is made.

A thank-you letter should be sent to every nonclient who attended, including an invitation to meet for lunch or to discuss a specific question that may have been raised during the informalities of the cocktail hour.

Everyone who attends the seminar should be placed on an appropriate mailing list to regularly receive material issued by your firm. This might include reprints of the presentations of the seminar. This same material, incidentally, can be sent to invitees who did not attend.

## Charging Admission

If you're going to use a seminar as a marketing tool, and you want to attract as many prospective clients as you can, why put up a turnstile?

There are some good reasons to charge admission, even in the context of developing new leads.

Consider, first, that the real value of a seminar is to demonstrate that expertise abounds in your firm. It's a showcase, both for your expertise and for your people. This means, of course, that the panel must offer substance.

But sometimes, charging for it has other purposes as well.

- It adds moment to the subject matter. "This information is so valuable we can hardly be expected to give it away."
- It allows you to afford a high-priced outside expert, whose name is so attractive that admission is really worth twice the price. "We have to pay him to come, so you have to pay to see him."
- The interest in the subject matter is so vast that you have to hire a large hall.
- The seminar is more than a one-day event.

There is, then, a distinction between the kind of seminar you can charge for and simply charging for a seminar because you want to recoup expenses. Charging for the latter can be counter-productive. It's much like charging people to come and watch you collect stamps.

There is an important consideration in charging for seminars. When you give a seminar to your clients and a few non-clients, you're still in the accounting or consulting or legal business. You are performing a public service, in a sense, and if you're a little slipshod about it, or the seminar isn't perfect, it really doesn't matter. You're doing everybody a favor.

But when you charge, you're not in the accounting or consulting or legal business—you're in the seminar business, and you've got to function accordingly. You've got to sell tickets, or you're going to lose some money. You're going to have to run it as a business. Mailing out simple invitations works for a free seminar, but not for a paid one.

Some thoughts on how it can be done effectively . . .

- Make sure you've got somebody assigned to do the job, and preferably a professional marketer. Just having a partner responsible for putting it together in his or her spare time may work for the free seminar, but not necessarily for the paid one.

- Make sure that your subject matter and your panel have sufficient selling power to make it worthwhile for participants to spend the time and the money. The time, incidentally, may be more valuable to attendees than the money.

- Don't overlook the value of a good partner. A joint venture with a university or a bank adds prestige, sounds a little less self-serving, and adds their potential audience to yours.

- Your mailing list must be a good one, and large enough so that if only 5 percent of the list is sold, your seminar will still be a financial success.

- Be sure to price realistically, in terms of your costs, the value of the seminar, and the competitive rates.

- Check your date very carefully. You don't want to book against another event that might draw part of your audience.

- Use a professional meeting planner, if possible. The myriad details can sink you, and if you're not experienced at it, you'll miss many details.
- Don't skimp on the design, writing, and production of announcement materials. They should be professionally prepared. Non-professional design and writing will diminish the announcement, and the attendance as well.
- Book the best hall your budget can afford. Luxurious surroundings take the onus off of the admission charge.
- Plan well ahead. Your first mailing should go out no later than six to eight weeks before the event. That gives people time to plan, and gives you time to do a second mailing if response is slow.
- Use publicity heavily, particularly if you've got good names on the panel and your subject matter is hot.

There is an inherent danger in charging for a seminar you sponsor. If a free seminar doesn't work, it's bad enough, but not fatal. But what will people think of your firm if they've paid money to see you fall on your face? That's why you shouldn't stint on any aspect of it. Do it well.

And if it works well because you've done it well, and you follow up assiduously, then you should reap benefits in both profit and new business prospects.

## Seminar Costs

The basic costs of a seminar include these elements:
- Mailing and production costs for invitations, press, and other materials
- Room rental, and subsidiary costs
- Food and beverages, snacks and cocktail party
- Transportation and housing for guests and out-of-town panelist
- Production of slides, etc.
- Tips
- Advertising (if appropriate)
- Promotional material for seminar to which admission is charged

### The Meeting Planner

The myriad details of seminars and other forms of meetings have given rise to the full time role of the meeting planner. Many larger firms have them on staff, but a number of excellent independent planners and planning firms are available.

The advantages to using meeting planners is that they arrange for and manage all the details and costs, and they do it from a base of extensive experience. Theirs is a full time role. For the non-professional, it's a part-time role, which means that many crucial elements are not attended to. This way lies failure and budget busting.

In making a seminar successful, and keeping within budgets, a meeting planner pays for himself or herself, more often than not, in cost savings and meeting effectiveness.

# 13

# Publications

Publications—newsletters, brochures, position papers—are venerable practice development tools.

They are not often flagrantly promotional, and so have never been questioned in an ethical context.

Brochures and booklets on new laws, or foreign currency, or new accounting principles, or describing the effects of a new tax code—all were favorable devices well before the change in the canons of ethics. A brochure on fluoridation, for example, written some 25 years ago, and distributed by dentists with their own imprints, was considered to be an important factor in the public acceptance of fluoridation, and was a major marketing device for many dentists as well. Doctors' and dentists' offices have been repositories of brochures on health, with the practitioner's imprint, for decades. Accounting firms and consultants have long issued periodic newsletters interpreting economic events.

Even though there are newer and perhaps more sophisticated marketing tools, publications, properly used, are still invaluable and widely used. They're valued by those who receive them because they're a source of useful information. They're valuable to professionals because they serve clients, and project the author's expertise to both clients and nonclients. Because they can be produced inexpensively, they're useful for both small and large firms.

So ubiquitous are publications from professional firms, in fact, that many business people have come to expect them from their professionals in response to new laws, or changed regulations. The other side of that coin, of course, is that brochures and other publications now compete against one another for a prospective client's attention. And in this competition, only the best designed and written publications—those that are the most useful and readable—serve as effective marketing tools.

There's a peculiar comfort in a brochure. It's easy to feel that if you've got one, you've taken care of marketing. Or most of it, at least.

Brochures, then, are too often done "...because everybody has one," rather than as part of a thoughtful marketing plan.

## Kinds of Publications

The major categories of publications used by professionals as marketing devices are:

- *Brochures.* A brochure may be anything from a pamphlet to an extensive booklet. *Facilities* brochures describe the firm and its services. *Technical* brochures may deal intensively with a specific professional or technical subject.

- *Newsletters.* These are periodical publications, distributed regularly to clients, prospective clients and influentials, usually dealing with either a narrow technical area, or a broader context relative to the profession. They may be inexpensive typed bulletins or expensive, elaborate newsletters or newspapers.

- *Position papers.* A position paper is a document that usually presents a point of view on a specific subject relevant to the profession, backed by facts and technical information.

- *Annual reports.* While the traditional annual report is a financial document issued by a public corporation, an increasing number of professional organizations are distributing them to serve as a combination of a facilities brochure and a progress report of the firm and its growth. The implication, of course, is that the growth is a function of the firm's superior ability to serve its clients.

- *Reprints.* A reprint of an article about the firm, or by one if its principles, serves as a powerful marketing tool because it's reinforced by the imprimateur of the publication in which it first appeared. A montage of press clippings, for example, says that the firm's expertise warrants the press' constantly turning to it as a prime source.

In a separate category is the *trade book*—the full-length book published and distributed by an outside publisher. This is usually done either as an individual endeavor in an author-publisher relationship, or as a firm-sponsored joint venture between a firm and a publisher. The work that goes into it is enormous, but the rewards are overwhelming. Witness, for example, the Ernst & Young & Co. Tax Guide, a superb and monumental work which became a national best seller, featured in bookstores from coast to coast.

### How Each Is Used

Singly or in concert with one another, each plays a significant role in marketing:

- *Brochures.* A brochure, in this context, is a pamphlet or booklet that describes a firm, a facility or a service. It may be used to explain all or a segment of the firm's services, or how it functions in a particular industry, or addresses a specific problem.

    Despite the values inherent in well-done brochures, there are some pervasive misconceptions that substantially undermine their very real value to sound marketing.

A *facilities* brochure is useful in describing a firm's capabilities and specialties. The nature of professional services, however, limits its usefulness as a selling tool in that as glowingly as the brochure may describe the firm's capabilities, it can't describe them competitively. A brochure for an accounting firm may talk about the firm's people and services, but can't say "We do better audits." The canons of ethics under which the professions still function clearly dictate discretion in this kind of brochure. At the same time, the brochure is useful in presenting the firm and its practice brightly and enthusiastically, and as a strong adjunct to other marketing tools.

A facilities brochure may describe the firm, its capabilities, its service concept, and its facilities. It may be used to explain the firm to prospective clients or to prospective recruits. It may discuss the entire firm, or one segment of its services, or how it functions in a particular industry.

*Technical* brochures serve an entirely different purpose, in that they offer information on a specific subject based upon the firm's expertise. These are the brochures that address such subjects as accounting for foreign currency under new regulations, or responsibilities of the trustee under a new estate law. The role of these brochures is to serve as an educational aid to the reader. In fact, they portray the firm as knowledgeable.

- *Position papers* afford a firm the opportunity to take a strong position, sometimes partisan, on a matter of interest and urgency to its clientele and prospective clientele. As a marketing tool they clearly demonstrate knowledge, interest, and concern in a matter that concerns the prospective clientele.

- *Newsletters* are particularly valuable in developing an ongoing relationship between your firm and your clients or prospective clients. A well-written and edited newsletter that deals with matters that are genuinely consequential to the reader, and that imparts really useful information, can be particularly helpful in enhancing reputation within the context of expertise. It can also serve as a source of material for publicity, by publicizing the content of a newsworthy article. The important thing to remember about a newsletter is that it will not automatically be read; it must survive and thrive independently as a valuable source of information to the reader. It can cover a wide range of subjects within a profession, and it affords the opportunity to quote everybody in the firm who has any expertise in any area.

- An *annual report*, for a professional firm, is a way of demonstrating facilities, capability, and most significantly, growth. It goes beyond a facilities brochure in that its point of view can be less objective in discussing a firm's business. It affords a firm the opportunity to be somewhat more dynamic, and perhaps a little freer in speaking of its own capabilities.

- A *reprint* can sometimes serve the same purpose as a brochure, depending upon the original article. Reprints have the additional value of the implied objective endorsement of the publication in which the article originally appeared. The reprint seems to say that because the publication chose to publish the article, there is an independent and objective assent to its premise and credibility to its content. The marketing power of a properly used reprint is extensive.

## Role in the Marketing Mix

For all that a good publication can contribute to a marketing program, it's rarely the keystone of a total marketing effort, nor should it be. But as an *adjunct* to a marketing plan, it can be powerful.

In conjunction with other marketing tools, publications have a specific role and value. They:

- Are tangible. Unlike advertising or editorial publicity, which are fleeting, publications can be held in hand and studied at leisure.
- Are capable of making a specific contribution to a client or prospective client's business. They can supply information that has its own value, and which therefore redounds to the benefit of the source.
- Afford the opportunity to present a firm in its best light.
- Give a visual dimension to a firm, at least in the context of the design of the publication. A well-designed, attractive publication implies a well-run, efficient organization.
- Have staying power. They give dimension and weight to anything you say about your firm and capabilities.
- Can demonstrate a firm's most valuable asset—its intellectual capital.
- Catalog and describe a firm's capabilities, facilities, expertise, or point of view, all in best light.
- Can supply valuable information, redounding to the benefit of the source.
- Give legitimacy to a new facility or service. A new practice in an existing firm, for example, becomes tangible to both its prospective clientele and the firm itself when it appears in print.

Perhaps the most expensive misconception is that publications *sell*—that a prospective client will read a brochure loaded with glowing adjectives, and sign a contract as a result of it.

To assume, too, that people read brochures thoroughly and carefully is another trap. In fact, a brochure, no matter how attractive or thorough, is simply glanced at. It may be read in conjunction with other material, to get an overall impression of a firm. But it's rarely devoured like a novel.

There's a tendency to forget that publications strongly compete against one another—and against other marketing literature—for a prospective client's attention. Your brochure is rarely the lone voice in a wilderness.

Nor can a publication be merely self-serving, ignoring the needs of the reader. The brochure that sings the praises of oneself may fulfill egos, but rarely will it fill coffers.

A newsletter, for example, functions well to sustain an ongoing relationship with a client or prospective client, but only if it's a valid newsletter that contains information that contributes substantially to the reader's advantage.

Technical brochures, position papers, and reprints serve in the same way to contribute to the reader's store of information and education.

Annual reports, or reprints of an article about a company, fall into a different category, since they tend to be frank marketing pieces. A facilities brochure contributes to the reader's well-being only to the degree that the reader wants to know about your capabilities. But it's still self-serving.

Recognizing the distinction between those pieces that are self-serving and those that contribute to a reader's education and information helps to understand how each is to be used. It helps to understand, as well, the kind of readership that can be anticipated. A well-produced newsletter or technical brochure is likely to have greater readership than a facilities brochure or an annual report. And each must be accompanied by a different kind of cover letter, and served to the client or prospect in a different context.

## Constraints on Publications

Because of the long tradition of using publications as marketing devices in the professions, there tends to be a too easy use of them; a proclivity to use them pointlessly, and to produce so much printed material that prospective clients are inundated. This, of course, causes a reaction that's precisely opposite to the one you want.

In larger firms, the problem is magnified, because every partner in charge of an area of the practice, or responsible for serving a specific industry, tends to feel naked without being represented in print. The result, in firm after firm, is that practice offices throughout the country warehouse unopened cartons of brochures, which will never be used.

The publication's role in meeting the objectives of the marketing program must be determined. Without clarifying this role, the effort behind a publication can be wasted.

Under no circumstances should a publication be produced if it can't be done professionally and skillfully. Newsletters that impart no knowledge are junk mail, and counterproductive. Technical brochures or position papers that make no genuine contribution, or that are superficial, are also counterproductive.

Any publication is distinctly contraindicated when . . .

- It's not part of a plan that delineates why it's being done, and how it's going to be used.
- There's no clear view of how it will demonstrate the firm's intellectual capital.
- There are better ways to accomplish the objectives set for the publication.
- It can't be done with a professional and businesslike appearance.

## Objectives

A publishing program should, in all aspects, conform to objectives. The objectives, more than anything else, shape the format, the design, the content, the distribution, and the longevity of all publications.

Because every publication you issue must compete with a great many other publications for the limited time and attention of your chosen readership, publications that aren't focused, useful, and readable, with superior and professional design, writing, and production, are an absolute waste of money.

Publications that meet no specific objectives, or that try to meet objectives that are best met through other marketing devices (such as advertising or public relations,) are expensive, waste time and money, and serve no valid purpose.

No publication should be produced without answering at least the following questions:

- Who is my audience? Is it a broad audience consisting of all my clients or prospective clients, or a narrow audience consisting of those with a specific interest?
- What am I trying to accomplish with this publication in terms of the overall marketing program? Will something else better accomplish what I want?
- How will the publication be used in conjunction with other marketing tools? Will it be offered in ads? Mentioned in press releases? Used in direct mail?
- How will the publication be delivered? Will it be mailed ahead? Left behind after a meeting? Mailed after meeting?
- What do I want my audience to know, to do, or to think after they've read my publication?

- Will some other marketing tool better accomplish what this publication is being asked to do?

The answers to these questions will, in turn, focus the objectives of the publication, and lead to developing a more effective document.

When the audience is clearly defined and the objectives are clearly understood and stated, then the likelihood of the publication's serving a significant purpose is substantially increased.

## The Brochure

The format and content of a brochure are not arbitrarily dictated, but are chosen by the role the brochure is to play in the marketing plan.

Too often, the graphic designer is called in before the writer, and before the brochure's marketing role is defined. This subordinates the message to the design, almost invariably resulting in a visually attractive publication, but one that diminishes or fails to serve the communications or selling objective.

Still, publications should be professionally designed, written, and produced. Amateurism will say things about your firm that are unflattering and counterproductive. If appearance is not the primary factor, desktop publishing may be sufficient. But a brochure to rest on the desks of CEOs of major corporations should not be home produced.

The art of writing a brochure is exactly that—an art. But in writing brochures for a professional service there are some distinct considerations that can make the difference between a brochure that accomplishes your objectives and one that doesn't.

The thoughtful, and most useful, brochure for a professional service firm must solve a major problem—how do I describe my facilities and services in ways that differentiate me from my competitors, and at the same project quality? Ethics, of course, preclude comparison, which forecloses a classic marketing device.

### What Works?

The answer is still emerging, but we do begin to see some things that do work.

Clear objectives seem to make a difference. If you know exactly what you want the brochure to accomplish, then it's more likely to work well.

One of the great exercises in frustration is trying to get some sell into a brochure for a professional firm.

It's easy for products. "We make the world's best Gizmo!" Or, "With our Hotchkiss, you can go faster than ever!"

But how do you use an exclamation point in a brochure about a law or accounting or consulting firm? "Our offices have cleaner windows!"? How about, "Our thoughts are assembled faster than anybody else's in the profession!"?

231

Having gotten over that hurdle—by realizing that there's no way around it—try thinking about words like "honest", or "service", or "creative." This is where you try to tell other people what they should think of you. "We give creative service to your needs." What does that mean? Does it mean that you give clients what they pay for? Does it mean that they get their money's worth? Does *creative* mean you make it up as you go along?

The problem is that brochure writers—and ad and direct mail writers, too—are trained to sell, to use adjectives and emotionally laden words that move you toward a purchase. They're trained to find distinguishing factors, and unique selling propositions, and all those Madison Avenue words.

Unfortunately, that's not how it works in professional services marketing. You can't say, remember, "We do better audits," or "We write better briefs."

In other words, you can't use hard sell.

But that's not so horrible. In fact, it's what professional service marketing is all about. What you can do is really more interesting.

You can deal with facts. You can say, "Every client's account is managed by a partner, no matter how small the account." That's a fact that says more than all the adjectives you can summon up.

You can say, "We deal with problems in patents and copyrights with more than just attorneys. We have a full staff of physicists, chemists and other scientists who work closely with our attorneys." You can say that every person on the staff functions with state-of-the-art computer software, to increase efficiency and lower costs of serving your clients. These are statement of fact, and they're more compelling than any slick selling technique.

You can describe specific problems, and explain how you deal with them. "The strategies we design for controlling the flow of commodities to our clients' plants have increased our clients' productivity by 35 percent." If this is true, then it says more to sell than does any selling language.

You can write about your solution or services as if you invented them, even if you know you didn't. It may be the first time your reader has seen that capability or solution delineated.

If being *creative* is really important to you, you can make the point without using the word, by describing several situations in which your innovative approaches solved specific problems. Case histories do a better job of describing what you do than can any descriptive phrases.

Perhaps the guiding rule is in the old saying, "What you are speaks so loudly that I can't hear what you *say* you are."

One of the reasons this approach is so much more compelling than the old techniques of adjectives and hard sell is that nobody hires a lawyer or an accountant or a consultant from an ad or a brochure. The marketing devices may generate an interest in a firm that clearly offers a solution to a problem. They may cause a predilection towards a specific firm. But in the final analysis, brochures and ads don't sell professional services; only professionals do.

Hard sell, then, rarely has a place in professional services marketing, and that's good. It forces us to be thoughtful and innovative. And that's *really* creative.

The operative word, implied or in fact, is "you." Most brochures die when the first word is "we." Your brochure must be cast, invariably, in terms of the needs of the market—what the prospective client needs, not what you have to sell.

The art of writing a brochure, then, is exactly that—an art. But in writing brochures for a professional service, there are some distinct considerations that can make the difference between a brochure that accomplishes your objectives and one that doesn't. For example:

- *The audience.* A brochure describing your firm for prospective clients will be very different from one you'll use to recruit college students to join your firm. A technical brochure for middle management might be written very differently than one for senior management. The reasons, obviously, are that you have different things to say to different audiences. The advantages of working for your firm are not the same as the advantages of retaining your firm. How you write anything is a function of who you're talking to. The brochure is very much subject to that dictum.

- *Purpose.* A brochure to be sent ahead as a forerunner to a presentation or a meeting has a very different point of view than one to be left behind following a meeting as a summary or reminder, and to reinforce points made in person. The brochure that's sent ahead, for example, has as its job to explain who you are, what you do, and how you do it. You're presumably talking to somebody who doesn't know you. The brochure you leave behind assumes some measure of knowledge about you and your firm, and should reinforce points you've made in person. Thus, purpose alters the format and text of a publication.

- *Illustration.* It's very difficult to illustrate a brochure for a service organization. All lawyers and accountants and consultants seated at desks look alike. Illustration is the toughest part of any brochure, and the burden is heavy on designers. Photography that shows as much action as possible is an improvement over static, posed shots. The visualization of your message, then, must ultimately rely upon the writing, not artwork.

- *Distribution.* How a brochure is to be distributed affects it's design. If it's to be mass mailed, it should be remembered that postage costs are a major consideration. Odd shapes that use custom designed rather than stock envelopes may be attractive, but increase costs substantially. Here, too, return on investment must be considered. Brochures that cost $5 each may be well worth it if they contribute to getting clients that pay fees in multiples of that.

- *Longevity.* How long will the publication be expected to do its job? A publication on a new tax law will have a shorter life than one on how to keep records. Thus, a brochure with an intended long life shouldn't have references that can become dated.

It helps to limit the brochure to a single purpose. A service. A facility. A single problem and its solution. Omnibus brochures seem to be less effective than the single-purpose document, although that's precisely what you have to do for a brochure that describes an entire firm.

Writing a technical brochure is simpler than writing a facilities brochure. In the former, one deals with professional skills. How to understand a new law, for example. It is, in effect, simply a matter of practicing a segment of one's profession on paper.

But how do you write a facilities brochure when your ability to use adjectives is clearly proscribed; when the service you perform is precisely the same as everyone else's? (We do better audits? We write better briefs?)

If there's any answer, it's to write simply and clearly about what you do—whether its to describe the range of services you perform or your approach to addressing specific problems, such as personal finance, or cash management. And if you write it all simply, and as if nobody else is performing the service, then a selling impact may emerge. And because it must not be assumed that any reader will devote an extensive amount of time to any single publication that might be construed as promotional, the message should be clear, simple, accessible, and not embroidered in too many words.

The objective and the target audience should always be kept in mind, to avoid unfocused writing. Objectives for publications should be simple, and no publication should be expected to carry too much weight.

Relevance is significant. What you put into any publication must be relevant to the needs of your prospective reader, and address those needs without deviating from the point and without clutter. When you do that, then the publication works for you the way you mean it to. This, by the way, is as true of a technical publication as it is of a promotional one.

A brochure, in a sense, is no different from any marketing tool. Properly used, it works. Improperly used, it not only doesn't help, but it lulls you into thinking that you're accomplishing more than you really are. Better to take the larger view; to develop the larger marketing context in which the brochure is a working cog.

### Newsletters

Picture all those prospective clients out there, waiting eagerly each month...watching the mails with bated breath . . . for your newsletter. Never mind *Time,* or *Newsweek,* or *Business Week.* It's your newsletter they want.

Picture dozens of your competitors, as well as practitioners in other disciplines, all thinking the same thing—that readers are waiting eagerly for just their newsletters.

The funny thing is that this is only a slight exaggeration, because the decision to do a newsletter usually stops at the point where somebody says, "OK, let's do a newsletter." Nobody asks the hard questions—the why and the how. The result is that so many newsletters are badly done. Imitative, amateurish, irrelevant—and unread.

And yet, there are still a number of newsletters put out by law, accounting, and consulting firms, as well as those provided by professional newsletter publishers and distributed under the banner of individual firms, that are effective and sometimes powerful contributors to practice development. Certainly, there are enough successful ones to demonstrate that a newsletter is still a good marketing tool, despite the apparent glut of them.

What makes the difference? Why do newsletters work for one firm and not another? Is it slickness that counts? Must they be professionally designed? Many questions—but all worth looking at.

### It's the Reader That Counts

While all marketing should be done in terms of the prospect's needs and not simply what the seller wants to sell, this rule becomes more cogent in newsletters than in many other marketing areas. This is because the competition for the reader's attention is not with other competitive firms, it's with all reading material that the reader receives. You are indeed competing, in this context, with *Time*, or *Newsweek*, or *Business Week*. And so all newsletter planning begins with the reader. This applies as well to a newsletter you buy from a service to redistribute as it does to one you write yourself from scratch.

In fact, a newsletter, properly used in an appropriate context, can be a powerful marketing tool. Either as part of a larger marketing program or standing alone as the major marketing tool, it contributes several valuable factors:

- It's a communications vehicle from the sender to the receiver, allowing valuable and relatively current information to be conveyed in a controlled context.

- It conveys up-to-date technical information that can be helpful in the reader's own business or personal business. This redounds to the credit of the sender. As a service to the reader, it has good will—or good public relations—value.

- The quality of the newsletter speaks to the quality of the sender. A valuable and useful newsletter implies a valuable and useful firm. By imparting good technical information, it implies that the publisher is a good source of technical help.

- By judicious use of mailing lists, it focuses on precise target companies and prospective clients.

- It adds an informational dimension to direct mail.

- It frequently serves as a feedback device to the sender, in that it invites inquiries, discussion, and sometimes requests for further information, which opens the door for further selling activities.

- In a fuller marketing program, it serves as a vehicle for public relations, direct mail, and even advertising. Articles in the newsletter can be quoted in releases, for example, or published in the trade press as by-lined pieces.

And all this assumes, of course, that the newsletter is of a quality that gets it read by the recipient.

## The Newsletter Plan

With the reader always in mind, planning a newsletter begins with a clear view of objectives. Rather than just accepting the idea of a newsletter because it's there to do, at least the following questions should be asked . . .

- Why are we doing a newsletter? Is it the best way we have to reach this audience with the message we want to deliver?

- Who is the audience? How do we define it in terms of what our service is? How will we identify the audience, and develop the mailing list? How do we keep the list purged and up-to-date?

- What are our objectives in publishing or distributing this newsletter? Is it pure good will? Is it name recognition? Is it a door opener to allow followup by phone, letter, or in person? Is it to demonstrate your expertise in the area or industry covered by the newsletter? Is it to establish a franchise in a particular industry you serve or want to serve?

  While delineating objectives may seem academic, they are, rather, the key to determining most of the aspects of your newsletter that are important—its format, its content, its voice, its audience, its method of distribution, and its role in the total marketing program.

- How will it be used? Alone, as a sole marketing tool, or in conjunction with other marketing tools? If it's to be used alone, it may lean more heavily on the firm and its individuals. If it's to be used in other contexts, content and format will reflect that.

- What do you want your readers to know, to think, or to feel after they've read each issue?

- Should you do it yourself, or use one of the excellent prepared newsletters supplied by specialized publishers, to which you simply add your own identification?

- If you do it yourself, who's going to do it? Do you have top-notch staff, or will you hire freelance writers and editors? Will you produce it in-house, with desktop publishing, or will you have it designed and produced outside?

- What will be your source of material? Will it come entirely from your own expertise, or will you be abstracting from other material? Who's going to do it—one of your partners? A staff editor? An outside service?

- How frequently will you issue the newsletter? Have you budgeted properly for it? Do you have enough material to issue it with that frequency?

- What arrangements will you make for mailing it? In-house? An outside mailing house?

- How about the lists? Where will you get them? Who will maintain them? Mailing lists can be very difficult. Names, address, and titles change. Even the best lists from mailing houses have mistakes, and at today's mailing rates, mailing mistakes can be costly. Maintaining lists—keeping them up-to-date, changing and correcting, recording returns—can be a full time job for a clerk, who'd better be a very smart and dedicated clerk.

## The Answers to the Questions

If these are the kinds of questions that must be asked before you do a simple newsletter, then you have a sense that choosing to do one is not an arbitrary decision. It's clearly very complicated, which is why so many firms, both large and small, use prepared newsletters supplied by outside firms. These firms specialize in producing newsletters professionally, covering a range of topics.

Consider, also, this problem of competing for the reader's attention. There are two ways to do it successfully, in view of the fact that you may be competing with *Business Week*.

The first is to have one that's more interesting to read than anything else your reader will get in the mail. You or someone on your staff may very well be a superb writer, capable of producing a period report that's actually fun to read. Or your audience may be small enough—or intimate enough—to accept a personal newsletter from you. This is one way to go, and if it's the wrong way, you'll find out soon enough.

The other is to be able to supply information that's not readily available anyplace else. Nobody else may cover those aspects of litigation support that you can. You may have a nationally recognized economist on your staff. You may know more about inventory control in the retail food industry than anybody else. The point is that if your newsletter is covering an area intensively that others cover only generally, then you've got a fighting chance to become important to your reader.

If you're a generalist, capable of dealing authoritatively with only general material in your profession, then your best, cheapest, and most cost-effective way to go might very well be to use a prepared newsletter supplied by one of the outside houses.

### The Newsletter as a Marketing Tool

Assuming that you've got a terrific letter, by any of the foregoing criteria, how does it become a marketing device? It's quite possible that one of your readers will be so taken with the newsletter, and so immediately recognize your expertise, that he or she hires your firm on the spot after reading the first issue. But don't count on it. That's the reason for followup.

If the value of a newsletter is your ability to target individuals, then that means that you can follow up with letters or even cold calls to a subscriber. You can say, for example, *"You may have read about the problems of dealing with the new employment laws in the last issue of our newsletter. If it doesn't affect you now, it very well may in the near future. Because you want to be prepared, why don't we sit down and discuss ways in which our firm can help you protect yourself when..."*

Every opportunity that kind of letter gives you to meet a prospect multiplies many times the value of your having published a newsletter.

Or you may want to issue a news release after each issue that says, *"The fall of the Berlin Wall may have been many miles from Peoria, but the repercussions in Peoria business can be more profound than you realize, according to an article in the current issue of ...."*

Increasingly, firms issuing newsletters are learning to subtly insert marketing messages in the text—unobtrusively, but effectively. Others are sure to end technical letters with a commercial message. Some firms see newsletters as frank direct mail pieces, and include inserts that pitch services quite specifically. These inserts are a way to generate feedback—to make the newsletter interactive.

There are many ways in which to use a newsletter in marketing, and they should all be considered. But what should be considered as well is that you can spend a lot of money to produce a newsletter that nobody will read or care about if you don't ask the right questions before you start. The problem, you see, is that it costs as much to feed a bad horse as to feed a good horse.

The same is true of newsletters.

## Internal Communications

It's not reasonable to talk about publications without dealing with internal communications.

Time was when an effective internal communications program consisted of a well-placed source on the grapevine, a newsletter, and the periodic department meeting. However, today's business environment, as well as the very nature of professional service firms, have necessitated a whole new approach to internal communication.

Kim A. Buckey, Director, Recruiting and Human Resources Communications of KPMG Peat Marwick, writing in *The Marcus Report*, points to reasons for a growing urgency for firms to communicate internally.

"The accelerated pace and increased complexity of business events, the globalization of markets, and the world's rapidly changing geopolitical structure," she says, " have contributed to an unparalleled external demand for information and advice from today's service organizations—and a corresponding internal demand for a highly responsive and informed employee base. Today's employees, no matter where they are, must be kept current with the firm's activities and focus."

Moreover, the needs to communicate internally are very real and practical. Buckey notes that . . .

- In many professional service firms, a high percentage of the staff may be out of the office on client assignments, or traveling for long periods of time, effectively placing them outside the reach of traditional communication media such as meetings, newsletters or bulletins, and video presentations.

- There is a dichotomy among employees themselves— *professional* versus *administrative; partner* versus *staff*—which requires the communicator to balance different information needs with very different levels of education and sophistication. One area where this is particularly apparent is employee benefits. Partners frequently have similar, but differently structured, benefit plans than employees, and are usually interested in more detailed, financially oriented analysis of information such as pension fund performance. While multiple publications may provide a simple answer to employees with a diverse reader profile, budget constraints often require the communicator to work within the confines of a single publication, trying not to insult the intelligence of one group while not going over the head of another.

- High turnover is inherent in service firms. Today's worker feels less loyal to his or her employer, frequently moving from firm to firm in quest of different experiences and more money. Many service organizations have come to expect—if not encourage—this turnover, knowing as they do that vagaries in the business environment and the inevitable loss of clients may cause them to generate some economically or financially induced turnover of their own. In CPA or actuarial firms, where employees may stay only long enough to achieve professional certification, turnover can exceed 20 percent each year. Whatever the cause, this ongoing change of audience requires repeating key messages to ensure consistent delivery and universal understanding.

- The very nature of service businesses requires better informed employees, because there are more—and more frequent—points of contact between employees and clients, customers, potential customers, suppliers, and vendors. Employees need to be able to adequately and appropriately respond to questions from their constituencies to ensure future business growth.

Many of the traditional techniques for internal communications still work in a professional service environment, but maximum effectiveness can be realized only when these techniques are part of a comprehensive internal communications program, says Buckey. "The effective communicator must find a way to combine media to ensure that messages reach all audiences in a timely manner," she says, "and that those messages can adequately compete for the audience's attention in the information-intensive environment of professional services."

Internal newsletters, bulletins, and other printed material have a lot to recommend them—they are portable; they can be distributed as necessary to one site or many, to the home, or to the office; they have a long shelf-life; and they can easily be shared and discussed with others. Unfortunately, says Buckey, printed information may also get lost in the sheer volume of material that people receive. The communicator always runs the risk of coming across someone like the accounting firm partner who said, of a newsletter he received on a regular basis, "I didn't know I was supposed to read this."

Buckey points out that in our TV-oriented society, videos and audio-visual presentations still carry a lot of impact, particularly when they reinforce printed or interpersonal messages. To get around the difficulties of absentee audiences, many firms are making copies of videos (and videos of slide shows) available to employees for viewing at home or at their on-site living quarters. This enables the off-site employee to participate and share information on a timely basis.

"Face-to-face communication, of course, remains the communications method preferred by both communicators and audiences," she says. One inherent problem is the need to have the communicator in several locations at more or less the same time. While new technologies, such as closed-circuit television and satellite teleconferencing, can solve that problem, the communicator still runs into an even bigger one—such communications, at least in the form of large group meetings, often require pulling professional staff off the job, thereby interfering with chargeable hours. If your partners or management are particularly preoccupied with the bottom line, you may never be able to pull everyone together—at least not during office hours. You will have to rely on your management to convey information personally when they meet with their staff on the job or in regularly scheduled sessions.

Electronic mail and voice mail offer tailored broadcasting, enabling the communicator to reach the entire office or selected employees simultaneously and immediately, or with a programmed delay. And for those technology-intensive firms, interactive computer disks can provide an inexpensive, portable way of conveying extensive information in a consistent format—which the employee can access when it's most convenient, and he or she is the most receptive.

"While today's internal communicator must be more creative in terms of the format and media he or she uses to convey the firm's messages," says Buckey, "the basic fundamentals of internal communications haven't changed. The failure to communicate will still result in employees creating their own version of the truth. An employee's ability to contribute meaningfully to the future of a firm is still directly related to the degree to which he or she is kept informed about the firm's business and the complex business issues that face it. No communications program will be successful without the support of top management. And a good program still requires regular evaluation and multiple media to reach all audiences appropriately, to reinforce messages received under one medium, and to ensure timely and consistent delivery."

## Design

A firm publication, whether it's typed or typeset, must be readable and attractive, printed on good quality paper and laid out so as to avoid a formidable crowded look. A standard letterhead for a newsletter should be designed for consistency and easy recognition. The masthead should be printed even if the newsletter itself is simply to be typed. The format of any periodical publication, such as a newsletter, should be designed to be instantly recognizable by the third or fourth issue. Brochures should be attractive. If you plan to publish more than one brochure, you may find it useful to try for what's known as a "design family" feel. This is a consistency of design from one publication to another that makes the series of publications instantly recognizable as coming from one source, but still distinguishes each one so that they're not confused with one another.

## Production

The production process is much the same as in advertising. Here too, professionalism saves money by making the process smoother and faster, and by avoiding waste.

There is some measure of flexibility and control of the costs of publications, but there are still certain cost elements that are consistent. Inherent in the cost of all publications are:

- The time of the professionals involved in producing the publication.
- The time and cost of professional editors or writers.
- Design costs, including design, layout, and preparation of camera-ready mechanicals.
- Typesetting, proofing, and printing costs. Even if the publication is done in-house by desktop publishing, these are costs that must be calculated.

- Photography.
- Paper.
- Printing and binding.
- Distribution, including bulk distribution and shipping, bulk packaging, and mailing.

Publications showcase a firm, and frequently act as a major tool in presenting the firm to its prospective clients. Like the good suit, tie, and polished shoes, the appearance of a firm's publication bespeaks the firm itself, and so care should be taken in designing, producing, and distributing publications. There are no savings in cutting costs to the point of producing shoddy work.

The time and care put into carefully planning and professionally executing publications—newsletters, brochures, etc.—can result in a profound return on investment. Poorly planned and executed publications, on the other hand, are expensive and counterproductive.

# 14

# The Logo and Firm Graphics

Graphics—the design factors used in a firm's literature, stationary, and other printed material—may not contribute the fire power of other marketing disciplines, nor the gravity in the marketing mix suggested by graphic designers, but they're nevertheless a significant marketing factor.

Just as clothes project an instant impression of the individual, so do the graphics of a firm. A dull and mundane letterhead, an undistinguished business card, an uninspired sign over the door, will give the casual observer the impression of a dull, mundane, and uninspired firm. A badly designed and unattractive brochure or newsletter won't be taken seriously, and without a uniform graphics look, won't be readily identified with the issuing firm. The facts may belie the impression, but if the first impression is negative then the observer may never get past it to the facts.

This is why attention to the design of all firm graphics is an important marketing element. It's an escutcheon, a shield, a banner that sets a primary mood to invite people to want to do business with you.

A well-designed graphic representation used consistently in your printed, advertising, and display material conveys a feeling of substance, of professionalism.

The consistent use of good graphics throughout all your material reinforces identification and recognition. The graphic impression of the letterhead, of the business card, of the ad, of the billboard—all reinforce one another, and speed up and enhance recognition to the point of comfortable familiarity.

Distinctive graphics serve yet another important role. They distinguish you and your firm from your competitors. What the coat of arms of heraldic times was to the noble family, so are distinctive graphics to today's business firm. Name alone may not be as memorable as name in an attractive graphic representation.

As real as are these advantages to a good graphics presentation, there is, on the other hand, the danger of being overwhelmed by the value of graphics in other aspects of public relations. Your firm is not what your graphics imply that it is—rather, it's the other way around; your graphics must represent your firm as it really is.

Several years ago, a major national airline spent almost $1 million on a particularly successful corporate identity program. It modernized its logo, its graphics and the appearance of its outlets and personnel. After a short time, every aspect of the appearance of the airline, from its advertising to its airplanes, was readily identifiable.

This graphics program, however, did nothing to improve the quality of the airline's service or its management. It still maintained poor on-time performance; its personnel did not improve their efficiency or their manners, nor could all the graphics and advertising improve the quality of its operations. It achieved instant and consistent identification of an operation that was considered so generally inferior that its profits were well below those of its competitors' for many years. It has since disappeared from the scene for many reasons—but many would no doubt still recognize it today from its graphics.

In other words, all of the good will, the attention, the identification, the implied professionalism of your graphics can be denied in one rude phone call, one muffed assignment.

### What Are Company Graphics?

Company graphics, sometimes called the corporate or firm identity, are the visualization of your signature in a uniform, attractive, and distinctive style, used consistently everywhere your name might reasonably appear. This might include:

- Letterheads
- Business cards
- Advertising
- Office sign
- Publicity material
- Promotional material
- Company vehicles
- Signs and billboards

The impression is achieved by a distinctive design of your firm name and logotype, and the way they're used.

### The Trademark

There's a subtle distinction between trademark and logo. The names Kodak, Xerox, Kleenex—are trademarks. They are distinctive company names, registered as such with the U.S. Patent Office. The products they make are the Kodak camera, the Xerox copier and the Kleenex tissue. These names are protected by law. "Kodak" doesn't mean all cameras or films, "Xerox" doesn't mean all copiers and "Kleenex" doesn't mean all tissues.

A logo (short for *logotype*), on the other hand, is a distinctive design or design device that, like an escutcheon, represents a firm. The logo need not be a separate design device; it can be the design style of the firm name. Coca-Cola, and its distinctive script form, is at one time a firm name, a logo, and a trademark. The word "Coke" is also registered as a trademark and so precludes calling any cola drink a Coke except Coca-Cola. But visually, the distinctive style functions as a logo that's consistently used on all the Coca-Cola firm's materials, from their letterhead to their product and their trucks.

In professional services, you and your firm are your product, and so the concept of trademark doesn't necessarily apply. This is particularly true if your own name is the name of the firm. Firms in most professions, in many cases mandated by canons of ethics or local law, use the names of their principals, which takes them out of the category of trademark. This may ultimately change as concepts of governance change.

Sometimes a distinctively designed typeface is sufficient to serve the graphic needs of a firm when it's used for the firm's name. The firm name is, of itself, a logo. But sometimes the firm's concept of itself can be enhanced and projected by an additional design device that's distinctive, attractive, and memorable. Properly designed and used, a distinctive firm name can fulfill all of the needs of a good graphics program.

The visual distinction of logos becomes increasingly important as marketing heightens competition. Firms need the visual aspect of graphics to help distinguish themselves from other competitors, and to build substantive identification.

## Making a Logo Work

A logo—or any firm graphic—will not work on its own. It must be used in a planned, carefully devised way. Attractive though it may be, if it's not placed in positions where it's constantly visible it will achieve only a fraction of its potential purpose and value. This is why firm identity programs require more than just a design of a logo and a signature. Every piece of printing on which the logo and signature are to be used must be considered, and a full design program must include consistency for all possible uses. In a graphics program, designers usually issue complex instructions on when and where each iteration of the logo may be used, including size, proportion, and color.

Like slogans, logos, as attractive as they may be, are useless without constant repetition. They must be visible in many forms—stationery, signs, advertising, and promotion. Logos must be made to do a job by constant exposure.

## Elements of Design

All firm graphics, including the logo, should attempt to reflect the firm itself. They should spring from your marketing objective and the position you've chosen in the market. As you've seen, different typefaces and different designs convey different feelings. An accountant or lawyer seeking business in a conservative world would hardly use a jazzy or cartoon-like logo. But for an innovative designer, or a specialized consultant, an unusual logo might well be appropriate.

If the word *image* comes to mind here, it should be an image based on reality, or else the inconsistency would quickly confuse the prospective client. The reaction might be subliminal and the prospective client might not be able to put a finger on it, but the feeling would be there.

A good design program begins, then, not with the preconception of a visual image but with an analysis of the firm and the purposes to which the graphics will be put. Professional designers charged with developing a firm graphics program spend a great deal of time analyzing the firm, its objectives, its positions, its market, its target audience, and management's own attitudes and feelings about the firm and its future growth areas.

The designer then analyzes all of the uses of the graphics; all forms of communications, vehicles, stationery, signs, advertising, and so forth.

The design consists of more than just a drawing or a rendering of a logo and a signature. It must be scaled to every communications piece. How large should it be in proportion to the rest of the space on a letterhead? On a business card? On an envelope? On a brochure? A professional design program isn't complete without a graphic standards manual for firm-wide use, and an instruction sheet to printers about color, size, and scale.

Color, when it's used, is as much part of the design as the style of the typography. While the logo may at times be used in black and white, when it's used in situations where color is appropriate, the color should always be coordinated. Color is as much a part of the identification as type, and in fact, some designers deliberately blend a distinctive color that isn't likely to be duplicated. But since logos are used in black and white in some advertising, they should be designed to be as distinctive and memorable without color as with color.

The design should always be simple and clear. And while it should reflect your business as it currently exists, your future business should be considered as well, unless you want to go through the expense and trouble of redesigning the logo every time your business shows substantial growth or changes in any way.

## The Designer

Not only should firm graphics, and especially a logo, be designed professionally, but the designer should have extensive experience in logo design. An advertising designer, or one who specializes in brochures, may be extraordinarily talented, but unless there's a specific experience in developing a firm identity program the likelihood is that the result will be less than satisfactory.

Before ordering a graphics identity program from a designer you should see many samples of the designer's work, asking in each case about the firm behind each design and its marketing objectives. This allows you to judge not only the attractiveness of the design but also its appropriateness and the degree to which it meets objectives.

The cost of design can vary from a few hundred dollars to many thousands of dollars, although cost alone is no guarantee of superiority. A few years ago, a most expensive corporate identity designer charged hundreds of thousands of dollars for a new logo for NBC's television network. Not included in their services, apparently, was research. It was only after the new logo went on the air that NBC discovered that its new logo was almost exactly the same as the logo done for a very small television station in the Midwest. This was not only embarrassing but expensive, because NBC's design had to be modified, and the smaller station had to be compensated.

When selecting a designer beware of being oversold. Understandably, designers ascribe magical qualities to firm graphics and identity programs. They have no magical qualities. Good graphics serve a purpose—an important one. But they cannot accomplish more than you can accomplish for yourself. They cannot project an image that is greater than your firm. A stranger having met Albert Einstein walking through the Princeton campus, and not knowing who he was, might have assumed that he was a sloppy old man rather than a genius with one of the greatest minds in history. Many a charlatan is finely garbed. If the reality of your firm is less than you would have it, don't depend upon a graphics program to change your firm into what you think it should be.

Graphics and a well-designed logo are important, but they're only part of a total marketing program.

# 15

# The Public Relations Agencies

The technical skills necessary to function effectively in public relations are quite different from those used in advertising, and are in many respects more complex. The tasks are different, as are the kinds of creativity. Moreover, public relations has its own professionalism. Naturally, then, the structure of the public relations firm is very different from that of an ad agency in more than just organization.

## Internal or External?

Which is not to say that, perhaps more than with advertising, a modicum of public relations activity can't be performed by the inexperienced public relations person functioning in his or her own behalf. Using the techniques in chapter 11, a small professional firm or sole practitioner can indeed perform many of the public relations tasks, and do so effectively and profitably. The entrepreneurial bent, drive, and outlook that made you a successful professional in the first place are the same attributes that can often supply the imagination to learn what's newsworthy and what's not, to establish friendly relations with the local press or the appropriate editor of the larger press, to develop the kinds of newsworthy events discussed in previous chapters, and to function generally on a small scale in pursuing a publicity program. It should be noted, however, that doing your own publicity can be tremendously time-consuming, and that the time and energy given to it might better be spent in other aspects of your business.

But sending out an occasional news release or letter to a journalist, or being interviewed now and again, don't constitute an effective public relations program. A program of any magnitude must be planned and executed by public relations professionals, either internally—on your staff—or by an external public relations agency. There are both advantages and disadvantages to internal staffs and external agencies. On the obverse side of the coin, the mutual disadvantages can, in most circumstances, be offset by using both internal and external staffs at the same time.

Sometimes it's difficult for a sole practitioner to be his or her own public relations agent, a position of blowing one's own horn to an editor. The outside agency, on the other hand, can sometimes do the job more effectively and more professionally. Agency staffs maintain ongoing relations with members of the press, which allows them to deal with the press more easily in selling story ideas and in channeling news. A good agency also has the experience of having worked for a variety of clients, and so can bring to bear a crosshatch of ideas and experience from other companies and other industries. An outside agency can spare you as well a great deal of time in performing the mechanics of publicity—writing and distributing releases, preparing press kits, wooing editors, and so forth.

In determining which route to take, the distinctions that are peculiarly those of professional services come to the fore.

In most cases, an external agency can deal very well with the public relations problems and opportunities of most companies. But in working with a professional service, it's the rare agency that can:

- Grasp the essence of professional practice, to the point of knowing what's newsworthy or important in a legal or an accounting or a consulting practice. Translating technical principles in law or accounting in ways that are useful to the prospective client is an essential part of public relations for professional services. And while this skill is not beyond the ken of an increasing number of public relations practitioners, it's essential, for the success of a public relations program for a professional firm.

- Be ubiquitous within the halls of a firm, to know what's going on that might be newsworthy in every area of the firm's practice, so that the latest nuance of an international tax ruling or Supreme Court decision can be caught and seized upon as a publicity opportunity.

- Deal with a partnership, as a source and as a program monitor, in which every partner is the client.

- Know and relate to the individual marketing plans and programs of each of the very many segments of virtually every professional service firm, regardless of size. Without this knowledge, the burden of performing successful public relations is unbearable and untenable.

Which is not to say that it can't be done. Indeed, it's not always done successfully by an internal staff, no matter how competent.

The arrangement is most likely to work successfully when there's a thoroughly professional internal staff, functioning as an internal public relations agency; an excellent outside agency; and a good marketing management structure in which the external agency functions as part of the team. Assuming a seasoned professional on the internal staff, the entire program is best coordinated and directed internally rather than externally. Then there are the advantages of each that overcome the disadvantages of each.

## Internal Public Relations

There are several distinct advantages to running the publicity program internally, for the firm that can develop and manage a good internal public relations department.

- It may be less expensive, although this is not categorically so. The salary spent on a publicity person, or the time a staff person allocates to publicity, might well add up to more dollars than the cost of an outside agency.
- The inside person is constantly in touch with your operation. He or she knows your firm intimately, knows the industry, and has the opportunity to see newsworthy activities firsthand as they develop.
- An internal program is usually more sensitive to—and exerts greater control on—both focus and activities. You and your partners know what's going on at all times, how much time is being spent on the program, what the press reaction is at any given moment.
- Your internal program can be supplemented with specialists as needed. For example, a photographer or a brochure writer or a meeting planner can be hired by the project.

In adding a staff person to handle the public relations and publicity function, there are only two hard and fast rules.

The first is that the person be properly qualified. There should be some verifiable experience in developing a public relations program, in writing releases and feature articles, in press contact and so forth. Don't underestimate the professionalism involved, or the value of experience—particularly if it includes work in professional services.

Second, it's next to useless to have an internal public relations person who doesn't have the ear, respect, and direct access to the senior or managing partners. The press will very quickly discern the degree of authority a public relations person has in speaking for a firm and in serving as a source of real news. There must be a genuine commitment to both the program and the person hired to do it, or else you can anticipate a lot of wasted time and money.

## External Counsel

A properly qualified public relations agency has several distinct advantages that go beyond the obvious ones of manpower and physical capability. These include:

- They are specialists, and as professional in pursuit of their craft as you are in yours. Public relations is their business, and the full focus of their business is on serving their clients in public relations activities.

- An agency is staffed and organized to deal with all aspects of a public relations program. It's equipped for the quick dissemination of releases, for direct contact with the press, and for planning and running newsmaking events. It maintains or has access to up-to-the-minute press mailing lists and lists of appropriate personnel in the press.

- Its liaison with the press is constant. Its staff should know of shifts in press attitude and personnel, and be able to supply an extraordinarily valuable perspective of changing needs.

- A good agency brings to each program the breadth of its experience in having served many companies with a wide variety of problems, and therefore having developed a broad experience in solutions.

- Its people are objective. Any good agency or public relations counsel must serve two roles—objectivity and advocacy. One is useless without the other. The agency will use its objectivity to help you make realistic public relations decisions. Advocacy—representing you to the public—that's not based on objectivity is weak, frequently irrelevant to your own objectives, and often borders dangerously close to creating problems of credibility.

- The agency staff represents the wide variety of skills necessary to conduct a well-rounded program.

- Agencies can be cost-effective. While there may be hidden overhead factors to be added to the cost of an internal public relations person, the expenses of an external agency can be budgeted. Agencies are accountable for fees and expenses. This is particularly true for those agencies whose fees are based on an hourly rate, where each month's bill itemizes the amount of time spent by each agency executive in each of the several categories in which he is functioning for the firm.

While this would seem to weigh the argument very heavily in favor of the use of an outside agency, the judgment is made, in many respects, no differently from the decision to retain inside or outside accounting or legal staff. Nor does the use of one necessarily preclude the other, and frequently they supplement one another. Indeed, an internal marketing director, who coordinates all marketing activities, can very well function as liaison between your firm and a public relations agency, advertising agency, and so forth.

## The Structure of a Public Relations Agency

In significant respects, a public relations agency is structured differently than an advertising agency. In an advertising agency, remember, there is a specialist for each skill and an account executive who functions as the agency's liaison with you, but is not expected to perform any of the skills of advertising. Few public relations firms are large enough to maintain specialists, and those that do have very few specialists in the same categories as in advertising.

And unlike advertising, the size of the public relations firm is no measure of its ability to serve you effectively. A small, well-run public relations firm that has imagination, skill, and energy can often accomplish more for even the largest professional service firm than can a giant public relations firm that has, as its most effective department, accounts receivable. Size, in public relations, is not of the essence—skill, and the imaginative and energetic dedication to using that skill in behalf of the client—is.

The service core of the larger public relations firm is predicated on the account executive and the account supervisor. In most public relations firms, the account executive performs the same liaison function as in advertising, but is expected to be capable of performing all of the skills of public relations—planning the program, counseling on all public relations attitudes and activities, writing all publicity material (releases, articles, brochures), dealing with the press, and so forth. In other words, the account executive is usually a well-rounded person who actually can perform all of the tasks of public relations.

The specialists and technicians in the larger agencies are usually specialists in media placement or writers. For example, a large agency may have a radio and television placement specialist, a magazine placement specialist, a newspaper placement specialist, and so forth. Some agencies have staff writers who do no placement or account liaison but may specialize in writing releases, feature articles, speeches, annual reports, brochures, or other material. If the agency has clients for whom it does financial public relations or investor relations, it will have staff people who are expert in that area.

Larger agencies with many clients in a particular industry may have industry specialists. For example, an agency with a great many food clients may have a staff home economist who tests and develops recipes for the client's products. Some public relations firms maintain their own art staffs for designing brochures, firm identity programs, and publicity reprints.

Many advertising agencies maintain separate public relations departments that are capable of performing the same functions as a separate public relations agency. Sometimes these ad agency public relations staffs are extraordinarily capable. The degree to which this is the case is a function of the advertising agency's own attitude towards publicity and public relations. Because advertising and public relations are so distinctly different, the ad agency public relations department should have a large degree of autonomy, rather than function merely as a creative subsidiary to advertising. The ad agency that perceives of its public relations department simply in terms of writing releases for its ad clients is not likely to have strong public relations capabilities.

In smaller public relations agencies, one or two people perform all the public relations tasks performed by the staffs in larger agencies. The restriction in terms of effectiveness for any client is the number of clients that any one individual can handle at one time without giving short shrift to other accounts.

## How to Work wth a Public Relations Firm

Because of the distinct differences between advertising and public relations, dealing with your public relations firm can be very different from dealing with your ad agency. In advertising, once the program is set, it's executed in a series of ads and perhaps promotional activities. Each ad can be seen and judged and, to some degree, its effectiveness can be measured.

A public relations program, on the other hand, is an ongoing activity with a constant flow of ideas and day-by-day effort to establish workable press relations, newsworthy activities, releases, feature articles, and so forth.

The relationship with your public relations firm begins with a program spelled out on paper so that you know at the outset exactly what your agency is going to do for you, and the timetable within which it's going to do it. What you may expect from the program should be made absolutely clear to you. Your public relations account executive should have constant access to you and your staff, without, of course, interfering with your day-to-day activities. If you're not experienced in public relations, his or her job is to train you to understand what kinds of material and activities the agency needs to know about to do its job. You should expect new and fresh ideas regularly from your agency.

You should also expect periodic meetings (at least once a week) with your account executive to review the week's activities and the status of the program. The account executive's supervisor should also meet with you periodically to review your program and its progress.

Written reports, no matter how brief, should be forthcoming regularly, and minutes—or at least notes—should be taken at each meeting. This avoids misunderstandings about what was promised and what was delivered.

A difficult part of a public relations program is that it frequently takes time and a great deal of work before the results begin to show up. Unfortunately, this is more often true with a smaller professional firm than with a larger one, because a smaller firm is less likely to generate the kinds of activities that are newsworthy; more must be developed for the smaller firm. Thus, no program you undertake should last less than three months. This should be time enough for a new agency to become familiar with your business, to prepare any necessary materials, and to develop some successful publicity. The nature of publicity is such that you can't always pick your dates and timing. A great many releases may have to go to an editor, over a long period, before he decides that you've said something newsworthy, or even before the editor decides to accept your firm as a news source. Feature material may also take a month to six weeks to develop and place. In publicity, you hear the word "no" more often than you do "yes," and it sometimes takes a great barrage of material to the press before a single clipping is produced. In the start-up period of a publicity program, the results may be slim but the effort isn't wasted. Contacts are being made in your behalf and a familiarity with your firm is being developed—all of which should pay off in the next three months.

But the program and the agency's activities must be carefully monitored even during that initial period to be sure that the pipeline is in fact being filled, and that the time isn't being used by the agency just to learn your operation and your industry at your expense.

If, during the first three-month initial period, you don't quickly discern that your agency is coming to understand your firm and is functioning successfully in your behalf, or if at the end of six months there have been no tangible results as measured against the original public relations program, then it's time to consider whether you've chosen the right agency. Any questions you have of that nature should be raised directly with the agency principals. If the program isn't working, then conceivably, it's their fault. Just as conceivably, it's your fault. They may not have made clear to you what they're trying to accomplish and how they work, or you may not be cooperating with them in areas that count. There may be personality problems with the particular account executive, or the agency itself may not be the right one for you. But if a program isn't working, it's the program and its performance that's at fault—not the validity of public relations and publicity as a marketing tool.

## Selecting an Agency

Public relations agencies come in all sizes and forms. They range from the one-person firm to major international firms with offices in many cities throughout the country and the world. Many advertising agencies have departments of various sizes.

Public relations firms are no different than your own professional service, in that regardless of the size of the firm, the success of the relationship is a function of the individuals involved—not necessarily the firm itself. So it is with public relations. You may retain the largest, most prestigious firm in town, and get a dud working on your account. It may not be the public relation's firm's fault—the account person may be terrific, but just not right for you. You may be the largest firm in town, but the individual who runs a small public relations firm may be just right for you. The point is that the success of the program is a function of the individual assigned to your account, more than the agency itself.

Choosing the appropriate agency for you is a function of your needs as well as your budget. If your program—and your budget—are small, then conceivably a one-person agency (who himself has a low overhead) can perform as successfully for you as can a large, major national firm (assuming that the one person isn't so overloaded with other accounts that you can command only the smallest portion of his time). If your program is of any size, then obviously it will require the manpower and the facilities of a larger firm. Note, though, that it's the size of the program, not the size of the firm, that dictates the size of the public relations agency.

In choosing a firm, a preliminary interview should establish at least the following:

- What are the size and nature of the agency? How many clients does it have and who are they? Are many of the clients the same size as your firm? What industries are its clients in?

- What successful programs for other clients can it show you? This should include a full presentation of the original objectives, the programs designed to meet those objectives, and clear evidence of the successful performance of those programs.

- How well established is the agency? A public relations agency is a business, just as yours is. It should be able to demonstrate that it's well established and financially sound. Getting a Dun & Bradstreet rating is helpful.

- What is the experience and what are the qualifications of the people who will work on your account? Are they senior people? Can you see samples of their work? What's the line of internal reporting responsibility? Who in the agency has the ultimate responsibility for performance on your account?

- Who will be working directly on your account, and what are their experience and qualifications? How many other accounts do they service? Do you personally like the account executive to be assigned to you? Since the working relationship will be close, this is extremely important.

- What is the fee structure, including the policy on out-of-pocket expenses?

- What contractual arrangements are offered? Agencies prefer a year's contract. This is understandable and usually acceptable, provided, however, that there is a three-month trial period and a 30-day cancellation clause.

- Do they ask the right questions? Even in a preliminary conversation you can tell pretty fast whether you're dealing with intelligent people who understand your business and who can quickly learn your marketing problems, your objectives, and the role that they will be expected to play in your marketing program.

- What references do they offer? This should include both present clients and business references. If possible, it should include references from the media itself. A well-established public relations firm should be happy to give you the names of several editors with whom they have long-standing relationships and who can vouch for their professionalism.

If possible, you should interview several agencies rather than allow yourself to be sold by just one. The relationship with a public relations firm is a close one—closer perhaps than with an advertising agency. A great deal depends upon a strong interplay of communication and ideas. Given all of the qualifications and appropriate answers to the list of questions you should feel comfortable with your choice.

## Serving Competing Clients

For professionals inexperienced in working with public relations firms, the question arises as to whether the agency you choose should be allowed to have competing clients (two or more law firms, accounting firms, etc.).

When an accounting or a law firm takes several clients in the same industry, it's a marketing device that projects an expertise in that industry. It's good marketing.

But can a public relations, marketing, or advertising agency take competing firms as clients, even when different account teams work on different clients? To some practitioners, it's thought to be unethical, and unsound business for an accounting or law firm to hire an agency that has competitive clients.

Go back, for a moment, to what the accounting and law firms do. First, they recognize that specific industries have singular bodies of specific guidelines, practices, jargon, rules and regulations, accounting practices, and nuances. There is a distinct advantage to having a law or accounting firm with expertise in your industry. It enhances the wisdom of the professional services offered.

But if you ask an accountant or a lawyer why his or her firm wouldn't hire an agency that has other law or accounting firms as clients, you might be told something about competitive secrets. Or, "If they have a marketing or public relations idea, how do we know that they'll apply it to us, rather than to the firm's other client?" Or, "How do we know if we can trust them with our firm's secrets?"

Are we assuming, then, that only accountants and lawyers and consultants can be relied upon to have a Chinese wall that separates one client's interests from another? Is this rational?

Granted, there is a canon of ethics-defined code of confidentiality that governs the professions, and that therefore exudes confidence to companies that their secrets will be respected. Is the feeling that marketing and its parts are too fragile—

its people too unprofessional—to understand the Chinese wall and the meaning of confidentiality?

We know better. We know that it's the firm, not the profession, that builds Chinese walls. Accountants and lawyers and consultants, with their canons of ethics, do have more of a stricture, and therefore more to lose if they violate client confidentiality, than do marketers. Marketers, lacking this ethical strictures, have nothing to lose but their clients.

Violating client confidence is not just—or even merely—unethical. It's dumb. Every profession has dumb people, and no dumb accountant or lawyer or marketer should be hired. But because Chinese walls are a function of sound business, and not arbitrary ethical structures, the choice of sharing confidential information with a client or an agency should be made on the basis of the individuals involved, not the profession.

One of the truly outstanding marketing communications agencies in the professional services marketing business, Torrance Associates, makes a point of not having two clients in the same industry or profession, unless the assignments are completely devoid of conflict or the clients are in different cities or market areas. This is a conscious choice of the principals of the agency. They feel that their clients are more comfortable with it, that they can concentrate better on solving the client's problems without diluting efforts, that there's enough anxiety about marketing for lawyers and accountants without adding the additional worry of confidentiality or dilution of creative efforts. It's the agency's choice, and they're comfortable with it, and they're a tremendously successful and well run agency.

But the paradox is that the people in this agency are so superior that, like accounting or law firms with industry expertise, they too have a singular and superior expertise in marketing professional services. The personalities are mature, and have the kind of integrity that can build better Chinese walls between clients of the same profession. And so the agency—and there are others like it—is actually depriving professional firms of potentially superior marketing support.

Marketing professional services is, after all, a distinctive and unique form of marketing, and for all who profess to understand it, there really are few who do. It's also, as is all of marketing, an art form, and as is true of all the world, there are very few artists. Unfortunately, there are more professional firms that need this expertise than there are experts to go around. Extending trust to a marketing firm that they will serve each client well, and confidentially, and with energy and artistry, can often be a wiser policy than one based upon suspicion.

Some marketing consulting firms, which are no different in practice than are any other kind of consulting firms, can serve the needs of competing clients because they don't actually perform the marketing function. They address each client's marketing problems, within the context of each client's own structures, objectives and marketing programs. And while it's true that they are privy to each client's secrets, they have track records of integrity, so that no question is ever raised about breaches of confidentiality. They are good business people, and are recognized for it.

The crux of the Chinese wall, and the essence of real service, is not arbitrary ethical codes, but rather, a sense of good business and sound judgment. Respecting confidentiality, and producing the best for each client, is good business and sound judgment. Nobody should work with or for anybody who doesn't have a dynamic sense of both.

The public relations agency, like your firm, is a service organization. You know how your firm deals with the problem of competing clients, and that offers some guidance. There are several questions that apply:

- What will the firm be doing for you that deals with sensitive information?
- Is the public relations firm large enough to maintain separate account teams for competitive clients?
- What safeguards do they offer to maintain security and discretion, as you do in your own firm?
- Is the firm really that good that raising the question is worth the effort, or should you look elsewhere?

When these questions are addressed head on, you're closer to knowing whether there is, in fact, a problem.


## The Request for Proposal

Too often, the lack of experience by most agencies in dealing with a professional service makes it difficult for them to propose properly. The subject, even now, is too new for even the best agencies to adequately address a program for you, without a great deal of input from you.

The solution lies in a formal *Request for Proposal*, in which you delineate on paper those facts that would help an agency propose intelligently.

The RFP (see appendix) should include at least the following information:

- A description of your firm
- A description of what you do, and how you're distinguished from others in your profession.
- Your general firm objectives
- Your general marketing objectives
- Your structure for dealing with marketing projects
- Your expectations from a public relations program
- An open invitation to ask questions before the written proposal is made.
- Mechanical information (timetable, how selection will be made, etc.)

- Any other information you yourself might like to have if the situation were reversed

Then, of course, there is the basic information that you want to know about the proposing firm, such as the factors that will help you judge the firm's experience, substance, and so forth. This includes their size and nature, number of clients, size of staff, fee structure, background and qualifications of the individuals who will be working on your program, and so forth.

Preparing a written RFP may seem to be an unnecessary use of your time, but it isn't. It will consume less time and effort than will reading proposals from agencies, including some good ones,that really don't understand how to propose to a professional service firm.

## Costs

Essentially, the expenses in a public relations program are:

- Consulting fees
- Reproduction costs for releases, etc.
- Mailing costs
- Travel costs for meetings, major press interviews, etc.
- Out-of-pocket and miscellaneous expenses, including long-distance phone bills, entertainment of editors, etc.
- Design and printing of special brochures, publicity, reprints, etc.
- Special projects, such as photography, opinion surveys, and other special events and contingencies

Fee structures vary from one firm to another, although basically there are only two types used by most public relations firms—straight fee and hourly rate. Fees for an effective program may range from $500 a month to $100,000 or more for a year. These days, for $500 a month you get virtually no service, and probably very little quality. Service and quality begin at about $1,500 a month. Average fees are about $2,000 to $5,000 a month.

Straight fee basis is usually a fixed amount, paid monthly. This has the advantage of simpler budgeting.

The hourly rate functions much the same as with accountants and attorneys. Usually a basic minimum fee is agreed upon, with hours charged against that fee, and the client is billed for hours in excess of the minimum. Sometimes a maximum is also agreed upon. The maximum allows for overall budgeting. The hourly basis functions best if there's a clear understanding beforehand of the hourly rate of each person who is to work on the account. Your bill might then consist of an hourly breakdown, person by person, with a portion of time allocated to each activity (client contact, press contact, planning, release writing, etc.).

Most firms bill a month in advance, with firms that use the hourly rate billing the agreed-upon minimum.

Prior to signing a contract with a public relations firm, you should have a general idea of the cost of each item. How much are reproduction costs for releases and other material? How large a mailing list is involved, and what will the mailing costs generally come to? If the public relations firm is located any distance from your office, who pays the travel expenses for meetings with you?

Normally, out-of-pocket and routine expenses include:

- Clipping services
- Photography and artwork
- Telephone, telegrams, Fax
- Special wire services for rapid distribution of urgent news
- Transportation other than for meetings with you
- Promotional expenses for meeting with the press, including press entertainment
- Postage
- Messenger services
- Photocopying
- Subscriptions to trade publications
- Secretarial overtime on special projects
- Miscellaneous minor expenses
- Press list maintenance

If your press coverage extends beyond local newspapers and other publications that you would normally read, a clipping service may be included. This allows you to determine the extent to which any publicity you've issued is printed. Unfortunately, no method has yet been devised to mechanize the essentially human job of scanning thousands of publications. As a result, the number of clippings found is usually a small percentage of material that actually appears.

Telephone and other means of communication are usually billed at exact cost, as shown on actual bills. Faxes may be billed at a fixed rate per page.

Transportation expenses usually include transportation within a city, such as cabs, buses, subway and so on.

In addition to postage for regular mailings of press releases, there's postage normally used in mailing letters and other material, fulfilling information requests, and for shipping quantities of background material and so forth.

During the course of a program, it's frequently necessary to conduct business with members of the press over lunch, dinner, or cocktails. These expenses must be documented by receipts.

Costs for messenger service are usually incurred within one city, although occasionally messengers or air couriers must be used to transmit important material between cities. These expenses are supported by copies of bills. Photocopying costs are usually calculated on a predetermined rate based on costs.

In order for your public relations firm to function well for you, it must keep abreast of your industry by reading trade publications. Subscriptions to such publications for that purpose are normally billed to the client.

Special wire services for rapid distribution of publicity releases normally charge a fixed rate for each day of operation. In other words, two separate releases for one firm on the same day cost the same as for one release. There are variations of cost if the release exceeds 500 words.

The costs of travel—indeed, all expenses on behalf of the client—are usually allocated on the same basis used by the Internal Revenue Service. This includes transportation, meals, hotel expenses, transportation within a city, auto mileage, tips, and miscellaneous out-of-pocket expenses.

While normal secretarial and office services are considered part of a public relations firm's or professional firm's own internal operating expenses, special projects frequently require additional expense, such as secretarial overtime or the use of temporary office help. Public relations firms normally include these costs in expense billings.

In the normal course of a program, miscellaneous minor expenses are sometimes incurred. These include additional copies of publications, tips, phone calls made away from the office and so on.

Even in the best planned program, situations frequently arise, often in the form of opportunities, for special projects or activities. This may include an opportunity for someone in your firm to participate as a panelist in a seminar, the need for a special brochure or pamphlet and so forth. While these occasions are normally unexpected, and unbudgeted, their extra costs can often be measured in terms of added value.

Granted the flexibility of expenses that tend to be variable, it's still possible to review a program well in advance and generally estimate what the expenses are likely to be. This should make it possible for any firm or experienced public relations firm to budget appropriately for the cost of the program.

Whether your public relations program is performed internally or externally, the objectives, and the relationship to the total marketing program and marketing mix, are the same. So too should be the quality of results. And except for fees, the expenses of a program will be basically the same whether you do it in-house or use an outside agency.

The idea, of course, is the result, not the path to get there.

# Part IV

# Proposals
and
Presentations

# 16

# Proposals and Presentations

The major thrust of the total marketing effort is to bring the prospective client to the point at which a proposal and presentation—written, oral, or just a simple request for the order—are requested and made. This is what marketing professional services is about. And it is here that the client is won or lost.

Clients are rarely won without a presentation and proposal, in one form or another, particularly in this competitive climate. It's a long way from "This is who we are—when do we start?" to the elaborate, competitive formal proposals, and dog-and-pony-show presentations, that are commonplace today. Still, nothing so cogently makes the point that marketing is a process, and not a configuration of isolated acts, culminating at the proposal stage.

Ideally, the sum total of the marketing effort should be sufficient to close the deal without the formality of a discussion and a proposal—but it rarely is. Such is the nature of professional services that the people who hire must feel comfortable with the people who are hired. Comfortable with them as both people and as professionals. In fact, even the most formal and elaborate proposal and presentation should drive to develop that comfort—to build confidence in individuals.

There are, of course, some professional services in which a formal proposal is neither required nor expected. No one asks a doctor or a dentist for more than a few words of explanation about the problem, the solution, and the charges. Lawyers, too, are rarely required to write proposals or to make formal presentations, although increasing competition is causing changes here, too.

On the other hand, no moderate or larger-sized company is likely to accept a bid from an accounting firm or a consultant without some clear picture of how the professional sees the prospective client's situation and needs, and how he proposes to serve them.

In professional services, proposals and presentations play an interesting role, part of which is predicated on the fact that buyers of professional services are poor consumers. Most individuals don't know much about how to choose a lawyer, an accountant, an architect, or any other professional. Even sophisticated business people, with experience in dealing with professionals, don't have much to guide them in choosing. Given a parade of any six professionals who perform the same service, who are of equal size and qualification, how do you distinguish one from the other? How do you make a choice, except on instinct or personal chemistry?

And if you're selling the service, how do you distinguish yourself from the others in the parade, particularly when you're down to the wire of a proposal and a presentation?

There are more responses to these questions than there are clear solutions. That's why proposals and presentations are getting more elaborate, if not necessarily better, as if splendor were a response to competition. That's why so many proposals from different firms in the same profession so often sound so much like one another, as if everybody subscribed to the same proposal writing service.

The answer, if there is one, perhaps lies in looking more thoughtfully at the process—trying to fathom what works for you and what doesn't; trying to bring more skill and imagination to it.

There are some hints. The way the proposal is written, and what it contains, must convey a sense of competence, intelligence, skill, and a service concept that inspires confidence in the firm, its people, and their ability to perform. The presentation must show a sense of stability and security in what's being presented. Thoroughness, and being meticulous, seem to make a positive difference.

In professional services, ultimately, people sell people. It's not the ad or the news story or the brochure that people buy—it's the faith that the people who perform the service can be trusted to do what the ads and all the other marketing tools say they can do. In fact, Ruth Sheridan, a particularly thoughtful specialist and expert in proposal writing whose track record for successful proposals is rarely matched, notes that proposals that aren't people oriented are doomed to failure. "A proposer must strive to achieve direct contact with the decision makers. Paper, no matter how well done, is no substitute for personal contact."

## The Proposal

If the proposal is part of a process, then the proposal is a process in itself as well. It's certainly more than just a document. Inconsistency in proposal success is as much a result of failure to follow the process as it is of competition. It's as much a failure to understand the primary focus of a proposal as it is of being outsold. It begins with the invitation to propose, and proceeds step-by-step to either getting the client or losing. At every step there is a potential obstacle or opportunity, which must be examined and seized or rejected.

And in the course of going through the process, the eye must never leave the objective of getting the client, nor the substance of good marketing technique.

For example, says Sheridan, "The fundamental thing the proposal process must accomplish is to generate a prospect's confidence in your firm. The prospect must be confident of his or her ultimate decision to chose the correct firm, and to be able to defend the choice. This comes through confidence in the firm's ability to do the work, and confidence that the firm's people understand the company management's needs—that they have the ability and resources to meet those needs."

And most of all, she says, "Proposals must clearly demonstrate why the proposing firm should be the prospect's choice."

In smaller firms, the proposal is usually written by a principal of the firm, or some senior member who's displayed a special capability to do it. In larger firms, proposals are considered to be of such consequence that teams of proposal writers are especially trained and dedicated to writing them.

Elaborate proposals for prospective clients can, in the larger firms, cost as much as hundreds of thousands of dollars. When a Fortune 500 company invites an accounting firm or a consultant to make a proposal, where the prospective fee is many times the cost of the proposal, then expense is no object. The higher the stakes, in terms of fees, the greater the expense that seems to be warranted.

### Deciding To Bid

Unfortunately, it costs the prospective client nothing to invite five or six firms to make that expenditure, too often knowing beforehand which firm will be hired. There seems to be no known solution to this deplorable practice, other than a frank request of the prospective client to clearly state that the competition is indeed open.

Each firm should develop its own criteria for making a bid or no-bid decision. While the criteria are subjective, they should certainly include an analysis of whether the firm is capable of handling the business with existing skills or facilities, whether the prospective client fits into the firm's own objectives, and whether the cost of getting the business is equal to the value of the business to the firm.

As for the assessment of whether there's a chance to get the client, if there's any doubt, a frank question of the prospect isn't out of line. It would take a cynical executive to lie about a wired—pre-agreed upon—arrangement. If you suspect it, it's worth asking.

## Types of Proposals

Proposals range from the simple to the elaborate.

The simplest type of proposal and presentation is the face-to-face statement in which the professional says to his prospect, "This is the problem, this is how I'm going to solve it, this is what I think will happen as a result of my efforts, and this is what it will cost."

A written proposal says essentially the same things, but may range from a simple one page letter to an elaborate document of many pages, illustrated and bound.

Other proposals may take advantage of graphic and visual techniques. Proposals have been done in the form of video tapes and motion picture films. A proposal may be in the form of a computer program supplied on a disk. Mixed media proposals may combine a written document with several different audio visual techniques. In fact, in requesting a prospective client's business there are no limitations, other than the imagination, to the form a proposal may take.

There are four basic categories of relationships with prospective clients, each of which requires a different view of the kind of proposal that may work:

- *The straightforward relationship,* in which the prospect has a strong feeling that the firm is exactly right. This may be the prospect's hunch, or the result of a strong recommendation. It usually requires little more than a discussion, and perhaps a letter outlining the approach to be used by the proposing firm to solve the problem.

- *The sole source,* in which no other firm is being invited to propose. This may be the result of a marketing effort, or it may be based upon the firm's reputation for a particular expertise. Here, too, the proposal may require little more than a descriptive letter.

- *The Request For Proposal (RFP),* in which the firm is one of several invited to respond to an RFP. Here, the thrust of the proposal must primarily be in careful response to the RFP, adding only that information thought to be significant, but not specifically requested by the RFP

- *The fully competitive proposal,* in which each firm invited to make a presentation is given little guidance in an RFP, but is expected to fully compete. This is the kind of proposal that results in costing a great deal of money, in which many people are involved, and in which there is opportunity to range free and be thoughtful and original in developing the proposal and presentation.

These are, of course, general categories, and general suggestions within each one. There are no hard and fast rules. In getting the business, the solution that works (ethically, of course) is the best solution—regardless of the rules.

## The Proposal Process

The proposal process begins with the marketing effort itself that either supports the actual selling effort or leads into the agreement to meet with the firm. There may or may not be an RFP, or there may be just a simple invitation to discuss a potential relationship.

A basic point here . . .

If the business is worth having, it's worth getting. That means being professional and meticulous in pursuit of it. If the client isn't worth the effort, then don't risk the firm's reputation by doing a shoddy proposal. If it is worth getting, then take the RFP very seriously. And if there's no RFP, function as if there is one, and respond accordingly. It's a way to avoid skipping a base or two.

Nor should the RFP be taken as a sole source of inquiry. It may be poorly written, forgetting to ask you to supply the very points about your firm that are most worthwhile. It may ask irrelevant and unknowing questions, the answers to which may be distractions from the real reasons that they should choose you. In that case, follow the RFP, but find a way to get the proposal back on track to what you want to say. Improvise if you must—but don't ignore the RFP—it's somebody's document written with pride.

At least the following steps should be taken as part of the process:

- Review the RFP. Look at it carefully, and respond to each request for information thoughtfully. What services are requested? What's the level of detail provided and requested? Can you easily answer the questions asked, or must you go to other sources for help? What are the special requests and limitations? Are the decision criteria clearly stated? Are the decision makers identified? Be particularly responsive, but try to go beyond the questions to get a sense of what is really being asked; what will really turn this company on.

- Research the firm carefully. Read its literature. If it's a public company, scour the databases and the printed material. Review the press coverage. Check out the backgrounds and histories of its officers—particularly those who will participate in the hiring decision. If an audit committee is being used, learn what you can of its members' backgrounds. Try to determine the problems faced by the company, beyond the reason for firing the existing firm. The more you know, the more useful will be your ability to demonstrate that you can help.

- Manage the effort. If possible, put a team on it, including experts on the problem, the individuals who will run the account, specialists in different aspects of the proposal. The team should plan the effort, and then manage every aspect of it.

- Develop a timetable, working backwards from the delivery deadline date. Write a schedule, allowing realistic amounts of time for everything from research and writing to printing and binding.

- It's more than appropriate to meet with those people in the prospect's management who will be influential in making the decision to get to know them (and for them to know you), to get further information about the company, and to determine how the proposal will be judged and how the final decision will be made.

- Follow up special opportunities, such as building an inventory of solutions to problems similar to those faced by the firm, and meeting with people outside the company who might be helpful.

- Plan your strategy to win. This is the point at which the team determines what strategy they think will win the contract competitively;

that will overwhelm and win the hearts and minds of the prospect's management team.

- Finalize the team that will actually make the presentation. Review the proposal with them in great detail. Assign different segments to each member of the team. And rehearse. Critique the rehearsal. Polish. Rehearse again—as often as it takes to get it perfect and win the account.

## Elements of a Proposal

Whether it be done in one page or a bound book, whether it be part of a written proposal or an oral presentation or a combination of both, prospective clients may be best persuaded to retain you if they're given the following information:

- An indication that you understand, or are capable of learning, the essence of the prospect's business and industry.
- An indication that you understand the nature of the prospect's problem, or the situation that warrants the need for your professional services.
- A sense of what the prospect really needs, or wants, or can be persuaded to want, in terms of the service you have to offer (this doesn't mean persuading the prospect that he needs something that you want to sell more than he needs buy). Ethics count, because win or lose, there's always another day.
- A persuasive argument for your ability to fulfill his needs or wants.
- The basic information about your firm . . .
  - Size and nature
  - Personnel
  - Structure, in terms of prospect's needs (Specialists? Access to outside experts? Levels of people responsible for the prospect's account?)
  - History of your firm
  - Track record, particularly in parallels to the prospect's situation or problem
  - Names and backgrounds of people who will be directly responsible for servicing the prospect
- A sense of program to address the client's needs—what you will do to meet those needs and how you'll do it.
- A timetable
- Costs and fee structure

- Any other information that the prospect may require to help him distinguish your firm from others, and to make a decision.

Just how this information is presented is a function of many factors. How big is the prospect's company? How large is the situation or problem? How many people make the decision about which firm to hire? Who will contribute to that decision? Increasingly, larger companies are relying upon committees of the board of directors to qualify and retain professionals, in which case you're facing a tougher audience, but one that's likely to have more experience in dealing with professionals. A two-edged sword.

## Proposal Rules

There are some basic general rules as well that must be considered. They simply encompass the most logical, reasonable, and effective use of marketing practices. And like all rules of marketing, they are not graven in stone, but rather, should be breached only for conscious and knowing reasons. In the final analysis, what works, works—and the only measure of success for a proposal is that it gets the client.

The rules:

- The proposal should be orderly and logical. It should state the prospect's problem or define his situation, your capabilities and approach to solving the problem, the forces of your firm that you will bring to bear in the prospect's behalf, a description of your qualifications, a breakdown of time frame and costs, and your fee. Try to keep the level of writing fairly high. Poor and unfocused writing says to the prospective client that you're a poor and unfocused thinker and practitioner. And watch the length. A proposal that's too long, too wordy, or too elaborate will lose a prospect's enthusiasm, attention, and focus.

- No matter how special or unique your services, they should be presented in terms of the client's needs—what he wants and needs, not what you have to offer. Merely to offer your capabilities is not sufficient. The wrong point of view, in which the emphasis is on who you are and what you can do, rather than on the client's needs, will almost invariably turn the prospect off.

- If there is a formal request for a proposal it should be read very carefully and the response should be precisely in terms of the RFP, even if it deviates from your normal proposal format.

- Because of the personal nature of professional services, every effort should be made to delineate precisely who will work on the account, including their personal backgrounds and experience.

271

- Prior to writing the proposal, as much research as possible should be done on the prospective client's company, the industry, the nature of the problem, and the people involved. Nothing turns a prospective client off so quickly as the feeling that the professional didn't take the trouble to understand what the client's company, industry, or problems were about. Do your homework. It's useful, too, to know against whom you're competing, if possible. This can sometimes give you an advantage, particularly if you have a sense of your competitor's strengths and weaknesses.

- Graphics and exhibits should be used very cautiously. The danger is that they will be a distraction, rather than support the points you want to make. Judgment should be exercised carefully.

- Be cautious of boilerplate—standard paragraphs or sections you include in all proposals. A proposal should look tailor-made, and focus specifically on the needs of the prospective client. Boilerplate has a way of looking and sounding like boilerplate. Moreover, a careless typist can pick up a boilerplate element from another proposal that may include something that clearly gives away the fact that it is boilerplate.

- Too much or too little sell are equal pitfalls in a proposal. Too much sell is irksome and distracts from the real message. Too little sell will not allow a proposal to achieve its ends.

- Don't forget to ask for the order. This is a basic tenet of selling—one that works and that's too frequently ignored.

- Whether the style is formal or informal, the proposal should have an element of personality in it. It's an individual talking to an individual—not a piece of paper talking to a machine, or an insurance policy. There should be a measure of humanity, warmth, and readability.

- Never promise more than can be delivered. Even the most naive prospective client will realize that you've done this, more often than not. It destroys credibility. And don't misrepresent. You'll pay for it sooner or later. Probably sooner.

- Not relating the proposal to the oral presentation can be confusing and distracting.

Essentially, the written proposal is another one of those anomalies of marketing—the mixture of technique and art. And while proposals for professionals are not new, doing them in the new competitive context is new, and creates new problems in that they must be done more thoughtfully than ever before. But it creates new opportunities as well.

## Presentations

A presentation is the primary selling point at which an individual or team explains in person why the prospect should retain the firm. It's the point at which the information and persuasive arguments of the written proposal are presented by the individuals who will perform—or supervise the performance of—the program. It's the point at which the important element of personal chemistry is added to the marketing mix, frequently for the first time.

While salesmanship is inherent in both proposals and presentations, their structured nature must be viewed apart from classical sales techniques. Selling is involved in both, of course, but within the framework of the structure.

Although a proposal is usually given in conjunction with a presentation (either before or after), and elements of both will appear in each, the two are quite separate. However, the nature of the relationship between the two dictates the format of each. The proposal may supplement an oral presentation—include information that's not part of the presentation—or complement it. The proposal may be sent ahead of the presentation, or left behind after the presentation has been made.

Presentations offer somewhat different, and usually more flexible, opportunities than do proposals. Proposals are words on paper. Presentations are people presenting themselves, as much as the information they impart. In professional services, it's people who get hired, and so the presentation offers the opportunity to focus on individuals.

Presentations offer the prospective client the opportunity to ask questions, and they afford the opportunity to respond immediately to those questions, to new information, to objections—none of which can be done with the same psychological advantages in a written proposal.

The presentation can be as casual as a dialogue with the prospect, or it can be formal, carefully designed and orchestrated, with several people from your firm participating, elaborate audio visual support (including slides and films), and a substantial proposal left behind or subsequently delivered.

The several considerations that affect the format of the presentation include, essentially, the same as those for proposals. The size of the prospective client company and the size of the prospective account and fee. The nature of your firm and its size. The nature of traditional or competitive presentations.

But to these considerations should be added concerns about the ability to deal well on a face-to-face basis, to think well on your feet, to inspire confidence in person.

Add to this both the wherewithal and the familiarity to use graphic and visual materials. If you haven't had experience in using an overhead projector or in making a slide presentation, a new business presentation isn't the place to learn.

The presentation may be made by one or two individuals, or it may use an entire team that consists of senior partners who are specialists in new business presentations, experts in specific areas of the prospective client's problems or business, and those partners and others who will be responsible for serving the account should it be won. Your firm's growth may depend upon having an increasing number of your firm's members participating in presentations.

Consider the individuals to whom you'll be making the presentation. Know about them beforehand, if possible. Then you can adjust your style to the personalities of the audience.

While a good deal of personal style dictates the nature of a presentation, it's useful to attempt to catalog what works for your firm and what doesn't, and then to train as many people as possible to make presentations.

It's not out of line, these days, to ask the prospect why you *didn't* get the account. You won't always find out, but when you do, the information is worth its weight in gold.

## Physical Arrangements

While the physical arrangements of the room in which you'll make your presentation are most often the province—literally and figuratively—of the prospective client, there may still be some flexibility in the arrangement. Ruth Sheridan suggests that you try to see the room in advance, to determine room dimensions, layout, location of outlets, and availability of easels and audio visual equipment.

To the degree that you can control the situation, what you're after are surroundings that are comfortable and receptive. For example, a conference room or the seating area of an office is preferable to an arrangement in which you're making a presentation to an individual seated behind a desk. The desk serves as a psychological barrier.

You want to be sure that there's enough light and that neither you nor your prospect are seated with a back towards a sunlit window. Certainly, if you're going to use visuals, you want to be sure that the facilities are compatible—that screens can be set up and equipment conveniently plugged in, that extraneous light can be blocked, and so forth.

Of course, if you can arrange to have the presentation made in your own offices, it's presumed that you will have set up the facilities to your advantage.

## Using Visual Aids

Your choice of visual aids is extensive. Among your many choice are, for example:

- Flip charts.
- Chalk boards
- Overhead projectors.

- Slide projectors.
- Video tape.
- Motion picture projectors.
- Multi-media presentations . Audio tapes
- Phonograph records

Using these devices can be very seductive. They're exciting and they're vivid, and there's a tendency to use them badly, or to use the wrong device for your material. But if they're used well they can capture and hold attention. And they should, of course, be thoroughly professional. Poor visual aids can do more damage than can no visual aids at all.

There is a danger, too, in forgetting that visual aids are *aids* to the presentation, which, after all, is a function of people relating to people. If they interfere with your establishing rapport with the individuals to whom you're making the presentation, scrap them. The focus of attention should be the individual—not the screen or flip chart.

The ultimate decision to use visual and audio visual devices should be a function of the information you want to impart rather than the sheer drama. The choice of using audio visuals, then, is a function of impact, but within a context of imparting information and selling. Dramatic presentations may be amusing, but if they don't sell they're expensive.

## When to Use Visuals

Beyond the context of imparting information, other factors that dictate using these devices are:

- Budget.
- Available production facilities.
- Available equipment.
- The room in which the presentation will be made (it's size, shape, lighting and so forth).
- Your experience in dealing with the equipment and with visuals.

Different media offer different capabilities, and it's extremely important to use each of the devices effectively within its own medium. To attempt to allow audio visuals to carry more than their weight can lead to confusion and distraction. The rule is to keep it simple, with each visual making no more than a single point. When an audience is reading a slide or a chart it's not listening to the speaker. Nothing should go on a slide or a flip chart that can't be grasped in a moment.

Films or videotape offer the opportunity to bring in outside experts or to dramatize a point. On the other hand, these are expensive devices to use for showing a chart or a graph, which can be done more effectively with slides.

Charts, photographs, and even a simple cartoon can be very effective in presenting a complex idea simply. Where words must be used in the graphic, use as few as possible.

Chalkboards or flip charts, on the other hand, are effective devices for riveting attention and making a point during an oral presentation. They also have the advantage of staying in front of your audience for as long as you need them, without being distracting.

In using flip charts and chalkboards, use them as carefully as you would electronic devices. Flip charts have distinctive advantages in that they supply a certain intimacy with the audience. They can be used almost anywhere and are simple and inexpensive. They can be flipped back and forth to refer to previous points more easily than can a slide. They don't require a darkened room, which means that you're always in sight of your audience and can maintain valuable eye contact.

Flip charts also have an advantage in that they can be prepared beforehand or used like chalkboards to make points as you need them.

A chalkboard, while it can show fine detail and is subject to the user's handwriting, has the same advantages as flip charts, plus additional spontaneity. They are a highly personal medium, with a great deal of flexibility. The only disadvantage is that you frequently have to turn your back to your audience to write.

Slides and other graphic media should be designed professionally by an art director. The additional cost is moderate and the return on the investment makes it worthwhile.

## Making the Presentation

In using audio visuals during the course of a presentation, it's extremely important to make the conscious decision beforehand about whether the slides are driving the speaker or the speaker is driving the slides. If the slides are an adjunct to the speaker they should aid, and not distract by being too elaborate or complex. At the same, time it's pointless to have the speaker simply read what the slide says and have no more to contribute to the presentation than that.

While you may have great confidence in your own ability to make a presentation, particularly on your own company, rehearsals are very much in order. This is particularly true if you're using new material or audio visuals, or if others are involved in the presentation. There is some peculiar notion held by those who haven't done it that rehearsal reduces spontaneity, or that the adrenalin rush of the moment will add an element of enthusiasm to the presentation. It simply isn't so. Rehearsal helps to familiarize all participants with the material, so that during the actual presentation the mind can be free and alert to reactions and other factors. It helps hone timing and smooths out difficult relationships with both other members of the team and with the audio visual material. There should be at least two rehearsals before a selected audience of your own associates. The comments of the audience allow flaws in the presentation to be seen and corrected after the first rehearsal; the second assures that all flaws are ironed out.

### Anticipate Questions

It's also a good idea to anticipate questions, particularly difficult ones, and to formulate answers beforehand. There should be no reason to be stumped by a trick question. While you may pride yourself in your ability to think on your feet, an anticipated question and a carefully worked out answer is more advantageous. Even for the experienced presenter there are a number of pitfalls to be avoided:

- Not knowing your prospect's needs and wishes.
- Not doing your homework on the prospect's company and industry.
- Focusing on what you have to sell rather than on what the prospect needs.
- Straying from the point and being overlong.
- Not being sensitive to your listeners. If they don't laugh at your jokes, stop telling them.
- Selling too hard.
- Personalizing, or overloading with irrelevant anecdotes.
- Not asking for the order.
- Lack of familiarity with the audio visual material.
- Being unprepared for questions.
- Not knowing your competition, and lack of competitive intelligence.

Most presentations conclude with some notion of when a response will be given. It's not untoward to ask for it if it isn't volunteered. It's sometimes useful to keep open avenues of continued contact until a decision is made. For example, casually mentioning an article or a brochure that wasn't mentioned in the presentation, and then offering to send it.

In marketing professional services, the sale is made only on a face-to-face basis. To spend a considerable amount of money on all of the tools of marketing, and then to short-change the presentation and proposal, is to lose the final advantage in a selling situation.

## Post-Presentation

To merely walk away from a presentation after it's been made, win or lose, is folly. Each presentation is a learning experience to improve the next one. Certainly, if you can learn why you lost, it's grist for the improvement mill. And even being told that price is the reason isn't valid—quality should have come through to overcome the price differences.

The post-mortem, then, is well worth the effort. It's a premium payment made to insure that the next proposal and presentation will be better.

# Part V

# Selling

# 17

# Selling

Sales people frequently note that "nothing happens until somebody sells something." Probably true, if not particularly profound. In professional services marketing, what's more significant is that all the marketing activities in the world don't sell—they merely lead to the selling activity.

What's even more difficult is that most—if not all—the selling must be done by the practitioner. If there's a role in professional services marketing for the sales person who is not an accountant, a lawyer, or a consultant, that role has yet to emerge in any focused view. True, experiments are taking place, and some delineation is coming clear (certain legal, consulting, and bookkeeping services may possibly be sold by non-professionals), but on the larger scale, the final selling must be done by the professional.

Nor is it likely that a salesman, no matter how bright, can learn enough of a profession to sell its services without actually being a professional.

Add to this the ramifications of selling a complex professional service to a sophisticated business person—and particularly if you believe that the kind of selling in which intensive personal relationships between the buyer and the seller are established is necessary for successful professional services selling. This new kind of selling requires that the person doing the selling has a full understanding of the problems and needs of the prospective client, which can be somewhat more technical than you'd expect an ordinary salesperson to handle. Legal and accounting services—most of them anyway—aren't exactly Electrolux vacuums.

Based on current experience, salespeople can develop leads, but only professionals can turn those leads into jobs. But that's the way things are currently structured. Who says that accounting firms and law firms and consulting firms, and the businesses they serve, will be the same a decade from now? Or that they'll have the same relationship?

## Learning to Sell

The paradox, of course, is that few lawyers, accountants, or consultants are prepared to do it, either emotionally or by training. That means that several difficult things must happen . . .

- The professional must learn to accept that he or she has got to learn to sell

- The professional must learn the selling skills
- The body of selling skills and techniques must be refined for professional services

These are three tasks that are easier said than done.

As for the first—learning to accept the need to learn to sell—there's an irony. "If I wanted to be a salesman," says the lawyer, the accountant, the consultant, "I would have gone to sales school, instead of accounting or law or consulting school."

In fact, the true professional recognizes that he or she only has to learn . . .

- How to identify a prospective client
- How to identify the prospects needs or problems
- How to make clear to the prospect that he or she understands those needs or problems
- How to make clear that he or she can meet those needs and solve those problems
- How to get the client to agree to start Monday

If the professional can become proficient in these five things, all of which are themselves within the context of professional practice, then that's all he or she needs to know.

And at no time was the word *selling* used.

Sales training for professionals has become an industry in itself, with the range of quality from very bad to very good. Fortunately, a great deal of new work has been done to determine what works and what doesn't work. What's even more important, the major problem that's being addressed is whether a non-salesperson can be taught selling skills that really work.

Selling is, after all, a talent. It's at least the ability of one individual to persuade another to do something he or she might not have done on his own. People *buy* what they need. They are *sold* what they are persuaded they need. People *buy* bread. They are *sold* fur coats. Or more pertinently, people *buy* accounting and legal and sometimes consulting services. They are *sold* the particular services of the particular lawyer or accountant or consultant and the particular firm. And that, in professional services, is what selling is mostly about.

Selling is also about people buying services they either don't want (nobody wakes up in the morning pining for a good audit that day), or wish they didn't need (a defense in a law suit), or don't, at the outset, understand that they need (a new computer or cash flow management system). This puts a burden on the professional to sell something complex—our firm rather than his firm. Or, yes you really do need, or can benefit from, this system or study I'm trying to sell you. Difficult enough for a professional salesperson—doubly difficult for the professional with little or no valid sales training beyond a three-day session in a dreary airport motel basement room.

The problem is two-fold . . .

- Can selling really be taught, or is it a talent you have to be born with?
- Is selling the same for professional services as it is for products?

The answers, we now know very well, are that yes, some techniques of selling can be absorbed by non-professional sales people. And no, the skills and techniques that sell vacuum cleaners and Xerox machines will not sell professional services.

### Learning Selling Skills

There was once a Russian fellow by the name of Constantin Stanislavski who noticed that sometimes an acting performance was so realistic that you seemed to be seeing, on the stage, real people doing real things for the first time in history. Other performances he saw were imitations, posturing, unbelievable, and artistically unsatisfying. Stanislavski then devoted his life to finding techniques and methods by which the ordinary but dedicated actor could distill elements from the talented actor's techniques that would allow the mundane actor to enter the realm of talent. The famous Stanislavski method.

All methods of selling, from the best to the worst, are an attempt to distill the intuitive and experiential techniques used by the talented "natural" salesman, and use those techniques to synthesize competent sales people from ordinary mortals. You have only to review any book on selling to see that sales trainers attempt to break down the process into its parts to drive the process to its conclusion—the sale. In fact, too often the focus is so heavily on the process that there's a tendency to forget the purpose of the exercise. The process then becomes so rigid that it locks out the learner's natural ability to relate to individuals.

This is the fault with most selling training. It relies too heavily on jargon and process, and too little on intuition. Selling is a personal skill—or rather, an interpersonal skill, and techniques are the aid, not the process itself.

## The Selling Skills

At the same time, in the rush to teach professionals how to sell, a great many trainers simply imported the training and selling tactics of other disciplines. The Xerox programs, for example, were very popular. After all, you can see how good the Xerox salespeople are.

It didn't work. Selling products is *not* the same as selling professional services.

Fortunately, the work of an extraordinary researcher, Neil Rackham of Huthwaite, Inc., came up with the answer. *(Spin Selling,* by Neil Rackham, McGraw-Hill, NY 1988, and *Managing Major Sales,* by Neil Rackham and Richard Ruff, Harper Business, NY 1991.)

Following years of research, Rackham discovered that a major factor was in the difference between the small dollar volume sale and the large dollar volume sale. The difference is also in the one-time sale (the Electrolux salesman), in which the salesman sells the product and disappears, compared to the relationship sale, in which the seller is selling a sustaining relationship with the buyer, as in a professional service. There are, he says, many important distinctions arising from the differences between the two types of sales.

The small, low dollar value sale is usually made in a single call. It's made by relating to the buyer's personal interests, rather than to a larger need. The customer is less conscious of value, and can take more risks because the price is low. And because the sale is made in one call, it's made in the presence of the salesman, rather than requiring the buyer to consult with others in a firm.

The interesting thing about this kind of sale is that it readily responds to almost all of the standard techniques of selling—the personal relationship opening ("I see you like golf"), the listing of the product's benefits and advantages, the litany of objection handling, and the array of standard closings, some of which were first codified in the 1920s and are still used.

### The High Value Sale

The large, high dollar value sale, such as a professional service, is very different. It's not made in a single call, the decision is rarely made on the spot by one person, and, unlike the product sale, the relationship between the buyer and the seller (or at least, the seller's firm) goes on well beyond the sale itself.

Rackham did more than theorize about the differences between the large and the small sale; he did intensive research, over a period of several years. In the course of developing selling techniques that do work, particularly in selling professional services, he learned that in large sales and in selling professional services, that . . .

- The standard opening conversational gambits not only don't work, but they make no difference at all.

- Different techniques are used to investigate the nature of the problem the service will address. In fact, the crux of selling success in professional services lies in asking the right questions in the right way.

- Merely delineating the benefits of your service, as you would with a product, doesn't work. On the other hand, you must build the perception of value.

- Objection handling, which is a classic technique taught by most sales trainers, is not the desirable aim. Objection prevention, which is very different, is.

- There is no closing, in the classic sense, because the entire context is different. In fact, in most cases, using a standard closing technique becomes totally irrelevant and counter-productive.

Rackham's work led to a number of precepts, many of which are revolutionary in traditional selling techniques. He discovered that there were still four basic stages to a sale—*the preliminary, the investigative, demonstrating capabilities, and obtaining commitment.* But there's a difference in the same thing. In the preliminaries, for example, he discovered that it's important to . . .

- Get down to business quickly
- Not talk about solutions to the prospect's problems too soon
- Concentrate on questions in the investigative stage, and not on abstractions

It's in the investigative stage where, Rackham says, that success or failure lies in this kind of selling. The technique is to fathom the nature of the prospect's need, or to learn enough about the prospect's business problems to be able to cast those problems into a condition that your service solves, and that fulfill his needs. This is where the process he calls SPIN selling comes in. SPIN is . . .

- *Situation,* in which you ask questions to gather data about the prospect's current situation, relative to the service you're selling.
- *Problem questions,* which explore the problems the prospect perceives, the situations causing trouble, and his or her dissatisfactions.
- *Implication questions,* the answers to which imply the value of the solutions to the prospect's problems.
- *Need-Payoff questions,* such as, if my service meets your needs, how much will you benefit?

Given a clear understanding of the prospect's needs, the sales discussion then evolves to one in which your firm's capability, in terms of the ability to meet those needs, emerges. Rackham warns about demonstrating capabilities too early in the sales discussion, and of focusing too heavily on the advantages of your services rather than on your ability to serve his specific needs. Precluding objections by focusing on the prospect's needs rather than on the benefits of your service prevents the discussion from getting sidetracked.

And finally, by setting action oriented objectives for each meeting with the prospect, you seek to obtain a commitment to further action from the prospect. In professional services, this could be a promise to have you discuss your service with a ranking executive, or to invite you to submit a written proposal.

Rackham, and those professional services marketing directors who use or train in his technique, says that SPIN selling works when . . .

- You don't get bogged down in irrelevant small talk in the preliminaries
- You use the SPIN approach in the investigation segment of the effort, asking...
  - *Situation questions*—just enough to establish background
  - *Problem questions*—to uncover implied needs
  - *Implication questions*—to make implied needs larger and more urgent
  - *Need-Payoff questions*—to encourage buyer to focus on solutions and benefits of solutions
- You demonstrate to the prospect's need, and not the services' advantages
- You seek commitment from the prospect by clearly defined objectives

Does this selling process indeed work? Ask any marketing director or any individual practitioner who uses it. They claim tangible success. Considering its consistency with everything we now know about marketing professional services, it seems logical that it should. It's certainly consistent with the nature of professional services.

Can selling be taught to people for whom selling was far from the original career goal? It's likely that certain basic skills can be imparted—how to identify a prospect, how to understand that prospect's problems and needs, how to demonstrate the ability to meet that prospect's needs, and how to get the prospect to make a commitment. That's quite specific, and not really the same thing as turning an accountant or a lawyer into a professional salesperson.

Can it turn anybody into a supersalesperson? Probably not everybody. Not every actor who studied the Stanislavski method is worth the price of admission, either. But there are more good actors because of it, and undoubtedly more good salespeople because of SPIN selling than there would be without it.

## Giving Over

When the superstar rainmaker in the firm wins a client, the real selling effort has just begun, noted Mary R. Mola of SD Management in *The Marcus Report*, because it's just after that beginning that the new client is most often lost. It all occurs in the process of *giving over*—turning the new client over from the person who closed the deal to the staff group that's actually going to perform the engagement. And *giving over* successfully is as much a part of the marketing process as advertising, public relations, or any other marketing tool.

Frequently, the firm's star salesperson can hardly handle all the business he or she sells, and the new client must often be turned over to others. This process of itself brings the sales process back to the point where credibility must be re-engendered.

It's clear that the process won't work if the sale itself is predicated solely on the individual sales person. If, in the selling process, he or she is selling personally, rather than selling the firm, then the problem is foretold. The person who will be in charge of the engagement must resell.

On the other hand, if the firm, and not the individual, is sold, says Mola, then the process becomes easier. Then, in the *giving over* process, the engagement person's qualifications alone have merely to be established, and a relationship based upon personal chemistry must be instituted. It's assumed that the firm is behind the individual. When the engagement manager has sold him or herself, and the credibility is established, the first aspect of successful giving over has taken place.

Unfortunately, Mola says, the process is still not complete, usually because the client has to deal with more than one person. No doubt, the partner in charge of the engagement is charming, bright, efficient, self-confident, and all those wonderful things that earned the partnership in the first place. But what about the army of service people behind the partner? Where do they stand in relation to the client?

As a service consultants and trainer, Mola has found that the giving over usually breaks down in the following areas:

- *Motivation.* The partner who sold the account, as well as the partner in charge of the engagement, is motivated to provide superior service. In a sense, the firm belongs to the partners, and they're motivated by at least profit. But what of the non-partners? What's their motivation for service? Loyalty? Only if the firm has tangibly demonstrated loyalty to them. A sense of belonging to a "family" or firm community? Only if the firm has consciously engendered that feeling. By now, every business person understands that compensation alone won't buy loyalty. There has to be a sense of participation—of pride in a superior firm and a manifestation that the firm is proud of all of its individuals, regardless of their positions.

- *Respect.* Respect to those outside the firm, Mola finds, is given only by those employees who are themselves shown respect inside the firm. The partner who bullies those under him or her simply cannot expect that the employee will show respect to anyone else—including the client.

- *Information.* Little erodes client confidence faster than talking to a firm employee who is uninformed. No, it's not expected that the non-partner, professional or otherwise, will know as much as the partner in charge of the engagement. But when ignorance of details on the account is rampant among those below the partner level, the client is on the way to being lost.

- *Class illiteracy.* Not just knowing how to read, but being comfortable talking to others, particularly those in positions of great responsibility.

When the receptionist can't deal comfortably with the chairman of the client company, it makes the chairman uncomfortable.

- *A service concept.* Partnerships, it sometimes seems, tend to have an underlying feeling that nobody matters in the firm but the partners. Everybody else is replaceable. This results in not only a failure in motivation and respect, but, as well, in not engendering a service concept—an understanding that the firm lives or dies on service to its clients, and not just on technical expertise, and that service must be given all the way down the line.

Most of these factors seem obvious, we know, in retrospect. But most professional firms have grown and lived, until very recently, in a non-competitive environment. Service has always mattered, but not as much as it does now in the new competitive arena. The result has been that these otherwise obvious factors have had no fertile ground in which to root, and so are still ignored today.

The distinction between partners and others that hinders the service concept manifests itself in many subtle ways. The separate dining room for partners and others. The disparity in employee benefits. Male (and sometimes female) chauvinism—*I'll have my girl call your girl.* A management style that demeans and bullies. In the old days, before competition, and when firms were small and collegial, these factors meant little to building a clientele. Today, when even the smallest firm must compete, and in an environment that's all business, these factors are anachronisms.

It costs less to keep a client than to get a new one, Mola reiterates. It costs less to train people—on all levels—in all aspects of a service concept then to lose a client.

What's more important is that it not only costs less—it pays more.

## Telemarketing

Telemarketing—selling services by cold calls on a telephone—is a relative latecomer to professional services marketing. Still a somewhat controversial marketing tool, it's increasingly being used by both large firms and small, with varying degrees of success. But one thing is certain. It is now an accepted marketing tool in professional services.

Telemarketing is most often perceived as those annoying intrusions that come just at dinnertime, trying to sell you magazine subscriptions or stocks. You can tell that the person on the other end of the phone is reading a script. It would seem to be so *undignified* to sell accounting, legal, or consulting services.

But properly done, professional telemarketers have been well received by business executives on all levels. That's because there's a vast difference between business-oriented telemarketing and consumer telemarketing.

Consumer telemarketing is mass marketing—indiscriminate calling of purchased lists. It's a numbers game. If one person says no, then the next person will say yes. It's virtually mechanical, and indeed, there are software programs that will automatically dial a number while the marketer is still talking to the last caller.

Business telemarketing, however, functions well, and is accepted by business people, because it doesn't try to sell so much as accomplish a single mission that business might find genuinely useful. It's used most often to establish appointments for professionals to discuss real business problems and potential opportunities. Most often, it's targeted to specific companies and categories of potential clients. Business people tend to accept this as a normal way to do business, and whether they are persuaded to accept the basis of the call or not, most often they don't object to it.

In the early days of marketing professional services, there was concern that the clients would think that advertising in any form was undignified and unprofessional. One of the then Big Eight firms did an extensive survey. The reaction was startling.

Overwhelmingly, the reaction was, "We advertise and market to sell our products. How can it be wrong if you do the same?"

There is a paradox, however, in the selling aspect of telemarketing. Conventional wisdom says that only an accountant or a lawyer can sell accounting or legal services. Professional services can't be sold by professional sales people.

But according to August J. Aquila, Senior Vice President, Practice Development Institute, studies have shown that in selling products, telemarketing actually increases the response/sales rates. These studies also show that when direct mail and telemarketing are used together, direct mail results can increase substantially.

Says Steven R. Lebetkin, a telemarketer and CPA, "An effective lead generation program will produce 50% of the appointments from *inventory*. *Inventory* in this sense constitutes the prospects that need to be contracted two or more times before an appointment can be arranged. This is because the process of telemarketing professional services is one of making friends, and building relationships takes time."

One point that seems to have been sustained by experience is that with certain exceptions, most professional services can't be sold on the *telephone* by telemarketing.

## When Telemarketing Works Best

It seems to be clear that telemarketing is emerging as a useful tool under carefully controlled conditions. While mass marketing of consumer products has its own experience, telemarketing professional services seem to work best when the focus is on a single objective. For example . . .

- To qualify the business owner as a valid prospect
- To engender his or her interest in finding out more about a specific service
- To pre-sell a specific service
- To generate the opportunity to meet with the prospect.

If the object is to get an appointment, then using the same call to accomplish something else seems not to work well. For example, when trying to get an appointment to sell a service, to describe the service in any detail in the same call is giving away the purpose of the appointment, and defeats the objective. Success is almost invariably a function of focussing on a single point, and deflecting all questions and objections to that single point.

Experience shows that other factors seem to apply as well to successful telemarketing . . .

- As in direct mail, the list is crucial. The finer it's tuned for applicability to a particular problem or need, the better the list.
- Qualification is important. While it's virtually impossible to guarantee that everybody who says "OK," is a legitimate prospect, a great deal of screening can be done.
- It's crucial to avoid a hard sell, in which the prospect agrees to an appointment simply to get the caller off the phone. When you go to the meeting, the prospect isn't interested, and you've wasted your time.
- Keep your eye on the objective, which in most cases is simply to get an appointment. The worst trap is to try to sell on the phone, thereby precluding the opportunity to sell in person. If you're doing it yourself, selling on the phone might work, depending upon the service you're selling and the nature of the prospect. If you're using a telemarketer who isn't a lawyer or an accountant, it's at least unlikely and probably impossible.
- Telemarketing is enhanced, in most cases, when it's combined with direct mail. The two-pronged approach has been shown to be very powerful. Moreover, when this approach is properly used, it tends to take the hard-sell onus off of telemarketing.

  In many successful programs, a preliminary call qualifies the prospect in a conversation in which name, title, nature of business, etc. are verified. A carefully crafted letter is then sent. The letter is followed up by a phone call. This is a very powerful approach.
- Even the best professional telemarketing firms, including those that specialize in business marketing, often don't understand the difference between selling professional services and selling consumer products. Plan, then, to spend more time working with them on scripts. And fol-

low your instincts. You know your target markets better than they do, even if they know more about telemarketing than you do.

- In telemarketing, you've got little more than a moment to make your point. If the original pitch, and the response to inquiries and counter-arguments, in any way strays from that point, then the call is a waste.

- Don't hesitate to test. Check the reaction from the first twenty or thirty calls, and then reevaluate the script, the telemarketer, the timing, and so forth. This is still a learning process, no matter what the professional telemarketers say. Don't be afraid to change what you're doing in mid-campaign.

## The Program

There is more to a telemarketing program than just the phoning, even if it's done by an outside agency. Indeed, the pre-call planning can be more important than the call itself. The crucial elements include . . .

- Choosing the right service to market
- Choosing the right list of target prospects
- Determining the thrust of the selling message
- Writing the script
- Training and monitoring the telemarketers
- Tracking and analyzing results
- Using results to fine tune the script and delivery
- Followup

### The Service and the Selling Message

As in most of professional services marketing, broad-scale firm marketing rarely works as well as does selling a single service, or a single benefit. A consulting firm can't sell its total services so well as it can sell, for example, its computer networking analysis. A law firm can sell its estate planning or will making expertise. An accounting firm can sell its tax planning service.

For the firm seeking retainer relationships for total services, the emphasis must still be on benefits. "We'd like to show you how we can use your own data to give you a more effective marketing tool."

There's a danger, in choosing a marketing thrust and writing a script, to generalize in terms of what you want the prospect to think of you—to tell the prospect how he or she should perceive you. It rarely works. To say, for example, "We perform with great integrity" is not only impossible to prove, or to serve as a means to distinguish your firm from others, but is a cliche that falls on deaf ears. It's a question of the weakness of such incredible statements, if you could make them, as "We do better audits," or "We write better briefs." As the song says, "Don't speak of love, show me." State a fact that offers a specific benefit.

## The Target Audience

If you're going to address a single service, or a single benefit, then you've got to limit your target audience to those most likely to benefit from—and therefore be more responsive too—that service or benefit. If you're selling a service that integrates estate planning with personal financial, planning, then your target is not only smaller closely-held businesses, but those that have been established longer, and are run by family heads. If your service is immigration law, it may well be larger corporations and law firms that function internationally.

The point is that the finer you can narrow your target audience, the greater the likelihood of success—and the more cost-effective the program.

## Training

As part of Practice Development Institute's training program, says Aquila, the telemarketers were taught to use words that sell. For example, words such as "results," "proven," "guarantee," "how to . . . " would often be used in written, as well as in verbal, communications.

The most difficult aspect of training is in skillfully overcoming objections. This skill can be more important than the phone call itself. The key to handling objections is not so much to create answers as to put answers in the proper form. In PDI's experience, some of the typical objections CPAs will face, for example, are . . .

OBJECTION:  *I'm not your client. Why do you want to talk to me?*

RESPONSE:  *We are currently engaged by one of our clients in your industry to find a qualified buyer for that company. Are you interested in expanding your company through an acquisition? Can we get together next week for a meting?*

OBJECTION:  *I've never heard of [your firm's name].*

RESPONSE:  *We are the fourteenth largest CPA firm in the state. We specialize in small- to medium-sized closely-held and family-held businesses. We offer assistance in acquisitions and divestitures of businesses, financing, business planning, tax planning, and accountancy. Our clients tell us we're a profit center for them. May I set up a meeting with you for next _____?*

OBJECTION:  *Send me something (e.g., more literature).*

RESPONSE:  *A request for literature, Mr. Jones, usually means that you have some questions I haven't answered yet. What questions do you have?*

292

The point is to keep getting back to the original objective, which is the appointment, and to avoid any sidetracking discussion.

### The Phone Call

The call itself, says Aquila, is broken into six parts:

- Reach the decision maker
- Open
- Body
- Answer questions, overcome objections
- Close
- Confirm

Inherent in the successful phone call are such strategies as penetrating secretarial barriers—getting through the gatekeepers. One way used by many telemarketers is to call early in the morning or after hours. Most business owners will answer the phone themselves at these times.

If you do need to deal with secretaries, say the experts, be professional and polite. Develop a positive relationship. "This can usually be accomplished by recognizing her as a person," says Aquila, "and calling her by name." For example:

| | |
|---|---|
| You: | *Good morning. This is Dick Adams. I'm a partner in the firm of Koltin & Grinde. Is. Mr. McCord in?* |
| Secretary: | *No, he's out for the day.* |
| You: | *Are you his secretary (assistant)?* |
| Secretary: | *Yes.* |
| You: | *What's your name?* |
| Secretary: | *Lisa.* |
| You: | *Lisa, when would be the best time to reach Mr. McCord?* |

By developing name recognition, you'll be less of a stranger the next time you call. Get the secretary on your side and many things will flow smoother, says Aquila.

It's important to open your call with statements that build rapport. "You have to make your offer hard to resist," says Aquila. "Here's a good place to distinguish between minimum service requirements (i.e., what the client expects from a service provider) and value-added services (i.e., services that are above and beyond what a customer has become accustomed to expect). For example, by presenting benefits and keeping it simple, you make it easy for the prospect to say yes." Here's a good benefit statement:

> "We have assisted twenty-two firms in the past twelve months to successfully package their businesses for sale. Each company sold for 10 percent more than the owner originally thought he could obtain."

The call should conclude with a thrust at the objective—in a sense, asking for the order. If you're after a meeting, it's important to say, "Can we set up a meeting next Tuesday?" It works better than when you don't ask for the order.

### Record Keeping

Meticulous record keeping is crucial to successful telemarketing. Each call should be recorded, with full details on . . .

- Who was called, and who in the company was reached.
- The time and date
- What was said, by all parties
- What objections were raised, and how were they met
- What followup is expected

A system of qualifying and judging each call and each prospect can be useful, to maximize the time of whoever must do the followup.

Fortunately, contact software is now available to make the task easier. Increasingly popular is a program called ACT!, which not only logs the information (some of it automatically) but can even dial the call for you.

Telemarketing does work when it's done well, and particularly when it's part of an integrated marketing program that includes direct mail and other marketing structures. It works when expectations for it are realistic, and when it's pursued seriously and assiduously.

And as an increasing number of accounting, law, and consulting firms are learning, it doesn't diminish or tarnish a professional reputation for quality.

# Part VI

# Marketing Management

# 18

# Managing Marketing

The apparent lack of effort with which the tightrope walker dances across the wire belies the difficulty of the art. Anything well done, particular when there's a lack of familiarity with the process, looks easier than it is. So it is with marketing.

In fact, managing the marketing effort can be as complex as is the effort itself.

In a corporation, marketing is managed by professional marketers, in a context in which marketing is familiar. A Xerox or IBM or Kodak is built as much upon marketing as on product. The marketing professionals usually report directly to the top, and sometimes the marketers rise to the top of the management pyramid. The production people, the finance people, and others in management usually have little or nothing to do with marketing.

In a professional service, however, the difference is substantial. Professional firms are usually partnerships. Marketing is relatively new to the professions, and so there's little experience in managing or even accommodating a marketing effort, and certainly no marketing tradition that readily accommodates the marketing professional.

This means that marketing must be managed by people who, all too often, are total strangers to the process, or to whom marketing is known more by its myths and misconceptions than by reality. And all too often, this is exacerbated by not only a failure to recognize the cultural differences between the professions and the marketer, but by an hostility that frequently exists towards the non-lawyer in a law firm and the non-accountant in an accounting firm.

One of the reasons that marketing professional services is in such a primitive state is that accountants and lawyers come out of school devoid of any understanding of the process. It's anathema to them, and by the time they come into positions in which they must address marketing, it's a foreign subject.

This attitude is perhaps best summed up by a statement made by a lawyer in a law journal. "If you're smart enough to be a lawyer," he said, "then you're smart enough to do your own advertising." Absolutely true. You're also smart enough to be a nuclear physicist. But that doesn't make you one.

The paradox is that in most cases, regardless of the skills or experience of the resident or external marketing professional, the marketing effort is managed by someone whose profession didn't recognize marketing as a valid discipline until just about a decade ago. Judgments must be made about marketing thrusts, marketing budgets, and marketing plans, even when they're all devised by experienced and skilled professional marketers, by people who were until recently far removed from the process. An odd situation.

Bound in the partnership are many traditional tenets of professional ethics, all of which are rooted in solid ground. The partnership precludes sharing fees with non-lawyers and non-accountants, which would be fee splitting. The partnership prevents conflicts of interest by avoiding situations in which independence is jeopardized by serving those who might profit from that service. The partnership, and its collegiality, sustains that isolation from corrupt sources that might injure independence and objectivity, the very essence of the value to business and society of the lawyer and the accountant.

In a corporation built upon products, marketing is ingrained in the company. The corporation's professional managers are trained either as marketers, or are conversant with it. The marketers are professional, and are understood and respected as professionals by managers in other disciplines.

But in professional firms, where marketing is very new, and the managers are accountants or lawyers or consultants, and not professional managers, marketing is impeded by lack of understanding of the marketing process. It sometimes even faces hostility. A corporation is home to individuals of every discipline needed to produce and distribute the product. In a partnership, hostility of varying degrees is the lot of any non-lawyer or non-accountant.

The paradox is that the accountant and the lawyer rarely sublimate their professionalism to the wishes of the client when those wishes run counter to the professional's technical skill and knowledge. And yet that is precisely what the practitioners, lacking a full understanding the marketing process, demand of the marketing professional. This, despite the fact that doing so runs counter to the well being of the firm.

But it's not a lost cause. As the need for greater marketing sophistication grows, so too does accommodation by the partnerships of the law, accounting, and consulting firms for the professionalism of marketing.

## The Partnership

It seems likely that the exigencies of contemporary business will ultimately obsolesce the partnership structure as a viable business and governance structure. But until that time, in the smallest and largest professional firms, the partnership structure still prevails.

That means that in most firms, and to varying degrees, each partner functions as an entrepreneur, serving the firm ultimately, but primarily serving his or her own businesses. Theory aside, in practice this can mitigate against good marketing by putting as many pressures on the marketing structure and the marketing staff as there are partners. Each partner has his or her marketing agenda and attitude toward marketing, and each exerts pressures on the marketers that reflect the power of the partner, and not the value of any aspect of the marketing program to the firm.

In fact, it's virtually axiomatic that the greater the entrepreneurial isolation of the partners, and the more they fail to pull together to create what consultant David Maister wisely defines as *the one-firm firm*, the less likely is marketing successful. In those firms in which the partners are competitive with one another, and where there's no unity of firm purpose, marketing is rarely successful, highly qualified and experienced marketers shy away, and the turnover of marketing staff is excessive.

## Making It Work

In any firm, the ideal solution to most effective marketing is to have a skilled and experienced genius as marketing director, and to leave him or her alone to function. Like most ideals, this happens only by the rarest chance—and you can't run a firm on chance.

The next choice is to find ways to function within the partnership system. This requires several elements . . .

- *The one-firm firm.* When you have a unified firm, or at least a firm whose partners are unified in purpose, and the leadership of that firm sees marketing as a process that's crucial to the future of the firm, then the firm has a chance to use the partnership successfully in marketing.

- *Leadership.* If the leadership of a firm, and particular the managing partner, sees marketing as important, then the attitude passes down through the rest of the firm. If leadership sees marketing skills as important to partnership growth path, then marketing—and marketers —have a chance. If not, then the greatest marketing activity will be the turnover of marketing personnel.

- *Understanding marketing skills.* If the partners who are in any way involved in the marketing effort understand the process, and the skills used in the process, then marketing moves forward successfully. The right marketing people are hired, the program is supported, it's effectively monitored, and the firm's contribution to marketing is substantial—with attendant rewards.

- *The partner in charge of marketing.* Until such time as professional firms can function as do corporations, with a discrete marketing operation that reports and is responsible to only the firm's chairman, marketing can work only with a partner in charge of marketing. Without a partner who has some status in the firm to act as a buffer and translator between the marketer and the firm, and as a liaison between the firm and the marketer, marketing becomes chaotic and ineffective. And even in a firm that's small enough to do it without outside professionals, lack of a single marketing coordinator can be a serious and deleterious problem.

It seems odd that a process like marketing should require this kind of structure. But it's precisely because of the amorphous state of marketing in professional services that structure is needed.

### The Partner in Charge of Marketing

It's probably more a matter of the newness of marketing to professional firms than anything else. With marketing a discipline new to most professional firms, the professional marketer is a stranger, someone not readily to be trusted with the firm's good name. The marketing partner also allows the firm to move more slowly, more cautiously, into marketing.

Too, many firms move into marketing as a home grown process, without hiring marketing professionals. Somebody, then, has to be responsible for *practice development*. In some firms, this is a partner who has shown some talent or predilection for the process. In others, unfortunately, it's awarded to an otherwise underutilized partner. As the firm moves toward accelerating its marketing efforts, outsider are hired, but the original structure remains. But for whatever reasons the partner in charge of marketing is in place, it's a reality.

What, then, is the role of the partner in charge of marketing in an effective program?

- To act as a liaison between the marketing professionals and the partnership, acting for each as an advocate to the other.
- It's not important that the partner be a skilled marketer. He or she should, on the other hand, be a knowledgeable consumer of marketing services, capable of understanding what the marketing professional is talking about when the marketer discusses every aspect of marketing.

  The partner should be able to hire, monitor, judge, and guide the marketing professional. The partner should not, on the other hand, presume that his or her marketing skills are equal to those of the marketer. When this happens, then the marketer becomes little more than an administrator. If you don't trust the marketer, get a new one.
- The partner should understand precisely what the partnership wants and expects from the marketing program, and transmit that clearly to the marketing professional. If the partner doesn't understand that, and can't function as the partnership's advocate to the marketing professional, then the program is likely to fail.
- The partner should be a strong advocate of marketing to the partnership, understanding the value of marketing to the firm, the firm's role in the process, and the need for the firm's commitment to the marketing program. He or she should help to educate the firm about the tenets of marketing, and rally the partners behind the marketing effort. If the partner can't do that, then the marketing professional will be

crippled beyond repair in that firm, and will never be able to make any kind of substantive contribution.

If the marketing partner sees the role as minor, or administrative, or as non-productive, or if the firm sees the role as one relegated to the least valuable partner, or as a way station to the pasture, then everybody's time is wasted, and the firm will suffer more than will the marketing partner or the marketing professional.

Ultimately, the success of the marketing partner will result in not only a strong program, but also in eliminating his or her own job. This will happen when the marketing operation is so successful that the firm's leaders recognize that further success depends upon elevating the marketing professional to the partnership, or at least to a position of comparable status and authority, thereby giving him or her access to the kind of information, on a timely basis, needed for a truly competitive marketing program. Then you have a mature marketing operation in a growing and successful firm.

### The Marketing Professional

The marketing professional is an individual who, through education, training and experience, is capable of developing, executing, and managing a marketing program.

He or she may or may not be totally proficient in every skill of marketing, but absent that proficiency, there's at least an understanding of each of those skills, how they function, and how they contribute to the total marketing effort.

A mistake that's easily made, in looking at a marketing professional, is that a specialist in any of the disciplines—public relations, advertising, and so forth—is a fully qualified marketing professional. Not necessarily so. Marketing, remember, is the way in which all of those disciplines are used to accomplish marketing objectives. And in fact, marketing may be considered a discipline of its own.

There are many definitions of the word *professional,* but as they pertain to someone who isn't a lawyer, accountant, consultant, architect, etc., it's tough to find one that makes sense. And without a reasonable definition, how do you classify someone who hasn't been to a graduate professional school leading to a licensed occupation as a professional? And even an MBA in marketing doesn't lead to a license.

What's tough about it is that the skills of a marketing professional are not only many and multifarious, but include both the tangible and the intangible.

The tangible is the array of specific skills and experience in the mechanics of marketing.

The intangible is a talent that incorporates imagination, intuition, and artistry. You can be a competent marketer without the intangible, but you're not likely to be a great one.

Cn the other hand, if you're too imaginative, intuitive, and artistic, you're going to have a devil of a time serving those who aren't attuned to those qualities. In fact, so pervasive is the intangible that it frequently defines the tangible.

The ultimate skill of the marketing professional is in planning—in understanding the profile of the market, understanding the profile of the firm, knowing how to combine that understanding with the skillful use of the tools, and managing the effort in ways that meet the firm's own objectives.

There are many areas in which the qualifications and skills of the marketing professional parallel those of any other profession. For example, he or she must be skillful in client relations, and sensitive to the reactions of his or her clients at all steps along the way. In this case, however, the client is the partnership. Moreover, the partnership of a professional firm may include individuals who resist marketing, who object to its costs and practices, and who are otherwise hostile to anyone who isn't a member of the firm's profession. The successful marketing professional is one who can cope with that attitude without losing stride in performing the marketing function.

Too often, the difficult part of the professional marketer's job in a professional services firm is not the mechanics of marketing, nor the imaginative aspect of the job. It's the context.

## Hiring a Marketing Professional

Considering the newness of marketing to the professions, it's understandable that hiring a marketing professional is beyond the experience of most practitioners. Moreover, the marketing discipline is new to the professions, and is viewed from as many different perspectives as there are partners. The mythology about marketing subscribed to by non-marketers everywhere is as pervasive and appalling as is the mythology about lawyers and accountants held by non-lawyers and non-accountants.

This poses a very difficult problem for the marketing professional, particularly one who comes from an environment in which the professionalism of marketing is recognized and understood. The frustrations can be overwhelming, and there's no doubt that more good marketing professionals fail in professional service firms from the causes of these frustrations than from insufficient capability. And so a distinctive talent for the marketing professional is the ability to survive and thrive in a sea of frustrating jetsam.

This is too often compounded by the battle between the partnership and the marketer for authority, in the fullest sense. If the partnership doesn't recognize the professionalism of marketing, there is a disequilibrium—an attempt to drive the marketer to a subservient position of reactive performance, rather than one in which there is the authority to originate and manage. The burden is constantly on the marketer to function as a marketing professional, and not merely as a marketing administrator.

There is no fiat likely to transform overnight the role of the marketing professional in a professional service firm. It will evolve, however, over a period of time, as the need for professional marketing in an increasingly competitive environment continues to press.

Until then, until the professional services marketing professional is given the cachet to function as he or she does for a manufacturing company, the marketing professional must simply hone capability, and push forward to make marketing work for the professional firm.

With professional firms tending to be structured for the personality and skills of a single profession, it's difficult to hire—and to work with—people from other professional disciplines. This difficulty, notes Elaine Goldman of the executive search firm Goldman Associates, is probably the greatest obstacle to successfully hiring and managing marketing professionals. There is the further challenge, Goldman wrote in an article in *The Marcus Report,* in the profound and important differences between working for a corporation and working for a partnership. In practice, more marketers seem to stumble on this obstacle than on marketing skills.

Because the history of professional services marketing is relatively short, traditional job design, pay, reporting practices, and monitoring techniques have not been developed sufficiently to help guide most personnel professionals. Nor have the differences from other forms of marketing been fully integrated into personnel structures. That many of the same tools and skills of other forms of marketing are used adds to the confusion.

There are, however, some general guidelines that Goldman suggests might find useful in hiring a marketing professional:

- Before you begin the hiring process, the partnership—and the hiring partner—should have a clear concept of what's expected from a marketing program. Even if lack of experience results in the partners having a skewed view of how marketing works and what it can do for the firm, debating expectations with a candidate is a fine way to learn a great deal about both marketing and the candidate. It also tells the candidate something about the interviewer's perception of the job, and the kind of skills and experience being sought. This can result in a more informative interview for both parties.

- You want a marketing professional—somebody who has actually done it successfully for other companies. On the senior levels of marketing, the number of experienced professionals is growing. But there still might not be a vast pool of talent with specific professional services experience on the lower echelons. Look, then, for comparable experience. Financial services, for example, is generally more useful than hard goods or consumer product experience.

- Don't be overwhelmed by academic credentials—even an MBA in marketing. Degrees are useful, but few graduate schools give courses in marketing professional services. Much of what is taught about marketing is simply not relevant to marketing for professionals. Someday, maybe, but not now.

- Look for at least a general recognition of the unique aspects of marketing a professional service, as compared to marketing a product. These differences should be a major topic of discussion in an interview.

- You want a person who understands—or seems capable of quickly learning—the technical aspects of your profession.

- Practitioners in your profession quickly learn to fit into the culture of your firm. Marketers may not. Look for someone who won't rub the partnership the wrong way, and yet can assert his or her marketing professionalism. At the same time, you should recognize that the marketing professional's expertise and culture may indeed conflict with the traditions and culture of your profession and your firm. Still, there is the reality that you and your partners are going to have to delegate some responsibility to the marketing professional you hire.

Judging the skills being offered you by a marketing professional, beyond the evaluations you would normally make based on education, prior experience, and personal presence, might best include:

- The candidate should be able to explain plausibly the capabilities listed on his or her resume, and to do so without using marketing jargon. The candidate should also be able to relate prior experience to marketing for your profession.

- The candidate should be able to explain achievements in concrete terms, and not merely recite a job description. What were the objectives of programs he or she worked on? How were they met? What programs were undertaken? Using what skills? With what new initiatives and what results? And be sure to probe the candidate's actual contributions to each of these achievements. Beware the pronoun "we" in an interview—it's the one place that it's inappropriate.

- Analyze the candidate's career history for a pattern of consistent growth and progress, or one that indicates his or her having reached a plateau. Is there enough room for growth in your organization for a fast-track performer? Or do you have to settle for the plateaued—but not burned-out—candidate?

- Look for consistent growth in responsibilities and skills development. Why was each job move made? Is the candidate a planner, or one who simply reacts to events? Has he or she been recruited for positions before (a sure sign that an individual is sufficiently outstanding to have come to the attention of an executive recruiter)?

Hiring, ultimately, is an art, not a science. There is no guarantee that any individual will succeed in your organization. There are, however, ways to help assess whether the candidate will fit into your firm.

Chemistry in hiring means a match between many elusive aspects of the firm and the individual. Partnerships, in which a marketing executive must work closely with many more individuals than he or she would in a corporation, require greater emphasis on personal chemistry. Does the candidate move at the same pace as your firm? At the same level? Is there a good balance between the assertiveness required of the successful marketer and the partnership?

Consider how well the candidate prepared for the interview. Did he or she know the firm? Its accomplishments? Its news? The profession?

Probe, too, for the candidate's ability to withstand some indifference, and even hostility, to the marketing function. After all, not everyone in professional services has fully accepted the need for marketing, nor understands its practices. Candidates with low levels of frustration tend not to last long in the professional services environment.

Goldman recommends multiple interviews. The hiring manager should see the candidate at least twice, with other managers and partners involved in the process as well. If the candidate is to have any relationship with the managing partner or chairman, that person should also be involved.

One last word—*let the candidate talk.* Ask good, open-ended questions, and listen carefully to the answers. It's more important that you learn from the candidate than the other way around.

Hiring a marketer—or anybody else not from your own discipline—can be complex, says Goldman, and there are never any guarantees. These few suggestions, however, should help you reduce some of the variables.

## Using a Consultant

There are two circumstances under which calling a consultant is clearly indicated. When there's expertise you need but don't have. When you need perspective.

This is a further paradox, because you don't always know what expertise you need, particularly in marketing, and it takes perspective to know that you need perspective.

And there's yet another paradox in that many professionals don't seem able to see other professionals in the same light in which they themselves want to be seen. "How do I work with these consultants?", they ask. Simple. The same way you want your clients to work with you.

Despite the broad umbrella of marketing, many internal marketing people come from a single discipline. They may have been in public relations, or advertising. No matter how good they are—and most of them are very good—no individual is likely to be brilliant at everything.

The problem is that a well-rounded marketing program requires using a full menu of marketing skills—advertising, public relations, printed material, direct mail, and so forth. Even if you start with a small program, such as public relations alone, sooner or later you're going to have to add something. A brochure or a newsletter. A direct mail campaign. A sales training program.

If you have a marketing person you know and trust for his or her skill, competence and originality, you jeopardize that trust when you ask that person to function outside his or her experience and expertise. It's not fair to you and it's not fair to your marketing director. That's the time to think about an outside expert and specialist.

Which is not to say that your in-house marketing person should be superseded or shunted aside. Quite the contrary. Your marketing director knows the firm in ways that you may not—in its marketing context. The marketing director, even if he or she is not expert in the specialty, knows the thrust of your marketing program, knows how the firm is perceived in the marketplace, knows how to deal with the expert as one professional to another.

It can be a major mistake for you to bring in a specialist without the full participation of your in-house marketing person. In fact, the chances are that your professional marketing director knows the sources for outside expertise other than—or supplemental to—his or her own experience.

There are, of course, other reasons to bring in outside specialists. You may want a different point of view. You may want a particular style in a brochure, or a newsletter. You may want more marketing hands on a temporary basis, or for a particular project.

There are other outside capabilities that may exist in-house in only the largest firms. Design, for example. Few firms are large enough to have design and production capabilities in-house.

Advertising requires a far greater range of capabilities than are likely to be found in even the largest professional firms.

Your marketing director may be the finest writer on the horizon, but no writer is capable of meeting every writing need. And if the writing load is heavy, more hands are needed.

Many marketing directors are skilled trainers, and in some areas, may be better than you can get outside. But not in all areas.

Again, outside experts can make a terrific contribution, but they need inside marketing experts who know the firm and the culture and the thrust of the overall marketing program to function most effectively.

## Hiring Consultants

How do you know the right questions to ask a marketing consultant? How do you know what problems to ask a consultant to solve?

You've made a commitment to marketing, and hired a marketing person. What can a consultant do, other than second-guess you?

A great deal, if it's the right consultant. A consultant with specific experience in professional services marketing can give perspective to your marketing program, thereby making your existing marketing structure more effective.

A consultant can answer some crucial questions, and answer them objectively. Have you fully identified your potential markets? Are they the right markets for your firm's size and range of skills? Are there any markets you should be in, even if you have to develop the skills or bring them in from the outside?

How about budgets? Is your budget for marketing appropriate to your needs and objectives? Are you getting an appropriate return on your investment?

Then there's personnel. It's tough enough for lawyers to hire the right lawyers for their firms, or for accountants to get the best accounting staff. But how do lawyers and accountants find, qualify, train, and monitor the best marketers, when marketing isn't their business? A good consultant can help.

There are a range of audits that a good consultant can perform. Communications, for example. Are you structured to deal most effectively with the press and other target audiences? An organizational audit will tell you whether your marketing structure is the most effective one for your firm and your marketing needs. It will tell you whether you're using your marketing people most effectively or not.

A training consultant will determine what kind of training is needed, and then supply it—not the other way around. There are a great many training consultants who have a package that's the same for everybody, even though everybody's needs are not the same.

And ultimately, there's perspective—the overview that, objectively, looks at your firm, and looks at your firm's objectives, and helps you relate your firm's objectives to its marketing needs—and then looks at your marketing program and tells you whether the program is equal to your needs. Or if you don't have a program yet, the consultant will help you determine what kind of program you really need, how to get it, how much it will cost, and what you can expect to get for your money.

If you're not a marketing professional, can you do this by yourself, or with a committee of your brightest partners? Yes, to about the same degree that a marketing professional can do a corporate audit or file and win its own lawsuit.

You are better able to survive without a consultant if you've got some good in-house people. They may even have the same skills, capability and experience as an outside consultant. But they are not likely to have the perspective. That can put unreasonable demands on your in-house professionals, which isn't fair to them and isn't fair to you.

## Finding the Consultant

Finding experts isn't as difficult as qualifying them. The chances are that the experts will find you—they do have their own marketing.

Specialists are known to your in-house people. But if you don't have anybody in-house, ask people who do. References are still the best way to find and qualify experts, although not everybody is everybody's cup of tea. It's a good start, though.

Consultants, if they don't find you first, can be found by reading the trade press and seeing who's writing what. A good consultant is constantly writing and publishing, or appearing on seminar panels, or making speeches. And not only for his or her own marketing. Knowledgeable people in every profession tend to want to share what they know; to improve the state of their arts. In hiring, there's an interesting difference between hiring the specialist and hiring the consultant.

Your relationship with a specialist—a writer or public relations consultant, for example—is more a function of that person's skills, rather than personality. You may not want to take the brochure writer or direct mail specialist home for dinner, but you do want to know that the quality of the work is equal to your needs.

Your relationship with a consultant, on the other hand, is much more personal. There must be a feeling of trust and confidence. You'll share much more information and concepts with a consultant, and you'll have to take much more of his advice on faith. Is it any different, by the way, in your own profession, and in your own relations with your clients?

This is not to say that the specialist shouldn't be able to get along with you and your people, or that the consultant needn't be technically sound. It's a question of degree.

In bringing any outsider into your firm, there are some basics that seem obvious. Given qualifications, there should be proof of experience and of specialized skill. There should be checkable references, and the references should be checked. Samples should be available. The outsider should be business-like, no matter what the level of the skill or relationship.

These are the obvious questions. Not so obvious are . . .

- Is there an experience, in that specialty, in professional services? It need not match your profession, but it should be professional services marketing experience.

- Does the specialist demonstrate a clear understanding of you and your needs? Does he or she understand what you're trying to accomplish? Do you sense that the specialist is on your agenda or his or hers? Does the specialist ask you intelligent questions, or just listen and nod in agreement?

- When you look at samples, whether it's a press release or a direct mail letter or a brochure, ask what the objectives were for that particular piece. There's no such thing as a good ad or brochure or press release in the abstract. These works are good only to the extent that they meet a clearly-defined objective.

- If you have an in-house marketing person, is that person part of the hiring process? Is his or her role in the project clearly defined? Have you gotten your marketer's input?

- What are the business structures? Will there be a contract or letter of agreement? Are the terms clearly understood, so that you know exactly what you can expect for your money, and how much you're going to pay for it, and at what stages of the project?

While these questions are the right ones for both a specialist and a consultant, your relationship with a consultant is likely to be more involved, and on a higher management plane. The additional questions are . . .

- How did you come by this person? Is this somebody whose articles or books you've read? Was it a recommendation or referral?

- Is this person indeed published? While not every qualified consultant is widely published, there's no better way to know how a consultant thinks about a problem than to read his or her writing on the subject.

- Is the consultant an academic only, or is there some real hands-on experience? Some terrific consultants are academics with experience, but not all academics are good consultants. And in this field, there are very few academics who understand the difference between marketing professional services and marketing other things.

- Here, personal chemistry is as important as experience and intelligence. A good consultant has to talk to—and get along with—a lot of people. Does the candidate understand the culture of your profession and firm? Will he or she be able to gain not only your confidence, but those of your partners? Will the candidate listen, or just talk?

- What form will the consultant's report take? How far does it go? Does it include implementation of recommendations?

There are other questions to be asked, but they needn't be spelled out, because they're the same questions all professionals get asked by their potential clients.

What's important in hiring a consultant, as you well know, is that the person be as qualified in his or her profession and specialty as you are in yours. As a relatively new field, there aren't many people with longevity in marketing professional services . There's a tendency, then, to settle for an experienced product marketer, with too little experience in professional services marketing. This is the consultant who'll treat your firm as a corporation, and not as a partnership.

When a consultant functions properly, the marketing program not only has relevance and perspective, but it's cost effective as well.

## Organizing to Manage

While most professional service firms are still limited to one or two marketing professionals on staff, an increasing number of firms are expanding marketing departments to substantially increase the marketing effort.

How best to structure the marketing department is a problem that faces every company, professional service or not. And marketing departments are constantly being reorganized, whether they need it or not, often to serve the needs of the firm other than marketing.

There are few rules to govern the organization of a marketing department, but there are some guidelines that might help.

The real strength in a chain of command in a marketing organizational structure comes from its ability to communicate both ways—to flow ideas back and forth. The other roles—to monitor, to control, to enforce execution—may exist, but they are less important than the flow of ideas.

The reason is simple. In the normal corporate chain of command, ideas normally emanate from the top, and flow down. In marketing, and particularly in marketing professional services, integration of marketing disciplines is the guiding force, and not simply translating a basic idea into the different disciplines at each level. And because marketing is a business of ideas, ideas may flow upward, from the levels of each discipline.

It may be easy to say, then, that public relations is subsumed under the marketing director. But of what value is that if public relations must be integrated with advertising and direct mail, for example, in order for public relations activities to have any tangible impact?

Another very real consideration is that the newness of marketing in the professions has given seniority, and therefore cachet, to individuals whose roles might ordinarily be subsumed by others.

For example, in the early days of marketing, many firms responded to marketing by hiring public relations experts. Many of these people succeeded, and hold responsible marketing positions. And then, an enlightened firm realizes that public relations is only one part of marketing, and should be subsumed under a marketing director with broader experience in all marketing disciplines. But does it make good sense to insist upon a rigid organizational structure in which a valued and experienced public relations person must now report to a newer and less tried marketing director? The word "rigid", then, has no place in a marketing organization.

In fact, the sound organizational structure is designed to bring together the elements of marketing so that they support one another, to expedite marketing activities, and to integrate the several marketing activities to achieve the marketing objectives. This, and not classic organizational chains of command, is what should be kept in mind in organizing a marketing department.

Under an organizational structure for most professional services firms, the Partner In Charge of marketing is usually the firm's Marketing Director, and every other responsibility is subsumed under him. For the most part, and for operations, the organization reports in a direct line to the National Director of Marketing, who in turn reports to the Partner in Charge of Marketing.

This is the way many structures have grown in the first decade of marketing. By putting a partner rather than a marketing professional in charge of the marketing operation, even a partner without the slightest experience in professional marketing, the firm feels protected from the ministrations of someone from a different culture.

Is this efficient in terms of marketing? Not really, unless the partner is intuitively a good marketer, able to translate the feelings of the partnership to the marketing professional, and to sell the marketing programs back to the partnership.

Thus, an effective marketing organizational structure is a matrix. The Partner In Charge of Marketing doesn't abdicate his direct involvement in all aspects of marketing, but focuses on those aspects that require the input of the partnership and policy, to supplement the marketing expertise of the marketing professionals.

The matrix organization works best because it's construed, and performed, in a spirit of cooperation, rather than chain of command. And it works even better when, as in a corporation, the marketing director—a marketing professional—reports directly to the CEO—the chairman of the firm or the firm's managing partner.

Ideally, the matrix structure has each of the disciplines of marketing reporting directly to the marketing director, who reports to the firm chairman, the managing partner, or the partner in charge of marketing. But each of the disciplines is, at the same time, interrelated with the others. However, each of the directors or managers may have positions that report directly to him or her. For example, in a large, multi-office firm:

**Partner in Charge of Marketing**

**National Director of Marketing**

*Public Relations Director*

National Staff

National Public Relations firm

Local Office Public Relations managers

Local Public Relations firms

(While the local PR managers and agencies report directly to the Office Managing Partner, or the Office or Regional Marketing Director, they should be monitored and guided by the National Public Relations Director for consistency with objectives and firm practice.)

*Advertising and Direct Mail Manager*

National advertising agency

National Direct Mail staff

Direct mail and advertising for practice offices

*Sales Manager and Sales Training Director*

*Product Managers* (A sufficient number, with staff, to cover every practice and industry specialty)

*Research Manager*

*Publications Director*

*Proposal Director*

*Regional Marketing Directors*

*Practice Office Marketing Managers*

(In multi-office firms governed by region, The Regional Marketing Directors, under the professional guidance of the National Director of Marketing Planning, are responsible to the Regional Managing Partners. The Practice Office Marketing Managers are guided by the Regional Marketing Directors, but report to the partner in charge of each practice office.)

Each discipline functions independently of the others, and on a par. All work toward the same objectives, under the same banner, and all activities are integrated for support and impact.

There is, of course, no single structure that is ideal. Because it's relationships that count, and not structures, different firms will function best with different structures. The guiding factors are:

- *The objectives of the program.* In some cases the scope of the program precludes emphasis on some marketing disciplines, and stresses others. Proposal writing in a law firm, for example, may not be as important is it is in accounting firms. In some programs, such as for certain kinds of law practices, advertising is crucial. In others, it's not.

- *The size of the firm.* Small firms generally don't need large marketing staffs. Perhaps large firms don't either, unless their practices encompass many specialties. A one- or two-office firm has very different organizational requirements than does a national multi-office firm.

- *Budget.* Obviously, on small budgets there are no large marketing departments.

- *Availability of skilled and talented people.* Marketing is still a function of skill, talent, and experience. There's no point in having an organizational slot for a direct mail specialist if you can't find one. Use an outside firm.

- *Firm culture and attitude toward marketing.* If marketing is considered a routine function, and not an integral part of practice growth and management, all the organization in the world is not going to allow professional marketers to accomplish much. If, on the other hand, the firm and its senior partners recognize marketing as a significant force, the organization becomes a phalanx that fulfills a serious mission.

Ultimately, organizations don't solve problems—people do. The organizational structure that works best is the one that best allows people to function effectively to solve problems.

## Tasks

To better understand the basis for an effective marketing organization, it's helpful to look at the tasks, conditions, and ongoing activities necessary for successful marketing. These would include:

- *Liaison with the partnership.* There must be a strong and effective liaison between the partnership and the marketing professionals. Without this relationship, there is conflict, misunderstanding, lack of communication of information essential to marketing, failure to understand methods or to properly evaluate results, and general confusion.

  This liaison must be a dynamic two-way street, with the ability to communicate the needs and wishes of the partnership to the marketing professionals, and the ability to communicate marketing plans, skills and activities to the partnership.

- *Managing the marketing function.* As with any activity, the marketing function must be managed, in both the planning and the everyday activity. This is best done by marketing professionals, working in conjunction with a partner dedicated to the marketing process. The high rank of the marketing professional is necessary because experience and an intensive knowledge of marketing skills is required. The partner is necessary to assure consistency with the firm's objectives, and to act as liaison with the partnership.

- *Program Management.* Each program within the marketing function, for each discipline and each project, must be managed to assure that professional marketing skills are aptly and effectively performed, and that the program conforms to the firm's marketing objectives.

- *Planning.* No marketing program, no matter how casual, can function without planning. The planning must be done for both short and long-term; to engender quick results even as it plans for the larger future. Each segment must be planned, for relationship to the larger program and for cost-effectiveness.

- *Research.* An effective marketing program begins with understanding the market. This means more than the demographics; it includes a full understanding of the changing needs and demands of the prospective clientele.

  From the point of view of market development, it must be capable of providing pertinent information, both nationally and locally, on industries, economic trends that can affect firm directions, and specific companies that are prospective clients.

  It must include transmitting market intelligence, and the techniques for gathering it, to the practice offices.

  It should help keep abreast of competitive activities, as a way to develop better competitive programs and techniques.

- *Advertising, Public Relations, and other tools of marketing.* These are functional tools that must be at the base of any marketing program. They include such practice development tools as organized networking, speeches, seminars, direct mail, etc..

  They must be performed both nationally and locally, and must be structured to deal with every discipline of the firm, as well as within every target industry in which the firm perceives its potential growth. They must be performed and managed professionally, not only for professional results, but for cost-effectiveness as well.

- *Publications.* Producing effective publications, and using them properly, requires not only skillful writers and technicians, but planning and integration with other elements of a marketing program. Publications have for so long been a marketing tool for professional firms that they have tended to lose a clear purpose in a total marketing program. In most firms, they have tended to grow farther and farther from realistic marketing objectives.

- *Proposals.* Proposal writing and oral presentations are processes that seem to have developed a life of their own. Subject to the exigencies of marketing planning, and creative and imaginative development, proposal writing requires a special writing staff, and the ability to support the practice office efforts.

  At the same time, there has developed a body of proposal writing skills. But that can work adversely by closing out the opportunity to be thoughtful and imaginative; to break away from established techniques, the origins of which may have been long forgotten.

- *New Product development.* Developing new products and services to meet the changing needs of the marketplace requires a full spectrum of both marketing and professional firm skills, working in conjunction with one another. This ranges from identifying the market need and then identifying the firm's skills and resources to meet that need, to developing and executing marketing programs to introduce and market new products.

- *Selling and sales training.* In marketing accounting services, no matter how extensive the marketing efforts, nothing happens until somebody sells something. Unfortunately, the people who perform the services are the ones who must do the selling—and they are the very people least trained to do so. Therefore, it's necessary to train non-selling professionals in selling skills, and to have a structure to supervise that effort, such as a sales manager.

## The Staff

This means that at least the following positions should be structured, including appropriate support staffs:

- *Partner in Charge of Marketing.* This is the liaison partner. This partner should be a dynamic individual, with the trust of, and access to, both the senior management structure and the partnership at large. He should be able to understand, deal with, and manage marketing professionals, and have an effective and productive relationship with the National Director of Marketing Planning. He is, in effect, the Marketing Director, and is directly responsible for executing marketing policy.

- *National Director of Marketing Planning.* This is the lead and managing marketing professional. He should be a consummate marketing professional—knowledgeable, experienced, and imaginative, with good management and planning skills. All professional marketing operations are his direct responsibility.

- *Director of New Products Development.* This is a difficult position to fill, because it requires skills that few professional marketing people have had time to develop in the few years of marketing's history in the profession. It requires understanding the full spectrum of the firm's capabilities, as well as the marketing profession, determining where the needs are, relating the firm's skills to those needs (including recommending developing new skills if necessary), developing marketing programs to introduce the new services, and structuring for ongoing marketing.

  It's conceivable that this position should be filled by an accountant or consultant, rather than a marketing professional. However, the exigencies of designing a new product to meet the needs of a market, and an appropriate marketing program, require more marketing skills and experience than accounting skills.

- *Product managers.* Product managers, in firms large enough to have them, should be trained and experienced marketing professionals, assigned to and immersed in specific disciplines (auditing, tax, etc.), and specific target industry responsibilities. Their job is to help develop marketing programs for their clients, and to execute them professionally. This should include functioning both nationally and for the practice office. They are the captains of the marketing army, with both strategic and operational responsibilities within the framework of the marketing program. They report to the service or industry partner, but for professional marketing coordination, they report directly to the National Director of Market Planning.

  The concept of the product manager stems from product marketing. In professional services, there are pros and cons. On the one hand, they allow intensive marketing coverage for a discipline. On the other hand, not every discipline warrants equal attention. For example, the health care and retailing industries may warrant separate product managers; the steel industry may not.

  The question is, who covers the gaps in the declining industries and services, or those that are not firm priorities? An answer may lie in using general marketing managers who serve several internal clients, rather than as consistent one-to-one product managers for each industry or service.

- *Public Relations Director.* The public relations director must develop, manage, and execute a broad spectrum of relevant programs. The programs must take advantage of the firm's activities in every discipline, and in every target industry. This includes publicity, speeches, seminars, issues programs, special events, and all other public relations activities. It includes working nationally, and developing and coordinating local practice office public relations structures. It includes supervising and effectively using the firm's national public relations consultant.

- *Advertising and Direct Mail Manager.* The advertising and direct mail manager must also develop and manage a broad spectrum of both national and local programs. He should be the source of expertise in his skills, and make them actively available to the practice offices. He should be able to manage outside agencies, and develop or supervise direct mail programs, which are best done in-house.

  This is not a simple job, as it might be in a corporation with an advertising history. New concepts must be related to the ad agency; the partnership must be made to understand the nuances of the ad and direct mail campaign. Mythology abounds, and must be transcended.

- *Research Manager.* This should be a professional research person, with experience in both market research and competitive research.

- *Publications Director.* This should be an experienced editor and publications manager, to supervise the writers, designers and production people who produce the firm's publications. An important skill, beyond the editorial abilities and understanding how to integrate publications with other marketing programs, is the ability to deal with the partners, and to understand the technical aspects of the subject matter.

- *Proposals Director.* A superior writer and editor, and manager of writers, to supervise the proposal writing staff. This should be a person with a full understanding of not only the writing skills, but the proposal and presentation process as well. The techniques of proposal writing and presentations can be expected to change radically in the future, an imaginative person is needed to cope with—and to lead—the change.

- *Sales Manager and Training Director.* This should be an individual who functions as a sales manager, even within the unusual context of non-professional sales people. He or she should not only manage the function, but be responsible for using outside consultants in sales training.

  *No such position appears to exist today in any accounting, law, or consulting firm. Yet, it is one of the most important functions in marketing an accounting firm.*

## National/Practice Office Organization

No matter how large the firm, no matter how effectively national marketing programs enhance the firm's reputation and enhance its capabilities, the preponderance of clients are sold at the practice office level. This is true of even the multinational client.

This clearly dictates that distinctions must be made between marketing activities that are national in scope, and those that work most effectively at the *practice office level.*

And because national and local marketing activities are different from one another, it's necessary to organize the program so that the activities are performed at the appropriate level, with the appropriate support, and that they are all well integrated and coordinated.

Some examples:

*Some activities can be only local*

- Identifying specific prospective clients for a practice office

- Identifying specific marketing opportunities, by company, by industry, or by business need
- Networking in a community

*Some can be only national*

- Overall national marketing policy
- Coordination of all firm marketing activities
- National advertising
- Most firm publications

*Some can be both national and local*

- Some seminars
- Some publicity to both national and local press
- Some industry marketing programs

*Some can be performed locally from national headquarters*

- Where there is no local capability (e.g. press relations), it can sometimes be done locally from national headquarters

*Some local activities can be fed by national material*

- Marketing material (press releases, publications, seminar packages) prepared by national for adaptation locally
- Some standard advertising formats
- Selling material

*Some activities are regional*

- Marketing activities that are responsive to firm regional control, as a cost-saving and management device to serve several offices in a region.

## National

Those activities that can or should be national, or that must stem from a national office of a multi-office firm, include:

- Overall marketing policy, which guides, and serves as a yardstick for, both national and local marketing programs.
- Coordination of all marketing activities, to integrate, reinforce, and maintain consistency with firm and marketing objectives.
- Training capability, to assure the best available skills for all segments of the firm.

- Basic national market and economic research, to assure consistency with the firm's long-term planning.
- Technical marketing help, based upon the assumption of stronger and more experienced professional marketing expertise at the national level such as . . .
  - Identifying, qualifying, and helping to hire local marketing professionals and outside agencies
  - Help with specific marketing problems
  - Developing technical marketing programs in such areas as advertising, direct mail, public relations, etc.
- National press relations, to deal with the major national press, and to coordinate local accesses to the national press.
- National advertising (when appropriate)
- Basic national material for local adaptation...
  - By department (tax, audit, consulting, etc.)
  - Printed material, particularly technical and firmwide
  - By marketing discipline
    - Press material
    - Advertising matrix
    - Seminar packages
    - Direct mail matrixes

## Practice Office

Those activities that function best at the practice office level include:
- Market identification
  - By industry
  - By specific company
- Selling
- Public relations
  - Predicated on practice office capabilities and activities
  - Local press
- Direct mail
  - Specific capabilities and services
  - Specific problem
- Seminars
  - Local audience

- – Local problems
- Speeches
  - – Local audience
  - – Local problems
- Practice development
  - – Networking
  - – Memberships in local organizations
  - – Influentials
    - - Local bankers
    - - Local lawyers
    - - Other local consultants
- Advertising (except that professional quality advertising should be developed under National direction)
  - – Specific capability
  - – Specific problem
  - – Specific solution
  - – Local media
- Printed material
  - – Localized problems
  - – Localized use of National material
  - – Localized distribution
- Follow-up on all marketing activities

# Regional

- Those activities that might be local, but are controlled regionally rather than locally as a function of administrative decision.

This organizational structure is a concept—a general matrix—predicated upon experience of what works and doesn't work, assuming the proper staffing of each position.

Ultimately, the success of a marketing program is not a function of the organizational structure, nor of abstract marketing theory, but of some very real activities. More crucial to marketing success than organization is planning, motivation, skill, training, and imagination.

When there is strong motivation, skill, well-trained and imaginative people, this organizational structure will facilitate effective and successful marketing. It will get clients. It will build a firm for the future.

## Industry Specialty

Many professional firms tend to have clientele concentrated in specific industries in which the firm has expertise and a successful client base. The marketing program projects the firm's expertise to target prospective clients in these industries. Industry and practice managers and marketing staff can be assigned to cover specific target groups.

Increasingly, firms are recognizing the value in marketing by industry, and are organizing for it. In some larger firms, particularly in accounting, industry groups are being organized as profit centers, with separate leadership structures, marketing programs, and identities within their own firms. It all falls under the rubric of *niche marketing*, or marketing segmentation.

While there can be no argument with the concept of the industry group, or even organizing vertically to attack that market, it's difficult to say that there's validity in isolating the marketing structure. It's a question in pragmatism. If it works, it's the right thing to do.

## Training

In the professions, continuing education is a deeply ingrained process. Training in aspects of marketing, on the other hand, is a relatively new process.

Marketing training has been going on for more than a decade, but unfortunately, on a basis so random, and with such spotty results, that the process is generally viewed with more skepticism than enthusiasm.

The paradox is that the nature of marketing professional services requires some degree of participation by the practitioner, no matter how good or thorough is the professional marketer. Some training, then, is indeed warranted. But what kind? Certainly, one doesn't turn a professional into a marketer overnight.

Experience thus far has shown that most training programs have failed to resolve the marketing problems in any magnitude. While there have been some short-term successes, they've been few and far between. Several talented individuals have had their natural selling skills honed and focused, and there's been some improvement in understanding the effective use of specific skills, such as networking, seminars, prospect identification, and direct mail.

But thus far, and with notable exceptions, most attempts to use training sessions to inculcate marketing into the professions have been, for a great many firms, unsatisfactory. Some of the problems have been:

- Too much is taught at once. Many of the programs attempt to teach the entire marketing discipline in a three-day seminar. It simply can't be done. The result is a superficial skimming of the marketing process.
- Too little is known about what should be taught. The state of the art of marketing professional services is still, after a decade of experience,

too primitive, and much of what's taught is residual from other marketing disciplines. The result is that people are being taught techniques that simply don't work, which is profoundly discouraging to their accepting the whole marketing process.

- Too little is known about how to hire or judge trainers who understand the distinctive nature of marketing professional services. While there are many fine trainers and training firms, there are a lot of promoters in the training business who know more about how to sell their own services than about marketing professional services.

- Too much that's taught is theory, rather than useful and practical activities. The basic lesson of educational motivation—small successes lead to larger ones—is ignored. People are being taught more than they can absorb, more than they can perform, and more importantly, more than they can succeed with.

These are probably the most flagrant failures in marketing training. It can be done better. For example:

- There should be a clear delineation between what the *professional* marketer can and should do, and what the *non-professional* marketer can and should do. For example, even the best trainers are not likely to be successful in turning accountants, lawyers, and consultants into public relations specialists, but they can teach the professionals how to be better consumers of public relations services.

   They can, on the other hand, learn better personal selling skills and techniques, and to improve the skills they already have.

- A training program should be designed for quick, tangible success. The segment on identifying prospects should be capable of producing real prospects within a reasonably short time. The segment on direct mail should result in direct mail campaigns that produce invitations to present and propose. The selling segment should teach people how to turn prospects into clients.

- The program should be taught by people who clearly understand the difference between marketing a product and marketing a professional service. At least one segment of the training program should involve the firm's best and most productive marketers, in the attempt to distill from those who are naturally talented marketers those elements that can be passed on to others.

- The program should be geared to a specific office, with considerable planning and homework done beforehand. The homework should consist of intensive study of the office, its strengths and weaknesses, its history of market development, its relations with its present clients, its market and market potential, and its current marketing efforts.

- The program should be participatory, with all of the group brought into the discussion, rather than one in which an instructor lectures.

- In a multi-office firm, there should be sufficient time between programs to allow each office to put the process learned into effect, so that there are merchandisable results for other offices.

- The practical elements of a training program should include hard and real skills, not theoretical ones, that are relevant to a professional's needs. Selling. Identifying markets and prospects. Dealing with marketing professionals. These are subjects that don't require reaching beyond the non-marketing professional's skills, nor do they reach beyond the capability of successful performance. They are skills that work.

As competition in the professions heats up, there's naturally a drive to garner and apply as much marketing skill as possible, in the shortest possible time.

There is indeed an urgency to learn marketing skills. But that urgency, particularly in planning a training program, is best met by making haste slowly and thoughtfully.

## The Retreat

In their extraordinarily fine book, *Practice Development*, Gerald Riskin and Patrick McKenna refer to the retreat as the most effective tool for change, and the least damaging. True—at least, if it's done right.

"It's most effective," say Riskin and McKenna, "because it encourages personnel to buy into the process of change itself—people like to implement their own ideas. It's least damaging for the same reason—participatory change is far easier to accept than change by edict, which usually results in subtle sabotage of the entire effort. Because the concept of retreat is to allow an individual or a group to withdraw to a place, and at a time, insulated from the pressures of every day's routine activities, and to use that withdrawal to bring perspective to various problems, there are few rules that should apply."

The concept of retreat comes from a religious practice of withdrawal from society for spiritual introspection. The process, for professional firms, is essentially no different.

What has evolved in the process, however, is the opportunity for a firm or a group within a firm to bring perspective to its daily practices, and to explore the validity of views on different aspects of a practice that have arisen during the course of that practice. And frequently, as happens in processes such as these, other factors enter, such as the attempt to educate a group to a firm policy.

While this last strays from the original purpose of a retreat, who's to say that it's inappropriate? A firm, gathering its members in an out-of-town conference center or a downtown hotel on a Saturday morning, has the right to make its own rules. The question, though, is whether that opportunity is being well used.

The introspective nature of the retreat may or may not be observed, but certainly, the time and effort is best spent if clear objectives for the exercise are delineated, as are the steps to be taken to assure that those objectives are met.

It would seem obvious that the objectives set for any retreat, and its agenda, be realistic in terms of what can be accomplished. Too ambitious an agenda will result in either failure to accomplish objectives or meeting them superficially.

Experience shows that retreats work best if specific topics are addressed, and if those topics are those that most intensively concern the assembled group. Frequently, large firms will divide a retreat into several parts—one for the partners, one for the associates and middle management, and one for the staff. There is then a plenary session at the end that delineates conclusions that mutually concern all groups. This brings the concept of the retreat to one of education.

Frequently, retreats are reinforced with outside speakers. During the past several years, for example, speakers from outside the firm have addressed the subject of marketing. It would be hard to say that this isn't perfectly appropriate, simply because there is no subject that has a greater impact on the future of a professional firm than marketing, and a professional firm's relationship to its markets.

Increasingly, the subject of governance is pervasive, as questions increasingly arise as to the relevance, in today's economic climate, of the partnership structure. Not to be overlooked is the role of marketing, and dealing with markets, in the need to change the governance structure.

The success of a retreat depends as much upon the ability of the retreat's facilitator as on the retreat's objectives.

In their book, Riskin and McKenna note that an effective facilitator should . . .

- Understand that the objective of the retreat is to help the firm to understand itself better and to arrive at some achievable goals that are consistent with its vision.

- Have the skill and experience to keep things in perspective when an individual or an issue is assuming an importance that is exaggerated beyond the purposes of the retreat, and must encourage those who hold less power to risk expressing their views.

- Know how to move the firm from that retreat to a path of implementation that will lead to measurable successes. In other words, given the ideas and concepts, what do we do on Monday morning.

The successful retreat, they say, shapes the mindset of its participants, who have journeyed together through a mind-altering experience. The real change will come, however, when the firm begins to steer toward the future it has chosen for itself. The firm becomes a ship with a charted course and destination.

A good facilitator, they note, will set everyone at ease by . . .

- Acquainting the participants with the agenda. The more the participants know about the design of the retreat, the less tension they will feel.

- Trying to ascertain what expectations the participants have of the retreat.

The facilitator does well to ask all participants, at the outset, to imagine for a moment that the retreat is coming to an exceptionally successful conclusion and that everything they hoped would happen did happen.The facilitator now asks each participant in turn to describe some of the things that would have happened over the course of this perfect imaginary retreat. This, they suggest, is an effective way to move everyone into the realm of effective objectives.

It may be difficult to put a retreat into the boundaries of rules. It should be sufficient to say that self-exploration is always useful, but that it's more so with a little foresight and planning.

## Productivity

It's difficult to talk of managing anything, much less a marketing program, without considering the problem of productivity.

American productivity, we are told, is falling off, which is why the Japanese are turning us into a second rate power. All those words about productivity, but never a clear picture of it.

And certainly, no words about productivity in marketing. Why not? Doesn't productivity matter in marketing? Can productivity even be measured in marketing, particularly for the smaller firm, and why should it be?

In fact, very little has been written about productivity in marketing, precisely because it's so hard to define and measure. And in professional services marketing, the challenge is even more daunting. Still, because marketing is demanding so much attention in professional services—and so many dollars—it's important to at least open a discussion about it.

Not being able to measure productivity in professional services marketing is possibly at the root of a great deal of resistance to it. Like a rich uncle who's uncouth, it lurks in the background, not discussed in polite company. Not only is it difficult to measure the contribution marketing activities make to building a practice, it's virtually impossible to put a dollar value on the cost of it to the professional firm. If you don't know what you're getting for what you're paying, why should you buy it? Measuring productivity, then, is not an arbitrary exercise in economics.

On a grander scale, productivity might be defined in this way . . .

- The *resources* of the world—labor, capital and commodities—are finite. There is just so much of each.

- The *needs* of the world are infinite. More and more is demanded of the outputs and combinations of the limited world resources.
- Productivity is the degree to which the *finite* resources of the world can be leveraged to meet the infinite needs of the world.

In manufacturing, the real world of daily concern, productivity can be defined rather simply, despite all attempts to complicate it:

- One person is paid $5 an hour, and produces 5 widgets an hour.
- A means is found to have him produce 6 widgets in the same hour, for the same $5.
- His productivity may then be said to have increased by 20 percent.

Now ... increasing productivity in a competitive world is important, obviously, because the more you can get for the same or less investment, the greater the profit. The greater the profit, the more there is available to invest in new and competitive machinery, raw material, and labor. And you can charge less for the same product than your competitor can, if your productivity is better than his.

A simplistic lesson in economics, perhaps, but it really is what productivity, for all the talk, is about.

But looking at the manufacturing example, which, for all its simplicity, is an effective economic definition of productivity, how do you increase productivity in marketing? For that matter, how do you measure productivity in marketing? Or to make the problem more difficult, how do you measure productivity in professional services marketing?

It might be said (with only partial accuracy) that one measure of productivity in marketing is the return. A campaign either produces sales or it doesn't, and presumably those sales can be measured against the effort and cost to produce those sales. The "partial accuracy" is because you don't always know what part of the marketing campaign actually produced the sales, or what each part of the campaign contributed how much to the result.

But it does indeed get more difficult in measuring productivity in professional services marketing, because the reach from the effort to the result is so great. An ad, remember, may sell a product, but it can only contribute to getting a client. The client must be sold by the individual who performs the service.

If you were to apply the industrial formula to professional services marketing, your best measure might be purely quantitative. How many press releases get written in one day. How many brochures get produced in one month. But clearly, this doesn't work, at least because quantity doesn't relate to quality. Even in the widgets example, if the sixth widget doesn't work as well as the other five, then there's been a decline, not an increase, in productivity.

And since so much creativity goes into the marketing effort, how do you measure that? Can you say, on an arbitrary scale of one to ten—how creative is this idea or that ad? Not likely.

Still, measuring productivity is consequential to the marketing process, and so a method must be found.

Perhaps a good starting point would be to look at the elements of productivity. They are . . .

- Time
- Labor cost
- Labor input
- Overhead (rent, lights, paper, equipment, secretarial help, etc.)
- Objectives

In this interesting array of elements, perhaps the most significant is *objectives*, because output of any kind is meaningless unless it meets stated objectives. If the objective of an action is to produce a client, pure and simple, measurement becomes relatively easy. If the objective is to enhance name recognition, or understanding of a practice, then measurement is infinitely more difficult.

The three fixed and measurable elements are time, labor cost, and overhead.

The amount of time any individual puts into a project is measurable. Now here, productivity—whatever it is in this context—can sometimes be improved by several factors. A computer used for word processing, for example, can reduce the time spent on writing. No secretary need get involved, which cuts overhead, and composition on a computer is faster and more efficient than it is by hand or on a typewriter. Ask any writer.

Time can also be reduced by a peculiar element called either skill, experience, or both. A skilled writer can produce a press release, a newsletter or a brochure in less time—and more effectively—than can a beginner. This, incidentally, is why we pay people with proven ability and experience more than we pay a beginner. The experienced person is more productive.

Overhead, because it costs a measurable amount of money, can also be measured. Rent, and the portion allocated to the individual performing the marketing function. Electricity, taxes, supplies, and other support services can also be measured relatively easily. A secretary's salary is part of it.

Within the overhead category, there are elements of productivity that can be measured. A secretary's typing speed, for example, is one such factor—the faster and more accurately she types, the greater her productivity and the greater the return on her services. Other than giving clerical or typing tasks to a receptionist, on the other hand, it's more difficult to measure the receptionist's productivity. A writer who is skilled with a word processor, though, increases productivity because the need for a secretary is eliminated. Other technology, such as phone mail, reduces clerical costs, and increases office productivity. Machines are paid for once, amortized quickly, and are tax deductible on a depreciated basis. They don't require fringe benefits, by the way.

Allocation of rent can be reduced—up to a point. You can put two people in one office, which halves the overhead cost of rent. But then you run into another problem. Marketers are creative people—another wild card in productivity. Two geniuses in one space may save on rent, but may also reduce creativity, which means the saving is illusory.

So not only are the fixed and measurable costs somewhat flexible, but it still leaves the wild card—labor. Until we can measure labor input in a creative and marketing context, we can't solve the problem of productivity in professional services marketing. Nor can we solve it until we can in some way quantify or evaluate the quality of output and its contribution toward meeting objectives.

As of the moment, this is a very wild card. There is little room in most professional firms, for example, for the creative genius who has difficulty fitting into the professional firm's culture. An obnoxious lawyer who writes brilliant briefs, or a tax genius with stains on his tie, will be tolerated more readily than a brilliant marketer or writer whose flamboyance rends a traditionally staid atmosphere. And yet, this flamboyant character may have the very answer to moving the practice to new heights. In terms of output relative to input, he or she may be a bargain in productivity—but the firm may deem the price to be too high in terms of other values.

Beyond individuals, the sheer risk inherent in choosing one marketing plan over another is another wild card in productivity. Beyond the break-in point, a law or accounting firm that institutes a new area of practice exposes itself to very little risk when it agrees to perform that service for a client. But a new and expensive marketing program, logical as it may seem on paper, faces the risk of failure each morning of the career of that program. The concept of productivity is left in the closet for awhile.

## Risk

This adds, incidentally, another new element to the mix—risk. In manufacturing, risk is sharply reduced by the time a product goes into production. The product has been tested and found sound, or it wouldn't be in production. It may fail in the marketplace at some point, but the likelihood is that it's been market tested before production. Risk is minimized.

In marketing, on the other hand, each new idea, and each element of marketing practice, carries with it fresh risk. Will the press release be published and have its desired impact? Will the direct mail campaign work? Will the brochure be appropriately distributed, read, and perceived by the reader in the intended way?

Regression analysis has quantified risk in the investment world. Not so in marketing, despite the inherent importance of risk in the marketing context.

And so, in part, the problem is stated, and the solution yet unborn. Is this just an intellectual exercise for marketers, or is it of consequence to every partner in every law, accounting, consulting or other professional firm, regardless of size?

Well...look at it this way. More professionals have one foot on the boat and one on the dock, when it comes to commitment to marketing. Now, millions of dollars are spent on marketing professional services, and nobody knows how well or ill those dollars are spent. Without the ability to understand or measure productivity, it's unlikely that a large body of professionals will be persuaded that marketing is a serious and consequential business for their firms and their professions. Of all marketing questions, addressed or ignored, productivity may be the most important.

## Budgeting

A recent survey of attendees of the AICPA National Marketing Conference, as reported by Donis Ford in the *Accounting Office Management Administration Report*, showed that accounting firms allocated an average 2.4 percent of their annual fees for marketing in 1991. This was down, says the survey report, from 3.0 percent the year before.

Basing a marketing budget on a percentage of revenues is the time honored way to do it. That's the way product manufacturers and non-professional services (banks, airlines, dry cleaning establishments, etc.) have always done it. Logically then, it would seem that that's how accountants, lawyers, consultants, and other professionals should do it too. Unfortunately, it's not that simple.

Budgeting can indeed be done for professional services marketing—and done with reasonable accuracy. But not the way it's done for products or non-professional services.

There are some cogent reasons why the classic budgeting techniques must be revisited when they're applied to professional services marketing. They're based upon the distinctive nature of a professional service, and must be considered in budget development if marketing is to have any chance for success. Most relate to the nature of analyzing professional service revenues.

Peter Horowitz, the Marketing Director of the international law firm, Morrison & Foerster observes that there is a profound distinction between those services that are perceived as commodities, and those that are perceived as value-added.

"For example," he says, "the statutory audit versus strategic tax planning, or legal documentation versus defense in a major law suit, or installing a transactional system versus designing a complex system to capture customer information."

The importance of that difference, notes Horowitz, is two-fold. First, the profit on a commodity, in most cases, is substantially lower than on a value-added service. Second, it costs more to market a commodity than to market a value-added service. Why?

Because, says Horowitz, everyone who performs the same service generally can offer no discernible advantage in having it performed by one firm rather than another. That means that twice as much effort must go into marketing that commodity to overcome the lack of distinction. In a value-added service, the performance itself contributes to the marketing effort. "And frequently at the client's expense," adds Horowitz. "Litigation, for example, makes the litigator and his or her firm visible with very little effort. And if the case is big enough, the visibility is salutary."

The point is that this peculiar phenomenon, distinctive to professional services marketing, makes it almost impossible to apply traditional budgeting techniques to the process. This is in addition to other factors. For example . . .

- There's a direct and readily measurable relationship between most marketing efforts and product sales. Thus, there's a potential for predicting the return on marketing investment. But marketing works differently in professional services (nobody hires an accountant or a lawyer from an ad, etc.), and the return on marketing effort is very different than it is for products. And the time frame is different. People tend to respond almost immediately to most product marketing. The response to service marketing is rarely immediate, unless you happen to hit a prospective client who was on the verge of making a hiring decision. Marketing a professional service, then, is a longer range investment, with a greater time span for the return on that investment.

- There's a vast experience in calculating return on investment in product marketing—and virtually none in professional services marketing. Product marketers have been at it for a long time, and know a great deal about cause and effect (not everything, of course, but still a great deal). Except in very rare instances (legal clinics, personal injury attorneys, and tax preparers—and these services are virtually products), few professional service firms have done sufficient marketing to have much valid evidence of marketing cause and effect.

  In this context, one need only look at the details of the AICPA survey. The marketing activities are all over the map, including everything from Yellow Page advertising to newsletters, with little cohesive program that would give any clue to what is working and what isn't.

- The cost structure of a product tends to be fixed, with the margins either constant or readily measurable. The cost structure of professional services, no matter how carefully controlled, is varied. In fact, the distinctive nature of a professional service means that each time the service is performed, it's done distinctly and differently. It is, in essence, a new product, with a new cost structure and new margins. You don't know, across the board, how long it will take you to perform most services, or what your revenues are likely to be. The personality of a client, or the intrusion of circumstances beyond one's control—all contribute to an infinitely variable cost structure.

- Projections for most professional services firms are made in terms of billable hours, not revenues or earnings. The aim is to achieve, each year, an increase in billable hours. But the revenues—and certainly the earnings—are impossible to project with any accuracy. Gross revenues are calculated by multiplying billable hours by billable rates. But to get a net revenue you have to deduct such factors as discounts, withdrawals, and so forth. Where a product might have a fixed price, with perhaps a volume discount, professional fees—even those predicated upon an hourly rate—tend to be negotiable in one form or another. And so if there's no revenue predictability, how can anything, much less a budget for marketing, be predicated accurately on revenues?

- The marketing efforts for most manufacturers are discrete and measurable. Marketing is done by the marketing department, and costs are definable. But in professional services marketing, you must draw on the efforts of individuals in the entire firm. What's the cost of a brochure—or even an ad—in terms of a partner's time? Partners' time is the major wild card in budgeting for marketing.

- Because marketing is so traditionally integral to products, the cost of marketing is built in to the price of the product, and passed on to the consumer. Because there's no tradition of marketing in services, and because the cost of marketing a service is so little known, there's no way to build the cost of marketing into the price of a service, nor to pass it on to the consumer. Without this relationship, there's no way to relate the cost of marketing to the revenue from the service.

These are only a few of the factors that preclude applying product marketing budgeting criteria to professional services marketing.

Does this mean that there's no way to budget for a professional service?

No. There are a number of possibilities—but they all require a thoughtful and original approach.

### Return on Investment

First, the objective in preparing a budget should be to consider return on investment, not amount. The concept of "We have X dollars to spend" without the respondent questions, "On what?" and "What will you get for it?" really seems to be little more than arbitrary. True, there are limits to what even the largest firm can spend on marketing (although few firms have any concept of what those limits really are), but isn't the idea of the expenditure to get clients? To build or shape a practice?

Consider . . .

- The most effective marketing for most professional firms is not institutional marketing ("Everything about our firm is better than everything about everybody else's firm"), it's marketing the individual service. Litigation. Auditing. Tax planning. Cash management. Expatriate taxation. Intellectual properties. Maintenance cost management. The most effective marketing seems to be done for the specific service, and not for the firm as a whole. (Consider, here, the distinction Horowitz makes between the commodity and the value-added service.)

- A firm that fully understands the research aspect of marketing can usually define a market for each of its specific services. That definition usually includes magnitude and potential buying power.

- A reasonable estimate can frequently be made of the potential of that universe. An accounting firm offering financial reporting services to middle market companies in a defined geographic area generally knows just how many companies in that area fall into the firm's bailiwick, and therefore, the firm may be able to discern approximately how large that universe is in potential revenue. This figure, for all the reasons given earlier, is at least an educated guess.

- Given that potential, a firm can set its objectives on a reasonable portion of that market potential. Realistically, no firm can expect to get every potential client for its specific services. Nor would a firm want that, without some larger plan to expand its capability to service business beyond a definedpoint.

- And given that prescription, the final determinations are, first, how much will it cost to get that reasonable portion of the potential market, and second, is it worth it—is the return on the investment great enough to warrant the investment.

- Because there is rarely an immediate reaction to marketing efforts in professional services, and even a different lag time by marketing activity (a brochure versus a newsletter versus a press release, for example), the time frame must be different. A time frame can be a year or less to measure a program to move an inventory of products, or to sell airline trips to the Bahamas. But it can take as much as two years to penetrate a market for a professional service, and that must be considered in budgeting. Horowitz advises that a distinction must be made between the costs of *marketing* and the costs of *supporting selling efforts*.

In other words, if you know how many clients, and how much revenue, you can get from specific marketing efforts, you can ask whether those results are worth that expenditure. If the answer is yes, then that expenditure becomes the budget.

This approach, while not without its inadequacies, is certainly more accurate than taking an arbitrary percentage of revenues. The percentage of revenues, in fact, must always be arbitrary, because in professional services marketing, there's simply no way to accurately relate that kind of figure to results.

This approach also has the added advantage of offering a way to measure success, even over a longer time period than a single budget year.

And the cautions?

- In some services, the fees may vary too widely to be predictable. An engagement for one client may produce fees many times that of an engagement for the same service for another client. This is in addition to the distinction between the commodity and the value-added service.
- Because so many people beyond the marketing professional are involved in any professional services marketing effort, it's extremely difficult to allocate costs to a marketing program. It's one thing to know the cost of producing a newsletter, but how about the time of the partners involved in writing and producing the material?
- In a multi-office firm, it can be difficult to appropriately allocate costs to an office or to the national budget.

What this all adds up to is that budgeting a marketing program for professional services doesn't readily respond to the pat formulas of budgeting a program for a product. It requires a great deal of skill, imagination, and understanding of objectives.

But clearly, it's not logical to budget as a percentage of revenues—past or future.

### Budgeting Factors

While the decision regarding total amounts may depend upon the foregoing factors, there are still the specific items to be budgeted. A checklist would be predicated upon the nature of the marketing plan, and the people and tools to be used. It might include the following. . .

- *People.* Staff salaries and standard personnel costs, obviously. Support services from within the firm. Outside and freelance help. And what might be considered here is the cost of time for professionals who must contribute to the program.
- *Outside consultants.* Even with staff, outside consultants are frequently used. This can include specialists (marketing planning, research, direct mail, etc.) or public relations firms or advertising agencies. One advantage of outside agencies is that their services can be costed beforehand, for the most part, and so can be budgeted quite precisely.
- *Research.* Secondary research can be mostly people costs, but it could also be computer database time. Primary research, if it's done in-house, has attendant costs, and outside research can be budgeted by the agency performing the research.
- *Promotional expenses.* These are advertising and public relations costs. Advertising costs are more easily budgeted, because unless the work is done in-house, the agency will work from your space cost allocations,

on either a straight fee basis or a commission. Public relations costs, beyond time in-house and fees for outside agencies, are for releases, mailing, list maintenance, and so forth. Seminars can be large promotional expenses. Not to be overlooked are such out-of-pocket expenses as travel, editorial lunches, etc.

- *Administrative and overhead.* This includes both space and furniture allocations, stationary, and daily expenses, such as phones, telecopying, reproduction, and so forth.

- *Publications.* The costs involved in publication are the editorial costs of time for both writers and contributing professionals, the production and printing costs, and the distribution costs (including mailing).

- *Direct mail.* The costs of direct mail are plan development, writing and producing the package, list acquisition and development, mailing, and followup.

- *Selling.* This includes the time of professionals who participate in the selling effort, research on prospective clients, telemarketing costs (including outside agencies, list development, script development), and presentations and proposals.

As noted, some of the costs of marketing, while quite high, are difficult to discern or to budget. How do you budget professional time for contributing to a brochure, participating in a seminar, or making a sales call? It might be argued that these are intangible costs, and should not be budgeted, but certainly they should be considered a valid cost of any marketing program budget.

The question of how much to allocate to a marketing budget is a different matter, requiring different criteria. It's a function of judgment in several areas:

- How large is the potential growth of a market or a firm, measured in terms of dollar volume on an annual (or budget year) basis?

- How professionally run is the program to be?

- What percentage of current income shall be used to allocate a marketing budget, using any criteria as a guide?

- Will it be necessary, or even desirable, to alter pricing structure to accommodate marketing costs?

- What percentage of a future income shall be designated for marketing? Using what criteria?

- How much money is actually available to invest in marketing, regardless of ratios to current or projected sales?

- How seriously and carefully will the effort be managed?

- What are the local cost factors (e.g. advertising and public relations costs, etc.)?

- How should these expenses be allocated back to various profit centers?
- What relationship is to be established between expectations and time frame?

Theory aside, these are realistic factors to be considered. Money for marketing must come from somewhere, and be measured by one set of criteria or another.

### Client Retention

Nor should the costs of client retention be overlooked. It's almost a cliche—almost, but not quite—that it costs more to get a new client than to keep an old one. But the old one must be kept, and that includes not only consistent quality service, but keeping the client informed of what you're doing in his or her behalf. This is a process that must be assiduously pursued—and not without attendant expenses.

At the heart of client retention, of course, is the nature of the service and the way it's performed. The word *quality*, a difficult concept because it's difficult to define, comes to mind. If the client is given precisely what he expects to get for his money, and it's given promptly and smoothly, then it's half the battle.

But if you add to that those aspects of client relations that make a difference, such as communication, frequent contact, and so forth, you have the essence of client retention. You also have the costs, which must be calculated.

## Measuring the Effort

That marketing is an effort that functions well only as a totality is yet another reality we know from experience. No ad will so bestir a reader that he responds by retaining a professional on the basis of it. A knowledgeable article in a respectable journal may engender new respect for the expertise of its author, and that respect may well result in further discussion between the author and the reader, but ultimately the author of that article will have to personally convince that reader to retain him.

A profoundly successful marketing program may educate, persuade, enhance reputation and perception, and build unique and extraordinary proclivities toward a firm, but an individual will ultimately have to make the sale. How much toothpaste would Colgate sell if each tube had to be sold by Colgate's president? How many mainframe computers would IBM sell if each one had to be sold by IBM's chairman?

A direct mail letter offering a bible bound in genuine leather for only $9.95 may result in five percent of the recipients' sending in checks and order forms, and be deemed a success. But how do you judge the success of a hundred letters sent to business people, offering assistance in improving cash management? And if ten of those recipients ultimately do become clients, how much of it was attributable to the letter, how much to a firm's reputation that might have been enhanced by having been quoted on the subject in *INC Magazine*, and how much to the ability of the partner or partners who closed the sale?

Still, there must be a measure of the marketing effort—a way to know, as precisely as possible, what actually happened as a result of the time, money and effort spent on marketing.

According to PDI's August J. Aquila and Jodi M. Hier, one way to accomplish this is to establish a system of breaking the business development process down into concrete, measurable events and tracking the results of each event.

Each piece of new business that a law, accounting, or consulting firm brings in will go through the following stages:

1. *Generating the lead.* Where did the lead originate, and by whom? The firm can track trends in this area.
2. *Setting the appointment.* This may be the most difficult step. Identify the individual in the firm who is able to contact the prospect and set the appointment to discuss service needs.
3. *Conducting the interview.* Who in the firm is talented in the fact-finding process and can clearly and effectively communicate how the firm can meet the prospect's needs? Tracking this information is valuable in measuring who are the most gifted in this area by the proposal win/lose ratio.
4. *Preparing the proposal.* Involving others in the marketing process includes those responsible for helping to develop the written proposal as well as the oral presentation.
5. *Asking the prospect to buy.* The final step is asking the prospect for the business. Many an opportunity has been lost because the accountant or attorney was reluctant to ask this important question.

By establishing a system of measuring the results of the sales cycle, you can track progress, credit those who participate, and most importantly, identify trends in the sales process.

It's a kind of reverse measuring process. While most product marketing is measured by counting the number of units sold, this process starts with the sale and works back up the chain.

Ultimately, the measure of a marketing program is in the growth of the firm. Practically, the measure of a program is the degree to which the marketing objectives have been met.

Managing the marketing effort, then, is not an arbitrary task. It is perhaps the most sensitive and fragile aspect of the entire marketing effort, in that the most imaginative and powerful marketing program can be destroyed by being mismanaged.

In marketing, marketing management might well be where the greatest professionalism is demanded.

# 19

# The Computer in Marketing

The computer, like the hammer or screwdriver, is a tool that's only as useful as the hand that wields it. The personal computer is, in fact, almost exactly as old as professional services marketing—about a decade. Using the PC in marketing, however, is relatively new.

The question is whether the demands for computer applications for marketing become a self-fulfilling prophecy—or do computers really add a dimension to marketing that's especially useful?

In most ways in which the computer is applied to marketing, and in which specific programs are applied to marketing, the computer makes a substantial difference.

True, there are times when a computer is misused, simply because a computer exists in a marketing department. A press release done on a laser printer in a fancy typeface that looks like an ad, for example, can be self-defeating. And there certainly are programs with more bells and whistles than anybody can use.

But in other areas, there's no doubt that the intelligent use of a computer enhances the marketing process. And to avoid wasteful and ineffective computer use, it's necessary to explore how these now ubiquitous machines can be used most effectively and productively to enhance or aid the marketing process.

## Desktop Marketing

Desktop marketing is a new and useful term to define the use of technology in marketing. Clearly, it's not a single resource. Rather, it's a series of information tools to help marketers do their jobs more efficiently and effectively.

These tools encompass a range of technologies, including:

- *Hardware.* Computers, modems, fax boards, laser printers, local area networks, CD-ROM readers
- *Software.* Word processing, desktop publishing, mailing list managers, contact managers, statistical analysis, CD-ROM disks

---

Much of the material in this chapter is derived from the column, The Marketing Machine, by Tim Powell, a research director at Find/SVP, and appeared in editions of *The Marcus Report*.

- *Communications tools.* Electronic mail, voice mail, bulletin board systems
- *On-line services.*
- *Telephone systems.* Interconnect systems, telemarketing programs, electronic phone books, autodialers

In fact, just about anything a marketer does—from naming a new service to building a dossier on a prospect—can be assisted with a computer.

Desktop marketing applications can automate a process, in which the drudge work of marketing (like typing out mailing labels) is done by the computer. This brings to the process exceptional accuracy and efficiency. Productivity—increased output per unit of input—is improved.

Desktop marketing also increases effectiveness by making some of our tools more *intelligent*—capable of sensing and responding to the environment.

For example, an automated letter that addresses a prospect by name is a more effective marketing tool than one that begins "Dear Small Business Owner:". The letter can even make reference to the prospect's previous service history or other relevant data. It's no wonder that the computer has made such inroads into marketing.

## The Three General Areas of Computing

There are three general areas of computing that apply—the all-purpose computer program that can be used in marketing as well as elsewhere; the all-purpose program that can be adapted to specific marketing uses; and the marketing-specific program. Let's look at each area in the marketing context.

### The All-Purpose Program

These are programs that can be used in many different contexts. The obvious example is word processing. It's used for normal office correspondence and memos and personal letters. It's also used for writing brochures and press releases and advertising copy.

In this context, it's fascinating that we don't hear much, any more, about executives with computer phobia. Or with status problems ("I'm an executive. I don't type.") Today, the computer is a tool, like a staple machine or scotch tape. It sits comfortably on every executive's desk, a status symbol of its own, like having an office with a window.

In fact, an increasing number of executives, in marketing as well as other disciplines, now use a wide range of general programs, such as scheduling, to-do lists, and so forth. And many marketing executives are literate in two or more word processing programs (such as *WordPerfect* or Microsoft *Word).*

With the advent of Microsoft *Windows* and Quarterdeck's *Desqview*, programs that allow the user to run two or more programs at the same time (word processing and a spreadsheet, for example), and to swap information between programs, computer literacy goes to new dimensions. It now includes the ability to do things that had never been done before. Today, the hip marketing executive starts the day by turning on his or her computer, checking the to-do list, reading the electronic mail, and then going to work on a brochure or a press release. *Windows* and *Desqview* allow the user to interrupt work on a brochure text to bring up a database, slot some figures into the brochure, and close the database to go on with the brochure.

A spreadsheet program, such as Lotus *1-2-3*, Microsoft *Excel*, or Borland's *Quattro Pro*, is normally thought of as an accounting or financing tool. But the ability to display numbers in spreadsheet fashion, and to use the what-if features inherent in spreadsheet programs, makes them useful in looking at research figures, planning marketing campaigns, and budgeting. A template program (a program that pre-formats another program) called *The Budget Express* (Symantec) specifically sets up Lotus *1-2-3* to do budgets, an absolute necessity for a marketing plan. Numbers and projections are an integral part of marketing. To be able to ask the computer, "What if I shift X dollars to Y category. What result will I get?", and to see the answer immediately, adds a new dimension to marketing planning.

Here, efficiency—and productivity—is enhanced by using regular commercial off-the-shelf software effectively. And now, it's so easy, and most professional service people are so computer literate, that few marketing professionals are without the skills and the capability to use this kind of system.

### The Adaptable Programs

Some all-purpose or off-the-shelf programs particularly lend themselves to marketing. Prime examples are database and desktop publishing programs.

Database programs take standard information, such as all facts in a particular category, (names and addresses and telephone numbers, for example) and allow this information to be retrieved in formats that are particularly useful to the user. If you have a mailing list of several thousand names, and the list includes such information as the industry in which each person on the list works, you can summon up only the names of the people in a particular industry. Or all of the people in a particular ZIP code. This brings mailing list management—once the most difficult task in all of marketing—to a realm of manageability by the average user. You no longer have to be a specialist.

This ability to correlate information quickly and effectively has other marketing purposes. Results of surveys, for example, can be tabulated quickly and accurately. Market research characteristics can be sorted out. Target marketing, for example, becomes feasible in a way that never existed before. If your prospective clientele has twelve or twenty or even more specific characteristics, if the names of prospective clients in your geographic area have been entered, and those characteristics have been included, you can say to this marvelous machine, "Give me the names of the 100 largest companies in this category, with these specifications and those qualifications, including the person responsible for making the buy decision in each company."

Before the computer, this was never really possible. It could have been done manually, to some extent, but by the time the job was done, the configuration had changed, and the information was dated and useless.

The other kind of software in this category is desktop publishing, in which standard software (and appropriate hardware) is used to produce essentially the same results that once had to depend upon the trained designer, typesetter, and layout artist.

Now, in the hands of a capable user, it takes very little skill and talent to lay out a brochure or a newsletter or even an ad.

There are cautions. A graphics designer is an artist, not a mechanic. Being able to make the machine do what you want it to doesn't make you an artist. Still, with a little training, and perhaps some guidance from a designer, the average marketer can do some extraordinary things with desktop publishing. It's been a boon to marketers in doing simple brochures, newsletters, presentations, and even memos that are improved by graphics.

## The Marketing-Specific Program

There are indeed programs designed specifically for marketers, and particularly for specific disciplines.

For example, programs designed to do regression analysis for market researchers make it possible to do more sophisticated research than has ever been done before, and do it on more timely basis. And while database programs, in the hands of an experienced researcher, can be used to tabulate survey results, now there are special programs designed for statistical analysis.

There are special programs designed to calculate demographics, and for the product marketer, there are programs designed to find product names.

Another category of specialized products are contact programs. These are programs that allow you to keep track of sales or marketing contacts, and to record and update the results of meetings, the necessary followup, and the status of relationships. They are increasingly popular, for the very good reason that they are marvelous organizers that save time and preclude lost sales opportunities.

Still another category is the automatic record keeping program, such as *Timeslips* (Timeslips Corp.) that allow highly accessible and convenient logging of time spent on each client. The program then automatically generates bills, as well as myriad other information that's invaluable to any professional.

## *The Marketing Computer*

The computer, then, is now a valuable tool in the hands of experienced market-ers. It's more than convenient—it brings a new dimension to the marketing pro-cess, and quite literally increases productivity by producing more output without increasing input of time and effort.

Where earlier computer developments produced new products that did things that computers had never done before, the focus now seems to be on improve-ments of existing products, updating of programs—including those used in mar-keting—to make them easier to use and more useful. This includes windows-based programs and networking and LAN programs. LAN (local area network) programs allow many users of a core computer and core software to work from remote ter-minals. The value is to allow many individuals to benefit from the input of large groups, such as a whole marketing department. That means that it's no longer necessary for each individual to have, for example, a database on an individual computer. Each user can draw from the master base on a central computer. This can open up even more uses, and greater usefulness, for the marketer.

Looking at each category in greater detail, we get a better sense of how com-puters are becoming integral to marketing.

## Memory and Windows

It's impossible to talk intelligently about computers today without recognizing two new concepts that are becoming pervasive in the industry—*extended memory* and *Windows*. They're a function of DOS and computer memory in general.

## *DOS*

DOS is the disk operating system. It's the internal program that makes it all happen. Without DOS, or one of the other systems (such as Unix or the new OS/2), you'd have to be an engineer to control and execute computing processes from your keyboard. The only competing program that comes anywhere near it is the separate and different system used by Apple and MacIntosh.

## *RAM*

RAM stands for *random access memory*, which is the amount of memory you have available to work with on any application you use. This is the memory capa-bility built into the machine to run applications, not for storage on disks, which is another matter.

When the first PCs came out, 16K of memory—16 kilobytes—was sufficient, because that's all it took to run the first applications. Then, as programs got to be more complicated, they required more memory. In the early days, this was done by adding chips to the computer, or plug-in memory boards, which eventually got the computer up to 640K.

And then we had to stop, because 640K was all that DOS could handle. But the more that people learned to use computers, the more they demanded of them, and so the more complicated became the applications.

You can, for example, run Lotus 1-2-3 version 2.0 on 640K. But version 3.1, and the new versions of Microsoft *Excel*, require considerably more (in return for which they do considerably more than the simpler and earlier versions of the same programs).

The technicians were able to give us more memory in later models of IBM and IBM-compatible machines with relative ease. The later models, with advanced high speed computing chips (such as the 286, 386, and 486) now consider as much as 5 or 10 megabytes as standard. (It takes a thousand kilobytes to make one megabyte.)

But if DOS can handle only 640K, what good are all those megabytes? The answer lies in understanding two more concepts, and then looking at the programs that function in those concepts. Those are the concepts of *expanded memory* and *extended memory*.

### Extended and Expanded Memory

Without getting into the technical aspects of it, we're talking about usable memory beyond 640K.

*Extended memory* is memory beyond 640K. Technically, it's more complicated than that, but let the computer technicians worry about it.

*Expanded memory* is really a technique that allows a computer that's equipped with the hardware and software to do so to use extended memory. Using software designed for the purpose, it works by playing programming tricks on your computer.

We're really talking about a concept that physically uses addresses on memory boards, but it's the process we're concerned with here, not the technical aspects of mechanics.

In practice, suppose you had some work going in Lotus 1-2-3 that was using most of the 640K memory. You have a TSR (terminate and stay resident) program, such as *Info Select*, a program that makes it possible to jot notes and retrieve them as you need them. A TSR program, remember, is one that loads up when you start up your computer, but doesn't become available to you until you summon it from your keyboard. TSR programs usually take up a lot of memory, which is why it's best to use them with expanded memory programs.

When you hit the key to bring *Info Select* into play, it swaps places in memory with Lotus 1-2-3. When you're finished, you hit the clear key and it swaps it back.

## Expanded Memory Programs

With the ability to reach into this vast new memory arena come programs that facilitate the process, and take advantage of it.

For example, a major new program—Microsoft's *Windows 3.0*, is actually a core program for a whole series of applications programs designed especially to work under Windows.

*Windows 3.0* is a graphical user interface (GUI),which means that each letter or figure on the screen is actually a little picture—a graphic. This is why you can customize the typeface on the screen, for example.

This also means that all commands can be pictured—*icons*—rather than words or letter commands. *Icons* work best with a *mouse*.

The mouse is a hand-held and operated device that moves the cursor on the screen. It's very fast. If you have a mouse and icons, instead of typing a command, you simply use the mouse to move the cursor to an icon representing that command, click a button on the mouse, and the command is executed. And so *Windows 3.0* with a mouse means speed and efficiency.

*Windows 3.0's* most valuable advantage is its extraordinary ability to manage memory. It simply breaks the 640K memory barrier, allowing access to the memory your computer has beyond that. Thus, the power of contemporary programs becomes available to you, by virtue of being able to access the megabyte realm.

But the best part of *Windows 3.0* is that by using extended memory, it gives you access on screen to many programs at one time, and allows you to move data, text and graphics from one program to another. If you're working on a sales report with your word processing program, and want to integrate some figures from a spreadsheet, you open a window for your spreadsheet and move the data to the word processing document. The same with, say, a graph from a separate graphics program. And if you change the data in the spreadsheet, it automatically changes that data in the integrated word processing document.

An increasing number of programs are being developed with special application to *Windows 3.0*. For example, *Crosstalk*, the communications program, now makes *Crosstalk for Windows*. If you're working on a report and need some figures, you open a window with *Crosstalk for Windows*, access a database, and download the figures you want directly into your document. Many other programs are similarly being adapted, including Microsoft's own *Word*, *Excel*, *Project*, and *Power Point*. These programs take advantage of the graphic beauty of GUI.

Other companies are producing a cascade of new windows products. *Lotus 1-2-3 For Windows*, for example, brings all of the power of the original program into a GUI mode, with enhancements that users will be very comfortable with. *WordStar*, the classic word processing system, has also moved its latest version into *Windows*, as has *WordPerfect* and Lotus *Ami Professional*, a particularly powerful program.

There are many more capabilities and small programs, such as a calculator, a calendar, a telecommunications program, and so forth, that add value to *Windows 3.0*, but these are all in addition to the major features.

*Windows* is enhanced by a program called *Norton Desktop For Windows* (Symantec), which manages and speeds up file access, helps launch programs from within the Windows environment, and performs a large number of other valuable tasks. It finds files, supplies a library of icons or allows you to make your own, provides instant system information, and performs the classic *Norton* data recovery services. It makes a good program better.

What it adds up to is that *Windows 3.0* brings the computer into the next generation of capability. It's a new way to function with computers. It's as if the rules of gravity have been repealed, allowing us to function effectively in all directions, as do space travelers enhanced by weightlessness.

The value of *Windows 3.0*, for the marketer is incalculable. Simply by moving all of computing into the new dimension of graphic facility, it makes any computer task easier and more effective. But when you apply that capability to marketing, you get the ability to produce memos, reports, proposals—any document—with data and graphics of such stunning effectiveness as to warrant calling it a new genre of communication.

*The applications programs being developed for Windows 3.0*, are, in their own way, just as innovative and facile as *Windows*. Because of GUI, as well as the additional development to make them more effective with *Windows 3.0*, many of these programs are substantially improved over their current DOS versions.

For the marketer, being able to control access to a great many sources, ideas, graphics, and data not only triggers imagination, but feeds it. Facts, figures, and graphics, seen in different juxtapositions, open possibilities for marketing ideas never before possible. Being able to see data in juxtaposition to context, or to be able to visualize information in a number of different graphic ways to choose the best way, gives it a new and valuable meaning.

## DOS-Based Programs

Clearly, for the next decade or so *Windows* will be the technology that will provide the environment in which the computer becomes an even more useful tool than it is now.

But if you want to work with either your existing DOS-based programs or the special *Windows* programs, you should look at *Desqview 386* and its companion program, *QEMM 386* (Quarterdeck Office Systems).

The *QEMM* part is the program that does the actual expanded memory act. But in combination with the *Desqview* part, it does some other extraordinary things. Essentially, it's a windows program, but one that can only work with expanded memory.

Let's say you're working on a document in *WordStar*. You want to get some information that's in *Lotus 1-2-3*. With *Desqview*, you can open *Lotus* in a window on the screen, without losing *WordStar*. You can load as many as five windows, showing five different programs, on your screen at the same time. The beauty of it is that you can transfer data from one program to another. If you're working on a document in word processing, and need some spreadsheet calculations, you open the spreadsheet in one window. Then you find you need some additional data from a data base. You open the database in another window. You switch information from the database to the *Lotus*, do the Lotus calculations with the new data, and transfer the results to the document in word processing.

And you can work from the keyboard in the standard way, or from a mouse, which can be very much faster. It's remarkable, and comes under the heading of things you can do with a computer that you couldn't do before the computer.

*Desqview* also supplies some interesting TSR programs as a companion. *Link* opens a window that serves as a communications program, so that you can use your modem to transmit data. *Desqview Notepad* lets you jot down notes or short memos and letters. *Desqview Databook* is a calendar and scheduling program. *Desqview Calculator* is a powerful calculator. All offer fine examples of the best use of TSRs.

### The RamPack

Another, and perhaps simpler, program is *RamPack* (Bloc Publishing, Coral Gables, FL).

*RamPack* actually consists of two programs—*Above DISC*, and *PopDrop PLUS*. *Above DISC* converts extended memory into expanded memory, pure and simple. It's compatible with all major applications, and has the distinct advantage of working on both 286 and 386 machines. It also can load certain network drivers into extended memory, which is useful for network users. It's easy to install and use, and a good bare bones answer to those who don't need or want the bells and whistles of windows-type programs.

*PopDrop Plus* enhances the process by deftly managing TSR programs, which it keeps and manipulates into expanded memory. Included are device drivers—programs that run networks, activate mouse controls, and so forth. With this program, TSR programs loaded into extended memory are readily accessible with *hot keys*—predetermined keys that you hit to bring up each TSR. This, too, is a sound program that's useful and cost effective—simple to install and use.

### Solving the Memory Problem

One would think that by this point DOS would be able to function beyond the 640K limit without the gimmicks, and indeed, the new iteration of DOS—*DOS 5.0*—will do so. The relatively new OS/2 does it, but is a long way away from universal acceptance and replacement of DOS.

### DOS 5.0

*DOS 5.0*, from Microsoft, is fast, facile, and formidable. Moreover, it's got a feature that should be dear to the heart of anybody who's ever changed his or her mind. If, after you install it, you don't like it, you can uninstall it, with no loss to anything you've got on your computer (including DOS 4.0).

But what's most important about *DOS 5.0* is what it does for memory. By residing in memory above the 1 megabyte boundary (in 286 or better computers), it saves about 45K in the lower 640K area.

On 386 and 486 computers, there's even more memory saved, because *DOS 5.0* loads TSRs (terminate-and-stay-resident programs) in upper memory. This can save as much as 133K of conventional memory. The particular value here to marketers is that for most daily uses of the computer, the TSR is a goldmine. Programs like autodialers, note takers, hourly record keeping and so forth, as TSRs, can be called to the screen instantly, no matter what else you're working on. And if you use Microsoft *Windows*, this memory feature is invaluable, because you get to use more conventional memory for DOS applications running under *Windows*.

If *DOS 5.0* did nothing more that break the barrier to memory above 640K, it would be worth its weight in gold. But it does do more.

For users who hate getting into an application with the old cd\ command, *5.0* has a new shell with a "point and click" operation. That means that you have rapid access to any application you run under DOS. The shell has a task-swapper that allows you to move from one application to another without having to exit the first application. There goes tedium.

### New Commands

A new feature called DOSKEY, which sits in TSR waiting to be used, allows previously executed commands to be recalled, edited, or re-executed without retyping.

And if you've got some applications that work only on earlier versions of DOS, a utility called *SETVER* allows you to control the version of DOS that you use on those programs. Several of the traditional commands have been improved. The *MEM* (memory) command can be used to show a summary of memory in use, the size of programs, and the memory blocks available. The *DIR* (directory) command can display file names in lower case, display files by attributes (size, date, etc.), search subdirectories to find any file on your disk, and so forth. A treasure chest.

One of the improvements that *DOS 4.0* made over previous versions was that it broke the limit on hard disk partition. If you had a 40 Megabyte hard disk, for example, you had to format it in two parts, with a C: and D: drive. The limit for the C: drive was 32M. *DOS 5.0* goes much farther in supporting hard disks. It can format as high as 2 gigabytes, which is, today, like building a car that can be adapted in the future to fly.

If you've ever had to edit a program in DOS with *EDLIN*, the old DOS text editor, you'll welcome the new *EDIT* program. It's commands are drawn from *WordStar* and *Microsoft Word*.

*Windows, DOS 5.0,* and the memory expanding programs open new worlds for the compute user.

## Database Programs

Facts have a way of accumulating beyond usefulness. Not only is the volume of facts overwhelming, but relating them to one another in ways that make facts useful information can be lost as well. Herein lies the value of the database program.

Accurate and up-to-date lists are now crucial for the any degree of control of client relationships, as well as for any sophisticated marketing program.

The cost of a single piece of mail, including addressing, stuffing, printing enclosures, postage, and the time in managing the process, seems to burgeon endlessly. Mailing to the wrong address, or misspelling a client's name, is costly.

Mailings must be tailored to reach specific groups with specific messages. Differentiated messages require differentiated lists to deliver those messages.

Sometimes, lists cross lines and overlap by purposes. A list of clients is different from a list of prospective clients. But a list of clients is also a list of prospective clients for a new service you have to offer.

Mailing lists are dynamic—constantly changing and needing updating. They seem to be alive, and it's been said that whom the Gods would drive mad, they first put in charge of mailing lists. Lists must be managed and attended to constantly, including grouping and regrouping names in order to reach different targets with different messages. Fortunately, contemporary software makes it possible without undue effort for those who want to manage smaller lists.

But for larger and more complex lists, the solution may be the outside list service bureaus, which usually use mainframe computers or minicomputers for list management functions. Their services may also include letter shop services, such as affixing labels, stuffing envelopes, and delivering the completed packages to the post office. They offer the advantage of greater facility and convenience, the benefits of information derived from their serving many customers (change of address, etc.), and the ability to track costs precisely. On the other hand, you own only those lists you supply, and so you can rarely control other of their lists.

Recent versions of major database programs for the personal computer are sophisticated, with interfaces that allow relatively easy use by non-technical users. *Paradox* (Borland) is a powerful program that's ease of use belies its power. It has exceptional presentation graphics that make it a favorite for those who turn data into presentations. The classic *dBaseIV* (Borland/Ashton Tate), one of the earliest of the database programs for the PC, now has simplified language commands and better memory management. Probably the most popular database program for non- professional computer users is *Q&A* (Symantec). While a powerful program that's readily capable of handling mailing lists and inventory systems, it's simple to use, has on-line help, and can exchange data with other databases. The interesting thing about Q&A is that it includes a word processing program that can very well stand on its own for simplicity and capability.

## Online Databases

If knowing your market is at the crux of an effective marketing program, then the computer, with it's vaunted access to databases, should be a crucial tool in market research.

There are two kinds of research that concern us—primary and secondary.

*Primary* research is when you go directly to your market and ask questions (surveys, interviews, focus groups). But most researchers start with *secondary research*, in which you explore material already available.

Secondary research used to be accomplished by going to a business library and physically scanning various business periodicals and reference works.

The advent of online databases has changed all that. Now research can be conducted by computer, via telephone connection to mainframe computers that store vast amounts of information electronically. The amount of business information available electronically has grown rapidly in the past few years, until now there are more than 3000 online databases. The list grows weekly, and the range of information online is extraordinary. Mailing lists, company background, biography, journal and other press abstracts, medical and legal information, bibliography, demographic information—a virtual cornucopia of fact.

While more useful than any secondary research tool we've ever had before, online databases are still far from the powerful tools they could be. The information may really be in the database. But getting at it is something else.

First, you have to know where to look. Because almost all online information is produced in electronic form after being published first in hard copy, online data follows the structure of the published sources. If you're researching a topic that you know was written about in *Grocery Store News*, you have to know which database carries that publication's material.

Searches are usually structured as keyword searches of abstracts or full-text articles. The commands for doing this involve a kind of mathematical logic not commonly used by business people.

And the user interfaces are typically obtuse. Searches are command-driven, and so the commands themselves must be committed to memory, or referred to on a printed sheet. While some vendors have front-end programs that improve this somewhat, most of the improvements are mainly cosmetic. Special knowledge or expertise is still often required to get useful online results. This means that information intermediaries—librarians or other researchers, or outside vendors—are too often needed to translate the end user's needs into search logic that can actually retrieve the information.

But this is less than a perfect solution. In using an intermediary, timeliness may be compromised. Or the researchers may be knowledgeable in the techniques of searching, but not necessarily in the business problems being researched. They may not understand the true strategic meaning of the information you need as thoroughly and as quickly as you'd like.

Should this discourage you, however, from attempting to come to grips with online data? Not at all. There are still extraordinary values in electronic information access that should be pursued.

### The Forms of Information Available

The kinds of available information online that would be of interest to a marketer of professional services include:

- *Periodicals.* General press (national and regional), business press, trade press, and newsletters. The information may be full text, prepared abstracts, or just citations.
- *News wire stories.* These are the classic news tickers that used to be found in brokerage firms and broadcast newsrooms.
- *Market research reports.* These are in-depth reports on a full range of information in a market for a particular product or service.
- *Investment reports.* Written by security analysts, this information can be valuable for company background and competitor data. It may also contain line-of-business data.
- *Financial data and annual reports.* Helpful in monitoring key clients, prospects, and competitors.
- *Executive biographies.* Especially helpful where the purchase decision will be made by one or a small group of individuals.
- *Company listings.* Selections can be done on industry, size, and location. Listings of directors and officers are typically included.
- *Trademark registrations.* Both Federal and state registrations are available online.

This list expands constantly. In fact, there is an online database of online databases to keep you current. Some of this information is also now available on CD-ROM disk (a compact disk optically read, for computers).

### How Much It Costs

Pricing for online databases is typically set by the originator of the data, not the electronic vendor. This means that the rate card is complicated, which can be intimidating.

Essentially, the costs are based on time logged onto a particular database, the time connected to a particular data vendor, and phone charges (usually at local call rates.)

The key to pricing is knowledge. The more skilled and adept you are at using the database, and at finding the information you want quickly, the less time you're online, and the lower the charges.

In the hands of an experienced researcher or search professional, search costs can be surprisingly low compared with the strategic value of the information, as well as the cost of obtaining the information by other means.

### How to Get Started

In practice using online databases shouldn't be difficult. If you're new at it, it may cost you a few dollars in line and time charges until you get the hang of it, but you'll more than make that up as you go along.

To go online, you need:

- A personal computer or terminal.
- A telephone line.
- A modem. This enables your computer to plug into the worldwide network of telephone lines.
- Modem software. This enables you to dial the phone line through the modem, access information, capture the information to disk or the printer.
- A valid online vendor account. Each vendor carries hundreds of databases, but you'll need several accounts to really have access to a useful range of information.
- Some training in search techniques and strategies. Vendors often offer this as a package when signing up for the service.

Your first step, though, should be to get more background information. A very good source book is Alfred Glossbrenner's *How to Look It Up Online* (St. Martin's Press).

### Word Processing

Once, word processing was merely the electronification of typing. Now, it's the sophisticated, complex manipulation of symbols to express ideas. Add to that the laser printer, which transforms the electronics of the computer into a seemingly limitless array images on paper— a variety of typefaces, type sizes, page layouts, and so forth. Word processing now takes the expression of ideas as far from the typewriter as the typewriter was from prehistoric wall painting.

There is, as well, the added element of communication. Ideas can now be transmitted around the world instantaneously. A writer in New York can transmit his copy directly to the typesetter in Los Angeles, and the typesetter turns it into the printed page without retyping.

*WordStar*, one of the earliest of the word processing programs, is now in version 6.0, with 7.0 on the way. The ability to produce complex documents with this classic system is astonishing, particularly to an early user. Today, there are special versions for both *Windows* and laptop computers. Still command based—it takes its commands from the keyboard in combinations of letters with control and *alt* keys—it's useful for writers and touch typists, who are at home on a keyboard.

Microsoft *Word*, on the other hand, functions best with a mouse to move the cursor through both the command screen and the editing screen. An extremely popular program, it leans heavily on menus to accept editing, filing, and formatting commands.

*WordPerfect* is probably the best-selling program. For office workers, it seems easiest to use. Most of its commands are from the function keys, at the side or top of the keyboard.

While most contemporary word processing programs have desktop publishing features, *Ami Pro* (Lotus) seems to be the most facile, both for straight word processing and for its desktop features. It works from either keyboard or mouse, as does *Word*, although the mouse is faster. *Ami Pro* is also made for Windows.

For the person who requires a less demanding word processing program, with fewer bells and whistles but the ability to produce creditable documents, there's always *Just Write* (Symantec). Simple though it may be, it does a number of useful and powerful tasks, such as file conversion from other programs and links with other applications.

There are, of course myriad other word processing programs, of varying configurations, purposes and uses. A wide variety, with literally hundreds of features beyond merely entering text.

While virtually every word processing program includes a built in spell checker and thesaurus, yet another breed of software checks grammar and syntax.

The leader in the field is *Grammatik* (Reference Software), which proofreads for grammatical errors, style, usage, and so forth. *Correct Grammar* (WordStar International) corrects inconsistencies, catches awkward phrases, and analyzes style. *Right Writer* (Rightsoft) parses sentences and analyzes style.

These programs can be useful for the non-professional writer, but they do tend to move all writing to a middle level. On the one hand, they might be good for catching accidents and mistakes in usage. On the other hand, the writer whose style is a reflection of his personality would find them oppressive.

### Communications Software

Communications by modem, from one computer to another and from a computer to an online database or service such as *CompuServe*, depends upon a reliable software program. There are a great many such programs, from those that are part of word processing programs to simple free or low cost programs available offline from services.

The standard for programs that perform a full range of services, including transmitting from one brand of computer to another, or to a computer using a different system, is *Crosstalk* (DCA). Constantly updated to include the ability to script a full spectrum of communications protocols and integrating the complex calling card protocols used in dialing for different phone services, *Crosstalk* seems to be the most reliable system for transmitting with the fewest errors caused by bad phone connections, and so forth.

Hayes, which makes the modem now considered the standard, has a program called *Smartcom,* which is also popular with computer users who communicate a lot by modem.

## Project Management

Most projects you do go in linear stages, with each task having to be completed before the next one can begin, and have subtasks that are concurrent and parallel to the linear tasks. A missed deadline for one critical subtask can cascade though the rest of the project, making every succeeding task late. What often happens then is that a window of opportunity can be missed, which amplifies the original error.

To take a concrete example, let's say you have a new firm brochure that you're preparing to mail the week after Labor Day. If you work backwards, you start by understanding that the brochure will be at the printer a maximum of two weeks, meaning that you have until the third week in August to complete it.

But there's a catch. The senior partner must approve the final proof before it goes to the printer. He's leaving to go fishing for a month in the Rockies on August 1, and can't be reached after then. An unanticipated production delay of even a day or two in July can set your promotion schedule off by a month or more. This would push the mailing to mid-October, which can adversely affect the impact of the promotion.

At the same time, several people, some of whom depend upon one another for input, must contribute different sections to the brochure. And while this is being done, the brochure must be designed, and photographs and other artwork arranged for. Some of these tasks must happen consecutively, and others simultaneously. How do we keep track of it all, so that the brochure comes out on time?

## Project Management Software

That's what project management software does—it tracks and schedules both simultaneous and consecutive tasks on one chart, including timetables. By visualizing it, the tasks of the project are easy to follow, and by timing it, they are easy to schedule. It also:

- Tracks dependencies between the tasks, e.g., the sign- off must be completed before the brochure goes to the printer.

- Tracks the person responsible for each task.
- Tracks the time for each task, including...
    - The resource time it will take to complete (person-hours)
    - The date by which it must be finished.

    Actual times can be entered and compared with the planned times. Slippage in the delivery date of a task can be addressed by either moving the due dates of later dependent tasks, or by adding other resources to keep the dates intact.
- Tracks the dollar costs associated with each task. Again, actuals can be entered and compared with the plan.

It can also visualize your projects in several useful formats, such as a Gantt chart, in which all of the tasks are listed down one side, followed by bars of different lengths on a calendar grid. This shows the length of time allocated to each task, its relationship to other tasks, and its relationship to the *critical path*, the main operational thrust. A *PERT* chart, on the other hand, graphically presents each task in a box, with lines relating one task to another. Having both charts of the same project allows different perspectives of the project. By entering actual performance to replace projected performance, the relationships are changed to keep the projections realistic.

## Applications

Project management techniques in marketing a professional firm can have several applications, such as producing brochures and other collateral materials, coordinating a rollout campaign for a new service, planning and promoting professional seminars, and planning and tracking personal schedules.

It can help you think through all the steps involved in completing a project and their relationship to each other. You can monitor the actual course of the project against the plan, and know immediately if you're going to be late or ahead of schedule, and perhaps make some adjustments to other parts of the project to correct for the schedule change.

It helps communicate the complexity of the project to those who might otherwise not understand a process. For example, things like lead times required for media placements and collateral production are often not understood by practitioners.

Tracking a project's actual performance against its plan can help make planning for future similar projects more realistic, since they're now based on experience. Certainly, being able to see the elements of a project in perspective, with all elements on display at once, can often show how the approach to the project can be improved, and how productivity can be increased. It helps, as well, to visualize total departmental effectiveness, productivity, and consistency to the overall marketing (or other) objectives.

Project planners range from the simplest schedule programs, such as *On Target* (Symantec), which is primarily a scheduling tool, to the high-powered and professional *Timeline* (Symantec), Microsoft *Project for Windows,* and *Project Scheduler* (Scitor) for the IBM, which can accommodate fairly complex planning, and do it with great graphics, and *Keyplan* (Symetry) for the Macintosh.

## Utility Programs

Some of the lesser tasks of marketing, including many that are just the everyday tasks of life, are also part of the computer world. The computer programmers have given us a number of mighty tools that simply make life easier. These programs come under a lot of different categories, such as contact software, personal information managers, and so forth.

There are a great many programs that will manage your desktop functions, such as calendars, phone lists, notetakers, etc. Each has advantages and disadvantages, and the choice among many is a very personal one.

Perhaps the most interesting in this class is a program called *Info Select* (Micro Logic Corp). *Info Select* is essentially a note taker. You write random notes on the screen, just as you used to do on a piece of paper. But instead of losing the paper, *Info Select* keeps each note in an easily retrievable window. The notes then stack up (within the computer, of course), but you can manage them at your convenience.

For example, with hundreds of notes (the program accepts many times that) you can retrieve any one of them by asking for any string of characters that might be included within that note. This could be a name, a date, a phone number, a code—anything. If you're on a phone call with Charlie and want to refresh your memory about something, you simply get "Charlie," and up comes every note you have on Charlie.

It's an auto dialer, too, so that if you want to call Charlie you simply put the cursor on his number and push the button.

You can combine notes, or separate a complex note into several simpler ones. You can delete or edit a note, or reorganize notes into separate distinct piles of notes, or files. You can find notes by getting the single string of characters, by calling for the first line of all the notes in a stack, or by browsing through all the notes you have. You can reorganize notes into an order of priority. And there's much, much more.

The point is that this is the computer at work, doing valuable and time-saving things for you that you could never effectively—or cost-effectively—do before. It's the real boon of the computer.

The most incredible program of this kind is Lotus *Agenda,* a program that takes the computer to its upper limits of performance.

*Agenda* starts by asking you to list facts, and then to decide the categories that might be concerned with those facts. The categories might be chronological, or a team of people, or an order of priorities. Every fact you then enter is distributed automatically to those categories. If you change a fact in one category, it changes in all the others.

You can then view each category separately, which gives you each fact in proper relation to the other facts in the category.

If it sounds complicated, it is. But once you learn the system, it's easy to use. And it's value is remarkable.

For example, if you're responsible for producing a brochure, you have all of the tasks involved, you have a timetable, you have a budget, you have expenses, and you have several people on your team, each with a different responsibility. Each of these become categories. As the project progresses, different tasks are assigned, different people complete certain of their tasks, different expenses are incurred, and the budget must be adjusted. *Agenda* records each of these events, reflects changes and progress throughout all categories, and allows you to take a view of the project at any moment from the perspective of each category.

*Agenda* is an extraordinary program that subjects managing a project to effective organization.

An unusual and particularly useful program, especially for the small firm, is *The Manager's Organizer*, by the remarkable MECA Software, Inc. (Westport, CT). MECA is the company that produces Andrew Tobias's *Managing Your Money* and *Tax Cut*, which puts it in the forefront of business-oriented personal programs.

*TMO* was designed as a personal program to be used by the managers at IBM, and so contains a number of applications not usually found in desktop managers.

For example, *TMO* has the standard time organizer, business card file, calender, calculator, and notepad. But it goes beyond that to include a personnel manager that allows you to keep track of all of the time and other records of employees, and an inventory of contracts and agreements you may have to refer to frequently.

It also goes beyond the standard expense report record to include an automobile log and trip report. Its business calculator allows you to quickly calculate business formulae. Its telephone log keeps track of messages.

The beauty of the program is that it integrates information so that a great deal of it can be at your fingertips in moments. For the active marketer, or the practitioner with a small firm, or the manager in a large firm with a range of responsibilities, it gives new breadth and dimension to the computer.

The classic program in this category is *Sidekick* (Borland), which takes notes, keeps appointment lists and telephone numbers, autodials, and performs myriad other such tasks.

*Who, What, When* (Chronos) has some added advantages in people and project scheduling that make it particularly useful in managing staffs and staff time.

*Polaris Pack Rat* offers the full range of personal information management, and integrates it with other programs as needed.

## Emergency and Program Control Utilities

Did you ever have a hard disk crash—and lose all the stuff you've input for the past year? Did you ever have a glitch in your spreadsheet or data base, because a floppy disk went bad? Did you ever find that your computer was getting very slow, because you had so much material on the hard disk? Did you ever lose a file because you accidentally hit a wrong key, or because you couldn't remember the name you gave that file?

These, of course, are the problems endemic to computers, and would seem to wipe out all of the advantages they have over the old typewriter and file cabinet.

Experts say that theoretically, a hard disk should last, on average, from 30,000 to 70,000 hours. That could be as much as 15 years, even if your computer were used 40 hours a week. Of course, it never happens that way. One reason is that preventative maintenance is often beyond the ken of most users.

Even a simple thing like parking heads can help. *Park* is a commonly available program that you use just before you turn your machine off. What it does is leave the disk reading heads in a position in which they're not resting on the disk. Over a period of time, heads resting on disks can cause undue wear and damage. The hard disk, unfortunately, may be electronic, but it's also mechanical, and the mechanical component can be fragile.

For the experienced computer user, there's always the knowledge that the cure for the massive depression caused by all these problems is in a group of tools that correct, save, and cure computer problems. And in some respects, these programs also serve to offer preventative maintenance to discs. Some programs, such as *Norton, Mace,* and *PC Tools Deluxe,* are dedicated to just solving disk and file problems. Other programs, including MS-DOS itself, contain programs that presumably perform specific aspects of repair and protection programs.

No one producer has a product that's absolutely best in all categories, but *Norton Utilities* (Symantec) comes close to it. Its range of capabilities is extraordinary, covering virtually every aspect of maintenance and repair.

*Norton Utilities* is actually comprised of a group of individual, easy-to-use programs, each of which performs a specific function, all of which are integrated under the Norton umbrella. For example...

*Unerase* automatically searches and restores erased files. When a file is deleted, it isn't actually destroyed unless a new file is recorded over it. What happens is that its directory access is deleted, which is what a restoration program reconstructs.

*Unformat* recovers data from a disk that's been reformatted, thereby destroying all the data on that disk.

*Safe Format* prevents accidental hard disk formatting.

*The Norton Disk Doctor II* analyzes a disk and fixes a large number of things that might have gone wrong with it.

*File Fix* finds and repairs damage to 1-2-3 and dBASE files. It automatically makes a new and corrected copy.

*Norton Cache* speeds up access to data by keeping your most often used data in memory.

*Speed Disk* performs one of the most useful tasks in computer maintenance — unfragmenting. As you save data, it goes to the most convenient spot it can find on your disk. This means that all of the data in a single file may not be contiguous on the disk. As a result, your disk arm has to search all over the disk to bring up the different segments of a file, thereby substantially slowing up the process of retrieving a file. Unfragmenting puts all the fragments together, thereby speeding up the computer's operation.

*Disk Monitor* prevents parts or all of your disk from being overwritten, whether by accident or by a deliberately planted computer virus. And since more and more computers are networked, and more files are brought in by modem, concern for computer viruses can be very real.

A computer virus, you undoubtedly know, is a bit of programming deliberately hidden in a file. It's designed to enter your system, causing other files to act independently of your commands. Some can be harmless pranks—others can be downright dangerous in that they can destroy files of data.

*Norton Control Center* allows you to change aspects of your computer operation, such as the speed of your mouse. It can allow you to change your cursor size, change screen colors, change keyboard speed, set the time and date, and adjust many other aspects of your computer.

*Diskreet* adds password protection to your files and disk for security, so that only you or those you authorize can use your computer.

*Disk Editor* gives you split screen editing, cut/paste editing, and other editing controls.

*File Find* locates files anywhere on your disk by name, contents, date, or any other information, and allows you to view the files.

And much, much more in the ways of maintenance and repair.

Unlike earlier versions of this kind of program, the Norton program protects against losing data during the course of its operation.

### Other Ways to Go

This is not to say that the *Mace* and *PC Tools* programs are not useful. Each has something to offer that the others don't. But for the non-technical user, *Norton Utilities* is the easiest to use, and has the broadest range of capabilities.

A word of warning, though. As good as programs such as the *Norton Utilities* are, they don't solve such problems as disks being physically or mechanically destroyed. *Always back up your work periodically.* Nothing will cause your heart to sink lower or faster than finding that you've entered crucial data on a disk that breaks down. *Norton* has a good backup program, and so too does Gazelle—*Back-It 4*. A memory resident program, it can back up a file or your entire hard disk to floppies and even some tape drives. It's incredibly fast, for even the largest hard disk. *Fastback Plus* (Fifth Generation), another excellent backup program, makes good use of the mouse, with a directory tree that's used to select individual files to back up.

Nor will disk tools save data that's still in random access memory when the power goes out. What hasn't been backed up is irretrievably lost.

There's also the problem of the defective floppy disk. While some brands are generally more reliable than others, every brand produces a few in every batch that don't hold up. Without a backup, when a disk goes, your data goes, and no maintenance tool can retrieve it.

## *The Disk Manager*

Another kind of utility that comes under the heading of disk manager is not a maintenance or repair program in the same sense of *Norton Utilities*, but rather one that allows you to view and manipulate your files. One such program, and probably the best of them, is *XTREE Pro Gold* (XTree Company, San Luis Obisbo, CA).

At the heart of the *XTREE* program is the tree—the diagramed structure of directories, subdirectories and files on your disk. When you boot up *XTREE*, the program reads your entire disk and displays the directory. But in a sidebar, you get such information as the amount of space taken and available on your disk, the size of each file, and the number of files on the disk. A list of each file in each directory also appears on the screen, and can be brought up to the full screen so that you can work with it. You can then perform a number of operations that allow you to organize your disk.

You can, for example, view any file. You can split the screen to compare files in two different directories, or even on two different drives. You can delete files, transfer them easily from one directory or disk to another, open or close directories, rename files or directories, and generally manipulate files as quickly and handily as you did when you were using the file cabinet.

You can also print the whole tree, giving you a view of the directories on your disk. If you have a lot of directories, it's sometimes hard to remember the designation of those you use the least. Most of those designations, for most people, are usually abbreviations. A picture of the tree can help.

While there are more elaborate programs to find a particular file, such as Lotus's *Magellan*, *XTREE* is very fast and useful in finding a file if you have some general idea where it might be. For example, if you need the form letter you used for a particular project you were pitching to prospects, and you can't remember the name, *XTREE* allows you to browse through directories and files until you do find it.

There are, of course, many more things that can be done with *XTREE* to manage files, and while there are other programs that do some of those things, it seems that *XTREE* is the only one that does all of them. It's fast and easy to use.

## The File Finder

With disks of today's size you can have several thousand files on your hard disk, not counting what you've got on your floppies. Then comes the time when you've got to find something you've written, and you can't remember the file you've got it on. And all you remember is a fragment of a sentence.

Lotus *Magellan* is the program to solve that problem. First it asks you what you're looking for—a word, a phrase, a number sequence, a fragment. Then it asks you if you can narrow the search to a group of files—but if you can't, that's okay. It will scan the entire disk for you. On one side of the screen, it will list every file that contains what you're looking for. On the other side of the screen, it displays the file itself, so you can see if it's the right one. And if you're not sure, it will run the program, including the file, for you. From within Magellan you can edit, move or copy a file, or delete a file.

The more files you have, the more useful is *Magellan*—a boon to computer users.

## Other Useful Utilities

*FormTool Gold* (Bloc Publishing, Coral Gables, FL) is yet another example of how the computer can be used to do something you might never have done before.

Every business has forms it uses to keep track of something. Expense forms. Time sheets. Signout sheets. These forms are usually designed with a pencil and a ruler, and then sent to an art director or a printer to do in final form, and then print.

With *FormTool Gold*, the form is designed right on the computer. By using sophisticated printer drivers (controls), *FormTool Gold* prints out a useful version of the final form, which can then be photocopied and reproduced, or sent to an offset printer for inexpensive copies.

A companion program from the same software developer, *FormFiller*, allows you to build a software template in your computer that matches any form you regularly fill out. This allows you to use your computer for the time-consuming process of filling out large forms.

Not a difficult program to master, *FormFiller* takes you step by step through the process of building a template for a form, including spacing instructions that match those of the form. When the template is complete, you simply insert the form in your printer, fill out the blanks on your screen, and print the final form as perfectly as if you'd typed it.

Obviously, there's no advantage to using a computer to fill out a single form. But if you have frequent occasions to fill out the same form, this can be a boon.

And the one function that most regular computer users have come to know and use—a function that's particularly useful to marketers—is *mail merge*.

While there are several programs that particularly simplify the process, virtually every major professional word processing program has a mail merge function. *FastPak Mail* (Bloc Publishing) is a stand-alone program that covers not only mail merging, but labels, list management, and so forth. It goes well beyond the mail merge capabilities of the average mail merge part of a word processing program.

Mail merging is essentially very simple. You write a standard document. Using the format of the program you're working with, you instruct the computer to fill in certain spots in the basic document with information keyed to it from mailing lists.

A letter to prospects, for example, can pick up the name and address of each prospect, a salutation based on first or last name, and if you choose, include that person's name in the body of the text. The computer then prints each letter, filling in the blanks with information from the mailing list for each successive letter.

The result is a letter that looks completely personalized. It's a simple process, but tremendously effective by virtue of its personalized addressing and salutation.

Mail merging has been around for some time now, but it's increasing in popularity. You've probably received many such letters yourself—sometimes without realizing that they're mail merged.

## E-Mail

The first telephone was nothing. It was the second telephone that made the instrument a communications device.

So it is with *E-Mail*, a form of computer communications that may ultimately revolutionize mail between companies or individuals. Or at least, it will when enough people are signed on to an E-Mail system and are using it.

Many professional firms are already taking advantage of *E-Mail* (short for electronic mail), and it seems to be growing in popularity.

Electronic mail sends messages—pure text, graphics, or binary files (computer programs)—from one computer to another, via ordinary telephone lines. E-mail is a system that usually works on a *store-and-forward* basis. Users send messages by computer to another user's private electronic mailbox on a central host computer, and get messages by using their computers to access their own mailbox on this host.

The electronic message can also be received by a FAX machine, or forwarded as a telex, or as hard copy that's delivered by messenger or by mail from a post office near the recipient.

E-mail can be accessed only by the addressee. *Electronic bulletin boards*, however, are public, and messages can be read by anyone logging onto the system.

Most electronic mail systems have these features:

- *Message answering and forwarding.* The ability to automatically answer a message you've received on the system, or to forward it to another user.
- *User directories.*
- *Security.* Identification codes and passwords keep someone else from accessing your mail or charging to your account.
- *Copying,* so that you can send multiple copies of your message.
- *Group addressing,* for simultaneous mailings to groups of users.
- *Archiving,* to store both your incoming and outgoing messages for future reference.
- *Message scanning.* The ability to read only the topic lines of all your messages first, and then to select those messages which you want to read full text.
- *Off-line composition.* The ability to create a message before you connect to the system to send it, thereby reducing telephone and on-line charges.

Electronic mail is really a hybrid of the telephone and regular mail. Like the mail, the sender and recipient use the system at different times. While this makes it inappropriate for interactive communications, it also means that time need not be wasted getting both parties on the line at once (less telephone tag).

Like the FAX, it can quickly transmit large amounts of text. Unlike the FAX, it is not yet very good at sending pictures. It can, however, send program files, which can't be done by FAX.

Messages can be stored centrally and retrieved at will by the recipient. FAX, a point-to-point medium, generally doesn't allow this.

### What It Means for Marketers

Clearly, E-Mail can replace mail, telephone, or inter-office memo for many messages. For professional firms, this could mean internal or external communications that are both fast and terse, and therefore cheaper than phone or direct contact. It can be used like direct mail, broadcast to a list or to selected names. Like the old telegram, hard copy E-Mail seems to offer a sense of urgency that supports a selling message.

Internal communications in large, multi-office firms are a much more common use of E-Mail, and could involve such activities as sharing proposal drafts among a geographically decentralized team, distributing market intelligence, distributing marketing support software or data, and distributing technical software or data.

E-mail can also be used for external communications, to clients or prospects, for example, although not many professional firms are doing this yet. Information, such as analysis of tax legislation and rulings, could be made widely available almost instantly.

## What Are the Options?

There are two basic options—established commercial E-Mail systems, and proprietary systems, run by the individual professional firm. One typical commercial system is MCI Mail, run by the MCI telephone company. It now has about 100,000 users. Other E-Mail companies include Western Union and Tymnet.

General user services, like *CompuServe, Genie,* and *Prodigy,* also offer electronic mail, although these are more for personal than professional use.

Proprietary in-house systems are typically run on a mainframe or minicomputer, but there are also systems that can be run from a powerful microcomputer. Although the software and hardware for such systems is inexpensive, they require advanced technical expertise to install and maintain.

A disadvantage that many people find with the in-house system is that it can quickly become cluttered with unnecessary and time-consuming memos and private notes. In some companies, fifty or more messages a day addressed to one individual is not unusual.

## What Are the Requirements?

To use electronic mail, you'll need a computer, a telephone line, a modem, communications software, and a valid user account with an E-Mail system. A Hayes-compatible modem made by any reliable manufacturer is relatively inexpensive. The current standard is 2400 bps.

You'll also need plenty of patience. Like other on-line systems, the user interfaces on most E-Mail systems are at best spartan, and the command syntax is not very intuitive.

There is a very good book on the MCI Mail (*The Complete MCI Mail Handbook,* Steven Manes, Bantam Press, NY), and a program that simplifies its operation (*Lotus Express,* Lotus Development Corp., Cambridge, MA).

## Sales Support Software

Sales support software essentially consists of an enhanced electronic call list. Like mailing list software, it includes a database of clients and prospects. Phone dialing is done though the modem at the push of a key. When the computer finishes dialing, you then pick up the phone and begin the conversation. Reports, usually including phone directories, follow-up lists, contact histories, and form letters can be printed. Many contact management programs include a telemarketing module, which can then be effectively integrated with a mail module.

## Contact Managers

Contact managers are sales support programs that help keep track of individual contacts with clients and prospects. They typically consist of:

362

- A database that includes useful information about a contact, including name, address, phone number, date, time and outcome of last contact, and specific instructions for followup.
- A simple word processor
- A telephone dialer (for which you need a modem)
- A calendar for scheduling and tracking follow-up phone calls and visits

*ACT!* (Contact Software International), for example, is a form of database that allows you to enter information on each person you contact for a business reason, and gives you the structure to record all aspects of that contact, including when the contact was made, for what reason, what material was sent, who said what, and when the next contact should be made.

In a selling situation, *ACT!* is superb because it allows you to keep fully abreast of the status of each and every sales contact you make, and to follow through in an appropriate and timely manner. It even allows you to autodial, if you have a modem. That means that with the material for a contact on the screen, you have only to push a key to dial the number. Very fast and very convenient. The contact you make that way is automatically recorded. Half the work is done for you, which means that time is saved.

### The Electronic Phone Book

A newer development is the electronic phone book. Rather than simply being a shell into which the user can put contacts, electronic phone books are becoming infoware products which include actual information content, not just information templates.

An example of this is the *Fortune 500 Prospector,* published by MZ Group of San Francisco in cooperation with *FORTUNE* Magazine. This package includes all of the information contained in the printed version of the 500, plus the names, addresses, and telephone numbers of key executives for each company, identified by function.

You can print out a number of pre-formatted reports, including follow-up sheets and mailing labels.

The time saved in keyboard input alone, not to mention research time, justifies the cost of the software, if the Fortune 500 is the market you're trying to reach. Other such lists are rapidly coming to market.

### Things to Look For

Some features are not consistent throughout contact or telemarketing software programs, and you must consider them in making your choice:

- *Flexibility.* Are the field definitions appropriate for your organization? If not, does the software allow them to be customized? Can you, for example, code prospects to the industry or functional specializations of your practitioners?

- *Data interfaces.* Automatic data exchange between other company systems—particularly mailing lists—can be especially valuable, as is the ability to read and write common PC data formats (1-2-3, dBase, ASCII).

- *Networking.* Where the work of several client contact people must be coordinated across either space or time, a local area network can be the answer. Can the software operate on a network? If so, are any of its operations limited in this configuration?

- *Scripting.* Some programs allow conversation scripts to be displayed for the sales people. This can help to control the quality of the phone interchange.

- *Accounting.* Some programs allow internal accounting, which can be helpful in monitoring both telephone costs and the labor productivity of the telemarketing function.

## Graphics Programs

The ability to produce graphics is virtually a basic requirement in the marketing computer. Whether it be graphics for desktop publishing, or to support a proposal or presentation with charts, or artwork to illustrate a point in a memo or an in-house newsletter, designing graphics are useful and important.

There are several excellent programs that make it easy to do. For graphs, for example, you can choose a style of graph, enter the numbers, and the computer does the rest. For others, you can actually draw on the screen, using a mouse.

Three of the top programs for graphics are *Harvard Graphics* (Software Publishing Company), *Freelance Graphics* (Lotus) and Microsoft *Power Point.*

All three bring relative ease of use to highly sophisticated programs that give extraordinary graphic designs. This includes a wide range of colors, a large choice of fonts, the ability to integrate with text from other programs, and so forth. Clip art (prepackaged drawings that you can integrate into the presentation) and templates for a wide variety of formats also enhance the programs.

Graphics programs bring a new dimension to computers and how they are used. For the marketer, the values and possibilities are limited only by one's imagination.

## Desktop Publishing

The ability to use the computer to manipulate and integrate pre-existing text and picture files, in a variety of type faces and sizes, and arrange them on the page as would a designer or layout artist, has opened a new world called *desktop publishing* (DTP). DTP would seem to put the ability to design and produce professional quality printed material in the hands of anyone who can use a computer. In fact, for all the marvel of it, DTP still requires the experience and training of an artist to produce quality work. Still, its facility and capabilities are so vast as to make its possibilities endless.

The page produced by DTP is then, presumably, *camera ready*—ready to be photographed on a lithographic plate for printing. DTP essentially serves the same role as the manual paste-up process. It's important to recognize that DTP can't be used to create graphic images, and generally shouldn't be used to create text files, because its text capabilities are quite limited compared to modern word processing software.

Once a document looks good on the screen, DTP software can then turn it into camera-ready hard copy. Unless very high resolution (exceptionally clear definition of gray tones, as in photos) is essential, this can be done on an office-model laser printer. Where higher quality output is required, DTP software allows you to send the document to a professional typesetting machine, either on-site or at an outside service bureau.

All of the features of DTP have been available for some time on expensive, dedicated hardware-based systems. The recent "DTP revolution" has come about because inexpensive software has been developed to run on generic machines (both IBM PC and Macintosh).

In a professional services marketing environment, DTP is most often used for newsletters, proposals, statements of qualifications, and direct mail pieces. It may be appropriate for non-complex advertisements, such as simple tombstones, complimentary ads in organizational journals, or display-sized classified ads. Other kinds of documents, such as technical monographs, can also be produced attractively by DTP.

## Benefits of Desktop Publishing

In high-volume situations, it may be *less expensive* to use DTP than to do paste-up manually. In low volume situations, a relative novice can create professional-looking results cost-effectively by following the design done by a professional layout artist. Of course, the costs of hardware, software, maintenance, and training must be factored into any break-even calculation.

Beyond the cost saving, the *quality of printed output can be raised considerably*. This is especially useful in a professional services marketing environment, where low volume documents, such as proposals, play a key role in new business development. Projects for which full typesetting might not be economically justified may also benefit from DTP treatment.

DTP can give you *greater control* over the final product. Creating the document becomes an interactive process, with active and dynamic feedback for changes and corrections before the final output is produced. In the traditional process, changes are communicated to the professional designer, who then prepares (and charges for) a new iteration of the document—a cumbersome and expensive process. It's also possible, in some instances, to use DTP output to reduce the margin of possible error on the printer's side. For example, copy can be sent containing crop marks (defining spacing), rather than indicating measurements of where the cropping should be.

DTP allows *design expertise* to be stored in the form of templates, standard design molds into which graphics and text can be poured. Templates for various kinds of documents come bundled with the major DTP packages, and an active third-party market to provide others is emerging. This minimizes the need to redesign a standard document format each time you need it, and may bring about greater consistency in the marketplace (especially for multi-location organizations). It also offers the ability to leverage the efforts of talented graphic designers.

## What Are Its Pitfalls?

First, despite the blandishments of DTP hardware and software suppliers, DTP is definitely not for the casual user. *Desktop publishing software is complex* and difficult to master, compared to other classes of software. Implementing a DTP workstation involves carefully selecting hardware and related software (word processing and graphics). Of course, all advertising for DTP products sports stunning output documents, with no mention of how long they took to produce, or how much training the system operators had.

Second, there is sometimes a tendency to rush into graphics import and page layout—the fun stuff—before the written text itself is satisfactory. Because the text editing within DTP programs is rudimentary, this may mean more effort than necessary spent on certain tasks.

Finally, related to the benefit of greater control, there is the temptation to nit-pick every design decision.

## Choosing the Right Tool for the Job

Just getting a DTP workstation set up involves choices among considerably different alternatives. In top-down order, these are:

- *Dedicated vs. software-driven system.* For some high volume applications, where a trained operator can be employed full-time, the right choice may still be a dedicated hardware/software package. The alternative is to get software that will run on a standard architecture machine.

- *IBM vs. Macintosh.* If you've chosen a standard-architecture setup, these are your two alternatives. Both have inherent advantages which should be explored in terms of your own specific needs. The software for each is different, with its own set of relative advantages. The desirability of compatibility with other office systems plays a large role here.

- *Software.* Different DTP software packages behave differently, and each has certain advantages in the context of the type of work being done. Some, for example, are better for single-page or short documents where the format varies a lot. Others are better for longer documents, where each page is formatted relatively consistently. The software that originally creates the text and graphics must, of course, be compatible with the DTP package.

- *Mix and match vs. turnkey system.* If you know what you're doing, probably the best DTP systems consist of components from various sources, as with stereo sound equipment. Alternatively, there are vendors who offer complete "turnkey" systems that simply need to be plugged in to be ready to operate.

## Implementing Desktop Publishing

Implementing a desktop publishing system is often an opportunity to re-examine design parameters and the organization of the design function in your firm. A good way to proceed might be to:

- Have a management-level group decide how it wants the final output to look.
- Hire a professional designer to create a design guide that describes the treatment of text and graphics.
- Implement the design guide as a re-usable template in the DTP software you're using.
- 

Desktop publishing can be a valuable competitive resource, if it's managed properly. Managing the DTP resource effectively involves knowing when to use it to best advantage, what people to assign to it, how to train them, and how to integrate DTP into the operating fabric of the organization. It includes, as well, knowing when not to use it.

Desktop publishing is a software application that's evolving rapidly, but which has reached the level of stability that warrants that every marketer of professional services should seriously consider using it for at least some of its applications.

## Measuring Technology Costs

Considering the initial cost of computer equipment, how does one determine the cost—and the return on the investment—of a computer operation? By the cost of the hardware?

Only partially, according to computer marketing specialist Timothy Powell. Citing a recent study, Powell notes that hardware expenditures are only about 15 percent of total lifetime outlays related to a microcomputer. The rest of the iceberg can include software, in-house and vendor support services, maintenance contracts, repairs, training, and fees paid consultants for developing custom applications.

Powell then looks at the return side of the equation. Positive incremental cash flows are a combination of net cost reductions and revenue enhancements. Cost reductions are based on the time and effort saved by working smarter through technology. These are usually pretty easy to evaluate.

Don't forget that savings may be a combination of one-time and recurring events. If we can eliminate a clerical position through technology, that money (salary and benefits) is saved year after year, hence the stream of positive cash flows, Powell points out.

Revenue enhancements may be harder to get a handle on, and often represent the key payoff for a marketing support technology. Here's where you literally use the machine to generate revenues for the firm. It takes some creativity to evaluate these, but it can be done.

One good way of measuring increased revenues is to look at the productivity of marketing activities. For example, let's take those "what have we done for you lately" calls to past clients. We can evaluate a desktop technology to help organize this function and make it more productive by increasing the number of calls that can be made within the time allotted (that is, with no increase or decrease in labor cost). The payoff from using the new technology can be calculated something like this:

Calls made per person per year with the new technology . . .

>     - calls made per person per year now
>     = incremental calls per person per year
>     X number of people making calls
>     = total incremental number of calls per year
>     X the proportion of calls that result in new leads
>     X the proportion of leads that result in new bookings
>     X the average net value of a new booking
>     = the incremental cash flow per year

This positive cash flow per year is then analyzed with any other positive benefits (revenues or savings) and the costs of the investment, using either internal rate of return or net present value.

A book that contains many examples of this kind of analysis drawn from real-world situations is *The Information Edge* by N. Dean Meyer and Mary E. Boone (Dow Jones-Irwin, Homewood, IL, 1989).

Its basic thesis is that desktop information technology can substantially change the way we do business, and can make us money, provided we subject it to the same analytic scrutiny we would any other investment decision.

Other factors contribute as well to the growth of desktop marketing. Burgeoning technology and increased sales make the computer and computer technology ubiquitous. Miniaturization has given us practical, efficient, and low cost laptops. The equipment gets better and cheaper, and the software continues to make inroads into new capabilities and efficiencies. Software continues to improve in its ability to interface with other software and other brands of computers, broadening the scope of computer capability. The growth of networking, in which more terminals have more access to more information—is becoming available at lower cost.

Desktop marketing, then, is here to stay, because it really does bring a new dimension to marketing.

# Part VII

# The Future

# 20

# The Future

It would have been impossible, except for those with a high aptitude for lucky guesses, to anticipate in 1977 the effect that the *Bates* decision would ultimately have on the economic world in which we live today.

It's difficult to say with certainty, even in hindsight, what events specifically altered the course of the professions, and to what degree.

It's a fairly safe guess that introducing competition into what had once been a pristine world contributed substantially to the changes that have led to megamergers, new contemplations in governance, and so forth. But what next?

So many factors—some new and some altered versions of old—enter into the dynamic of change that prognostication is impossible. The fight for share of market, among other factors, has led to increased mergers. Will the mergers work? Will there be more of them?

There is also the interesting effect that marketing itself has on the marketplace, in which marketing strategies and actions change the texture and dynamic of the market.

With a realtime effect, marketing activities generate new attitudes toward a profession and its professionals in the minds of the prospective clientele, and new ideas for using that professional service. Good marketing educates consumers. When law firms market their ability to deal with estate problems, it makes people aware of estate problems they didn't know they had. When accountants talk of tax planning, they are asking clients to anticipate, rather than to react.

The market is constantly changing, as well, of its own volition, assaulted as it is by random forces; constantly shifting; constantly reweaving itself in pattern and texture. A change in legislation or the economy can cause substantial change in the market for accountants and lawyers. Increased internationalization, new financial instruments, the breakdown of barriers between financial institutions—the list of events that affect professional practice is long.

Industries mature, and technology forces change. What's the impact on the accounting profession of a decline in the rate at which the number of public corporations come into being, and of mergers, and how does that affect the audit as a source of new business? Consider the effects on the legal profession, and on the medical profession as well, of changing attitudes towards negligence suits and malpractice suits. Consider the effects on the marketplace of the sophistication in computers and other technology. What do new concepts in financing and in taxation do to resegment the market's needs for new skills from a professional in any of the financial disciplines?

It seems certain now that the partnership structure, which the 1986 version of this book predicted would fall, is now in at least a metamorphosis. How will it emerge? What will replace it? How will new structures deal with the ethical and practical considerations that dictated the old structures? There's no question that these problems will be solved, as wise professionals pursue new structures in their own interest. And the prediction suggested here in the earlier edition, that a major corporation (such as Sears or Merrill Lynch) might someday own an accounting or law firm for the profit of it, seems almost more certain now than in 1986. A small suggestion, but one indicative of the potential for great change.

And certainly, competition, assisted by technology, will continue to alter the way in which accounting and the law are practiced. The IRS increasingly accepts electronic filing. This gives a better view of the effectiveness of tax law and tax practice. The information plays back in the form of both tax legislation and tax practice. And so forth.

The growth of the tax and legal clinic, and the institutionalization of the once controversial personal injury marketing approach, show a trend in professional practice driven by marketing considerations that, just a decade ago, was unimaginable.

And so on.

But what's to become of marketing and the marketing process?

Here, it's difficult to distinguish between what *should* happen and what *will* happen.

What *should* happen is that all the accountants and lawyers and consultants become wise and knowing in the ways of marketing, and understanding and tolerant of the ways and culture of the marketer.

What *should* happen is that marketers become universally wise and knowing in those aspects of marketing that work, and those that don't, and that the body of knowledge and course of marketing practice becomes truly professional. These are things that *should*, but won't, happen. At least not in a straight line, or a single stroke of lightning, or flash of revelation.

Process of this magnitude is necessarily gradual. There's an education process. A process of integration of information with established practice. And there's also prejudice, and perception and personality.

William Ruder, the co-founder of the international public relations firm, Ruder & Finn, put a finger on it. In a discussion of the changes in public relations practice since the early days, and the formalization of many of those practices, Ruder said, "Yes, but it's still an art form, and if I don't lose the artistry I'm still in business."

Precisely so. Marketing, with all its formal practices and jargon and experiences, is still an art form. And, unfortunately, no art is ever universally perceived, understood, or accepted.

Consider, for example, that there are a finite number of marketing tools, and it seems unlikely that any others will be invented in the foreseeable future. There is advertising and public relations and direct mail and telemarketing, and so forth. And within each of these disciplines, there are also limitations in media and techniques. The challenge, then, is to be successfully competitive with just these tools.

Not all that hard, maybe. There are only fifty-two cards in a deck, but look at the infinite varieties of hands that can be dealt in any card game, and the infinite varieties of ways in which each hand can be played. And so if we're limited in the variety of marketing tools, we're not limited in our imaginative skills in using these tools.

What we can predict for the future, perhaps with more hope than certainty, is that the artfulness will flourish. As we surge through a direct mail or telemarketing campaign, and learn what works and doesn't work, we polish the art. And this will most likely happen.

As professionals have more experience with marketing, they will better understand its principles and dynamics, and indeed become better consumers of marketing services.

As marketing professionals are given greater opportunity to hone their skills, perhaps they, too, will break away from repeating the cliches of marketing drawn from other marketing practices, and bring a new originality to the practices of marketing professional services.

While the range of capability among marketers, from one end of the spectrum to the other, is measured in light years, perhaps experience and education will shorten that distance. In every profession and every trade, there are bright people and not so bright people. Challenge drives the bright ones, and a definable body of knowledge sustains the others. In marketing professional services, the body of knowledge is still unfortunately smaller than most of us want to admit—but it will grow. And so will grow the professionalism of those who must rely on it.

It may seem smug, from a platform of a book on marketing, to say that the future of the professions resides in the future of marketing. After all, the professions got where they are well before they were lumbered with marketing.

But that's the fact of it. Nothing much changed, in the professions, before competition entered the picture. And then the change has been profound.

As marketing skills increase, and the body of knowledge grows, it's certain that the professions will change. The things that professionals do to meet changing needs of the marketplace will change. The structure of the professional firm as it gears itself to compete will change. The perception of the professional, already tainted by the light of reality, will continue to change as the professional stands more earnestly before his or her audience.

We don't know whether this dynamic—this change—is for good or ill. That's a judgment that can only be made in hindsight.

But we do know that it will change.

We should know, as well, that in a changing environment, we succeed best when we address not the events, but the dynamics of the change itself. That's how we best understand and cope with it.

But at the same time, on a day-by-day basis, we've got to deal with the mechanics of the practice. And that, for the most part, is what this book has been about.

# Appendices

# I

# A Sample Direct Mail Program

## The Problem

The company is one of several consulting firms competing in the highly lucrative area of maintenance management. Its direct mail letters have thus far failed to effectively produce a satisfactory number of opportunities to make presentations.

In selling this service, there are several considerations that must be addressed...

- Most prospective clients may not be aware of the full complexity of the problem of maintenance management, its cost, its potential for wasting money, and the danger of mismanagement of maintenance to the overall production process. This means that before you can offer a solution to the problem, the problem must be clarified and explained to the prospect in terms that are relevant to the prospect.

- While identifying the companies that serve as prospective clients for you is relatively easy, it becomes more important to identify the right people within the company to approach. In some cases, it may require approaching two or three people (i.e., the CEO, the VP Engineering, and the CFO)—each with a different approach.

- Timing is a major consideration. At what point following the mailing should there be a phone followup? How many letters should go out at one time? How many letters should there be to each recipient in the campaign, and how far apart should they be mailed?

- What do you say on the phone in the followup?

- Should a campaign be tested by letter, by list, by followup? For example, are some industries better sources of prospective clientele than others, and should they be the areas of primary concentration?

- Should literature be offered or enclosed in an initial mailing? Or does that interfere with the selling process?

- And finally, how can the letter be crafted so that it's read, believed, and the appeal to meet personally is accepted?

## A Program

With these factors in mind, the following basic program will serve as a test for you of the efficacy of a carefully planned direct mail program.

It's overall objective would be to substantially increase the number of opportunities to make presentations to prospective clients to sell maintenance management consulting services.

The strategy and copy platform would include:

- Focusing on target industries most likely to be subject to the need for maintenance management
- Analyzing the target companies to help determine the individuals (by title) within each company to be sent letters
- Planning the campaign for mailing, including determining the lists, the number of letters, and the timing
- Developing the copy strategy to be used in each of the letters to each of the recipients
- Developing the packaging—the appropriate letterheads, the envelopes, what goes into each mailing, and so forth
- Writing the letters
- Planning the followup strategy
- Monitoring results, and correcting strategy as needed

Essentially, only as many letters would be mailed at any one time as could be followed up by phone a week later. And despite the fact that each letter says "call us," the initiative for the phone followup will be taken by the firm's consultants.

## The Letters

### Letter Number 1 to CEO

Dear . . .:

With maintenance costs up more than 10 percent in your industry, you are aware, I'm sure, that constantly changing conditions in rapidly growing companies can result in waste in even the best run plant. In some plants we've looked at, maintenance waste has been as much as a third of the total maintenance budget.

We can help you, just as we have helped hundreds of companies in your industry.

As the leading consultants in maintenance management, we have saved our clients thousands—sometimes millions—of dollars.

We've written to your maintenance manager, asking for the opportunity to show how we can help him generate a maintenance program that's more efficient and cost effective.

If you feel that you, too, would like to discuss ways in which we can help you, please call me today at (212) 555-1212, and we'll arrange to meet at your convenience.

Thank you.


Yours truly,


*Letter Number 1 to Maintenance Supervisor*

Dear. . .:

No matter how efficient your maintenance operation has been until now, the chances are that changing conditions have bred waste and inefficiencies that cost you vast amounts of money. In fact, more than $100 billion is wasted on maintenance each year by American business, much of it in even the most carefully run plants—a cost that must be stemmed in even the best of economic times.

We can stop that loss.

We've done it successfully for hundreds of companies of all sizes, and in many industries—including yours—since we were founded in 1900. We can do it for you.

Typically, programs for our clients have helped to. . .

- Increase worker maintenance productivity by 50 percent or more
- Reduce maintenance materials inventory costs by 10 to 15 percent, while increasing serviceability and parts availability
- Improve machinery up-time, which boosts production capacity and product quality, and improves customer service

And, by bringing you both an objective view of your system and the experience borne of serving hundreds of companies like yours, we can do it for you, too.

Our professionals address each maintenance program as unique, and build solutions that are both relevant and susceptible to constantly changing conditions. We give you people solutions—not off-the-shelf computer programs that are more complex than the problems they attempt to solve.

Give me one hour, and I'll show you how The Maintenance Consultants —the most experienced in maintenance management—can help you. Call me today at (212) 555-1212, and we'll arrange to meet at your convenience.

Yours truly,

381

P.S. Because senior management support for your efforts is frequently necessary for you to embark on a program of maintenance management consulting, we've taken the liberty of availing your management of the facts about our service.

## Letter Number 1 to CFO

Dear. . .

With maintenance costs in the chemical industry up more than 6 percent this past year, maintenance is likely to be the point of greatest uncontrolled waste in your company's plants. In fact, more than $10 billion is wasted each year in maintenance systems in plants throughout the country.

We can help you stem that waste.

As leading consultants on maintenance management, we've saved untold millions of dollars for companies such as yours, and we can do it for you. The Maintenance Consultants have been serving industry since 1900, which means that the cumulative experience of our professionals is greater than that of any other consulting firm in the country.

We've written to both your senior management and your maintenance supervisor, requesting the opportunity to review your maintenance system and to demonstrate how we can help you. However, if you'd like to discuss with us the real savings and cost-effectiveness of a maintenance management system designed specifically for your company, please call me today at (212) 555-1212, and we'll arrange to meet at your convenience.

Yours truly,

## Letter Number 2 to CEO

Dear. . .

Of the $10 billion wasted on maintenance each year by American business, what portion is yours?

As tightly as you control costs in your company, are you aware of the myriad ways in which your maintenance costs can leach away your profits—particularly in a dynamic company trying to succeed in highly competitive environments? And particularly in today's precarious economic environment?

We're aware of how quickly—and sometimes surreptitiously—maintenance costs can burgeon, because over the years we've looked at the maintenance systems of hundreds of companies like yours. And we've found ways to save our clients thousands—and sometimes millions—of dollars.

As leading consultants in maintenance management, we can show you, in a very brief meeting, how and why your maintenance systems may be a drain on your profits. We can show you how to stem that flow of wasted maintenance dollars.

Give us a few minutes to discuss it with you. It may be the most profitable few minutes you can spend to keep your plant running efficiently. I'll call you for an appointment. Or you can call me at (212) 555-1212.

Yours truly,

## Letter Number 2 to CFO

Dear. . .

You're well aware of the causes of lost profits from such factors as rising production costs and inflation. But then there's the slow and quiet drainage that comes from maintenance. More than $10 billion is wasted on inefficient maintenance systems in U.S. plants each year.

We can help you stop the leak of profits that comes from maintenance costs.

As leading consultants on maintenance management, we've done it for hundreds of companies like yours, and saved millions of dollars for our clients. And we can do it for you.

Give me a few minutes to show you how we can substantially reduce the waste that seems to creep in to even the most carefully watched maintenance program. It will be time well spent for you.

I'll call you for an appointment. Or you can call me at (212) 555-1212.

Yours truly,

## Letter Number 2 to Maintenance Supervisor

Dear. . .

It's a slow leak.

The maintenance management program that worked so effectively for you last year doesn't work quite the same way today. New demands on the machinery...changes in your suppliers...new personnel...budget cuts to cope with today's difficult economic conditions—all these and more cause slow but persistent leaks and inefficiencies, and rising costs, in your maintenance management program.

We can help.

We can show you, as we have for hundreds of companies of all sizes in many industries, including yours, that we can improve your maintenance management program.

We've helped these companies develop programs that increase worker efficiency by more than 50 percent...reduce maintenance material inventory costs by as much as 15 percent...improve machinery up-time and productivity —all of which are crucial in today's economic climate.

Give me one hour, and I'll show you how The Maintenance Consultants —the most experienced in maintenance management—can help you. I'll call you in a few days to arrange an appointment at your convenience. Or call me today at (212) 555-1212.

Yours truly,

### Letter Number 3 to CEO

Dear...

Would you be willing to bet a few minutes of your time to learn how much your maintenance systems and programs are really costing you in lost time and money—and that the time and money can indeed be saved?

Today there's nothing that's harder for even the best management to get a handle on than maintenance costs—and that's why billions are lost each year in maintenance systems that have gotten out of hand.

We can help you—as we have for hundreds of other companies in your industry. And we can prove it to you in just a few minutes.

As the leading consultants in maintenance management, we've saved our clients thousands—sometimes millions—of dollars. We bet that in just a few minutes, we can show you how we can do the same for you.

Call me today at (212) 555-1212, and we'll arrange to meet at your convenience. It will be, for you, time well spent. I promise you.

Yours truly,

### Letter Number 3 to CFO

Dear...

There's enough drain on your bottom line, these days, without adding the hard-to-grasp maintenance costs. Billions of dollars are lost in maintenance each year—and it keeps getting worse.

In just a few minutes, I can show you how we can substantially reduce the waste that creeps into even the most carefully watched maintenance program—as we've done for hundreds of companies like yours.

As leading consultants on maintenance management, we've saved millions of dollars for our clients. And we can do it for you.

I'll call you for an appointment. Or you can call me at (212) 555-1212.

Yours truly,

### Letter Number 3 to Maintenance Supervisor

Dear...

It's bad enough if maintenance management is your full time job. It's overwhelming if it's just one of your many responsibilities. With new demands on the machinery...changes in your suppliers...new personnel...budget cuts to cope with today's difficult economic conditions—last year's systems don't seem to control it any more.

We can help.

We can show you how turn a difficult maintenance system into one that works smoothly...saves time...cuts cost.

As the most experienced firm in maintenance management, we can show you, as we have for hundreds of companies of all sizes in many industries, that we can improve your maintenance management program.

We've helped these companies develop programs that increase worker efficiency by more than 50 percent...reduce maintenance material inventory costs by as much as 15 percent...improve machinery up-time and productivity.

Give me one hour, and I'll prove it to you. I'll call you in a few days to arrange an appointment at your convenience. Or call me today at (212) 555-1212.

Yours truly,

# II

# Bibliography

While there are a great many books on marketing, few offer vast insights into the realm of professional services marketing. The following sampling of books contribute, to varying degrees, information that may be useful in understanding basic marketing concepts, and are more attuned to the problems of professional services marketing.

Adler, Elizabeth W. *Print That Works*. Palo Alto: Bull Publishing Co., 1991

Bobrow, Edwin E. and Mark, David. *Marketing Handbook*, Vols 1 and 2. Homewood: Dow Jones-Irwin, 1985

Breen, George and Blankenship, A. B. *Do-It-Yourself Marketing Research*. New York: McGraw Hill, 1982

Fueroghren, Dean Keith. *"But the People in Legal Said."* Homewood: Dow Jones-Irwin, 1989

Hiam, Alexander. *The Vest Pocket Manager*. Englewood Cliffs: Prentice Hall, 1991

Levitt, Theodore. *The Marketing Imagination*. New York: The Free Press, 1983

Marcus, Bruce W. *Marketing Professional Services in Real Estate*. Chicago: Realtors National Marketing Institute, 1981

Marcus, Bruce W. and Wallace, Sherwood. *Competing in the New Capital Markets*. New York: Harper Business, 1991

Rackham, Neil. *Spin Selling*. New York: McGraw Hill, 1988

Rackham, Neil and Ruff, Richard. *Managing Major Sales*. New York: Harper Business, 1991

Rapp, Stan and Collins, Tom. *Maximarketing*. New York: McGraw Hill, 1987

Ries, Al and Trout, Jack. *Marketing Warfare*. New York: McGraw Hill, 1985

Ries, Al and Trout, Jack. *Positioning: The Battle for Your Mind*. New York: McGraw Hill, 1981

Riskin, Gerald A. and McKenna, Patrick J. *Practice Development*. Toronto: Butterworths, 1989

Shenson, Howard L. *How to Create and Market a Successful Seminar*. New York: Everest House, 1981

Shenson, Howad L. *How to Select and Manage Consultants*. Lexington: Lexington Books/D.C. Heath, 1990

Shenson, Howard L. *Shenson on Consulting*. New York: John Wiley and Sons, 1990

Stever, Richard M. *A Guide to Marketing Law*. New York: Law and Business Inc./Harcourt Brace Jovanovich, 1986

Weinstein, Art. *Market Segmentation*. Chicago: Probus, 1987

## Directories

*Bacon's Publicity Checker*—Annual publication analyzing publicity requirements of almost 4,000 business, trade farm and consumer magazines (Bacon's Clipping Bureau, 14 East Jackson Blvd., Chicago, Il 60604, annual)

*Bacon's Publicity Checker-Newspapers*—Lists more than 6,500 daily newspapers in the United States and more than 8,000 weeklies (Bacon's Clipping Bureau, 14 Jackson Blvd., Chicago, IL 60604 annual)

*Broadcasting Yearbook*—(Broadcasting Publishing Co., 735 DeSales Street N.W., Washington, D.C.,annual)

*Chamber of Commerce Business Directories*—Directories of local Chambers of Commerce (U.S. Department of Commerce, Washington, D.C. 20036)

*College Alumni Publications*—Circulation, advertising rates and other data about over 500 alumni publications of colleges and universities in every state (Public Relations Publishing Company, Inc., 888 Seventh Avenue, New York, NY 10106, pub. 1980)

*Editor & Publisher International Yearbook*—A state-by-state and city-by city listing of daily newspapers in the United States and Canada with information on their circulation and names of executive personnel (Editor & Publisher Magazine, The Editor & Publisher Co., Inc., 850 Third Avenue, New York, NY 10022, annual)

*Gale Directory of Publications*—A complete directory of 1,900 daily newspapers, 8,200 weekly and 3,000 trade and consumer magazines, all listed alphabetically by state (Book Tower, Detroit, MI 48226)

*Hudson's Washington News Media Contacts Directory*—A directory of Washington, D.C. area news media, including editors (Hudson Associates, Rhinebeck, NY, annual)

*Middle West Publicity Media Directory*—A directory of Chicago area publications and news media, including key editorial personnel (St. Clair Press, Chicago, annual)

*New York Publicity Outlets*—Directory of New York City, metropolitan area and major national publications, including personnel and deadlines P.O. Box 1197, New Milford, CT 06770 CT)

*News Bureaus Contacts*—A directory of the locations and personnel of all news bureaus in the United States and their branch offices (BPI, 1515 Broadway, New York, NY 10036)

*News Media Yellow Book of Washington and New York*—A directory of those who report, write, edit and produce the news in the nation's government and business capitals; contains six specialized indexes (Monitor Publishing Company, 104 Fifth Avenue, 2nd Floor, New York, NY 10011)

*News Bureaus in the U.S.*—A directory of the locations and personnel of all news bureaus in the United States and their branch offices (Richard Weiner, Inc., New York City)

*N.W. Ayer & Sons Directory of Newspapers and Periodicals*—A complete directory of 1,900 daily newspapers, 8,200 weekly newspapers, and 3,000 trade and consumer magazines, all listed alphabetically by state (N.W. Ayer & Son, Inc., West Washington, New York, NY 10017)

*O'Dwyer's Directory of Public Relations Firms* (Annual), and *O'Dwyer's Directory of Communications Executives* (annual), J.R. O'Dwyer Company Inc., 271 Madison Avenue, New York, NY 10036

*Professional Guide to Public Relations Services*—Describes and evaluates 1,000 products and services, including names, addresses, fees, phone numbers, and personal observations; includes suggestions on techniques (Public Relations Publishing Company, Inc., New York)

*Professional's Guide to Publicity*—(Public Relations Publishing Co., Inc., New York, pub. 1978)

*Simon's Editorial Offices in the West*—A directory of western media and editorial personnel (David H. Simon, Los Angeles)

*Syndicated Columnist Contacts*—Complete information on where to find columnists, plus history and operation of newspaper syndicates (BPI, 1515 Broadway, New York, NY 10036)

*Ulrich's International Periodicals Directory*—Information on 50,000 periodicals from all over the world; almost all major language publications, with information on publisher, personnel, rates, circulation, frequency of issue, languages of text, where indexed or abstracted; plus money exchange table with conversion rates and formulas (R.R. Bowker Co., Ann Arbor, MI)

*The Working Press of the Nation*—A reference to basic communication media in the United States, in four volumes: Newspaper Directory, Magazine Directory, Radio & TV Directory, Feature Writer and Syndicate Directory; presents names of personnel, addresses of publisher, subjects covered, phone numbers, titles, etc. (The National Research Bureau, Inc., 424 N.Third Street, Burlington, Iowa)

*Writer's Market*—Annual directory for freelance writers, listing over 4,000 publications, including a section on trade, technical and professional (Writer's Market, Cincinnati, Ohio)

## Newsletters

There are several newsletters that may be of interest:

*Jack O'Dwyer's Newsletter*—a comprehensive report of activities in the public relations and financial relations fields (Jack O'Dwyer, New York, weekly)

*PR Aids Party Line*—a weekly newsletter of current placement opportunities in all media (PR Aids Periodicals, Inc., NY, weekly)

*PR Reporter*—a newsletter of activities of public relations and investor relations practitioners, including frequent discussions of current public relations problems (PR Reporter, Meriden, CT, weekly)

*Public Relations News*—a newsletter of activities of public relations and investor relations practitioners, including frequent case histories of successful programs (Public Relations News, New York, weekly)

*Writer's Market*—An annual directory of some 4,000 publications, with editorial requirements. (Writer's Market, Cincinnati, Ohio).

## Clipping Services

Burrelle's Press Clipping Service (75 E.Northfield Road, Livingston, N.J. 07039

Luce Press Clippings, (Box 379, Topeka, KS 66601)

# III

# Electronic Information Services and Databases

The following list of electronic data services, supplied by the international research firm, FIND/SVP, are a sampling of the many that are available.

| Vendor | Key Databases | Contains |
|---|---|---|
| *COMPUSERVE*<br>5000 Arlington Center Blvd.<br>P.O. Box 20212<br>Columbus, OH 43220<br>(614) 457-0802 | Business Information<br>Service | General and Business<br>articles, brokerage<br>reports, stock quotes |
| | Compustat | Historical data on over<br>5000 U.S. and Canadian<br>companies |
| *DIALOG*<br>3460 Hillview Ave<br>Palo Alto, CA 94304<br>(800) 334-2564 | Trade and Industry<br>ASAP | Full text of over 3400<br>trade journals |
| | Management Contents | Abstracts, 700 journals |
| | Computer Database | Abstracts, 600 journals |
| | ABI/Inform | Abstracts, 800<br>publications |
| | PTS Prompt | 1500 mostly trade<br>publications (incl. 200<br>non-U.S.) |
| | PTS Mars | 110 marketing journals |

| Vendor | Key Databases | Contains |
|---|---|---|
| | Investext | Wall Street analyst reports, over 60 major research firms |
| | Disclosure Financials | Corporate financial results 13,00 companies |
| | Disclosure Management | Management biographies |
| | Moody's Corporate Profiles | Overviews of 3600 corporations |
| | Dun's Market Identifiers | Directory of over 6.6 million companies |
| | Dun's Financial Records | Financials for 750,000 companies—mostly private |
| | D&B Business Credit Reports | Credit histories—11 million companies |
| | PTS Newsletter | Full text of over 250 business and industry newsletters |
| | PR Newswire | Updated every 15 minutes—press releases from over 12,000 companies |
| | Business Dateline | Full text of over 180 regional business publications |
| | IDD M&A Transactions | Includes data on all partial and completed merger, acquisition, or divestiture transactions valued at $1 million |

| Vendor | Key Databases | Contains |
|---|---|---|
| *DOW JONES*<br>P.O. Box 300<br>Princeton, NJ 08540-0300<br>(609) 452-1511 | News/Retrieval | Stock quotes; Wall Street Journal; Barrons: corporate performance data |
| | Tradeline | 15 years price history on 150,000 issues |
| NEWSNET<br>945 Haverford Rd.<br>Bryn Mawr, PA 19010<br>(800) 345-1301 | NewsNet | Full text of over 450 newsletters |
| | TRW Business Profiles | Payment history—8 million businesses |
| *REUTERS*<br>61 Broadway, 31st Flr.<br>New York, NY 10022<br>(800) 426-4318 or<br>(212) 493-7100 | Textline | Full text and abstracts; over 1,000 periodicals, many foreign |
| | Equities 2000 | Securities prices |
| *VU/TEXT*<br>325 Chestnut Street<br>Suite 1300<br>Philadelphia, PA 19106<br>(215) 574-4100 | VU/Text | Regional newspapers |

# IV

# Request for Proposal

*The following is a sample Request for Proposal from an accounting firm to public relations firms. It's value is to assure that public relations firms proposing their services understand precisely what is required, thereby sparing both the public relations and the professional firms the time spent on proposing irrelevant services. In one situation, an RFP not unlike this one was used to retain some twenty local public relations firms to serve the local practice offices of a major international accounting firm. The results were almost uniformly excellent.*

This is a request for a proposal for public relations services for the Albany office of Smith & Dale, an international accounting and consulting firm. We would appreciate your reading the following material carefully, and responding with both a written proposal and an oral presentation that specifically address the communications needs of this office, and responds to all the questions outlined.

If further information is necessary for you to make an effective presentation that delineates how you can best serve our needs, please feel free to call James Smith, managing partner of this office, at 555-1212.

## Background

Smith & Dale is an international accounting and consulting firm with 200 offices in twenty countries throughout the world, and more than fifty offices domestically. It is one of the Big Six accounting firms—the six largest accounting firms in the United States.

The distinction of the Big Six is not merely that they are the largest accounting firms, but that they hold a particular distinction and prestige in the eyes of the Fortune 500 companies, of investment bankers, of investors, and of all sources of capital. That sets them apart from those firms that are not in the Big Six, regardless of size. Currently, all but six of the companies in the Fortune 500 are audited and otherwise served by Big Six accounting firms.

Smith & Dale, as are most accounting firms, is a partnership—not a corporation. It has no investors other than the partners, and so is not legally required to issue financial statements. However, for its fiscal year ended September 30, 19—, total revenues were $xxx million. It has 20,000 employees worldwide and 1500 partners.

As an international accounting and consulting firm, Smith & Dale performs a broad range of services for its clients. The capability to perform these services are either resident in the Albany office or are available to clients and prospective clients of this office through the firm's national capabilities. While the range of these services is too extensive to list in its entirety, they essentially consist of:

- Auditing and Accounting Services, for both publicly and privately held companies, for public and not-for-profit institutions, and for government agencies.
- Tax and Financial Planning Services, for both publicly- held companies and for individuals (usually with large incomes and complex tax problems.)
- Computer-assisted auditing services.
- A Broad Range of Consulting Services, such as:
  - ° assistance in organizational structure
  - ° cash management
  - ° aid in capital formation
  - ° productivity programs
  - ° assistance in executive recruiting
  - ° litigation support services
  - ° budgeting
  - ° estate planning
  - ° a full range of services to assist in managing a company

These services are performed in a wide variety of industries for companies of all sizes. In addition to the expertise the firm offers, there is further expertise in industries that require specialized knowledge and techniques. Among the industries served by the Albany office are:

- Agribusiness
- Financial institutions
- Recreation
- Government
- Hotel
- Mining
- Oil and gas
- Real estate
- Retail
- Small business

A representative list of clients is enclosed.

## The Marketing Program

The purpose of the public relations program is to assist the Albany office of Smith & Dale, as part of its overall marketing effort, in projecting its expertise and capabilities to the prospective clientele in the office's market area. The marketing program functions on several levels:

- *The Firm's National Marketing Program.*
  This is an umbrella program that functions from the firm's national headquarters in New York City. It includes the complete spectrum of marketing activities—such as market research, long-range planning, and advertising and public relations. Its role is to market the firm nationally, as well as to support and coordinate the practice office marketing programs throughout the country.

- *The Practice Office Marketing Program.*
  This includes a wide variety of activities designed to develop the practice locally, and to project the specific capabilities, skills and experience of the local practice office. Public relations is just one segment of the practice office marketing program, and is intended to support the practice office's total marketing efforts.

## The Public Relations Program

The public relations program for which you are being asked to submit a proposal is designed to serve the needs of the Albany office of Smith & Dale. Your client will be just the Albany office. But while it is a stand-alone program for the Albany office, you may anticipate guidance, support, and coordination from the national public relations office, to help maintain a consistency with the firm's overall public relations objectives; with advice and guidance drawn from the experience of both the national public relations program and those of other practice offices; and with material developed nationally that you may localize and tailor to the needs of the program for the Albany office.

In performing these activities in your market area, you may find a number of activities that have possibilities for the national press. These are perfectly acceptable as long as they are cleared with the firm's national public relations director, to avoid overlap. The primary emphasis, however, should be on the local financial and business community.

## The Objectives

The objectives of the practice office public relations program are:

- To project the expertise, skill and experience of the Albany office of Smith & Dale to the business community and the prospective clientele of the office.

- To assist the Albany office partners and staff in their efforts to participate fully in the business and community activities of the market area, including significant business organizations, community organizations, and charitable and social organizations that afford high visibility for the Firm and its people in the business community.

The first objective is quite precise, in that merely to project the Smith & Dale name is not sufficient. It must be projected in the context of the Firm's and the office's skill and expertise.

## The Program

The elements of the program to which your proposal should address itself include at least the following:

- *The press.* A particular concern is the press in the Albany office's marketing area. While this obviously includes the Republic, it also should include every other possible press outlet, including regional magazines, industry papers and trade press, and any other press outlet that you know to be useful in reaching the business community.
- *Speeches.* Opportunities for Albany office personnel to give speeches and presentations before significant audiences of business people in the market area must be identified and arranged for. In your proposal, both your knowledge of the platforms and your experience in arranging for client participation should be described.
- *Articles.* In addition to interviews and other aspects of press relations, you should identify opportunities to place by-line articles by Albany office personnel in local publications serving the business community. Not to be overlooked, of course, are comparable articles for national publications, but again, these should be cleared with the national director of public relations to avoid duplications and overlap.
- *Seminars.* In the normal course of events, the Albany office will develop a number of seminars for clients and prospective clients in the business community. As you become acclimated to your client's business, you may propose other seminars ideas. In your proposal you should demonstrate how you will participate in these seminars including assistance in setting them up and running them, as well as appropriate press coverage.
- *Publications.* the Firm nationally prepares a large number of publications and newsletters. These will afford you opportunities for publicity geared to the Albany office. It is possible, however, that the Albany office may from time-to-time want to produce a brochure specifically for the office, tailored to its particular needs. You may be called upon to assist in preparing this material.
- *Direct Mail and Advertising.* All advertising in the Firm is cleared by the National office, which maintains the services of a major national advertising agency. Occasionally, however, direct mail campaigns will

originate from the Albany office, and your assistance may be solicited in preparing these campaigns. Your help may be needed to assist in preparing mailing lists. It should be noted that Firm policy is that direct mail material be cleared by the National office.

* *Other Activities.* Within the scope of the objectives of the program, and consistent with the professionalism inherent in both the Firm and the accounting profession, the range of other activities you may develop to fulfill the objective is bounded only by your imagination. They may include valid surveys that are publicizable, newsletters, and events appropriate to the Firm that will gain visibility within the context (and only within the context) of the Firm's expertise and capabilities. The objective, remember, is not merely to project the Firm's name, but to project the Firm's expertise.

## Target Audiences

The target audiences your program should be designed to reach are:

* The business community at large. This includes all aspects of commerce and industry in the area, including financial institutions and the legal profession.
* The senior officers—including chief executive officers, chief financial officers, and the boards of directors of all public corporations in the area.
* Large privately-held companies in the area.
* The management of smaller companies in the area, both publicly-held and private. This includes not only moderately-sized companies, but small companies, emerging companies and entrepreneurial operations. The Firm has an extensive program, in which you will be asked to participate, that particularly focuses on these emerging businesses with special services designed to meet their particular needs.
* Nonprofit organizations and institutions—such as, schools, charities, hospitals, and health care facilities, etc.
* Local county and municipal bodies that serve as a prospective clientele for auditing, accounting, and consulting services.
* Financial institutions and law firms are a target not only as prospective clients, but also as influential individuals and institutions in recommending the services of an accounting firm to their own clients.
* The regional academic community, from whom the Albany office recruits top graduates.

## The Competition

In considering your proposal, you should be aware of the fact that competition for the services of Smith & Dale in your area consists of the efforts of other accounting and consulting firms, including local offices of other Big Eight accounting firms. Many of the services we offer our prospective clientele are now performed by smaller and moderate sized local firms. Many of these organizations maintain their own marketing efforts, and they too will be competing in ideas and for space in the local business press.

## Your Proposal

The purpose of the foregoing material is to give you both background and guidelines to the scope of the program you're being asked to propose to the Albany office of Smith & Dale. Both your written and oral proposals should address at least the following issues:

- The structure of your organization.
- The length of time you've been in business serving this market area.
- Your understanding of the nature of the services performed by an accounting firm, and Smith & Dale in particular.
- Your approach to developing a program that addresses the stated objectives, including the elements of the program outlined in this document.
- Your knowledge of the community, and specifically the local press, community and business organizations, and the nature of the business community of the area.
- Your techniques of working with your clients, including methods of becoming indoctrinated in our Firm and our business; representing us to the community as our public relations firm; keeping yourself informed of our activities and public relations opportunities; and reporting activities, performance and results.
- The names and experience of the account personnel who will specifically work on this account.
- Your fee structure, handling and budgeting of expenses, and billing techniques.
- The experience of your firm in dealing with financially and business oriented clients and the business community and press.
- Your understanding of the differences between public relations for a professional service and public relations for a product or a service such as a bank.

- A list of your current clients, and past and current clients specifically in the service (not product) and corporate / financial area.
- Any other information, concepts or ideas that will demonstrate your ability to serve us with a knowledgeable, effective public relations program.

It is recognized that there is a distinction between public relations for a product or a service, such as a bank or airlines, and public relations for a professional service. It is also recognized that because the Canons of Ethics allowing frank marketing efforts for professional services, such as accountants and lawyers, was changed only a few years ago, there may have been very little opportunity for your agency to have developed an experience specifically geared to a professional service. In public relations for a professional service, the full participation of every professional who performs that services is required for an effective relations or marketing program.

In the final analysis, your firm will be judged on your ability to demonstrate that you perceive these differences, and can work effectively to project the expertise, skills and experienced of the Albany office of Smith & Dale to its target audiences.

# Index